Level 5

Cooperation and Competition

•

Astronomy

•

Heritage

•

Making a New Nation

•

Going West

•

Journeys and Quests

Level 5

— PROGRAM AUTHORS —

Marilyn Jager Adams	Iva Carruthers	Marsha Roit
Carl Bereiter	Jan Hirshberg	Marlene Scardamalia
Joe Campione	Anne McKeough	Gerald H. Treadway, Jr.
	Michael Pressley	

A Division of The **McGraw·Hill** Companies

Columbus, Ohio

Acknowledgments

Grateful acknowledgment is given to the following publishers and copyright owners for permissions granted to reprint selections from their publications. All possible care has been taken to trace ownership and secure permission for each selection included. In case of any errors or omissions, the Publisher will be pleased to make suitable acknowledgments in future editions.

From CLASS PRESIDENT COPYRIGHT © 1990 BY JOHANNA HURWITZ. Used by permission of HarperCollins Publishers.

"The Marble Champ" from BASEBALL IN APRIL AND OTHER STORIES, copyright © 1990 by Gary Soto, reprinted by permission of Harcourt, Inc.

"The New Kid" © 1975 Mike Makley.

"Good Sportsmanship" Copyright © 1958 by Richard Armour. Reprinted by permission of John Hawkins & Associates, Inc.

From JUGGLING by Donna Gamache. Reprinted by permission of the author.

From THE ABACUS CONTEST. Copyright © 1996 Priscilla Wu. Illustrations copyright © 1996 Xiao-jun Li. Used by permission of Fulcrum Publishing.

Reprinted with the permission of Atheneum Books for Young Readers, a Division of Simon & Schuster Children's Publishing Division, from S.O.R. Losers by Avi. Copyright © 1984 by Avi Wortis.

"The Founders of the Children's Rain Forest" from IT'S OUR WORLD, TOO! by Phillip Hoose.

Copyright © 1993 by Phillip Hoose. By permission of Little, Brown and Company (Inc.).

NAVIN SULLIVAN: "Galileo" from 'Pioneer Astronomers' by Navin Sullivan, copyright © 1964 by Navin Sullivan.

"Telescopes", from THE WAY THINGS WORK by David Macaulay. Compilation copyright © 1988 by Dorling Kindersley, Ltd. Text copyright © 1988 by David Macaulay and Neil Ardley. Illustrations copyright © 1988 by David Macaulay. Reprinted by permission of Houghton Mifflin Co. All rights reserved.

"The Great Dog" and "The Scorpion" from THE HEAVENLY ZOO: LEGENDS AND TALES OF THE STARS by Alison Lurie, pictures by Monika Beisner. Text copyright © 1979 by Alison Lurie. Illustrations copyright © 1979 by Monika Beisner. Reprinted by permission of Farrar, Straus and Giroux, LLC

Text for "Circles, Squares, and Daggers" by Elsa Marston. Reprinted by permission of the author.

From THE MYSTERY OF MARS by Sally Ride and Tam O'Shaughnessy. Copyright © 1999 by Sally Ride and Tam E. O'Shaughnessy. Reprinted by permission of Random House Children's Books, a division of Random House, Inc., New York, New York. All rights reserved.

STARS TEXT COPYRIGHT © 1986 BY SEYMOUR SIMON. Used by permission of HarperCollins Publishers.

From SPACE SONGS by Myra Cohn Livingston. Copyright © 1988 Myra Cohn Livingston.

Published by Holiday House. Reprinted by permission of Marian Reiner. Illustrations copyright © 1988 by Leonard Everett Fisher. All rights reserved. Reprinted from SPACE SONGS by permission of Holiday House, Inc.

From SPACE SONGS by Myra Cohn Livingston. Copyright © 1988 Myra Cohn Livingston. Published by Holiday House. Reprinted by permission of Marian Reiner. Illustrations copyright © 1988 by Leonard Everett Fisher. All rights reserved. Reprinted from SPACE SONGS by permission of Holiday House, Inc.

"The Book That Saved the Earth" reprinted with permission of Plays Magazine.

From THE LAND I LOST, TEXT COPYRIGHT © 1982 BY HUYNH QUANG NHUONG. ILLUSTRATIONS COPYRIGHT © 1982 BY VO-DINH MAI. Used by permission of HarperCollins Publishers.

Abridged from IN TWO WORLDS: A Yup'ik Eskimo Family, by Aylette Jenness and Alice Rivers. Text copyright © 1989 by Aylette Jenness and Alice Rivers. Photographs copyright © 1989 by Aylette Jenness. Reprinted by permission of Houghton Mifflin Company, Inc.

"History of the Tunrit" from SONGS AND STORIES OF THE NETSILIK ESKIMOS, translated by Edward Field from text collected by Knud Rasmussen, illustrated by Pudlo. Reprinted with permission of Sand & Sorensen Law Firm.

Copyright © 1972 by Peggy

Mann. "The West Side" published in HOW JUAN GOT HOME; published by Coward-McCann (now Penguin-Putnam). Reprinted by permission of Curtis Brown, Ltd.

From LOVE AS STRONG AS GINGER. Text copyright © 1999 by Lenore Look, illustrations copyright © 1999 by Stephen T. Johnston. Reprinted with permission of Atheneum Books for Young Readers, Simon & Schuster Children's Publishing Division. All rights reserved.

"Women" from REVOLUTION-ARY PETUNIAS & OTHER POEMS, copyright © 1970 by Alice Walker, reprinted by permission of Harcourt, Inc.

From The Night Journey by Kathryn Lasky, with drawings by Trina Schart Hyman. Copyright © 1981 by Trina Schart Hyman, illustrations. Used by permission of Viking Children's Books, a division of Penguin Putnam, Inc.

"Parmele" from CHILDTIMES, COPYRIGHT © 1979 BY ELOISE GREENFIELD AND LESSIE JONES LITTLE. Used by permission of HarperCollins Publishers.

From ...IF YOU LIVED AT THE TIME OF THE AMERICAN REVOLUTION by Kay Moore, cover illustration by Daniel O'Leary. Text copyright © 1997 by Kay Moore, cover illustration copyright © 1997 by Scholastic Inc. Reprinted by permission.

"The Night the Revolution Began" Copyright © 2000 by Russell Freedman. All rights reserved. Reprinted from GIVE ME LIBERTY! The Story of the Declaration of Independence by permission of Holiday House, Inc.

www.sra4kids.com

SRA/McGraw-Hill

A Division of The **McGraw·Hill** *Companies*

Send all inquiries to:
SRA/McGraw-Hill
8787 Orion Place
Columbus, OH 43240-4027

Printed in the United States of America.

ISBN 0-07-569249-X

10 11 12 13 14 15 RRW 08 07 06 05

— Program Authors —

Marilyn Jager Adams, Ph.D.
BBN Technologies

Carl Bereiter, Ph.D.
University of Toronto

Joe Campione, Ph.D.
University of California at Berkeley

Iva Carruthers, Ph.D.
Northeastern Illinois University

Jan Hirshberg, Ed.D.
Reading Specialist

Anne McKeough, Ph.D.
University of Calgary

Michael Pressley, Ph.D.
University of Notre Dame

Marsha Roit, Ph.D.
National Reading Consultant

Marlene Scardamalia, Ph.D.
University of Toronto

Gerald H. Treadway, Jr., Ed.D.
San Diego State University

Table of Contents
Cooperation and Competition 18

Table of Contents

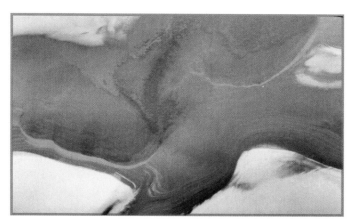

Table of Contents

Heritage

UNIT 4

Table of Contents
Making a New Nation

12

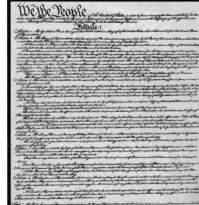

UNIT 5

Table of Contents

Going West 388

UNIT 6

Table of Contents
Journeys and Quests 508

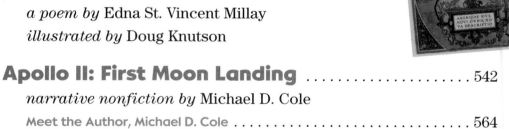

Cooperation and Competition

Sometimes we need to cooperate with each other to get things done. Sometimes, though, we find ourselves competing with each other. Sometimes we need to do both at the same time—cooperate with teammates while competing against an opposing team. Cooperation and competition play important roles in our lives and they take on many different faces. How do you see competition and cooperation at work in your life?

Focus Questions What qualities do good leaders have?
If you were running for class president, what would be your
strategy for winning the election?

Class President

Johanna Hurwitz
illustrated by Richard Hull

**To Delia and Bill Gottlieb
They get my vote every time!**

*Julio Sanchez is sure that fifth grade is going to be his
best year yet. On the first day of school, his homeroom
teacher Mr. Flores announces that this year the fifth grade
will be electing a class president. To get ready for the
election, the students are to be thinking about who might
make a good leader.*

*In the meantime, while playing in a soccer game at recess,
Julio's classmate Arthur breaks his glasses. The fifth grade
pitches in to pay for the glasses by holding a bake sale. But
on the day of the bake sale, Arthur's mom finds out his
glasses can be replaced for free.*

*Now the class has two things to decide: who to elect as class
president and what to do with the bake sale money no longer
needed to pay for Arthur's glasses. . . .*

On Monday, Arthur came to school with new glasses. Cricket
came to class with a big poster that said, VOTE FOR CRICKET, THAT'S
THE TICKET.

The election was going to be held on Friday. That meant
there were only four days more to get ready. In the meantime,
they learned about how to make a nomination and how to
second it. It was going to be a really serious election.

At lunch, Cricket took out a bag of miniature chocolate
bars and gave them out to her classmates. Julio took his and
ate it. But it didn't mean he was going to vote for Cricket. He
wondered if there was anything Lucas could give out that was
better than chocolate. Nothing was better than chocolate!

"If you're going to run against Cricket, we've got to get to work," Julio told Lucas on their way home. Julio wasn't very good at making posters, as Cricket and Zoe were, but he was determined to help his friend.

The next morning, a new poster appeared in Mr. Flores's classroom. It said, DON'T BUG ME. VOTE FOR LUCAS COTT. Julio had made it.

Before lunch, Mr. Flores read an announcement from the principal. "From now on, there is to be no more soccer playing in the school yard at lunchtime."

"No more soccer playing?" Julio called out. "Why not?"

Mr. Flores looked at Julio. "If you give me a moment, I'll explain. Mr. Herbertson is concerned about accidents. Last week, Arthur broke his glasses. Another time, someone might be injured more seriously."

Julio was about to call out again, but he remembered just in time and raised his hand.

"Yes, Julio," said Mr. Flores.

"It's not fair to make us stop playing soccer just because someone *might* get hurt. Someone might fall down walking to school, but we still have to come to school every day."

Julio didn't mean to be funny, but everyone started to laugh. Even Mr. Flores smiled.

"There must be other activities to keep you fellows busy at lunchtime," he said. "Is soccer the only thing you can do?"

Lucas raised his hand. "I don't like jumping rope," he said when the teacher called on him.

All the girls giggled at that.

"You could play jacks," suggested Cricket. Everyone knew it wasn't a serious possibility, though.

"Couldn't we tell Mr. Herbertson that we want to play soccer?" asked Julio.

"You could make an appointment to speak to him, if you'd like," said Mr. Flores. "He might change his decision if you convince him that you are right."

"Lucas and I will talk to him," said Julio. "Right, Lucas?"

"Uh, sure," said Lucas, but he didn't look too sure.

The principal, Mr. Herbertson, spoke in a loud voice and had eyes that seemed to bore right into your head when he looked at you. Julio had been a little bit afraid of Mr. Herbertson since the very first day of kindergarten. Why had he offered to go to his office and talk to him?

Mr. Flores sent Julio and Lucas down to the principal's office with a note, but the principal was out of the office at a meeting.

"You can talk to him at one o'clock," the secretary said.

At lunch, Cricket had more chocolate bars. This time, she had pasted labels on them and printed in tiny letters, *Cricket is the ticket*. She must be spending her whole allowance on the campaign, Julio thought.

After a few more days of free chocolate bars, everyone in the class would be voting for Cricket.

At recess, the girls were jumping rope. You could fall jumping rope, too, Julio thought.

Back in the classroom, Julio wished he could think up some good arguments to tell the principal. He looked over at Lucas. Lucas didn't look very good. Maybe he was coming down with the flu.

Just before one o'clock, Julio had a great idea. Cricket was always saying she wanted to be a lawyer. She always knew what to say in class. Julio figured she'd know just what to do in the principal's office, too. He raised his hand.

"Mr. Flores, can Cricket go down to Mr. Herbertson's office with Lucas and me? She's running for president, so she should stick up for our class."

"Me?" Cricket said. "I don't care if we can't play soccer."

"Of course," teased Lucas. "You couldn't kick a ball if it was glued to your foot."

"Cricket," said Mr. Flores, "even if you don't want to play soccer, others in the class do. If you are elected, you will be president of the whole class, not just the girls. I think going to the meeting with Mr. Herbertson will be a good opportunity for you to represent the class."

So that was why at one o'clock Julio, Lucas, and Cricket Kaufman went downstairs to the principal's office.

Mr. Herbertson gestured for them to sit in the chairs facing his desk. Cricket looked as pale as Lucas. Maybe she, too, was coming down with the flu.

Julio waited for the future first woman President of the United States to say something, but Cricket didn't say a word. Neither did Lucas. Julio didn't know what to do. They couldn't just sit here and say nothing.

Julio took a deep breath. If Cricket or Lucas wasn't going to talk, he would have to do it. Julio started right in.

"We came to tell you that it isn't fair that no one can play soccer at recess just because Arthur Lewis broke his eyeglasses. Anybody can have an accident. He could have tripped and broken them getting on the school bus." Julio was amazed that so many words had managed to get out of his mouth. No one else said anything, so he went on. "Besides, a girl could fall jumping rope," said Julio. "But you didn't say that they had to stop jumping rope."

"I hadn't thought of that," said Mr. Herbertson.

Cricket looked alarmed. "Can't we jump rope anymore?" she asked.

"I didn't mean that you should make the girls stop jumping rope," Julio went on quickly. He stopped to think of a better example. "Your chair could break while you're sitting on it, Mr. Herbertson," he said.

Mr. Herbertson adjusted himself in his chair. "I certainly hope not," he said, smiling. "What is your name, young man?"

"Julio. Julio Sanchez." He pronounced it in the Spanish way with the *J* having an *H* sound.

"You have a couple of brothers who also attended this school, Julio, don't you?" asked the principal. "Nice fellows. I remember them both."

Julio smiled. He didn't know why he had always been afraid of the principal. He was just like any other person.

"Julio," Mr. Herbertson went on, "you've got a good head on your shoulders, just like your brothers. You made some very good points this afternoon. I think I can arrange things so that there will be more teachers supervising the yard during recess. Then you fellows can play soccer again tomorrow." He turned to Cricket. "You can jump rope if you'd rather do that," he said.

Cricket smiled. She didn't look so pale anymore.

Julio and Lucas and Cricket returned to Mr. Flores's classroom. "It's all arranged," said Cricket as soon as they walked in the door.

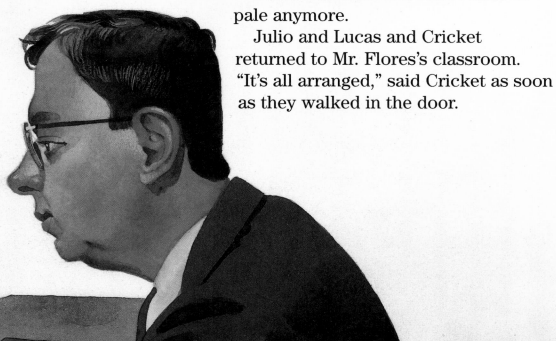

The class burst into cheers.

"Good work," said Mr. Flores.

Julio was proud that he had stood up to Mr. Herbertson. However, it wasn't fair that Cricket made it seem as if she had done all the work. She had hardly done a thing. For that matter, Lucas hadn't said anything, either. For a moment, Julio wished he hadn't offered to be Lucas's campaign manager. He wished he was the one running for class president. He knew he could be a good leader.

There was bad news on election day. Chris Willard was absent. Since there were twelve girls and twelve boys in Mr. Flores's class, it meant there were more girls than boys to vote in the election. If all the girls voted for Cricket and all the boys voted for Lucas, there would be a tie. Since one boy was absent, Lucas could be in big trouble. Julio hoped it didn't mean that Lucas had lost the election before they even voted.

Then Mr. Flores told the class that the Parent-Teacher Association was going to be holding a book fair in a few weeks. With more than seventeen dollars from the bake sale, the class could buy a good supply of paperbacks for a special classroom library. Cricket seemed to think it was a great idea, but Julio didn't think it was so hot. After all, there was a school library up one flight of stairs. Why did they need extra books, especially books the students had to pay for out of their *own* money?

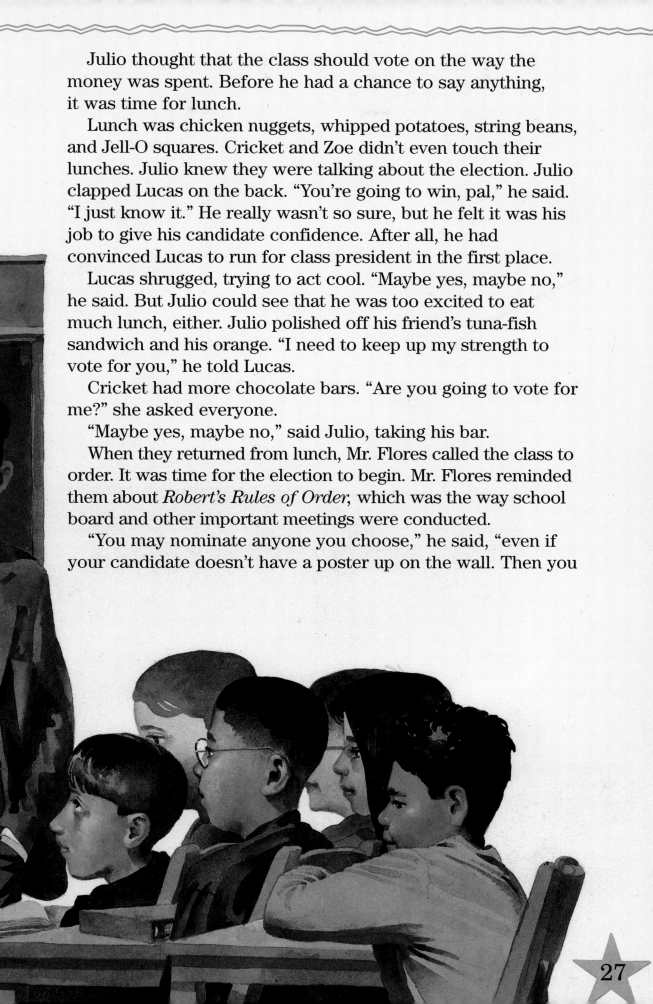

Julio thought that the class should vote on the way the money was spent. Before he had a chance to say anything, it was time for lunch.

Lunch was chicken nuggets, whipped potatoes, string beans, and Jell-O squares. Cricket and Zoe didn't even touch their lunches. Julio knew they were talking about the election. Julio clapped Lucas on the back. "You're going to win, pal," he said. "I just know it." He really wasn't so sure, but he felt it was his job to give his candidate confidence. After all, he had convinced Lucas to run for class president in the first place.

Lucas shrugged, trying to act cool. "Maybe yes, maybe no," he said. But Julio could see that he was too excited to eat much lunch, either. Julio polished off his friend's tuna-fish sandwich and his orange. "I need to keep up my strength to vote for you," he told Lucas.

Cricket had more chocolate bars. "Are you going to vote for me?" she asked everyone.

"Maybe yes, maybe no," said Julio, taking his bar.

When they returned from lunch, Mr. Flores called the class to order. It was time for the election to begin. Mr. Flores reminded them about *Robert's Rules of Order*, which was the way school board and other important meetings were conducted.

"You may nominate anyone you choose," he said, "even if your candidate doesn't have a poster up on the wall. Then you can make a speech in favor of your candidate and try to convince your classmates."

Uh-oh, thought Julio. He was ready to nominate Lucas but he didn't know if he would be able to make a speech. He wasn't good with words, as Cricket and Lucas were.

Zoe Mitchell raised her hand. "I nominate Cricket Kaufman," she said. No surprise there. Julio wondered if Zoe had wanted to run herself.

"Does anyone second the nomination?" Mr. Flores asked.

Julio thought the class election sounded like a TV program, not the way people talked in real life.

Sara Jane seconded the nomination, and Mr. Flores wrote Cricket's name on the chalkboard.

"Are there any other nominations?" he asked.

Sara Jane raised her hand again.

"Do you have a question, Sara Jane?" asked Mr. Flores.

"Now I want to nominate Zoe Mitchell."

"You can't nominate someone when you have already seconded the nomination of someone else," Mr. Flores explained. "That's the way parliamentary procedure works."

Cricket looked relieved. She hadn't been expecting any competition from Zoe.

Julio raised his hand. "I nominate Lucas Cott," he said.

"Does anyone second the nomination?"

"Can I second myself?" asked Lucas.

"I'll second the nomination," said Anne Crosby from the back of the classroom.

"*Ooooh*," giggled one of the girls. "Anne likes Lucas."

"There is no rule that girls can nominate only girls and boys nominate only boys," said Mr. Flores. He wrote Lucas's name on the board. "Are there any other nominations?" he asked.

Arthur Lewis raised his hand. "I want to nominate Julio Sanchez," he said.

"Julio?" Sara Jane giggled. "He's just a big goof-off."

"Just a minute," said Mr. Flores sharply. "You are quite out of order, Sara Jane. Does anyone wish to second the nomination?"

Julio couldn't believe that Arthur had nominated him. Even though Arthur had said that Julio should run for president, Julio hadn't thought he would come right out and say it in front of everyone.

Cricket raised her hand. "Julio can't run for president," she said. "He was born in Puerto Rico. He isn't an American citizen. You have to be an American citizen to be elected President. We learned that last year in social studies."

"Yeah," Lucas called out. "You also have to be thirty-five years old. You must have been left back a lot of times, Cricket."

"Hold on," said Mr. Flores. "Are we electing a President of the United States here, or are we electing a president of this fifth-grade class?"

Cricket looked embarrassed. It wasn't often she was wrong about anything.

Julio stood up without even raising his hand. He didn't care if he was elected president or not, but there was one thing he had to make clear. "I am so an American citizen," he said. "All Puerto Ricans are Americans!"

Julio sat down, and Arthur raised his hand again. Julio figured he was going to say he had changed his mind and didn't want to nominate him after all.

"Arthur?" called Mr. Flores.

Arthur stood up. "It doesn't matter where Julio was born," he said. "He'd make a very good class president. He's fair, and he's always doing nice things for people. When I broke my glasses, he was the one who thought of going to Mr. Herbertson so that we could still play soccer at recess. That shows he would make a good president."

"But Julio is not one of the top students like Zoe or Lucas or me," Cricket said.

"He is tops," said Arthur. "He's tops in my book."

Julio felt his ears getting hot with embarrassment. He had never heard Arthur say so much in all the years that he had known him.

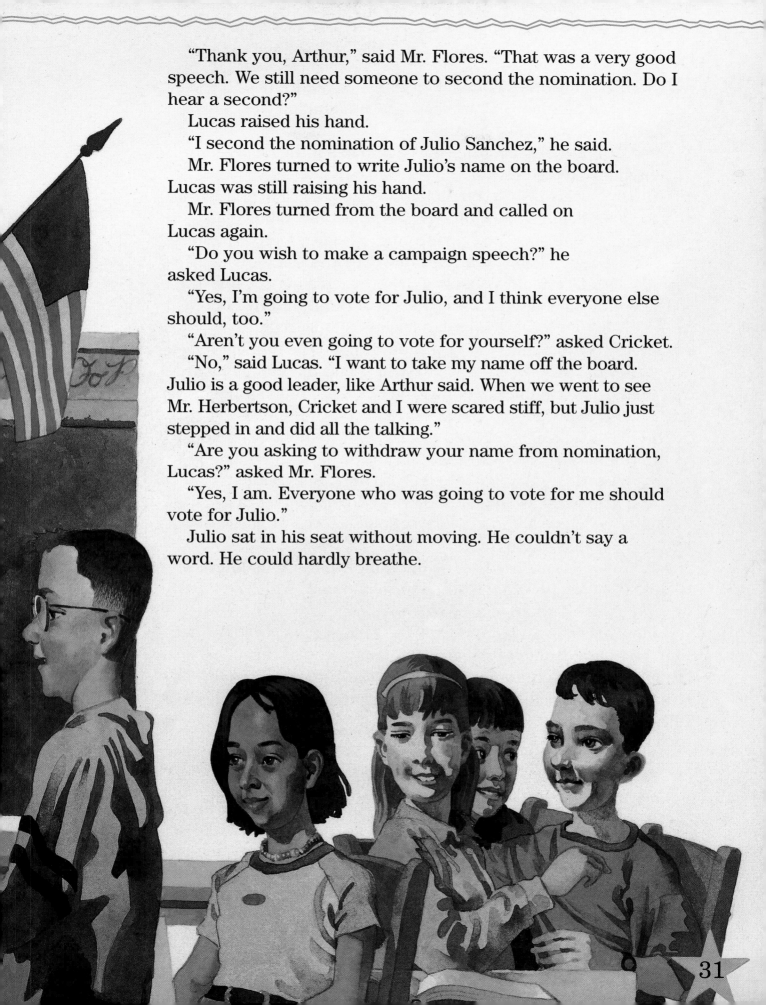

"Thank you, Arthur," said Mr. Flores. "That was a very good speech. We still need someone to second the nomination. Do I hear a second?"

Lucas raised his hand.

"I second the nomination of Julio Sanchez," he said.

Mr. Flores turned to write Julio's name on the board. Lucas was still raising his hand.

Mr. Flores turned from the board and called on Lucas again.

"Do you wish to make a campaign speech?" he asked Lucas.

"Yes, I'm going to vote for Julio, and I think everyone else should, too."

"Aren't you even going to vote for yourself?" asked Cricket.

"No," said Lucas. "I want to take my name off the board. Julio is a good leader, like Arthur said. When we went to see Mr. Herbertson, Cricket and I were scared stiff, but Julio just stepped in and did all the talking."

"Are you asking to withdraw your name from nomination, Lucas?" asked Mr. Flores.

"Yes, I am. Everyone who was going to vote for me should vote for Julio."

Julio sat in his seat without moving. He couldn't say a word. He could hardly breathe.

"Are there any other nominations?" asked Mr. Flores.

Zoe raised her hand. "I move that the nominations be closed."

"I second it," said Lucas.

Then Mr. Flores asked the two candidates if they wanted to say anything to the class.

Cricket stood up. "As you all know," she said, "I'm going to run for President of the United States some day. Being class president will be good practice for me. Besides, I know I will do a much, much better job than Julio." Cricket sat down.

Julio stood. "I might vote for Cricket when she runs for President of the United States," he said. "But right now, I hope you will all vote for me. I think our class should make decisions together, like how we should spend the money that we earned at the bake sale. We should spend the money in a way that everyone likes. Not just the teacher." Julio stopped and looked at Mr. Flores. "That's how I feel," he said.

"If I'm president," said Cricket, "I think the money should go to the Humane Society."

"*You* shouldn't tell us what to do with the money, either," said Julio. "It should be a class decision. We all helped to earn it."

"Julio has made a good point," said Mr. Flores. "I guess we can vote on that in the future."

Mr. Flores passed out the ballots. Julio was sure he knew the results even before the votes were counted. With one boy absent, Cricket would win, twelve to eleven.

Julio was right, and he was wrong. All the boys voted for him, but so did some of the girls. When the votes were counted, there were fourteen for Julio Sanchez and nine for Cricket Kaufman. Julio Sanchez was elected president of his fifth-grade class.

"I think you have made a good choice," said Mr. Flores. "And I know that Cricket will be a very fine vice-president."

Julio beamed. Suddenly he was filled with all sorts of plans for his class.

Mr. Flores took out his guitar. As he had said, they were going to end each week with some singing. Julio thought he had never felt so much like singing in all his life. However, even as he joined the class in the words to the song, he wished it was already time to go home. He could hardly wait to tell his family the news. Wait till he told them who was the fifth-grade class president. Julio, that's who!

At three o'clock, he ran all the way home.

Class President

Meet the Author

Johanna Hurwitz was born in New York, New York. It's not surprising that Ms. Hurwitz knew from the age of ten that she wanted to be a writer. Her parents met in a bookstore. She grew up in a New York City apartment where the walls were lined with books. Her father was a journalist and bookseller, and her mother was a library assistant.

She began her career with books working at the New York City Public Library while still in high school. She then got two degrees in Library Science. She published her first book while in her 30s and has been writing books for children ever since. In one interview she revealed, *"It seems as if all my fiction has grown out of real experiences."* She has written books about her children's love of baseball, her own childhood and summer vacations, her mother's childhood, and even her cats and their fleas!

Meet the Illustrator

Richard Hull teaches illustration at Brigham Young University. He has also worked as an art director and graphic designer with a magazine for fifteen years. Other books Mr. Hull has illustrated include *The Cat & the Fiddle & More, My Sister's Rusty Bike,* and *The Alphabet from Z to A (With Much Confusion on the Way).* He and his wife currently reside in Orem, Utah.

Theme Connections

Within the Selection

Record your answers to the questions below in the Response Journal section of your Writer's Notebook. In small groups, report the ideas you wrote. Discuss your ideas with the rest of your group. Then choose a person to report your group's answers to the class.

- How did the class cooperate to help Arthur? How did cooperation play a role in their effort?
- In what way are the methods that Cricket uses in the competition for class president unfair? Is competition always this way?
- Even though Julio didn't plan to run for class president, he was still nominated. What qualities did Julio have that would make him a good class president?

Beyond the Selection

- Describe a time when you or someone you know worked for the good of a group rather than the benefit of only one person.
- Think about how "Class President" adds to what you know about cooperation and competition.
- Add items to the Concept/Question Board about cooperation and competition.

The Marble Champ

from *Baseball in April and Other Stories*
by Gary Soto
illustrated by Maren Scott

Lupe Medrano, a shy girl who spoke in whispers, was the school's spelling bee champion, winner of the reading contest at the public library three summers in a row, blue ribbon awardee in the science fair, the top student at her piano recital, and the playground grand champion in chess. She was a straight-A student and——not counting kindergarten, when she had been stung by a wasp——never missed one day of elementary school. She had received a small trophy for this honor and had been congratulated by the mayor.

But though Lupe had a razor-sharp mind, she could not make her body, no matter how much she tried, run as fast as the other girls'. She begged her body to move faster, but could never beat anyone in the fifty-yard dash.

The truth was that Lupe was no good in sports. She could not catch a pop-up or figure out in which direction to kick the soccer ball. One time she kicked the ball at her own goal and scored a point for the other team. She was no good at baseball or basketball either, and even had a hard time making a hula hoop stay on her hips.

It wasn't until last year, when she was eleven years old, that she learned how to ride a bike. And even then she had to use training wheels. She could walk in the swimming pool but couldn't swim, and chanced roller skating only when her father held her hand.

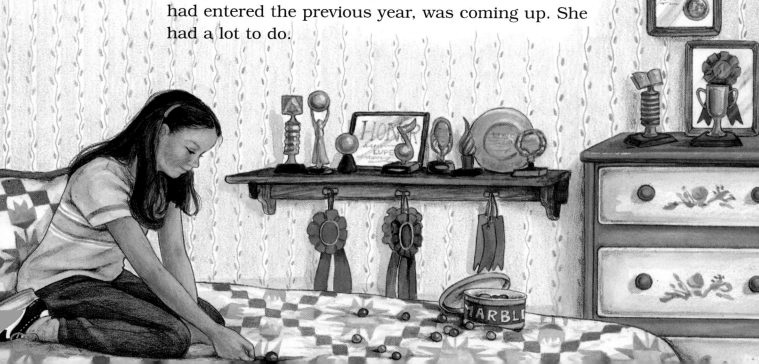

"I'll never be good at sports," she fumed one rainy day as she lay on her bed gazing at the shelf her father had made to hold her awards. "I wish I could win something, anything, even marbles."

At the word "marbles," she sat up. "That's it. Maybe I could be good at playing marbles." She hopped out of bed and rummaged through the closet until she found a can full of her brother's marbles. She poured the rich glass treasure on her bed and picked five of the most beautiful marbles.

She smoothed her bedspread and practiced shooting, softly at first so that her aim would be accurate. The marble rolled from her thumb and clicked against the targeted marble. But the target wouldn't budge. She tried again and again. Her aim became accurate, but the power from her thumb made the marble move only an inch or two. Then she realized that the bedspread was slowing the marbles. She also had to admit that her thumb was weaker than the neck of a newborn chick.

She looked out the window. The rain was letting up, but the ground was too muddy to play. She sat cross-legged on the bed, rolling her five marbles between her palms. Yes, she thought, I could play marbles, and marbles is a sport. At that moment she realized that she had only two weeks to practice. The playground championship, the same one her brother had entered the previous year, was coming up. She had a lot to do.

To strengthen her wrists, she decided to do twenty push-ups on her fingertips, five at a time. "One, two, three . . ." she groaned. By the end of the first set she was breathing hard, and her muscles burned from exhaustion. She did one more set and decided that was enough push-ups for the first day.

She squeezed a rubber eraser one hundred times, hoping it would strengthen her thumb. This seemed to work because the next day her thumb was sore. She could hardly hold a marble in her hand, let alone send it flying with power. So Lupe rested that day and listened to her brother, who gave her tips on how to shoot: get low, aim with one eye, and place one knuckle on the ground.

"Think 'eye and thumb'——and let it rip!" he said.

After school the next day she left her homework in her backpack and practiced three hours straight, taking time only to eat a candy bar for energy. With a popsicle stick, she drew an odd-shaped circle and tossed in four marbles. She used her shooter, a milky agate with hypnotic swirls, to blast them. Her thumb *had* become stronger.

After practice, she squeezed the eraser for an hour. She ate dinner with her left hand to spare her shooting hand and said nothing to her parents about her dreams of athletic glory.

Practice, practice, practice. Squeeze, squeeze, squeeze. Lupe got better and beat her brother and Alfonso, a neighbor kid who was supposed to be a champ.

"Man, she's bad!" Alfonso said. "She can beat the other girls for sure. I think."

The weeks passed quickly. Lupe worked so hard that one day, while she was drying dishes, her mother asked why her thumb was swollen.

"It's muscle," Lupe explained. "I've been practicing for the marbles championship."

"You, honey?" Her mother knew Lupe was no good at sports.

"Yeah. I beat Alfonso, and he's pretty good."

That night, over dinner, Mrs. Medrano said, "Honey, you should see Lupe's thumb."

"Huh?" Mr. Medrano said, wiping his mouth and looking at his daughter.

"Show your father."

"Do I have to?" an embarrassed Lupe asked.

"Go on, show your father."

Reluctantly, Lupe raised her hand and flexed her thumb. You could see the muscle.

The father put down his fork and asked, "What happened?"

"Dad, I've been working out. I've been squeezing an eraser."

"Why?"

"I'm going to enter the marbles championship."

Her father looked at her mother and then back at his daughter. "When is it, honey?"

"This Saturday. Can you come?"

The father had been planning to play racquetball with a friend Saturday, but he said he would be there. He knew his daughter thought she was no good at sports and he wanted to encourage her. He even rigged some lights in the backyard so she could practice after dark. He squatted with one knee on the ground, entranced by the sight of his daughter easily beating her brother.

The day of the championship began with a cold blustery sky. The sun was a silvery light behind slate clouds.

"I hope it clears up," her father said, rubbing his hands together as he returned from getting the newspaper. They ate breakfast, paced nervously around the house waiting for 10:00 to arrive, and walked the two blocks to the playground (though Mr. Medrano wanted to drive so Lupe wouldn't get tired). She signed up and was assigned her first match on baseball diamond number three.

Lupe, walking between her brother and her father, shook from the cold, not nerves. She took off her mittens, and everyone stared at her thumb. Someone asked, "How can you play with a broken thumb?" Lupe smiled and said nothing.

She beat her first opponent easily, and felt sorry for the girl because she didn't have anyone to cheer for her. Except for her sack of marbles, she was all alone. Lupe invited the girl, whose name was Rachel, to stay with them. She smiled and said, "OK." The four of them walked to a card table in the middle of the outfield, where Lupe was assigned another opponent.

She also beat this girl, a fifth-grader named Yolanda, and asked her to join their group. They proceeded to more matches and more wins, and soon there was a crowd of people following Lupe to the finals to play a girl in a baseball cap. This girl seemed dead serious. She never even looked at Lupe.

"I don't know, Dad, she looks tough."

Rachel hugged Lupe and said, "Go get her."

"You can do it," her father encouraged. "Just think of the marbles, not the girl, and let your thumb do the work."

The other girl broke first and earned one marble. She missed her next shot, and Lupe, one eye closed, her thumb quivering with energy, blasted two marbles out of the circle but missed her next shot. Her opponent earned two more before missing. She stamped her foot and said "Shoot!" The score was three to two in favor of Miss Baseball Cap.

The referee stopped the game. "Back up, please, give them room," he shouted. Onlookers had gathered too tightly around the players.

Lupe then earned three marbles and was set to get her fourth when a gust of wind blew dust in her eyes and she missed badly. Her opponent quickly scored two marbles, tying the game, and moved ahead six to five on a lucky shot. Then she missed, and Lupe, whose eyes felt scratchy when she blinked, relied on instinct and thumb muscle to score the tying point. It was now six to six, with only three marbles left. Lupe blew her nose and studied the angles. She dropped to one knee, steadied her hand, and shot so hard she cracked two marbles from the circle. She was the winner!

"I did it!" Lupe said under her breath. She rose from her knees, which hurt from bending all day, and hugged her father. He hugged her back and smiled.

Everyone clapped, except Miss Baseball Cap, who made a face and stared at the ground. Lupe told her she was a great player, and they shook hands. A newspaper photographer took pictures of the two girls standing shoulder-to-shoulder, with Lupe holding the bigger trophy.

Lupe then played the winner of the boys' division, and after a poor start beat him eleven to four. She blasted the marbles, shattering one into sparkling slivers of glass. Her opponent looked on glumly as Lupe did what she did best——win!

The head referee and the President of the Fresno Marble Association stood with Lupe as she displayed her trophies for the newspaper photographer. Lupe shook hands with everyone, including a dog who had come over to see what the commotion was all about.

That night, the family went out for pizza and set the two trophies on the table for everyone in the restaurant to see. People came up to congratulate Lupe, and she felt a little embarrassed, but her father said the trophies belonged there.

Back home, in the privacy of her bedroom, she placed the trophies on her shelf and was happy. She had always earned honors because of her brains, but winning in sports was a new experience. She thanked her tired thumb. "You did it, thumb. You made me champion." As its reward, Lupe went to the bathroom, filled the bathroom sink with warm water, and let her thumb swim and splash as it pleased. Then she climbed into bed and drifted into a hard-won sleep.

The Marble Champ

Meet the Author

Gary Soto was born into a Mexican-American family in Fresno, California. Growing up, he worked alongside his parents, grandparents, brothers and sister, as farm laborers in vineyards, orange groves, and cotton fields around Fresno.

As a young person, Mr. Soto was never very interested in books or schoolwork, but he decided to enroll in college anyway. He discovered he wanted to be a writer at the age of 20. In one of his classes he read a poem called "Unwanted." It had a big effect on him. He started taking poetry classes and writing his own poetry. Mr. Soto continues to write for both adults and children, and he produces short films.

Meet the Illustrator

Maren Scott lives in Utah with her husband and three sons. Besides illustrating, she also enjoys designing quilts. She has won many awards for both her art and her quilts. Ms. Scott advises young people interested in being artists to draw every day. She says, *"Draw what you see and don't be concerned about mistakes. It's okay to make mistakes; just learn from them and you'll get better and better!"*

Theme Connections

Within the Selection

Record your answers to the questions below in the Response Journal section of your Writer's Notebook. In small groups, report the ideas you wrote. Discuss your ideas with the rest of your group. Then choose a person to report your group's answers to the class.

- Why did Lupe care about being successful in a sports competition?
- What did Lupe do to win the marble competition? What role did her family play?
- How did Lupe treat the students she defeated in the competition? How did they respond?

Across Selections

- Which character in "Class President" is more like Lupe, Cricket or Julio? Explain why you think so.
- Compare the methods Lupe uses to win her competition with those that Cricket uses in "Class President."

Beyond the Selection

- Tell about a time when you worked hard to achieve a goal. What was your goal? Who and what helped you? What was the result of your effort?
- Think about how "The Marble Champ" adds to what you know about cooperation and competition.
- Add items to the Concept/Question Board about cooperation and competition.

The New Kid

Mike Makley

illustrated by Tony Caldwell

Our baseball team never did very much,
we had me and PeeWee and Earl and Dutch.
And the Oak Street Tigers always got beat
until the new kid moved in on our street.

The kid moved in with a mitt and a bat
and an official New York Yankee hat.
The new kid plays shortstop or second base
and can outrun us all in any race.

The kid never muffs a grounder or fly
no matter how hard it's hit or how high.
And the new kid always acts quite polite,
never yelling or spitting or starting a fight.

We were playing the league champs just last week;
they were trying to break our winning streak.
In the last inning the score was one-one,
when the new kid swung and hit a home run.

A few of the kids and their parents say
they don't believe that the new kid should play.
But she's good as me, Dutch, PeeWee, or Earl,
so we don't care that the new kid's a girl.

Good Sportsmanship

Richard Armour
illustrated by Tony Caldwell

Good sportsmanship we hail, we sing,
It's always pleasant when you spot it.
There's only one unhappy thing:
You have to lose to prove you've got it.

Juggling

Donna Gamache
illustrated by Daniel Powers

In gym class on Monday, we started volleyball, and I hit seven straight serves just over the net, hard and fast. Mr. Braden called me over at the end of the class.

"You've got a good serve, Kyle," he said. "How about coming out for the junior team?"

"Sorry, Mr. Braden," I said, without looking at him. "I'm busy every afternoon." I knew the practices were three times a week, right after school, and that's when I delivered papers. I'd started a paper route two years ago when I was ten, but this year I'd taken over a second route—a long one, too. I never finished delivering before 5:30.

"Well, think about it," Mr. Braden called as I left for my next class. "We could use a serve like yours. Couldn't you juggle your time a little?"

My friend Dave was waiting for me outside the gym door. "Did Mr. Braden ask you to join the team?" he asked.

I nodded. "I told him I was busy."

"You're a lot better than I am," said Dave as we got books from our lockers. "I wish you'd join. We need good servers."

Our next class was math, but it was hard to keep my mind on fractions and percentages. I kept thinking about how good it felt to hit that ball and see it sail over the net. Somehow I managed a spin on the ball that made it hard to hit back.

I'd have loved to say yes to Mr. Braden, but I couldn't afford to. I needed that paper route—or rather, my mom and I *both* needed it. We lived alone in a basement apartment about three blocks from school, and Mom worked at the Cramer Clothing

Factory sewing winter jackets. She didn't earn that much money, and most months her whole salary went for food and rent. Any clothing or school supplies had to come out of what I earned delivering papers. That's why I'd taken on the second route, but there still wasn't any money to spare.

The next day in gym class, Mr. Braden watched me again, and when class ended, he called out loudly, "Think about joining the team, Kyle."

Everyone heard him, and soon several other boys started trying to persuade me. "We haven't got any strong servers," said Jason. "Come on and help us out."

"I bet you could learn to spike the ball," said Billy. "You're tall enough."

They didn't seem to hear me when I mentioned my paper routes.

"We finish at 5:15," Jason persisted.

"I'm sorry!" I said. "I can't make the practices." It wouldn't have been so bad if I didn't *want* to play on the team.

"Volleyball season only lasts about two months, you know," said one.

"Where's your school spirit?" asked another.

"Leave me alone!" I finally snapped.

I decided I'd have to see Mr. Braden and tell him the truth—that I couldn't *afford* to play volleyball. But that night I found he'd phoned my mother. I knew right away something was up, but she didn't say anything until we'd finished our spaghetti.

"Your gym teacher called," she said then. "He says he wants you on the volleyball team, but you turned him down."

"Did he tell you the practice times?" I said sharply. "Yes."

"Then you know why I said no."

Mom sighed. "I told him about the paper routes. He said the practices are over by 5:15."

"My papers have to be delivered by then," I reminded her. "And when there are games, they'll play later than that." I knew my voice was shrill, but I couldn't help it. Everyone was pushing me to do something I already wanted to do, but *couldn't*.

But Mom didn't quit. I guess she knew how much I really wanted to play. "Maybe you could get someone else to deliver the papers on those nights."

"I'd have to pay someone nearly twenty dollars a week to do both routes three times," I said. Abruptly, I shoved my chair back from the table and stamped into my room. I flung myself on the bed and I didn't go out to help Mom with the dishes, either.

The next day in gym class, I deliberately hit all my serves low into the net and I messed up several setups, too. I saw Mr. Braden looking at me in a funny way, but he didn't say anything then. I kept away from Dave all day and ignored the other boys from the team.

At 3:30 I grabbed my homework from my locker and was just heading out the door when my name was called on the intercom. "Kyle Kreerson, please report to Mr. Braden's office."

I thought about ignoring the announcement, but I didn't want to get into trouble. When I reached the office, I saw that Dave was already there. I didn't give Mr. Braden time to speak. I just started right in. "Mr. Braden," I said, "I'm sorry I can't join your team. Will you please stop asking me about it? And ask the other guys to stop pestering me? I'd join if I could. But I *can't!* O.K.?!"

Nobody spoke for a minute, and then Mr. Braden took a deep breath. His face was red, almost like his hair. "Kyle," he said, "I understand. I'm sorry to pressure you, but I called you here to suggest something. Maybe *I* can do the juggling, instead of you."

"What do you mean?"

"As you know, Miss Foxon coaches the girls' team. Right now, they practice after us, but she's offered to trade practice times. That would start our practices at 5:15."

"I'm not finished with my routes by then," I said sharply.

"If you had some help, you could be, right? Dave is offering to help you."

"I can't afford to pay him," I insisted.

"I don't want to be paid," Dave said.

"Then why do it?"

Dave shrugged. "Because I want to. Because I want you on the team. And because you're my friend."

"Enough reasons?" asked Mr. Braden.

I looked at them both for a moment and I felt good for the first time in four days. "When do we start?" I smiled.

Juggling

Meet the Illustrator

Daniel Powers always loved
drawing and painting, but he did not go to
art school until recently. Mr. Powers lives in
the high desert country of New Mexico and enjoys
hiking there with his wife and two dogs. A couple
of times a year he works with children in the
schools of the nearby Zuñi Pueblo. He has
illustrated many children's books including
Jiro's Pearl, From the Land of the White Birch,
and *Dear Katie, The Volcano is a Girl.*

Theme Connections

Within the Selection

Record your answers to the questions below in the Response Journal section of your Writer's Notebook. In small groups, report the ideas you wrote. Discuss your ideas with the rest of your group. Then choose a person to report your group's answers to the class.

- In what way is Kyle a cooperative member of his family?
- How did the cooperation of the girls' volleyball team help solve Kyle's problem?
- How will Dave's help in delivering papers aid both Kyle and the team? Why did Dave offer to help Kyle?

Across Selections

- Compare how Dave, in this story, and Julio, in "Class President," cooperate for the benefit of the group.
- In what way are the families in this story and "The Marble Champ" alike?

Beyond the Selection

- Think about how "Juggling" adds to what you know about cooperation and competition.
- Add items to the Concept/Question Board about cooperation and competition.

Fine Art

Small Roman Abacus. Museo Nazionale Romano Delle Terme, Rome, Italy.

Footballers. **Ruskin Spear.** Private collection.

56

***Artist Pyramid.* Josef Hegenbarth.**
Oil on canvas. Private collection ©2001 Josef
Hegenbarth/Licensed by VAGA, New York, NY.

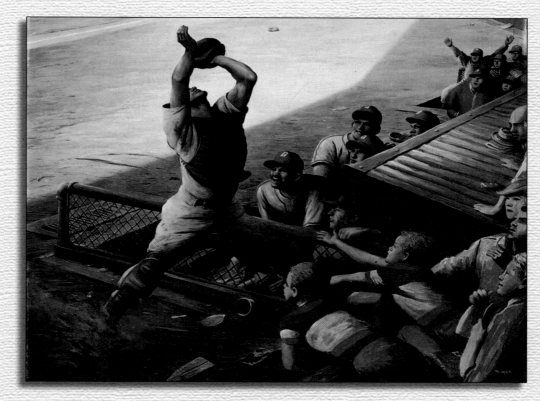

***Catcher on the Line.* Robert Riggs.** Oil on canvas.
Private collection.

Focus Questions Why is Gao Mai nervous about the upcoming abacus contest? Is it possible to be friends with one's rival?

The Abacus Contest

Priscilla Wu

illustrated by Yoshi Miyake

Gao Mai's fingers flew back and forth over the smooth black beads of the abacus.

Suddenly a wire snapped. The beads bounced onto the desk and rolled across the floor.

Gao Mai fell to her knees and crawled around after them. Just as she reached for the last bead, her best friend Li Zhi kicked it away from her hand. The other children giggled. Gao Mai's face burned.

Gao Mai opened her eyes wide and sat up in alarm. What an awful dream!

The comforting aroma of steamy, overcooked rice drifted in from the next room. She pushed aside the heavy quilt, got up from the floor and put on her school uniform.

"Are you ready for the big day?" Gao Mai's mother asked her as she came into the main room of the apartment. Gao Mai sat down at the table and helped herself to dried meat, eel and pickled cucumber.

The dream was fresh in her mind. "I'm not sure," she said.

"Remember what I told you," said Gao Mai's father. "Imagine the abacus is part of you." He smiled at her. "You did so well when we practiced."

It was true. During a few of her many timed drills she was even faster than her father. And he used the abacus every day at the bank.

"Don't worry," said her mother. "You're one of the best abacus students in your class."

"But what about Li Zhi?" asked Gao Mai. "She's beaten me every year."

"Last time it was only by one second. You've improved so much, I'm sure you'll win. Besides," continued her mother, as she lit the incense on the altar where the family ancestors were honored, "you were born under the lucky sign of the horse. I went to the temple yesterday and said a special prayer for you."

Gao Mai looked at her watch. "I have to go."

"Good luck," said her mother.

"Good luck," said her father. "I'll be thinking about you all morning."

Gao Mai ran downstairs to the street and walked quickly through the open market. One farmer had spread a piece of burlap on the pavement and piled it high with cut sugarcane. Her mouth watered as she thought of sucking the sweet juice from the snowy white center. Gao Mai glanced at the fish swimming around in a shallow metal pan. Tonight they would be on someone's plate, maybe even her own.

She reached the school just as the bell rang. Outside her classroom some boys were playing jian zhi. Her classmate, Kun Pei, scored one point after another by kicking the jian zhi into the air over and over again without letting it hit the ground.

Gao Mai walked into the classroom and Kun Pei yelled: "I won!"

During last year's abacus contest Li Zhi had beaten Kun Pei by four seconds, and Gao Mai had beaten him by three seconds. Today she was hoping to beat both of them.

Gao Mai watched Li Zhi's braids bounce as she tapped everyone on the way to her desk. She knew Li Zhi loved practical jokes and could tell by her mischievous look that she might play one at any moment. Gao Mai smiled while thinking of jokes they had played on their classmates together. Last week they had even played one on Li Zhi's mother. Yesterday Li Zhi had invited her to come over after school today so that they could think of a trick to play on her brother, Da Wei.

"Don't forget who won last year," said Li Zhi, sitting down behind her. She tugged on Gao Mai's ponytail and giggled.

"That was last year." Gao Mai leaned away and said, "If you pull my hair again, I'm not going to your house today."

Li Zhi leaned forward to grab Gao Mai's ponytail but only caught the tip. Gao Mai started to say: That's it, I'm not going to your house today. But the teacher arrived and the class stood up to greet him.

"Ni hao?" said Mr. Wang. "While everyone is nice and fresh, we'll begin with the abacus contest." He passed out booklets filled with addition, subtraction, multiplication and division problems.

"Open to the first page and begin with number one. When all the exercises are completed, return your booklet to my desk and I'll write the final time. Ready?" He paused. "Begin!"

Gao Mai's left hand moved down the column of numbers rapidly, wrote the answers and turned the test pages. The fingers on her right hand flew back and forth among the smooth, black beads of the abacus.

In a few minutes she was writing the last answer to the addition problems. Gao Mai began subtracting and a moment later heard pages turning. Everyone was right behind her!

She worked carefully. It was easy to make a subtraction mistake, especially when exchanging a higher bead for lesser ones.

After finishing the last subtraction problem she heard Li Zhi's page turn.

Gao Mai frantically turned to the multiplication but two pages were stuck together. She pulled them apart with shaking hands.

Barely breathing, Gao Mai sped through the multiplication and division. Finally she wrote down the last answer, jumped from her seat and collided with Li Zhi.

Two desks in front of them, Kun Pei rushed up and dropped his booklet on the teacher's desk.

"Oh, no!" yelled Li Zhi. "It's not fair!" She and Gao Mai dropped their booklets on the desk immediately after him.

"Quiet down, everyone," said the teacher.

Gao Mai returned to her desk and slumped in the seat, unaware of the other students handing in their booklets. Her bad dream had come true.

"Time for recess," said Mr. Wang, "while I check the answers."

Gao Mai was the last to go outside.

"Come on," yelled Ping Mei, wanting her to come and jump rope. But she shook her head. Across the playground, Li Zhi motioned for her to come and play tag with some of their friends. But Gao Mai turned away.

As he kicked the jian zhi into the air, Kun Pei bragged to a group of boys about winning the abacus contest. Gao Mai thought of her father's jian zhi at home on top of the TV. Father! Gao Mai knew he'd be disappointed that she hadn't won. The bell rang and everyone piled back into the classroom.

She heard Li Zhi behind her, laughing. "Hurry up, slowpoke!" she said, pushing past her.

Gao Mai secretly wished she could be carefree, like Li Zhi.

Mr. Wang stood up with the winning certificates in his hand. "Third-place winner of this year's abacus contest is Zong Zong."

The class applauded and a small girl with thick glasses walked quickly to the front of the room and shook hands with the teacher.

"The second-place certificate goes to Kun Pei," Mr. Wang continued.

Kun Pei came forward, looking as if he were about to cry.

"You were first to get your booklet in," Mr. Wang said as he handed him a certificate. "But one answer was wrong."

Gao Mai was confused. She turned around and looked into Li Zhi's bewildered face.

"Now," began the teacher, "we have an unusual situation——one that has never happened to me before. First place in speed and accuracy goes to Li Zhi, last year's first-place winner, and also to Gao Mai, last year's second-place winner."

Gao Mai turned and looked at Li Zhi. They burst out laughing and hurried to the front of the room.

"Here's a first-place certificate for both of you," said Mr. Wang.

As Gao Mai shook hands with the teacher, she decided it was a good day to go to Li Zhi's, after all.

The Abacus Contest

Meet the Author

Priscilla Wu comes from a family full of writers. Her father and grandfather write books, and her grandmother had some articles published in a newspaper. Says Priscilla, *"My dad, I remember him in the basement pounding away on a typewriter. . . . And from my dad's side—he was from the South—there was a tradition of storytelling. I grew up with many stories, or tall tales. . . . And I did the same thing with my own children. We had a lot of storytelling. We used to sit around in the dark at night, and sometimes, rather than read a story, we would tell stories."* Priscilla went on to become a writer herself, but not because writing came easily to her. *"I wasn't a very good writer in school. I've had to work very hard, and I think it is important to let students know that working hard does make a difference."*

Meet the Illustrator

Yoshi Miyake was born in Tokyo, Japan. She graduated from the Tokyo Metropolitan University with a degree in chemistry. While in college, she took a correspondence class in art. After graduation, she moved to Chicago to attend the American Academy of Art. She later opened a gallery called American West. Her long-time interest in Native American culture, and her study of the Blackfoot and Sioux languages inspired the theme of this gallery. Yoshi Miyake is the illustrator of more than a dozen children's books.

Theme Connections

Within the Selection

Record your answers to the questions below in the Response Journal section of your Writer's Notebook. In small groups, report the ideas you wrote. Discuss your ideas with the rest of your group. Then choose a person to report your group's answers to the class.

- How did the attitude of Gao Mai's parents toward the contest affect her own attitude?
- Why did Gao Mai feel it was unfair for Kun Pei to have his test booklet turned in before hers?
- What might have happened to Gao Mai's friendship with Li Zhi if there had been no tie?

Across Selections

- In what way is Gao Mai's attitude toward the abacus competition similar to Lupe's in "The Marble Champ"? In what way is it different?
- Compare the way Gao Mai responds to her parents' interest in the abacus competition with the way Lupe responds to hers.

Beyond the Selection

- Tell about a time when you competed against a friend. How did you feel? How did it affect your friendship?
- Think about how "The Abacus Contest" adds to what you know about cooperation and competition.
- Add items to the Concept/Question Board about cooperation and competition.

S.O.R. LOSERS

from the book by Avi
illustrated by Kate Flanagan

*Ed Sitrow and his friends have a big problem. All students at
South Orange River Middle School are required to play one sport
per year—only Ed is no jock and neither are his friends. Playing
a sport is sure to mean only one thing for them—total
humiliation. Somehow, they manage to slip through their first
year at S.O.R. without playing a sport. But when the school
catches on, they make up a special soccer team just for Ed's
crowd. This soccer team is anything but typical at a school
positively famous for its winning teams and all-star athletes. Mr.
Lester, the history teacher, has volunteered to be their coach. Little
does the team know that they'll be making history of their own.*

I should have guessed what was going to happen next when
this kid from the school newspaper interviewed me. It went
this way.

NEWSPAPER: How does it feel to lose every game?
ME: I never played on a team that won, so I can't compare.
  But it's . . . interesting.
NEWSPAPER: How many teams have you been on?
ME: Just this one.
NEWSPAPER: Do you want to win?
ME: Wouldn't mind knowing what it feels like. For the novelty.
NEWSPAPER: Have you figured out why you lose all the time?
ME: They score more goals.
NEWSPAPER: Have you seen any improvement?
ME: I've been too busy.

NEWSPAPER: Busy with what?

ME: Trying to stop their goals. Ha-ha.

NEWSPAPER: From the scores, it doesn't seem like you've been too successful with that.

ME: You can imagine what the scores would have been if I wasn't there. Actually, I'm the tallest.

NEWSPAPER: What's that have to do with it?

ME: Ask Mr. Lester.

NEWSPAPER: No S.O.R. team has ever lost all its games in one season. How do you feel about that record?

ME: I read somewhere that records are made to be broken.

NEWSPAPER: But how will you feel?

ME: Same as I do now.

NEWSPAPER: How's that?

ME: Fine.

NEWSPAPER: Give us a prediction. Will you win or lose your last game?

ME: As captain, I can promise only one thing.

NEWSPAPER: What's that?

ME: I don't want to be there to see what happens.

Naturally, they printed all that. Next thing I knew some kids decided to hold a pep rally.

"What for?" asked Radosh.

"To fill us full of pep, I suppose."

"What's pep?"

Hays looked it up. "Dash," he read.

Saltz shook his head.

"What's dash?" asked Porter.

"Sounds like a deodorant soap," said Eliscue.

And then Ms. Appleton called me aside. "Ed," she said, sort of whispering (I guess she was embarrassed to be seen talking to any of us), "people are asking, 'Do they *want* to lose?'"

"Who's asking?"

"It came up at the last teachers' meeting. Mr. Tillman thinks you might be encouraging a defeatist attitude in the school. And Mr. Lester . . ."

"What about him?"

"He doesn't know."

It figured. "Ms. Appleton," I said, "why do people care so much if we win or lose?"

"It's your . . . attitude," she said. "It's so unusual. We're not used to . . . well . . . not winning sometimes. Or . . . not caring if you lose."

"Think there's something the matter with us?" I wanted to know.

"No," she said, but when you say "no" the way she did, slowly, there's lots of time to sneak in a good hint of "yes." "I don't think you *mean* to lose."

"That's not what I asked."

"It's important to win," she said.

"Why? We're good at other things. Why can't we stick with that?"

But all she said was, "Try harder."

I went back to my seat. "I'm getting nervous," I mumbled.

"About time," said Saltz.

"Maybe we should defect."

"Where to?"

"There must be some country that doesn't have sports."

Then, of course, when my family sat down for dinner that night it went on.

"In two days you'll have your last game, won't you," my ma said. It was false cheerful, as if I had a terminal illness and she wanted to pretend it was only a head cold.

"Yeah," I said.

"You're going to win," my father announced.

"How do you know?" I snapped.

"I sense it."

"Didn't know you could tell the future."

"Don't be so smart," he returned. "I'm trying to be supportive."

"I'm sick of support!" I yelled and left the room.

Twenty minutes later I got a call. Saltz.

"Guess what?" he said.

"I give up."

"Two things. My father offered me a bribe."

"To lose the game?"

"No, to win it. A new bike."

"Wow. What did you say?"

"I told him I was too honest to win a game."

"What was the second thing?"

"I found out that at lunch tomorrow they are doing that pep rally, and worse. They're going to call up the whole team."

I sighed. "Why are they doing all this?" I asked.

"Nobody loves a loser," said Saltz.

"Why?" I asked him, just as I had asked everybody else.

"Beats me. Like everybody else does." He hung up.

I went into my room and flung myself on my bed and stared up at the ceiling. A short time later my father came into the room. "Come on, kid," he said, "I was just trying to be a pal."

"Why can't people let us lose in peace?"

"People think you feel bad."

"We feel *fine!*"

"Come on. We won't talk about it any more. Eat your dinner."

I went.

Next day, when I walked into the school eating area for lunch there was the usual madhouse. But there was also a big banner across the front part of the room:

**Make the Losers Winners
Keep Up the Good Name of
S.O.R.**

I wanted to start a food fight right then and there.

I'm not going through the whole bit. But halfway through the lunch period, the president of the School Council, of all people, went to the microphone and called for attention. Then she made a speech.

"We just want to say to the Special Seventh-Grade Soccer Team that we're all behind you."

"It's in front of us where we need people," whispered Saltz. "Blocking."

The president went on. "Would you come up and take a bow." One by one she called our names. Each time one of us went up, looking like cringing but grinning worms, there was some general craziness, hooting, foot stomping, and an occasional milk carton shooting through the air.

The president said: "I'd like the team captain, Ed Sitrow, to say a few words."

What could I do? Trapped, I cleared my throat. Four times. "Ah, well . . . we . . . ah . . . sure . . . hope to get there . . . and . . . you know . . . I suppose . . . play and . . . you know!"

The whole room stood up to cheer. They even began the school chant.

"Give me an S! Give me an O . . . "

After that we went back to our seats. I was madder than ever. And as I sat there, maybe two hundred and fifty kids filed by, thumping me hard on the back, shoulder, neck and head, yelling, "Good luck! Good luck!" They couldn't fool me. I knew what they were doing: beating me.

"Saltz," I said when they were gone and I was merely numb, "I'm calling an emergency meeting of the team."

Like thieves, we met behind the school, out of sight. I looked around. I could see everybody was feeling rotten.

"I'm sick and tired of people telling me we have to win," said Root.

"I think my folks are getting ready to disown me," said Hays. "My brother and sister too."

"Why can't they just let us lose?" asked Macht.

"Yeah," said Barish, "because we're not going to win."

"We might," Lifsom offered. "Parkville is supposed to be the pits too."

"Yeah," said Radosh, "but we're beneath the pits."

"Right," agreed Porter.

For a moment it looked like everyone was going to start to cry.

"I'd just like to do my math," said Macht. "I like that."

There it was. Something clicked. "Hays," I said, "you're good at music, right."

"Yeah, well, sure—rock 'n' roll."

"Okay. And Macht, what's the lowest score you've pulled in math so far?"

"A-plus."

"Last year?"

"Same."

"Lifsom," I went on, getting excited, "how's your painting coming?"

"I just finished something real neat and . . . "

"That's it," I cut in, because that kid can go on forever about his painting. "Every one of us is good at something. Right? Maybe more than one thing. The point is, *other* things."

"Sure," said Barish.

"Except," put in Saltz, "sports."

We were quiet for a moment. Then I saw what had been coming to me: "That's *their* problem. I mean, we are good, good at *lots* of things. Why can't we just plain stink in some places? That's got to be normal."

"Let's hear it for normal," chanted Dorman.

"Doesn't bother me to lose at sports," I said. "At least, it didn't bother me until I let other people make me bothered."

"What about the school record?" asked Porter. "You know, no team ever losing for a whole season. Want to be famous for that?"

"Listen," I said, "did we want to be on this team?"

"No!" they all shouted.

73

"I can see some of it," I said. "You know, doing something different. But I don't like sports. I'm not good at it. I don't enjoy it. So I say, so what? I mean if Saltz here writes a stinko poem—and he does all the time—do they yell at him? When was the last time Mr. Tillman came around and said, 'Saltz, I *believe* in your being a poet!'"

"Never," said Saltz.

"Yeah," said Radosh. "How come sports is so important?"

"You know," said Dorman, "maybe a loser makes people think of things *they* lost. Like Mr. Tillman not getting into pro football. Us losing makes him remember that."

"Us winning, he forgets," cut in Eliscue.

"Right," I agreed. "He needs us to win for *him*, not for us. Maybe it's the same for others."

"Yeah, but how are you going to convince them of that?" said Barish.

"By not caring if we lose," I said.

"Only one thing," put in Saltz. "They say this Parkville team is pretty bad too. What happens if we, you know, by mistake, win?"

That set us back a moment.

"I think," suggested Hays after a moment, "that if we just go on out there, relax, and do our best, and not worry so much, we'll lose."

There was general agreement on that point.

"Do you know what I heard?" said Eliscue.

"What?"

"I didn't want to say it before, but since the game's a home game, they're talking about letting the whole school out to cheer us on to a win."

"You're kidding."

He shook his head.

There was a long, deep silence.

"Probably think," said Saltz, "that we'd be ashamed to lose in front of everybody."

I took a quick count. "You afraid to lose?" I asked Saltz.

"No way."

"Hays?"

"No."

"Porter?"

"Nope."

And so on. I felt encouraged. It was a complete vote of no confidence.

"Well," I said, "they just might see us lose again. With Parkville so bad I'm not saying it's automatic. But I'm not going to care if we do."

"Right," said Radosh. "It's not like we're committing treason or something. People have a right to be losers."

We considered that for a moment. It was then I had my most brilliant idea. "Who has money?"

"What for?"

"I'm your tall captain, right? Trust me. And bring your soccer T-shirts to me in the morning, early."

I collected about four bucks and we split up. I held Saltz back.

"What's the money all about?" he wanted to know. "And the T-shirts."

"Come on," I told him. "Maybe we can show them we really mean it."

When I woke the next morning, I have to admit, I was excited. It wasn't going to be an ordinary day. I looked outside and saw the sun was shining. I thought, "Good."

For the first time I *wanted* a game to happen.

I got to breakfast a little early, actually feeling happy.

"Today's the day," Dad announced.

"Right."

"Today you'll really win," chipped in my ma.

"Could be."

My father leaned across the table and gave me a tap. "Winning the last game is what matters. Go out with your head high, Ed."

"And my backside up if I lose?" I wanted to know.

"Ed," said my ma, "don't be so hard on yourself. Your father and I are coming to watch."

"Suit yourselves," I said, and beat it to the bus.

As soon as I got to class Saltz and I collected the T-shirts. "What are you going to do with them?" the others kept asking.

"You picked me as captain, didn't you?"

"Mr. Lester did."

"Well, this time, trust *me*."

When we got all the shirts, Saltz and I sneaked into the home ec room and did what needed to be done. Putting them into a bag so no one would see, we went back to class.

"Just about over," I said.

"I'm almost sorry," confessed Saltz.

"Me too," I said. "And I can't figure out why."

"Maybe it's—the team that loses together, really stays together."

"Right. Not one fathead on the whole team. Do you think we should have gotten a farewell present for Mr. Lester?"

"Like what?"

"A begging cup."

It was hard getting through the day. And it's impossible to know how many people wished me luck. From all I got it was clear they considered me the unluckiest guy in the whole world. I kept wishing I could have banked it for something important.

But the day got done.

It was down in the locker room, when we got ready, that I passed out the T-shirts.

Barish held his up. It was the regular shirt with "S.O.R." on the back. But under it Saltz and I had ironed on press letters. Now they all read:

S.O.R.
LOSERS

Barish's reaction was just to stare. That was my only nervous moment. Then he cracked up, laughing like crazy. And the rest, once they saw, joined in. When Mr. Lester came down he brought Mr. Tillman. We all stood up and turned our backs to them.

"Oh, my goodness," moaned Mr. Lester.

"That's sick," said Mr. Tillman. "Sick!" His happy beads shook furiously.

"It's honest," I said.

"It's defeatist," he yelled.

"Mr. Tillman," I asked, "is that true, about your trying out for pro football?"

He started to say something, then stopped, his mouth open. "Yeah. I tried to make it with the pros, but couldn't."

"So you lost too, right?"

"Yeah," chimed in Radosh, "everyone loses sometime."

"Listen here, you guys," said Mr. Tillman, "it's no fun being rejected."

"Can't it be okay to lose sometimes? You did. Lots do. You're still alive. And we don't dislike you because of that."

"Right. We got other reasons," I heard a voice say. I think it was Saltz.

Mr. Tillman started to say something, but turned and fled.

Mr. Lester tried to give us a few final pointers, like don't touch the ball with our hands, only use feet, things that we didn't always remember to do.

"Well," he said finally, "I enjoyed this."

"You did?" said Porter, surprised.

"Well, not much," he admitted. "I never coached anything before. To tell the truth, I don't know anything about soccer."

"Now you tell us," said Eliscue. But he was kidding. We sort of guessed that before.

Just as we started out onto the field, Saltz whispered to me, "What if we win?"

"With our luck, we will," I said.

And on we went.

As we ran onto the field we were met with something like a roar. Maybe the whole school wasn't there. But a lot were. And they were chanting, "Win! Win! Win!"

But when they saw the backs of our shirts, they really went wild. Crazy. And you couldn't tell if they were for us or against us. I mean scary . . .

Oh yes, the game . . .

We had been told that Parkville was a team that hadn't won a game either. They looked it. From the way they kicked the ball around—tried to kick the ball around—it was clear this was going to be a true contest between horribles.

The big difference was their faces. Stiff and tight. You could see, they *wanted* to win. Had to win. We were relaxed and fooling around. Having a grand old time.

Not them.

The ref blew his whistle and called captains. I went out, shook hands. The Parkville guy was really tense. He kept squeezing his hands, rubbing his face. The whole bit.

The ref said he wanted the usual, a clean, hard game, and he told us which side we should defend. "May the best team win," he said. A believer!

Anyway, we started.

(I know the way this is supposed to work. . . . There we are, relaxed, having a good time, not caring really what goes on, maybe by this time, not even sweating the outcome. That should make us, in television land—winners. Especially as it becomes very clear that Parkville is frantic about winning. Like crazy. They have a coach who screams himself red-faced all the time. Who knows. Maybe he's going to lose his job if they lose.)

Well . . .

A lot of things happened that game. There was the moment, just like the first game, when their side, dressed in stunning scarlet, came plunging down our way. Mighty Saltz went out to meet them like a battleship. True to form (red face and wild) he gave a mighty kick, and missed. But he added something new. Leave it to my buddy Saltz. He swung so hard he sat down, sat down on the ball. Like he was hatching an egg.

We broke up at that. So did everyone else. Except the Parkville coach. He was screaming, "Penalty! Penalty!"

So they got the ball. And, it's true, I was laughing so much they scored an easy goal. It was worth it.

"Least you could have done is hatched it," I yelled at Saltz.

"I think they allow only eleven on a team," he yelled back.

Then there was the moment when Porter, Radosh and Dorman got into a really terrific struggle to get the ball–from each other. Only when they looked up did they realize with whom they were struggling. By that time, of course, it was too late. Stolen ball.

There was the moment when Parkville knocked the ball out of bounds. Macht had to throw it in. He snatched up the ball, held it over his head, got ready to heave it, then–dropped it.

It was a close game though. The closest. By the time it was almost over they were leading by only one. We were actually in the game.

And how did the crowd react? They didn't know what to do. Sometimes they laughed. Sometimes they chanted that "Win! Win!" thing. It was like a party for them.

Then it happened . . .

Macht took the ball on a pass from Lifsom. Lifsom dribbled down the right side and flipped it toward the middle. Hays got it fairly well, and, still driving, shot a pass back to Radosh, who somehow managed to snap it easy over to Porter, who was right near the side of the goal.

Porter, not able to shoot, knocked the ball back to Hays, who charged toward the goal–only some Parkville guy managed to get in the way. Hays, screaming, ran right over him, still controlling the ball.

I stood there, astonished. "They've gotten to him," I said to myself. "He's flipped."

I mean, Hays was like a wild man. Not only had he the cleanest shot in the universe, he was desperate.

And so . . . he tripped. Fell flat on his face. Thunk!

Their goalie scooped up the ball, flung it downfield and that was the end of that.

As for Hays, he picked himself up, slowly, too slowly.

The crowd grew still.

You could see it all over Hays. Shame. The crowd waited. They were feeling sorry for him. You could feel it. And standing there in the middle of the field—everything had just stopped— everybody was watching Hays—the poor guy began to cry.

That's all you could hear. His sobs. He had failed.

Then I remembered. "SOR LOSER!" I bellowed.

At my yell, our team snapped up their heads and looked around.

"SOR LOSER!" I bellowed again.

The team picked up the words and began to run toward Hays, yelling, cheering, screaming, "SOR LOSER! SOR LOSER! SOR LOSER!"

Hays, stunned, began to get his eyes up.

Meanwhile, the whole team, and I'm not kidding, joined hands and began to run in circles around Hays, still giving the chant.

The watching crowd, trying to figure out what was happening, finally began to understand. And they began to cheer!

"SOR LOSER   SOR LOSER   SOR LOSER!"

As for Hays, well, you should have seen his face. It was like a Disney nature-film flower blooming. Slow, but steady. Fantastic! There grew this great grin on his face. Then he lifted his arms in victory and he too began to cheer. He had won—himself.

Right about then the horn blared. The game was over. The season was done. Losers again. Champions of the bloody bottom.

We hugged each other, screamed and hooted like teams do when they win championships. And we were a lot happier than those Parkville guys who had won.

In the locker room we started to take off our uniforms. Mr. Lester broke in.

"Wait a minute," he announced. "Team picture."

We trooped out again, lining up, arm in arm, our *backs* to the camera. We were having fun!

"English test tomorrow," said Saltz as he and I headed for home. "I haven't studied yet. I'll be up half the night."

"Don't worry," I said. "For *that*, I believe in you."

"You know what?" he said. "So do I."

And he did. Aced it. *Our* way.

S.O.R. LOSERS

Meet the Author

Avi was born in New York City and raised in Brooklyn. His twin sister Emily nicknamed him Avi when they were children. To this day, Avi is the only name he uses. He was shy, uninterested in sports, and not a very good student. He failed at one school and nearly "flunked out" of another one before anybody realized he suffered from dysgraphia. This learning disability made writing very difficult for Avi. It caused him to reverse letters in words or spell them incorrectly. Reading, however, was not a problem. Though he hated Fridays in school because they were spelling test days, he loved Fridays because they were library days. He read everything he could find and even started his own library of favorite books.

Meet the Illustrator

Kate Flanagan graduated from Tufts University with a degree in fine arts. She was the assistant editor and a book reviewer for *The Horn Book Magazine,* a journal of children's literature, until leaving to have her first child. She now lives with her husband, three children, a cat and two fire-bellied toads in New Haven, Connecticut, where she is a free-lance illustrator. Some of the books she has illustrated include *Kids' Pumpkin Projects* (Williamson), *The Very Lonely Bathtub* and *My Gum Is Gone* (both Magination Press).

When she is not drawing, Kate enjoys quilting and sports. She runs in local road races, plays soccer and softball, and is a member of the Lady Lightning, a women's ice hockey team.

Theme Connections

Within the Selection

Record your answers to the questions below in the Response Journal section of your Writer's Notebook. In small groups, report the ideas you wrote. Discuss your ideas with the rest of your group. Then choose a person to report your group's answers to the class.

- Why were so many people at South Orange River Middle School surprised by the soccer team's attitude about losing?
- How did other students in the school cooperate to help the team? Why did they do so?
- How did cooperation among team members change the S.O.R. Losers? How did it affect their game?

Across Selections

- Compare the students on the S.O.R. Losers with Lupe in "The Marble Champ." Which other story characters from this unit are similar to the S.O.R. Losers?
- What other story about a sports team have you read in this unit? How are the S.O.R. Losers different from that team?

Beyond the Selection

- Think about how "S.O.R. Losers" adds to what you know about cooperation and competition.
- Add items to the Concept/Question Board about cooperation and competition.

FOUNDERS OF THE CHILDREN'S RAIN FOREST

from *It's Our World, Too!*
by Phillip Hoose
illustrated by Jim Effler

It all began in the first week of school when Eha Kern, from the Fagervik School, in the Swedish countryside, showed her forty first- and second-grade students pictures of hot, steamy jungles near the Equator. It was there, she said, that half the types of plants and animals in the whole world could be found. She read to them about monkeys and leopards and sloths, about snakes that can paralyze your nerves with one bite, about strange plants that might hold a cure for cancer, about the great trees that give us oxygen to breathe and help keep the earth from becoming too hot.

And then she told them that the world's rain forests were being destroyed at the rate of one hundred acres a *minute*. In the past thirty years, she said, nearly half the world's rain forests have been cut down, often by poor people who burn the wood for fire. Sometimes forests are cleared to make pastures for cattle that are slaughtered and sold to hamburger chains in the U.S. and Europe. Sometimes the trees are sold and shipped away to make furniture and paper. More often they are just stacked up and burned. At this rate, there might not be any rain forests left in thirty years!

The children were horrified. The creatures of the rain forest could be gone before the students were even old enough to have a chance to see them. It didn't matter that they lived thousands of miles away in cold, snowy Sweden. It seemed to them that their future was being chopped and cleared away.

During the autumn, as the sunlight weakened and the days became short, the Fagervik children continued to think about the rain forest. Whenever they went on walks past the great fir trees on the school grounds, they imagined jaguars crouched in the limbs just above them, their long tails twitching impatiently.

They begged Mrs. Kern to help them think of something—anything—they could do to rescue the creatures of the tropics. And then one afternoon during a music lesson, a student named Roland Tiensuu asked suddenly, "Can't we just *buy* some rain forest?"

The lesson stopped. It was a simple, clear idea that all the others understood at once. The class began to cheer, and then they turned to their teacher. "Please, Mrs. Kern," they said. "Please, won't you find us a forest to buy?"

"PLEASE BUY MINE."

Mrs. Kern had no idea how to find a rain forest for sale. But then, the very weekend after Roland's idea, she was introduced to an American biologist named Sharon Kinsman. As they chatted, Ms. Kinsman explained that she had been working in a rain forest called Monte Verde, or Green Mountain.

When Mrs. Kern told Ms. Kinsman of the nearly impossible mission her students had given her, she expected the biologist to laugh. Instead her expression turned serious. "Oh," she said quickly, "please buy mine."

Ms. Kinsman said that some people in Monte Verde were trying desperately to buy land so that more trees wouldn't be cut. Much land had already been protected, but much more was needed. Land was cheap there, she said—only about twenty-five dollars per acre.

Ms. Kinsman agreed to visit the Fagervik School. She would bring a map and slides of the Monte Verde forest and tell the children where they could send money to buy rain forest land. When Mrs. Kern told the children what had happened, they didn't even seem surprised. As they put it, "We knew you would find one."

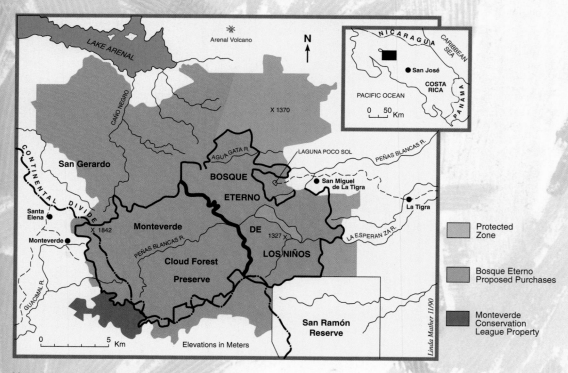

Here is a map of the Children's Rain Forest.

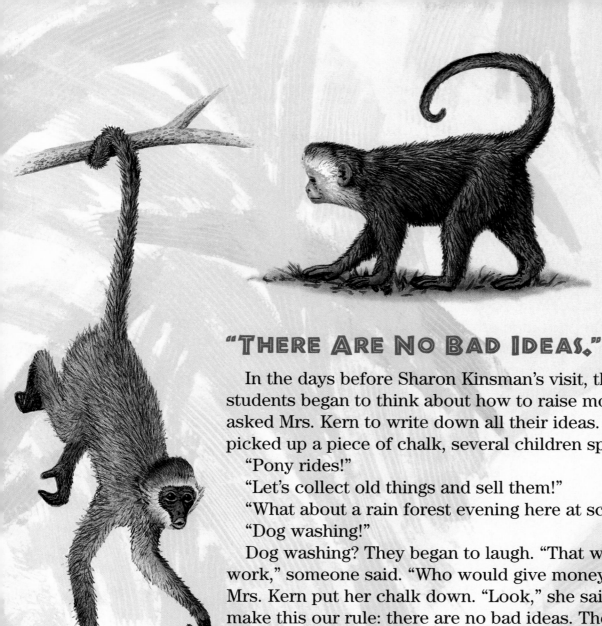

"There Are No Bad Ideas."

In the days before Sharon Kinsman's visit, the Fagervik students began to think about how to raise money. They asked Mrs. Kern to write down all their ideas. As she picked up a piece of chalk, several children spoke at once.

"Pony rides!"

"Let's collect old things and sell them!"

"What about a rain forest evening here at school?"

"Dog washing!"

Dog washing? They began to laugh. "That would never work," someone said. "Who would give money for that?" Mrs. Kern put her chalk down. "Look," she said. "Let's make this our rule: there are no bad ideas. The only bad thing is if you have an idea and don't say it. Then we can't use it." She returned to the blackboard. Were there more ideas?

"A rabbit jumping contest!"

"Rabbit jumping?" said Mrs. Kern. "Be serious. You can't *make* a rabbit jump."

"Oh, yes, we all have rabbits. We can train them. We can. We *can!*"

Mrs. Kern tried to imagine someone actually paying money to watch children try to make rabbits jump. She couldn't. This idea was crazy.

"Mrs. Kern . . . there's no such thing as a bad idea . . . remember?" She did. "Rabbit jumping," she wrote, dutifully putting her doubts aside.

GIANT SPIDERS AND DEADLY SNAKES

On November 6, 1987, Sharon Kinsman arrived at the Fagervik School. She was just as enthusiastic as the students. They put on skits for her about rain forests and showed her the many books they had written about tropical creatures. Then at last, it was her turn to show them slides of the Monte Verde forest.

First she unfolded a map of the forest and pointed to the area their money could preserve from cutting. She told them that 400 bird species live in the forest, more than in all of Sweden, as well as 490 kinds of butterflies and 500 types of trees. Monte Verde is also the only home in the world, she said, for the golden toad, a creature that seems to glow in the dark.

Then she showed her slides. As the room became dark, the students were swept into a hot, steamy jungle half the world away. The slides took them sloshing along a narrow, muddy trail, crisscrossed with roots and vines. A dark canopy of giant trees, thick with bright flowering plants, closed in above them.

They saw giant spiders and deadly snakes. Ms. Kinsman's tape recorder made the forest ring with the shriek of howler monkeys calling to each other and with the chattering of parrots above the trees. They saw the golden toad, the scarlet macaw, and the red-backed poison-arrow frog.

And they saw the forest disappearing, too. They saw hard-muscled men, their backs glistening with sweat, pushing chain saws deep into the giant trees. They could almost smell the smoke of burning tree limbs and feel the thunder of thick, brown trunks crashing down. Behind great piles of ragged wood, the tropical sky was hazy with smoke. Time seemed very short.

When the lights came on, the students were back in Sweden, but they were not the same. Now they had seen their forest—and the danger it faced. There was no time to lose. Mrs. Kern had inspired them with a problem, and Roland had given them an idea they could work with. Sharon Kinsman had shown them their target. Now it was up to them.

"We Knew What We Wanted."

Two weeks later, more than a hundred people crowded into an old schoolhouse near the Fagervik School for a rain forest evening. Students stood by the door and collected ten crowns (about $1.50) from each person. Special programs cost another crown. Even though it was winter, rain splattered steadily onto the roof, just as it must have been raining in the Monte Verde forest. To the students, rain was a good sign.

First they performed a play containing a dramatic scene in which trees of the rain forest were cut and creatures killed. That way guests would understand the problem they were trying to help solve. As the applause died down, the children passed an old hat around, urging audience members to drop money in it.

Then they sold rain forest books and rain forest poems. "We were not afraid to ask for money," remembers Maria Karlsson, who was nine. "We knew what we wanted was important." One boy stood at a table keeping track of how much they were making. Whenever a classmate would hand over a fresh delivery of cash, he would count it quickly and shout above the noise, "Now we've got two hundred crowns!!" "Now it's three hundred!!"

Here are the children from the Fagervik School in Sweden who started a multimillion-dollar effort to preserve rain forest habitats for endangered plants and animals.

The evening's total came to 1,600 crowns, or about $240. The next day, they figured out that they had raised enough money to save about twelve football fields worth of rain forest. It was wonderful . . . but was it enough space for a sloth? A leopard? They all knew the answer. They needed more.

They filled up another blackboard with ideas and tried them out. Everything seemed to work. Mrs. Kern brought in a list of prominent people who might make donations. Two girls wrote a letter to the richest woman on the list. A few days later, a check arrived. Someone else wrote to the king of Sweden and asked if he would watch them perform plays about the rain forest. He said yes.

One day they went to a recording studio and made a tape of their rain forest songs. From the very beginning, Mrs. Kern and a music teacher had been helping them write songs. They started with old melodies they liked, changing them a little as they went along. As soon as anybody came up with a good line, they sang it into a tape recorder so they would't forget it by the end of the song. They rehearsed the songs many times on their school bus before recording them, then designed a cover and used some of their money to buy plastic boxes for the tapes. Within months, they had sold five hundred tapes at ten dollars each.

The more they used their imaginations, the more money they raised. They decided to have a fair. "We had a magician and charged admission," remembers Lia Degeby, who was eight. "We charged to see who could make the ugliest face. We had a pony riding contest. We had a market. We had a lady with a beard. We had the strongest lady in the world. We tried everything." The biggest money maker of all was the rabbit jumping contest, even though each rabbit sat still when its time came to jump! Even carrots couldn't budge them. One simply flopped over and went to sleep, crushing its necklace of flowers.

Soon they needed a place to put all the money they had earned. Mrs. Kern's husband, Bernd, helped them form an organization called Barnens Regnskog, which means Children's Rain Forest. They opened a bank account with a post office box where people could continue to mail donations.

94

By midwinter, they had raised $1,400. The children addressed an envelope to the Monte Verde Cloud Forest Protection League, folded a check inside, and sent it on its way to Costa Rica. Weeks later, they received a crumpled package covered with brightly colored stamps. It contained a map of the area that had been bought with their money. A grateful writer thanked them for saving nearly ninety acres of Costa Rican rain forest.

In the early spring, the Fagervik students performed at the Swedish Children's Fair, which led to several national television appearances. Soon schools from all over Sweden were joining Barnens Regnskog and sending money to Monte Verde. At one high school near Stockholm, two thousand students did chores all day in the city and raised nearly $15,000. And inspired by the students, the Swedish government gave a grant of $80,000 to Monte Verde.

"I THINK OF MY FUTURE."

After another year's work, the children of Fagervik had raised $25,000 more. The families who could afford it sent their children to Costa Rica to see Monte Verde. Just before Christmas, ten Fagervik children stepped off the plane, blinking in the bright Costa Rican sunlight. It was hot! They stripped off their coats and sweaters, piled into a bus, and headed for the mountains.

A few hours later, the bus turned onto a narrow, rocky road that threaded its way through steep mountains. The children looked out upon spectacular waterfalls that fell hundreds of feet. Occasionally they glimpsed monkeys swinging through the trees.

Ahead, the mountaintops disappeared inside a dark purple cloud. For a few moments they could see five rainbows at once. Soon it began to rain.

The next morning, they joined ten Costa Rican children and went on a hike through the Monte Verde rain forest. Sometimes the thick mud made them step right out of their boots. But it didn't matter. "There were plants everywhere," says Lia. "I saw monkeys and flowers."

On Christmas day, the children of the Fagervik School proudly presented the staff of the Monte Verde Cloud Forest with their check for $25,000. They said it was a holiday present for all the children of the world.

The Monte Verde Conservation League used their gift, and funds that had been donated by other children previously, to establish what is now known as El Bosque Eterno de los Niños, or the Eternal International Children's Rain Forest. It is a living monument to the caring and power of young people everywhere. So far, kids from twenty-one nations have raised more than two million dollars to preserve nearly 33,000 acres of rain forest, plenty of room for jaguars and ocelots and tapirs. The first group of Fagervik students have now graduated to another school, but the first- and second-graders who have replaced them are still raising great sums of money. The school total is now well over $50,000.

The Fagervik students continue to amaze their teacher. "I never thought they could do so much," Mrs. Kern says. "Sometimes I say to them, 'Why do you work so hard?' They say, 'I think of my future.' They make me feel optimistic. When I am with them, I think maybe anything can be done."

Here is a view of a Monte Verde rain forest.

FOUNDERS OF THE CHILDREN'S RAIN FOREST

Meet the Author

Phillip Hoose likes to spend time with his family. When his daughter Hannah was younger, the Hooses had a family band in which they sang and wrote songs. One of their songs, "Hey Little Ant," later became a book by the same title. Phillip and Hannah got the idea for the song when they saw Hannah's younger sister squashing ants in their driveway. The book asks readers to question whether or not it is right to kill bugs.

Mr. Hoose has made a career out of his love of nature and music. He is a staff member of the Nature Conservancy and a founding member of the Children's Music Network.

Meet the Illustrator

Jim Effler has been drawing since he was two years old. That was back in 1958!

He has illustrated several children's books about animals. Jim's work has won awards from Art Directors' Clubs and the Society of Illustrators. He lives in Cincinnati with his wife Debbie and daughters, Jenna and Ariana.

Theme Connections

Within the Selection

Record your answers to the questions below in the Response Journal section of your Writer's Notebook. In small groups, report the ideas you wrote. Discuss your ideas with the rest of your group. Then choose a person to report your group's answers to the class.

- How did Mrs. Kern discourage competition among students as they brainstormed ways to raise money? Why did she do this?
- How did the students prove that the small contributions of many people can make a difference?
- Students carried out many different plans to earn money for the Children's Rain Forest. In what ways did students use competition as a way to raise money?

Across Selections

- Compare the cooperative efforts of students in Fagervik School with those of students in "Class President."
- Which character or characters from the other stories you have read in this unit would be most likely to lead this movement? Explain why you think so.

Beyond the Selection

- Tell about a time when you have seen people successfully work together to solve a problem that is too big for one person to solve.
- Think about how "Founders of the Children's Rain Forest" adds to what you know about cooperation and competition.
- Add items to the Concept/Question Board about cooperation and competition.

People have been gazing at the stars since the beginning of time. Some people just look and appreciate their beauty. Others ask, "What are those things in the night sky?" "How do they affect our lives?" "How can I find out?" In the search for answers, the science of astronomy was born. Find out how and why.

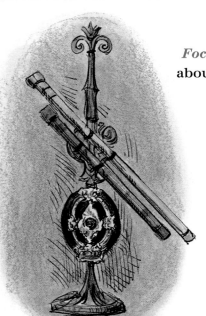

Galileo

from *Pioneer Astronomers*
by Navin Sullivan
illustrated by Jim Roldan

One May evening in 1609, a carriage rattled briskly through the streets of Padua, in Italy. In it was Galileo Galilei, professor of mathematics, returning from a trip to Venice. While he was there, he had received news from a former pupil named Jacques Badovere——news that had sent him hurrying home.

"A marvelous tube is on sale here," wrote Badovere, who was now living in Paris. "This tube makes distant objects appear close. A man two miles away can be seen distinctly. People call these tubes 'Dutch perspectives' or 'Dutch cylinders.' Some say that they were invented by Hans Lippershey, an obscure maker of eyeglasses in Middleburg, Holland. What is sure is that they employ two lenses, one convex and the other concave."

The carriage turned into the Borgo dei Vignali and stopped outside Galileo's house. Pausing only to glance at his garden, Galileo hurried indoors and went to his study.

"One convex and one concave," he repeated as though in a trance. He drew writing paper toward him, dipped a sharpened quill in the ink, and began to draw.

"Suppose the convex lens is placed in front, to gather the light," he muttered. "Then if the concave lens is placed the right distance behind, it should magnify the gathered light."

He only had to figure the distance and he would be able to make one of these marvelous "Dutch perspectives" for himself! He had already taken the precaution of bringing a good assortment of eyeglass lenses from Venice.

By the time that Galileo went to bed he felt fairly sure that he had solved the problem. Early the next morning he hurried to his workshop. The place was filled with gadgets he had already invented, including an apparatus for indicating temperature and another for timing the pulse of a patient. Now he would make a tube to demolish distance.

Seizing a handy piece of lead tubing, he cut it down to the length he wanted. Then he took a convex lens and placed it in one end, and placed a concave lens in the other. Excitedly, he held the tube to his eye and peered through. Immediately he gave a cry of delight. It worked! The church tower several streets away might have been just outside.

How much did his tube magnify? Galileo cut different-sized circles of paper and pinned them up on a wall. When he found that his tube made a small circle look the size of a larger one seen with the naked eye, he could figure the magnification by comparing the actual sizes of the circles. In this way he found that his telescope magnified three times.

Proudly he sat down and wrote to his friends in Venice telling them of his success. Then, after getting the lenses mounted in a more imposing tube made of wood, he hurried back to Venice himself. The Venetians were famous as sailors and navigators. This tube would show them ships out at sea long before they could be seen with the naked eye. Surely, thought Galileo, the nobles of Venice would pay well for such a device.

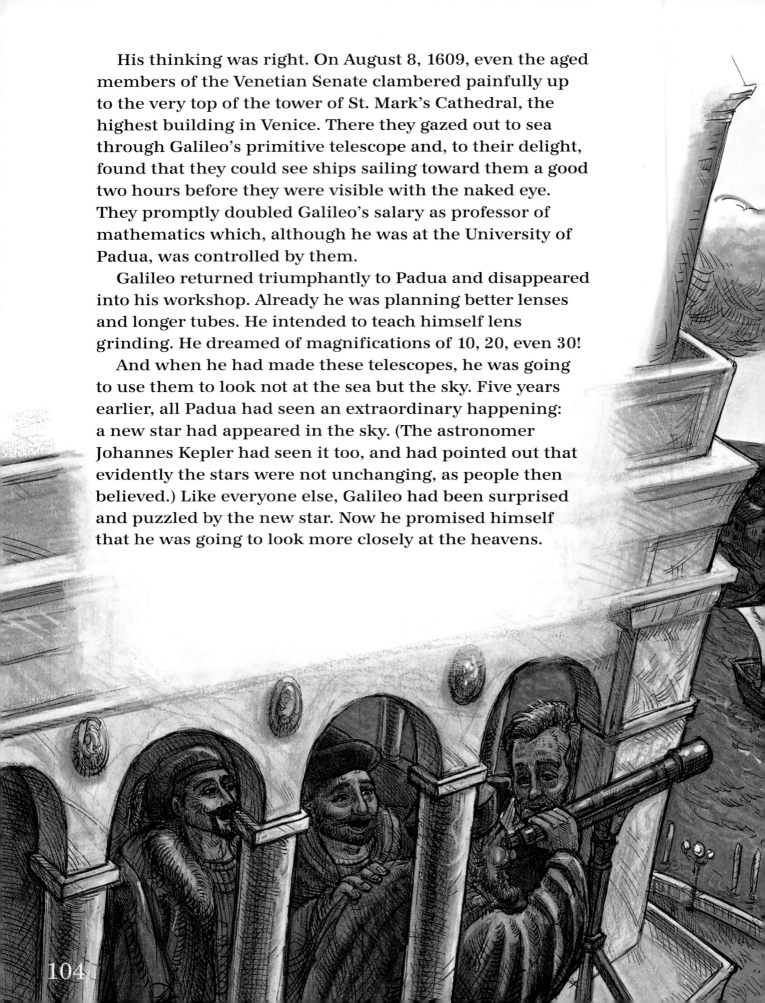

His thinking was right. On August 8, 1609, even the aged members of the Venetian Senate clambered painfully up to the very top of the tower of St. Mark's Cathedral, the highest building in Venice. There they gazed out to sea through Galileo's primitive telescope and, to their delight, found that they could see ships sailing toward them a good two hours before they were visible with the naked eye. They promptly doubled Galileo's salary as professor of mathematics which, although he was at the University of Padua, was controlled by them.

Galileo returned triumphantly to Padua and disappeared into his workshop. Already he was planning better lenses and longer tubes. He intended to teach himself lens grinding. He dreamed of magnifications of 10, 20, even 30!

And when he had made these telescopes, he was going to use them to look not at the sea but the sky. Five years earlier, all Padua had seen an extraordinary happening: a new star had appeared in the sky. (The astronomer Johannes Kepler had seen it too, and had pointed out that evidently the stars were not unchanging, as people then believed.) Like everyone else, Galileo had been surprised and puzzled by the new star. Now he promised himself that he was going to look more closely at the heavens.

It was four days after new moon. Galileo's newest telescope, magnifying 30 times, was resting in its cradle on a tripod stand. He squinted through it at the bright crescent, then drew what he saw by the light of a flickering candle.

The moon was, he knew, lit from one side by the sun. He noticed that the boundary between light and dark on the moon's surface was wavy and uneven. Also, he saw bright spots of light dotted over the dark area. What could they be?

He puzzled over them for a while, and then he made a bold deduction.

"These spots of light are mountain peaks just catching the sunlight," he decided. "And the wavy line at the boundary between light and dark exists because there are mountains there, too. It is sunrise up there and, just as on earth at dawn, the mountain peaks are bathed in sunlight while the valleys are still dark." It seemed incredible. Yet it must be true. There were mountains on the moon, as there were on earth!

Until then no one had seriously supposed that the moon might be something like the earth. People had thought of the moon and planets as heavenly bodies, things quite different in kind from the earth.

How high were the mountains? Galileo could not measure them directly, but he devised a way of comparing them with the diameter of the moon, which was fairly accurately known. When he had worked out the figures, he could hardly believe them. The moon mountains proved to be enormous, much higher than earthly mountains: up to four miles high.

It was a whole new world that Galileo was looking at. But was it full of living creatures or was it dead? He wondered if there was air on it, and shuddered at the idea that it might be cold and silent, a dead world forever circling the earth.

Then he began to explore the sky. Night after night he gazed upward, and what he found was a revelation. With the naked eye only about 2,000 stars are visible at any one time. Even with his relatively low-power telescope, Galileo found myriads more than that.

He examined the belt and sword of Orion: instead of the usual nine stars he found 89! The constellation of the Pleiades, in which sharp-eyed observers could only see seven stars, became a swarm of 43. As for the Milky Way——it was impossible to think of counting the stars in it. Wherever Galileo looked, his telescope showed crowded clusters of stars.

"Many of them are tolerably large and extremely bright," he noted, "but the number of small ones is quite beyond determination."

On January 7, 1610, while he was gazing at the sky an hour after sunset, he noticed that the planet Jupiter was visible. Immediately he turned his telescope onto it, eager to examine one of the planets for the first time.

He saw that it was a small, round disk that did not sparkle like a star. Peering more closely, he saw something else: three bright little points of light were grouped near it, two to the east of Jupiter, one to the west.

(East)  (West)

At first he told himself that these bright points must be three fixed stars. But the next night, to his astonishment, they were differently grouped: all three were to the west of Jupiter.

(East)  (West)

"Can Jupiter have moved past them?" Galileo asked himself in bewilderment. "If so, it is not traveling the way astronomers have always said it does."

He waited impatiently to look again the next night, but to his disappointment the sky was cloudy. However, the following night was clear. He rushed to his telescope and turned it with trembling hands toward Jupiter. This is what he saw:

(East)   X   XO   (West)

For a moment he wondered if he were going crazy. Now there were only two points of light, and both were to the east of Jupiter.

"Is Jupiter moving back and forth like a pendulum?" he muttered.

He searched the sky nearby, checking to see if Jupiter had moved in this way against the background of the fixed stars. It had not; it was on the course that astronomers had always charted for it.

"If Jupiter is not swinging to and fro, then the little points of light are," reasoned Galileo. "And since one of them has disappeared tonight, it is probably hidden by Jupiter——it has probably gone behind the planet.

It looks as if these points of light are swinging *around* Jupiter!"

This meant that the points of light could not be stars. To make sure that they were swinging around Jupiter, Galileo began a methodical series of observations.

On the next night, January 11th, he still saw only two of them, but now they had moved farther away from the planet. On the 12th they were closer again, and a third had appeared on the west of the planet. On the 13th, he had another surprise: there were four points of light.

(East) XOXXX (West)

He doubted no longer. "These are not fixed stars, but bodies belonging to Jupiter and going around it in various orbits," he decided. "Jupiter has four satellite moons of its own, just as the Earth has one!"

Full of excitement, he settled down to write a short account of all that he had discovered with his telescope. Two months later this was published in Venice, under the title *Messenger from the Stars*. His discoveries amazed the whole of Europe. Soon they were even being discussed in faraway Peking (now Beijing).

Galileo had opened up a new vision of the heavens. He had shown that the moon is a rocky, mountainous globe, that the earth is not unique in having a satellite moon, and that millions upon millions of stars exist. Soon he went further and discovered that Venus appears first as a crescent, then full, then dark, as it circles the sun and reflects light at different angles. He even traced the movement of mysterious spots across the face of the sun. The fact that the sun has spots shocked some people, who felt that a celestial object ought to be without blemish. Galileo, however, was very interested, for the movement of the spots, in one direction, indicated that the sun, like the earth, was spinning round on its axis.

To many people this probing of the skies was exciting. They realized that for the first time people had a means of exploring space. But to others it was unsettling, even dangerous. This was because, although they were living 70 years after Copernicus, they still believed that the earth did not move and was the center of the universe. The Church of Rome officially agreed with this belief, although some of its members did not.

Until now Galileo had not dared to defy the Church openly and declare that the earth moved round the sun.

"I would certainly dare to publish my ideas at once if more people like you existed," he had once written to Kepler. "Since they don't, I shall refrain from doing so."

However, his discoveries made Galileo a much more important man. He decided, finally, that the Church would not dare to curb him, and he began to state publicly that the earth circled the sun.

"Let them try to prove me wrong!" he exclaimed.

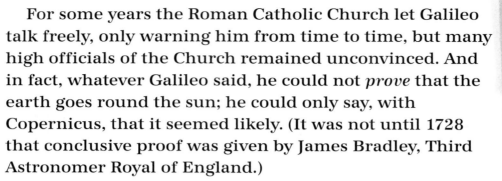

For some years the Roman Catholic Church let Galileo talk freely, only warning him from time to time, but many high officials of the Church remained unconvinced. And in fact, whatever Galileo said, he could not *prove* that the earth goes round the sun; he could only say, with Copernicus, that it seemed likely. (It was not until 1728 that conclusive proof was given by James Bradley, Third Astronomer Royal of England.)

In 1623 a new Pope was elected and the Church hardened against Galileo. He received more severe warnings than before, but would not give way. In 1632 he published a brilliant argument in favor of his beliefs, entitled *Dialogue on the Great World Systems*.

This was open defiance of the Church, and Galileo was summoned to appear before the Inquisition in Rome. Interrogation began on April 12, 1633. Galileo was asked to declare that he was wrong and that the earth stood still. The questioning continued for a month.

The great astronomer was now seventy years old, and he was worn out by fatigue and by fear of the Inquisition. In the end, Galileo did as he was told. Never again did he say in public that the earth moved.

Galileo

Meet the Author

Navin Sullivan has written and edited science books since he was a young man in his twenties. He is fascinated with people who make discoveries about things like outer space, medicine, and the human body. He calls them "pioneers" because they explore new territories in science. He has made it his goal to teach others about these scientists and their discoveries. He does this by writing books, like *Pioneer Astronomers* and *Pioneer Germ Fighters*. He also writes about these discoverers in short stories, magazines, and radio scripts.

Meet the Illustrator

Jim Roldan's first memorable gift as a child was a box of 64 colored crayons. He drew pictures of cartoon characters, animals, comic book heroes, dinosaurs and spaceships. He went on to earn a degree in Fine Art. After a few years working in a graphic design studio, Mr. Roldan started his own business illustrating ads, magazines, posters, books, and the occasional cartoon character. He currently lives and works in New Hampshire where he shares a house with his wife and their two cats.

Theme Connections

Within the Selection

Record your answers to the questions below in the Response Journal section of your Writer's Notebook. In small groups, report the ideas you wrote. Discuss your ideas with the rest of your group. Then choose a person to report your group's answers to the class.

- How did the telescope make a difference in Galileo's investigation of the stars, planets, and moon?
- Why did Galileo study the same objects in the sky night after night?
- Would Galileo have made even more discoveries if his efforts had been supported? Explain why you feel that way.

Across Selections

- In what way did the discoveries of early astronomers depend upon cooperation? How do you think competition might have affected them?

Beyond the Selection

- Does the night sky always look the same to you? What changes have you noticed in the sky from night to night?
- Think about how "Galileo" adds to what you know about astronomy.
- Add items to the Concept/Question Board about astronomy.

Telescopes

from *The Way Things Work*
by David Macaulay

TELESCOPES

A telescope gives a close-up view of a distant object, which, in the case of an astronomical telescope viewing a far-off planet or galaxy, is very distant indeed. Most telescopes work in the same basic way, which is to produce a real image of the object inside the telescope tube. The eyepiece lens then views this image in the same way as a magnifying glass. The viewer looks at a very close real image, which therefore appears large. The degree of magnification depends mainly on the power of the eyepiece lens.

REFRACTING TELESCOPE

In a refracting telescope, an objective lens forms the real image that is viewed by the eyepiece lens. The image is upside down, but this is not important in astronomy.

REFLECTING TELESCOPE

In a reflecting telescope, a large concave primary mirror forms the real image that is then viewed by an eyepiece lens. Usually, a secondary mirror reflects the rays from the primary mirror so that the real image forms beneath the mirror or to the side. This is more convenient for viewing.

Reflecting telescopes are important in astronomy because the primary mirror can be very wide. This enables it to collect a lot of light, making faint objects visible. Collecting light from an object is often more important than magnifying it because distant stars do not appear bigger even when magnified.

Reflecting Telescope

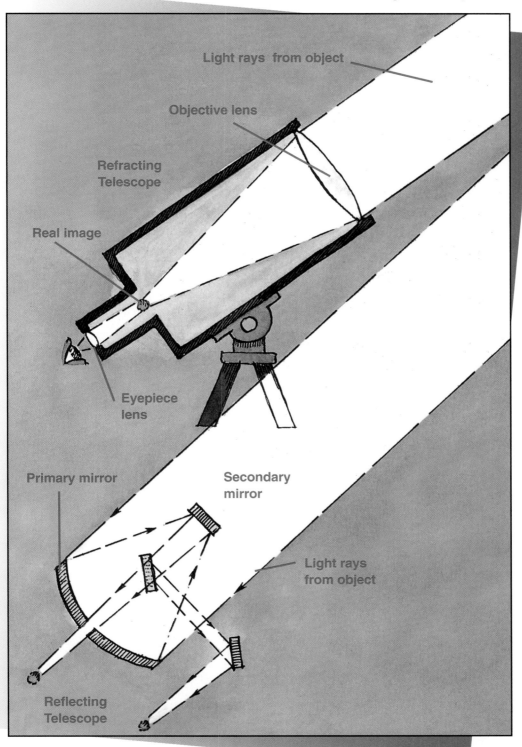

Light rays from object

Objective lens

Refracting Telescope

Real image

Eyepiece lens

Primary mirror

Secondary mirror

Light rays from object

Reflecting Telescope

RADIO TELESCOPE

Many objects in the universe send out radio waves, and a radio telescope can be used to detect them. A large curved metal dish collects the radio waves and reflects them to a focus point above the center of the dish, rather as the curved mirror of a reflecting telescope gathers light waves from space. At this point, an antenna intercepts the radio waves and turns them into a weak electric signal. The signal goes to a computer. Radio telescopes detect very weak waves, and can also communicate with spacecraft.

By detecting radio waves coming from galaxies and other objects in space, radio telescopes have discovered the existence of many previously unknown bodies. It is possible to make visible images of radio sources by scanning the telescope or a group of telescopes across the source. This yields a sequence of signals from different parts of the source, which the computer can process to form an image. Differences in frequency of the signals give information about the composition and motion of the radio source.

Radio Telescope

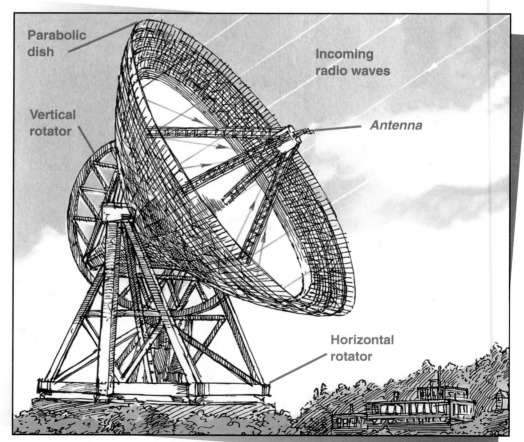

Parabolic dish

Incoming radio waves

Vertical rotator

Antenna

Horizontal rotator

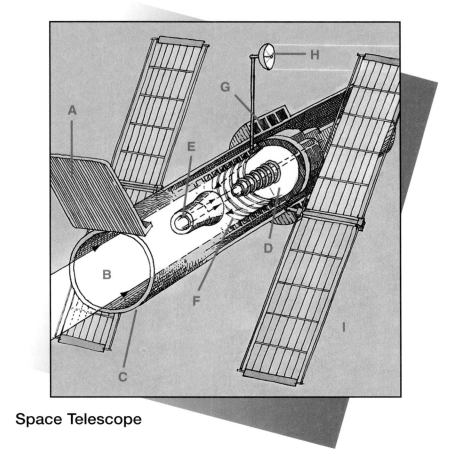

Space Telescope

A. Aperture door. B. Light rays from star or galaxy. C. Telescope tube. The main body of the telescope is 43 feet long and 14 feet across. D. Primary mirror. The space telescope is a reflecting telescope with a main mirror eight feet in diameter. E. Secondary mirror. F. Baffles. These ridges reduce the reflection of stray light from surfaces in the tube. G. Equipment section. Light detectors change the visual images produced by the mirrors into television signals. The space telescope also contains scientific instruments. H. Radio dish. The dish sends telescope images and measurements from instruments back by radio to ground stations below. I. Solar panels. The pair of panels provides electricity to work the instruments aboard the space telescope.

SPACE TELESCOPE

The Hubble space telescope is part optical telescope and part satellite. It promises to revolutionize astronomy because it operates outside the atmosphere, which hampers any observations made from the ground. The space telescope orbits the earth, observing distant stars and galaxies in the total clarity of space. It can peer seven times further into the universe than we can see from the ground, and can also detect very faint objects. The telescope may be able to "see" far back in time by observing ancient light waves from the most distant galaxies. Among these may be light waves produced just after the big bang that blew the universe into existence some 15 billion years ago.

Telescopes

Meet the Author and Illustrator

David Macaulay was born in England, but he moved to America at the age of 11. He went to college in Rhode Island and earned a degree in architecture. Afterward, he worked as a junior high art teacher, and an interior designer. He now writes and illustrates his own books. "Telescopes" was taken from his award-winning book, *The Way Things Work*. In it he explains how telescopes work, along with everything from nail clippers and zippers to a car's automatic transmission. Mr. Macaulay is the author of other fascinating books too, like *Pyramid*, *Black and White*, *Underground*, and *Motel of the Mysteries*.

Theme Connections

Within the Selection

Record your answers to the questions below in the Response Journal section of your Writer's Notebook. In small groups, report the ideas you wrote. Discuss your ideas with the rest of your group. Then choose a person to report your group's answers to the class.

- What types of information do telescopes gather?
- Why are reflecting telescopes especially important for the study of far-off planets and stars?
- What makes the Hubble space telescope different from other powerful telescopes?

Across Selections

- Has the basic principle of how telescopes work changed much since the early telescopes that Galileo used?
- Compare the purpose of the telescopes discussed in this selection with the purpose of the early telescopes described in "Galileo."

Beyond the Selection

- Have you ever used a telescope? Where were you when you did so? What did you observe?
- Think about how "Telescopes" adds to what you know about astronomy.
- Add items to the Concept/Question Board about astronomy.

Focus Questions How did some constellations get their names? What do these myths tell about the values and beliefs of the people who created them?

The Heavenly Zoo

from *The Heavenly Zoo: Legends and Tales of the Stars*
retold by Alison Lurie
illustrated by Monika Beisner

From the earliest times people have looked at the night sky and tried to understand what they saw there. Long before anyone knew that the stars were great burning globes of gas many millions of miles from the earth and from one another, men and women saw the sky as full of magical pictures outlined with points of light.

What shapes ancient people saw in the sky depended on who and where they were. Thus the group of stars that we call the Big Dipper, which is part of the Great Bear, was known to the Egyptians as the Car of Osiris, to the Norse as Odin's Wagon, and in Britain first as King Arthur's Chariot and later as the Plough. Many of the pictures that we see today are very old. The constellation we call the Great Dog was first known as a dog five thousand years ago in Sumeria; Taurus the Bull was already a bull in Babylon and Egypt.

Our ancestors saw all sorts of things in the stars: men and women, gods and demons, rivers and ships. But what they saw most often were beasts, birds, and fish. And for most of these creatures there was a legend of how they came to be there.

THE GREAT DOG

This story is from the Mahabharata, *which was written in India. Parts of this collection of stories were written more than two thousand years ago.*

Once upon a time in India there were five princes who left their kingdom to seek the kingdom of heaven. With them they took only food and drink for the journey; and the prince Yudistira brought his dog Svana.

Now besides Yudistira, who was the eldest, the brothers were Sahadeva the all-wise, who was learned beyond other men; Nakula the all-handsome, famed for his grace and beauty; Arjuna the all-powerful, who had never been defeated in any contest of arms; and Bhima the all-joyful, known far and wide for his good temper and love of pleasure.

So they set forth, and journeyed many days and many nights. Presently they came to a fair, where music was playing and people were drinking and dancing and feasting. Some of them saw Bhima the all-joyful, and called out for him to come and join them. Bhima said to himself, "I will rest here today and be happy, and seek the kingdom of heaven tomorrow." So he entered into the dance. And Yudistira and his brothers Sahadeva and Nakula and Arjuna and his dog Svana went on without him.

They traveled for many days and many nights, till they came to a broad plain where a great army was drawn up in ranks facing the enemy. When the soldiers saw Arjuna the all-powerful they shouted out, summoning him to come and lead them into battle.

Arjuna said to himself, "I will fight today for my country, and seek the kingdom of heaven tomorrow." So he joined the soldiers; and Yudistira and his brothers Sahadeva and Nakula and his dog Svana went on without him.

So they traveled for many days and nights, till they came to a magnificent palace surrounded by a garden full of flowers and fountains; and in this garden a beautiful princess was walking with her attendants. When she saw Nakula the all-handsome she was seized with love and longing, and she cried out for him to come nearer. Nakula too was struck with love, and said to himself, "I will stay with this princess today, and seek the kingdom of heaven tomorrow." So he went into the garden, and Yudistira and his brother Sahadeva and his dog Svana went on without him.

They journeyed on for many weary days and nights, until they came to a great temple. When the holy men who lived there saw Sahadeva the all-wise they ran out, inviting him to come and join them in prayer and study. And Sahadeva said to himself, "I will stay here today, and seek the kingdom of heaven tomorrow." So he went into the temple, and Yudistira and his dog Svana went on without him.

At last Yudistira came to Mount Meru, which is the doorway to heaven. And Indra the Lord of Past and Present appeared before him, and invited him to ascend. Yudistira bowed low and replied, "Very willingly I will do so, if I may bring my dog Svana with me."

"That may not be," said Indra. "There is no place in heaven for dogs. Cast off this beast, and enter into eternal happiness."

"I cannot do that," said Yudistira. "I do not wish for any happiness for which I must cast off so dear a companion."

"You traveled on without your four brothers," said Indra. "Why will you not ascend to heaven without this dog?"

"My lord," replied Yudistira, "my brothers left me to follow the desires of their hearts. But Svana has given his heart to me; rather than renounce him I must renounce heaven."

"You have spoken well," said Indra. "Come in, and bring your dog with you." So Yudistira and Svana ascended into paradise; and Indra, in recognition of their devotion to each other, set in the sky the constellation of the *Great Dog,* whose central star Sirius is the brightest of all in the heavens.

THE SCORPION

This story was told in ancient Greece.

Orion was one of the greatest of the Greek giants. Because he was the son of Poseidon, the god of the sea, he was as much at home in the water as on land. When he wished to get from one island to another he walked across on the bottom of the ocean; he was so tall that his head was always above the waves, and so large and broad that his travels caused high tides.

From childhood on Orion was famous for his beauty and his tremendous strength. He grew up to be a great hunter, able to track and slay all kinds of beasts with the help of his giant hound Sirius. When the island of Chios was oppressed and terrified by lions and wolves, Orion came to its assistance. He tracked down and destroyed every one, so that the people and their flocks could live in safety.

By the time Orion came to the large island of Crete, his fame was so great that Artemis, the goddess of the moon, invited him to go hunting with her. All went well until Orion, who had become vain of his skill, began to boast that he would soon have killed all the wild animals in Crete. Now the scorpion, who was listening, said to himself that this must not be. So he lay in wait for Orion, and stung him to death with his poisoned tail.

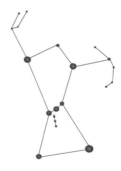

But Orion's spirit did not have to go down to dwell in the Underworld with the souls of ordinary mortals. The gods, who loved him, transported him instead to the sky, where he can be seen in his golden armor and sword-belt, holding up his golden shield, with his faithful dog Sirius at his heel. The scorpion who saved the wild animals of Crete was also raised into the heavens, and became a constellation in the southern sky.

Every night, as the *Scorpion* rises, Orion fades and vanishes.

The Heavenly Zoo

Meet the Author

Alison Lurie always felt like an outcast as a child. She was deaf in one ear due to an injury at birth. This injury also damaged the muscles in her face, causing her mouth to turn sideways. Often ignored by other children, she learned from an early age to entertain herself by making up stories and poems. Through writing, she could reinvent her world. This talent led her to study English in college. Today she lives in New York, and is an author and English professor. *The Heavenly Zoo: Legends and Tales of the Stars* was her first children's book. She went on to also write *Clever Gretchen and Other Forgotten Folktales* and *Fabulous Beasts*.

Meet the Illustrator

Monika Beisner is an author and illustrator who lives in England. She is fascinated with mysterious lands and creatures. One of her favorite things to imagine is what it would be like to live in a world where nothing is as you expect it to be. Reading her stories is like walking into just such a world, with a surprise around every corner. Her illustrations are also full of surprises and hidden meanings. The places she paints are odd, but almost life-like. In ways, her pictures are like beautiful puzzles. People who look at their details long enough, find that she tells as many stories through her paintings, as she does with words.

Theme Connections

Within the Selection

Record your answers to the questions below in the Response Journal section of your Writer's Notebook. In small groups, report the ideas you wrote. Discuss your ideas with the rest of your group. Then choose a person to report your group's answers to the class.

- What did this selection teach you about the beliefs and values of the ancient Indian and Greek cultures?
- What are some similarities between the two myths presented in this selection?
- Many ancient cultures devised myths about the constellations. Why do you think that people of long ago made up these stories?

Across Selections

- In what way were the goals of ancient Greeks and Indians similar to those of early astronomers?
- Compare what the ancient Greeks and Indians saw when they looked at the night sky with what Galileo saw through his telescope.

Beyond the Selection

- What other groups can you name who created myths about the world around them? What kinds of stories do the groups tell?
- Think about how "The Heavenly Zoo" adds to what you know about astronomy.
- Add items to the Concept/Question Board about astronomy.

Focus Questions How and why did Native Americans study the skies? What do Native American observatories tell us about how these people lived and adjusted to their natural environment?

Circles, Squares, and Daggers:

How Native Americans Watched the Skies

by Elsa Marston

You have probably heard about stargazers of the past such as the ancient Egyptians, the builders of Stonehenge, and the Mayas. Did you know that Native Americans, too, made astronomical observatories——long before Europeans arrived?

The study of these ancient observatories is called *archaeoastronomy*. By combining astronomy with archaeology, we are beginning to understand how people of the past observed the skies.

Archaeoastronomy is a very new field. The Native American observatories have been discovered——or their purposes understood——only recently. Most of the sites had been abandoned centuries ago, and their original uses had been forgotten.

Let's look at some of the different ways Native Americans devised to follow the movements of the sun and, in certain cases, the stars.

Medicine Wheels

One of the most dramatic observatories lies on a windswept plateau high in the Bighorn Mountains of Wyoming. It is simply a circle of stones that looks something like a wheel, 80 feet across. In fact, it's called the Bighorn Medicine Wheel ("medicine" means holy or supernatural).

In the center of the wheel is a large pile of stones called a cairn. Twenty-eight lines of stones lead like spokes from the "hub" to the rim. Just outside the circle stand six smaller cairns.

Though the wheel had been known for about a hundred years, it was not until the early 1970s that its secrets began to come clear. An astronomer, John Eddy, discovered how the wheel "works."

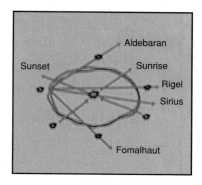

The Bighorn Medicine Wheel. The diagram shows cairns marking sunrise and sunset on the summer solstice and the rising of the bright stars Aldebaran, Rigel, Sirius, and Fomalhaut.

Bighorn Medicine Wheel

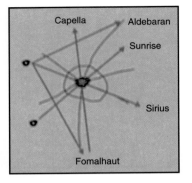

The diagram shows cairns marking sunrise on the summer solstice and the rising of the bright stars Capella, Aldebaran, Sirius, and Fomalhaut.

If you stand at a particular small cairn on the day of the summer solstice (usually June 21st), you will see the sun rise directly over the large cairn in the center of the wheel. At the end of the day, standing at a different pile, you'll see the setting sun line up with the center cairn. The medicine wheel tells almost exactly when the longest day of the year has arrived, the day we say summer begins.

The wheel shows other alignments as well. Pairs of small cairns were found to point to bright stars that shone briefly on the horizon on certain days before and after the summer solstice. These stars appeared roughly 28 days apart. Possibly the 28 "spokes" were supposed to help keep track of these intervals.

The Bighorn Medicine Wheel was probably built around 1700. The Ponca tribe claims that its ancestors constructed the original wheel. Other tribes probably added to it after moving into the area.

There is a similar medicine wheel in Saskatchewan, Canada. The Moose Mountain Medicine Wheel has cairns placed like those of the Bighorn Wheel. This gave a clue to its age. The point on the horizon where a star rises changes slightly over time. The wheel was dated by figuring out when bright stars rose closest to the points shown by the cairns. The calculations agreed with carbon dating for the site. The Moose Mountain Medicine Wheel was probably built around 2000 years ago!

Moose Mountain Medicine Wheel

Circles and Squares

At Cahokia, a major Native American site in western Illinois near St. Louis, archaeologists discovered traces of four large circles of wooden posts. They reconstructed part of one of these circles.

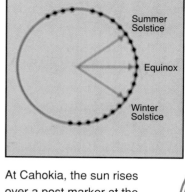

At Cahokia, the sun rises over a post marker at the equinox. The diagram shows posts marking sunrises at the summer and winter solstices.

Seen from the center at dawn, the sun lines up with certain posts at the summer solstice and winter solstice (the shortest day of the year, usually December 21st). A third post is aligned with the rising sun at the spring and fall equinoxes (usually March 21st and September 21st, when day and night are of equal length).

Another observatory was discovered near Kansas City, Missouri, in the early 1980s. Again, traces of posts were found, but this time in the shape of a square. About 35 feet long on each side, the square suggested a building such as a fort——except that the corners were open. A triangle of posts had stood in the center, and on the south side of the square was a double row of post marks.

A local astronomy society made a simple reconstruction of the square. They found that on the summer solstice, a person standing a certain distance from the center posts could see the sun rise and set through two of the open corners. The other two corners framed the sunrise and sunset at the winter solstice. On the equinoxes, the sun shone directly between the double lines of posts. Both observatories were made by Native Americans of the Mississippian culture, probably about a thousand years ago.

Cahokia

Sun Daggers

The Anasazi——a name that means simply "ancient ones"——lived in the beautiful but dry country of northern New Mexico, Colorado, Utah, and Arizona around 900 years ago. In Chaco Canyon, New Mexico, they designed an especially clever kind of observatory. It was discovered in 1977 by an artist, Anna Sofaer, who was examining rock carvings.

Near the top of Fajada Butte, a high rock that rises from the canyon floor, three large slabs of stone lean against a vertical rock face. About 9 feet long, they stand on end only a few inches apart, their narrow sides against the rock. On the shadowed rock behind them, two spirals have been cut.

At noon on the summer solstice, a tiny shaft of sunlight falls between two of the slabs. It makes a spot that looks like a dagger——cutting right through the middle of the larger spiral.

The solar marker in Chaco Canyon at noon on the summer solstice.

Fall equinox.

Winter solstice.

Spring equinox.

As the weeks pass, the "dagger" of sunlight moves to the right. Meanwhile, a second vertical streak of light appears. At the fall equinox, it cuts through the smaller spiral. By the winter solstice, the two "daggers" rest on the edges of the larger spiral. It's as though the spiral, now empty of sunlight, is a symbol of winter when the world is cold. Gradually, then, the sun daggers move to the left until, on the longest day of the year, the first one again strikes the center of the larger spiral.

All over the Southwest there are many such figures, called petroglyphs, cut in the rock. Spirals, crosses, rough outlines of humans, lizards, birds——all had meanings.

At many sites, the petroglyphs are touched by spots of sunlight, usually falling between two large rocks. Astronomer Robert Preston and his wife Ann, an artist, discovered many of these sites in Arizona. Light strikes the rock carving at the solstices, the equinoxes, or, in some cases, a point halfway between the fall equinox and the winter solstice.

"Sun Rooms"

The Anasazi thought of other ways to observe the travels of the sun. Between Tucson and Phoenix, Arizona, rises a three-story adobe building known as Casa Grande ("Great House"). At dawn, a person standing inside this ancient structure will see the sun shining through a small hole high in the east wall. The spot of light strikes the opposite wall, moves toward a small hole in that wall, and disappears into it. The spot of sunlight hits this bull's-eye only on the days close to the spring and fall equinoxes.

Casa Grande a little after dawn, at the time of the spring equinox. Sunlight passes through holes in two different walls, one behind the other.

Hovenweep Castle

There is a different type of Anasazi "sun room" at Hovenweep National Monument in Utah. Attached to a large stone structure called Hovenweep Castle is a tower-like room. At sunset on the solstices and equinoxes, the sun's rays enter small holes and a door, shine through the room, and strike doorways in the inside walls. The archaeoastronomer who studied Hovenweep Castle, Ray Williamson, determined that the beams of sunlight could not enter the room in this way merely by chance.

Why?

All over this country, Native Americans came up with ingenious ways to observe the skies. But *why* did they study astronomy?

The skies were the Native Americans' calendar. They had no fixed, written calendar as we do today. They relied on what nature would tell them about the changing times of the year. Important solar events such as the solstices and the equinoxes helped them know when to plant their crops, when to start preparing for the winter, when to move from one place to another.

The sun and stars told Native Americans when important ceremonies were supposed to take place. These ceremonies were usually concerned with the "return" of the sun and start of a new year, and with planting, harvesting, and hunting.

Other special occasions might have been for social purposes such as tribal rituals, gatherings of tribes, trade, or payment of tribute. For example, the most likely function of the Bighorn Medicine Wheel was to keep a calendar so large groups could assemble in summer for trading fairs.

It's probable that only special persons knew how to use the observatories and make the announcements awaited by the people. The observatories must have strengthened the power of the chiefs and religious leaders.

There is a deep religious meaning in Native American astronomy. The sun is a vital symbol in the beliefs of many Native American cultures. And something equally important: Native Americans' understanding of the heavens helped them feel in harmony with the universe——for in many Native American religions, human beings are only one small part of the world, living in peace with the rest of nature.

Today we are coming to recognize Native Americans' achievements in astronomical knowledge——and to appreciate the ways in which they used that understanding.

Circles, Squares, and Daggers:

How Native Americans Watched the Skies

Meet the Author

Elsa Marston was born in Newton, Massachusetts. Although she is a writer and an artist, she has had a wide variety of jobs and interests. She has lived both in Europe and the Middle East. In her lifetime she has taught English, been the head of an art gallery, and organized a jail improvement committee. She is also a nature lover and an active community worker. Her children's books are often based on experiences she has had. She says, *"My basic philosophy in writing for young people is that I want to share what is important to me."* Her favorite things to write about are the cultures of other people, both in the past and present. With her books, she hopes to *"encourage an awareness of the world beyond here and now."*

Theme Connections

Within the Selection

Record your answers to the questions below in the Response Journal section of your Writer's Notebook. In small groups, report the ideas you wrote. Discuss your ideas with the rest of your group. Then choose a person to report your group's answers to the class.

- Why did Native Americans want to track the movements of the sun and stars?
- What are some similarities among the observatories built by different Native American groups?
- What can the astronomical records and observatories that remain tell us about what was important to early Native American civilizations and about how they lived?

Across Selections

- Compare what you learned about Native American cultures in this selection with what you learned about ancient Greek and Indian cultures in "The Heavenly Zoo."
- Technology is the use of tools to solve problems. In what ways did the Native American groups described in this selection and the early astronomers in "Galileo" use technology?

Beyond the Selection

- Think about how "Circles, Squares, and Daggers: How Native Americans Watched the Skies" adds to what you know about astronomy.
- Add items to the Concept/Question Board about astronomy.

Pictorial Quilt, detail *Falling Stars*. 1895–98. Harriet Powers.
Pieced, appliquéd and printed cotton embroidered with cotton and
metallic yarns. 69 × 105 in. The Museum of Fine Arts, Boston.

Orion in December. 1959.
Charles Burchfield. Watercolor
and pencil on paper. $39 \frac{7}{8} \times 32 \frac{7}{8}$ in.
National Museum of American Art,
Smithsonian Institution, Washington, DC.

The Starry Night.
1889. **Vincent van
Gogh.** Oil on canvas.
$29 \times 36 \frac{1}{4}$ in. The
Museum of Modern Art,
New York.

Focus Questions What information about Mars has been retrieved by the *Viking 1, Viking 2,* and *Pathfinder* landers? How is Mars like and unlike Earth? Is it possible that there ever was or will be life on Mars?

The Mystery of Mars

Sally Ride & Tam O'Shaughnessy

In 1976 *Viking 1* and *Viking 2* settled softly onto the surface of Mars. They were the first spacecraft from Earth ever to visit the Red Planet. Twenty-one years later, *Pathfinder* dropped out of the Martian sky to join them. A parachute opened to slow it down, then giant air bags inflated to cushion it during impact. *Pathfinder* bounced hard more than 15 times before it rolled to a stop on the red Martian soil.

Pathfinder *landed in Ares Vallis, an ancient floodplain. Many of the rocks here were deposited by floods billions of years ago. This panorama also shows* Pathfinder's *deflated air bags and the ramp that its small rover,* Sojourner, *drove down to reach the surface. The rover is analyzing a rock a few feet from the lander. When* Sojourner *rolled down* Pathfinder's *ramp, it became the first rover ever to explore the Martian surface.*

The Pathfinder *lander. When the air bags that had protected it deflated,* Pathfinder *opened like a flower to reveal a camera, a weather station, and its rover,* Sojourner. *This photograph was taken by* Sojourner *after it had left the lander. The camera, at the top of the mast, is looking at* Sojourner.

Although the *Viking* and *Pathfinder* landers arrived at different locations, they landed in similar terrain. Engineers did not want to risk landing these precious spacecraft on the edge of a cliff or the side of a volcano. They guided them to different sites on the gently rolling Martian plains north of the equator. The pictures the spacecraft sent back showed flat, windswept landscapes strewn with gray rocks and covered with fine red dust.

The two *Viking* landers could not move from their landing sites. They could reach out only a few feet with their robot arms to scoop up small samples of soil. *Pathfinder* carried the first rover to Mars. The rover, *Sojourner,* was about the size of a small dog. *Sojourner* traveled on six rugged wheels at the end of flexible legs. It moved at a snail's pace, but was able to travel several yards from the lander.

The little robot geologist dug its wheels into the red Martian dirt, churning up the soil to analyze its texture and clumpiness. It roamed through a garden of nearby rocks, ranging in size from pebbles to boulders, and nuzzled up to several of them.

The Martian rocks and soil seem to be made of about the same minerals, though in different proportions, as the rocks and soil on Earth.

This dry, dusty world does not look very hospitable. But many scientists have wondered whether there might be microscopic life on its surface. The *Viking* landers performed three important experiments that scientists hoped would answer that question. Their long robot arms scooped up samples of Martian soil and carried them inside the landers, where instruments analyzed the red dirt for evidence of life.

Sojourner had TV cameras for eyes and was steered by drivers back on Earth. (Pathfinder)

Sojourner's cameras took these close-up pictures of interesting rocks in the Rock Garden. Above: A rock named Chimp, with small pebbles and wind streaks in the foreground. Below: A pitted rock named Half-Dome. It looks as if it has been sandblasted by the Martian winds.

In planning these experiments, scientists assumed that Martian microbes would be similar to those on Earth: they would take in food molecules, grow, and release waste molecules. In one experiment, nutrients were added to soil samples. Then an instrument looked for the waste gas carbon dioxide, which might signal that living organisms had eaten the food.

This experiment did not find evidence of Martian life. Results from the other two experiments were also negative.

But are the building blocks of life present in the Martian soil? Another experiment looked for organic molecules, the molecules that make up living things. Samples of soil were heated, and instruments watched for gases that would be released if organic molecules were present. It was a great surprise when none were found. Scientists know that meteorites and interplanetary dust deliver a steady supply of organic molecules to the Martian surface. So even if there are no living organisms, there should still be some organic molecules. Scientists now suspect that they are being destroyed by harsh chemicals present in the Martian soil.

Spacecraft that have followed *Viking* have not carried experiments to look for evidence of life. The few *Viking* experiments are all scientists have to go by. Most scientists do not believe that there is life on the surface of Mars today. But many believe it is possible that primitive life exists beneath the surface, or that life existed on the planet long ago.

The Viking 2 *lander's robot arm scoops up a sample of soil and leaves its mark in the ground.*

Earth is surrounded by an atmosphere that protects all the plants and animals on the planet from the extreme conditions in space. It shields us from the sun's radiation, helps keep our planet warm, and contains the oxygen that many of Earth's creatures need to survive.

Mars, too, has an atmosphere, but it is very different from Earth's. The Martian atmosphere is very, very thin and is made up almost entirely of carbon dioxide. Fine red Martian dust fills the thin air and creates a pink sky all year round.

Each of the landers set up a small weather station on the surface of Mars. While the stations operated, they radioed weather reports to Earth. Like the weather on Earth, the weather on Mars changes from day to day and from season to season. On some days the pink sky is mostly sunny, with light winds and wispy rose-colored clouds. On other days the sky is overcast, with strong winds and swirling cinnamon-colored dust.

The weather reports never included rain. There is very little water vapor in the Martian atmosphere. Martian clouds contain crystals of water ice, but the air is too thin and too cold for raindrops to form. In the early mornings, a thin veil of fog might fill the distant canyons, but there is no dew on the canyon walls. The rain that nourishes all life on Earth never falls on Mars.

Space shuttle astronauts took this picture of Earth's atmosphere at sunset. Storm clouds rise about eight miles above the planet's surface.

An unusually clear view of the Martian atmosphere. Thin layers of haze extend 25 miles above the horizon. (Viking)

Pathfinder's weather station. The windsocks on the far right are slightly tilted because they are being blown by the Martian wind.

During the late afternoon, clouds accumulate around and above Olympus Mons. (Mars Global Surveyor)

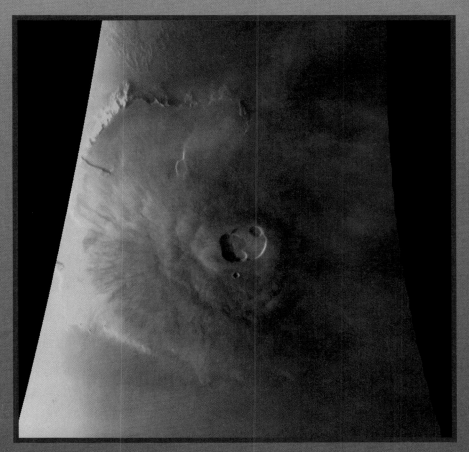

THE THIN AIR ON MARS

The air on Mars is very thin. Because it is so thin, water cannot exist as a liquid on Mars' surface. If an astronaut on Mars poured a glass of water, it would soon boil away.

The boiling point of water (the temperature at which it turns into a gas) depends on the pressure of the surrounding air. You can see this yourself if you go camping in the mountains. Near sea level, water has to be heated to 212 degrees Fahrenheit before it will boil. As you climb up a mountain, the air gets thinner and thinner, so water boils at a lower and lower temperature. On a 5,000-foot-high mountain (and in the mile-high city of Denver), water boils at about 203 degrees Fahrenheit (a few degrees lower than at sea level). At the top of Mount Everest, the highest mountain on Earth, water boils at only about 160 degrees Fahrenheit.

When spacecraft measured the air pressure on the surface of Mars, they found that it is the same as it would be on a mountain more than three times as high as Mount Everest. When the air is that thin, water boils at very low temperatures—temperatures near its freezing point. That means that water on Mars exists either as ice or as water vapor (a gas), but not as a liquid.

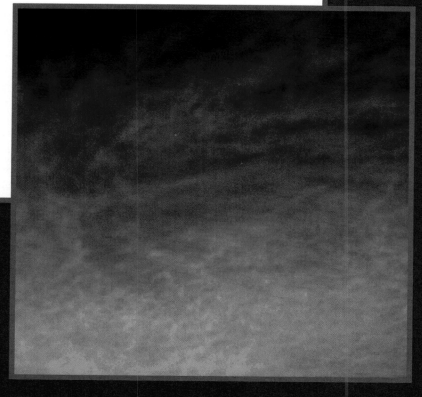

Wispy clouds about 10 miles high, made of water ice condensed on particles of red dust. (Pathfinder)

Mars is very, very cold. Even on bright summer days, temperatures may only reach 10 degrees Fahrenheit—22 degrees below the freezing point of water. When the sun goes down, the temperature falls to a frigid 110 degrees below zero. Earth's atmosphere helps keep our planet warm overnight. But on Mars the atmosphere is so thin that after the sun sets, the planet's heat quickly escapes to space.

If you were standing on Mars on a summer morning, your feet would be warm, but your ears would be freezing! As the sun warms the soil, the air a few inches above the ground is heated to nearly 50 degrees Fahrenheit. But just a few feet off the ground, the temperature plummets.

Winters on Mars are so cold that nearly 20 percent of the planet's air actually freezes out of the sky. Carbon dioxide gas in the air turns to ice and is trapped in Mars' polar icecaps until spring. Then when the temperature warms, the carbon dioxide goes back into the air as a gas.

Frost covers the Martian land-scape near the Viking 2 *landing site in Utopia Planitia in the Elysium region.*

A section of the north polar cap. Layers of white ice and reddish orange dust form terraces around both the north and south polar caps. (Viking)

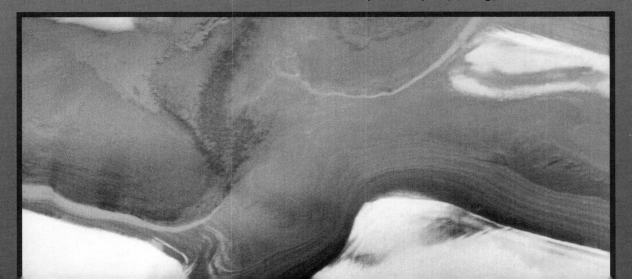

Mars is a windy planet. Dust devils whirl across the surface, lifting red dust high into the sky. During some parts of the year, ferocious winds stir up huge dust storms in the Southern Hemisphere that can grow to cover the entire planet. These dust storms are far worse than any on Earth and can completely block our view of the planet's surface for weeks at a time.

Over the ages, Martian winds have created complex sand dunes over much of the planet. Some dunes appear to be ancient remnants of an earlier time when the air was thicker and the wind could more easily blow sand around. Other dunes appear to be still active today.

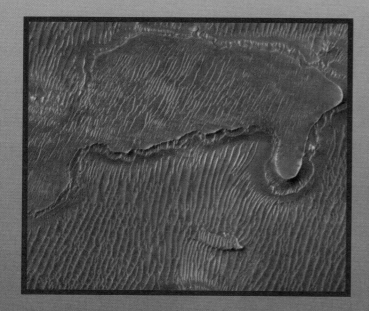

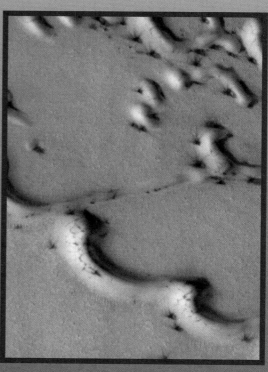

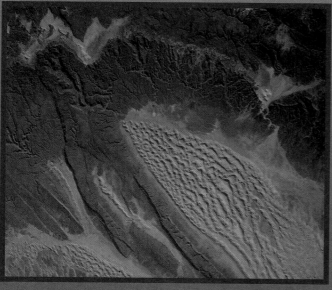

Top Left: *Sand dunes like these cover much of Mars.* (Mars Global Surveyor)

Top Right: *The north polar cap is surrounded by sand dunes. These dunes look bright because a layer of white frost covers the red sand.* (Mars Global Surveyor)

Bottom Left: *Sand dunes are also common on Earth. These dunes in Algeria were photographed by astronauts in the space shuttle.* (Mars Global Surveyor)

When the first astronauts visit Mars, what will they find? Though an astronaut could not survive without a spacesuit, she would feel more at home on Mars than anywhere else in the solar system. She could stand on a rocky surface, scoop up a gloveful of dirt, and explore extinct volcanoes and ancient canyons.

She would need the spacesuit to protect her from the thin Martian air and the extreme cold. The spacesuit would be bulky, but not heavy. Because Mars is smaller than Earth, the pull of gravity on its surface is lower. She and her spacesuit would weigh about one-third what they weighed on Earth.

As the astronaut hiked across the rugged, rocky terrain, her boots would leave deep footprints in the dusty red soil. Fine red dust would cling to her spacesuit. Even on days when the wind was calm, she would look up at a pink sky loaded with red dust. As she headed back to the warmth of her spacecraft at the end of the day, she would look past the silhouettes of crater rims at a dimmer setting sun.

The planet she was exploring would seem strangely familiar. But it would be missing the air and water that make Earth habitable, and the plants and animals that share her home world.

A Martian sunset.

The Mystery of Mars

Meet the Authors

Sally Ride never set out to become the first American woman in space. She really wanted to play professional tennis. Dr. Ride gave up her tennis dream to study physics because, her mother says, she could not make the tennis ball go exactly where she wanted it.

Ms. Ride became an astronaut by answering an ad she saw from NASA. Of the 8,000 people who responded to the ad, she and five other women were selected for a group of 35 new astronauts.

In 1983, Dr. Ride became the first American woman to travel to space. On the *Challenger* she performed experiments and tested the shuttle's robotic arm which she helped design. Now retired from NASA, Sally Ride is a physics professor at the University of California where one of her goals is to encourage young women to study science and math.

Tam O'Shaughnessy and Sally Ride have been friends since they were teenagers competing in junior tennis tournaments. Dr. O'Shaughnessy has played professional tennis, taught high school biology, and written several scientific books for young readers. She is a Professor at Georgia State University, where she researches ways to help children learn to read. Dr. O'Shaughnessy has collaborated with Dr. Ride on two other children's science books.

Theme Connections

Within the Selection

Record your answers to the questions below in the Response Journal section of your Writer's Notebook. In small groups, report the ideas you wrote. Discuss your ideas with the rest of your group. Then choose a person to report your group's answers to the class.

- Why do scientists on Earth want to gather as much information as possible about the other planets?
- How did the *Viking 1*, *Viking 2*, and *Pathfinder* landers collect information for scientists and engineers on Earth? How did the landers know what tasks to perform?
- *Viking 1* gathered information until 1982, *Viking 2* remained operational until 1980, and *Pathfinder*'s mission did not end until 1998. Why do you think all of the landers continued to collect data for so many years?

Across the Selections

- Compare Galileo's reasons for studying the stars and planets with scientists' reasons for studying Mars.

Beyond the Selection

- Which part of the Mars mission would you find most interesting, designing the landers or investigating the data the landers collected?
- Think about how "The Mystery of Mars" adds to what you know about astronomy.
- Add items to the Concept/Question Board about astronomy.

Focus Questions How are stars created? What are some of the different types of stars? Are there other galaxies like ours in the universe?

STARS

by Seymour Simon

Stars are huge balls of hot, glowing gases. Our sun is a star. It is just an ordinary star, not the biggest nor the brightest. But the sun is the star that is nearest to our planet Earth. Earth is part of the sun's family of planets, moons, and comets called the Solar System. All of the other stars that we see in the sky are much farther away from Earth. The stars are so far away from us that even through powerful telescopes they look like small points of light.

People long ago gave names to the brighter stars and learned where and when to look for them. They also gave names to the constellations, groups of stars that seem to form patterns in the sky. Usually these constellations were named after gods, heroes, or animals.

The photograph shows the constellation of Orion, the Hunter. Orion is visible during winter evenings. Look for the three bright stars in a row that form the belt of Orion. The bright red star in the upper left of Orion is named Betelgeuse (most people call it "beetle juice"). The brilliant blue-white star in the lower right is named Rigel. The brightest star in the sky is Sirius, the Dog Star. It is just to the lower left of Orion in the constellation of Canis Major, the Big Dog.

Thousands of years ago Orion looked different than it does today. And thousands of years in the future it will look different than it does now. That's because stars move in space. They move very rapidly, ten or more miles per second. But the stars are so far away from us that we do not notice their motion in our lifetimes.

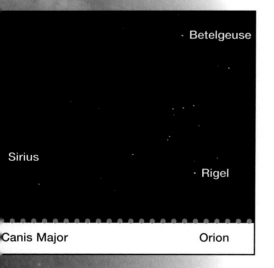

Betelgeuse

Sirius

Rigel

Canis Major   Orion

Imagine traveling in a spaceship going ten miles a second. Even at that speed, it would still take you about three and a half months to reach the sun. But it would take more than seventy thousand *years* to reach the next nearest star, Alpha Centauri.

Alpha Centauri is about twenty-five trillion miles away. There are other stars *millions* of trillions of miles away. These numbers are so big that they are hard to understand. Measuring the distance between the stars in miles is like measuring the distance around the world in inches.

Because of the great distances between stars, scientists measure with the light-year instead of the mile. Light travels at a speed of about 186,000 miles every second. A light-year is the distance that light travels in one year: a bit less than six trillion miles. Alpha Centauri is a little more than four light-years away. The stars shown in this giant cloud of gas in the constellation of Orion are fifteen hundred light-years away.

How many stars do you think you can see on a clear, dark night? Can you see thousands, millions, countless numbers? You may be surprised that in most places only about two thousand stars are visible without a telescope.

When the great scientist Galileo looked through his low-power telescope in the year 1610, he saw thousands and thousands of stars that no one on Earth had ever seen before. As more powerful telescopes were made, millions and millions of other stars were seen.

What look like clouds in the photograph of the Milky Way galaxy are really millions of stars too far away to be seen as separate points of light. With powerful telescopes we can see that the stars are as many as the grains of sand on an ocean beach.

Alpha Centauri

Some of the millions and millions of stars in the Milky Way.

A computer-colored photograph shows a newborn star in the cloud of gas and dust known as Barnard 5.

Stars are born in giant clouds of gas and dust called nebulas. Most of the gas is hydrogen with a small amount of helium. Over millions of years, gravity pulls the gas and dust particles together and squeezes them so that they heat up. When the gas gets hot enough, it sets off a nuclear reaction like that of a super hydrogen bomb and a star is born. This computer-colored photograph shows a newborn star (*arrow*) in the cloud of gas and dust known as Barnard 5.

Stars change as they grow older. For example, young stars (10 to 200 million years old) are very hot—with surface temperatures of more than 12,000 degrees (F)—and are usually blue or blue-white in color. Middle-aged stars like our sun are yellow and not as hot—10,000 degrees (F).

After about ten billion years stars begin to run out of their hydrogen fuel. Most of these old stars collapse upon themselves and they get hotter and hotter. Then, like a piece of popcorn when it "pops," the stars balloon out and become hundreds of times larger. They become what are known as red giant stars.

A red giant star may be 40 or 50 million miles across. Some are even larger. Betelgeuse is a red supergiant star 250 million miles across. If Betelgeuse were put in place of our sun in the center of the Solar System, it would swallow up Mercury, Venus, Earth, and Mars.

Some older stars go through a stage where they keep growing and then shrinking. These stars are called variable stars because at times they appear bright and at other times they are dim.

Other older stars shoot out a large cloud of gas into space. These stars are called planetary nebulas because through low-power telescopes they look like round planets. This photograph taken with a high-power telescope shows the real nature of a planetary nebula. This is the Ring Nebula in the constellation Lyra.

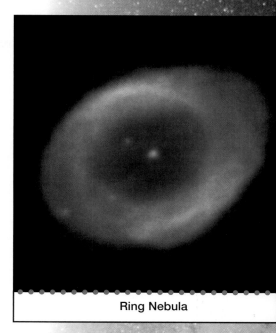

Ring Nebula

Finally, older stars cool and start collapsing. They shrink down to about the size of a small planet and are called white dwarf stars. As the white dwarfs slowly cool off they become black dwarf stars. And then the stars are dead.

Sometimes a star, usually a white dwarf, suddenly explodes and becomes much brighter. To people long ago it looked like a new bright star had appeared in the sky. They called the star a nova (*nova* means "new"). Even though most novas are too far away for us to see, scientists think that two or three dozen novas appear in the Milky Way every year.

Much rarer are the gigantic explosions known as supernovas. A supernova star flares up and becomes millions of times brighter than normal.

A supernova may appear only once every few hundred years. In the year 1054, Chinese astronomers saw a supernova in the constellation of Taurus. Today we can see the gaseous remains of that exploding star. We call it the Crab Nebula.

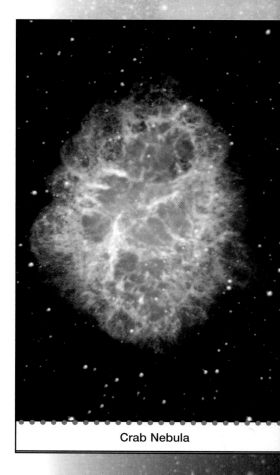

Crab Nebula

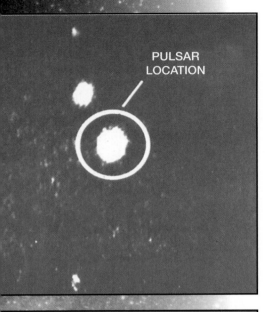

Some supernovas shatter completely, leaving behind only the wispy gases of a nebula. But a few supernovas leave a small, tightly packed ball of particles called a neutron star. A tiny drop of a neutron star would weigh a billion tons on earth.

The sudden collapse of a supernova causes a neutron star to spin very rapidly and give off a beam of X-ray radiation. Like the beam from a lighthouse, we can detect the X rays as a pulse. So a rotating neutron star is called a pulsar.

This X-ray photograph shows a pulsar in the middle of the Crab Nebula. The X rays from the pulsar in the Crab blink on and off thirty times every second. The star is visible when the X rays are "on" and invisible when the X rays are "off."

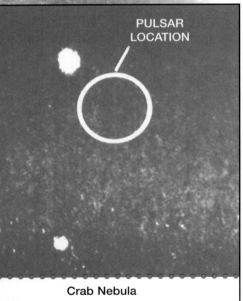

Crab Nebula

Some stars are much larger than the average star. When such a massive star cools and collapses, it becomes something very special. The star is crushed together by the huge weight of the collapsing gases. Gravity keeps squeezing and squeezing until the star seems to disappear. The star has become a black hole.

Anything passing too close to a black hole will be pulled into it and never get out again. Even light is pulled in and cannot escape, so a black hole is invisible. Yet, scientists think they have located several black holes.

This drawing is of a double star called Cygnus X-1. Only one of the stars is visible: a hot, blue giant star. Near it is a black hole that pulls gases from its neighbor. As the gases are sucked in they become so hot that they give off huge amounts of X rays. Some scientists think that there are many such black holes scattered throughout space.

Cygnus X-1

Our sun is an unusual star. It does not have any nearby stars circling it. Most stars have one or more companion stars and they revolve around each other. The star groups are so far from us that most look like single points of light to our eyes.

About half of all the stars we can see are double, or binary, stars. There are also many groups with three, four, a dozen, or even more stars in them. These groups of stars move through space together like flocks of birds in flight. Scientists think that the stars in such a group were all formed at the same time.

Very large groups of stars are called star clusters. This is a photograph of the Pleiades, an open cluster of stars. It contains several hundred stars that form a loose group with no special shape. These are young stars and they are surrounded by clouds of gas and dust.

Here is a different kind of star cluster called a globular cluster. A globular cluster contains many thousands, or even millions, of stars very close together.

This is the great globular cluster known as M.13 in the constellation of Hercules. It is visible just as a dot of light to the naked eye. But through a telescope we can see that it has at least a million stars. Most of these stars are very old and they have stayed together throughout their lifetime.

The biggest star clusters of all are called galaxies. Galaxies are the largest kind of star systems. Our sun and its planets are a member of a galaxy called the Milky Way. There are more than one hundred billion stars in the Milky Way galaxy.

Pleiades

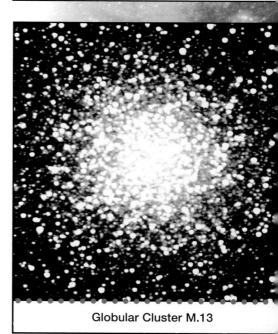
Globular Cluster M.13

Beta Pictoris

The sun is located almost out on the edges of the Milky Way. All the stars in the Milky Way whirl around the center of the galaxy, each at its own speed. The sun along with the Solar System moves at about 150 miles a second around the center of the galaxy. But the galaxy is so big that the sun takes about 225 million years to go around once.

Are there planets circling other stars in our galaxy? The answer is almost definitely yes. This picture shows a ring of material surrounding the star Beta Pictoris. This material is thought to be a young solar system in the making.

Planets form at the same time and from the same gases as do stars. So scientists think it is likely that some or even many stars have planets circling them. If even a tiny percentage of these planets are similar to Earth, then there may be millions of Earth-like planets in the galaxy.

Do any of these planets have life on them? No one knows. But scientists are using radio telescopes to listen for signals of intelligent life in outer space. They think the signals will come in the form of radio waves much like those of our own radios and televisions. So far scientists have not found anything, but they are not discouraged. Until they have examined every star that may have planets they won't know for sure.

The Milky Way is only one galaxy among millions of others in the universe. Galaxies——large and small, single or in groups and clusters, and in many different shapes——are found in every direction.

The Andromeda galaxy, shown here, is a spiral galaxy with almost twice as many stars as there are in the Milky Way. The Andromeda galaxy lies in far distant space, almost twelve quintillion miles away. That's 12,000,000,000,000,000,000! Light from this galaxy has been traveling for more than two million years by the time we see it in our telescopes.

Andromeda Galaxy

How many galaxies are there in the universe? No one knows. But scientists think that there are about one hundred billion other galaxies. And each one of these galaxies contains hundreds of thousands of millions of stars.

Many mysteries confront us in the distant reaches of space. Beyond most of the galaxies that we can see with our largest telescopes are bright starlike objects called quasars. Each quasar gives off more than one hundred times the energy of all the stars in the Milky Way galaxy put together.

This is a computer-colored photo of a quasar-galaxy pair. Scientists think that quasars may be the centers of young galaxies that are just forming. Light from most quasars has been traveling for ten to fifteen billion years by the time it reaches Earth. That means that we are viewing quasars as they were ten to fifteen billion years ago, just after the universe began.

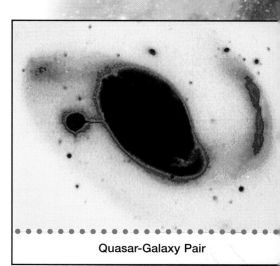
Quasar-Galaxy Pair

Powerful telescopes orbiting above Earth's atmosphere may soon show us the very edges of the universe and the beginning of time itself. Will all our questions about stars then be answered? It's not likely. Each mystery that we solve about space seems to lead to many more unsolved questions about the nature of the universe.

STARS

Meet the Author

Seymour Simon taught science in the New York City schools for 23 years but now devotes all of his time to writing. Simon is the author of nearly 150 science books written especially for students from preschool to junior high. Most of his books are about astronomy and animals. One of the reasons why his books are so wonderful is because they contain many spectacular photos. He likes picture books because, unlike television, they can "freeze" images for as long as the reader wants to look at them. He hopes children will be as amazed as he is by the photos' subjects. He says, *"Children need to develop a lifelong enjoyment and appreciation for science. Science is fascinating stuff like dinosaurs, space, earthquakes, and the human body."*

Theme Connections

Within the Selection

Record your answers to the questions below in the Response Journal section of your Writer's Notebook. In small groups, report the ideas you wrote. Discuss your ideas with the rest of your group. Then choose a person to report your group's answers to the class.

- What are stars? What is a galaxy?
- Why would it be important for scientists to learn about the life cycles of stars?
- What are scientists doing to listen for signs of life on other planets? What have they found?

Across Selections

- Compare ancient people's impressions of the stars with those of modern scientists.
- Compare what Galileo saw when he looked through his telescope with what scientists can see today.

Beyond the Selection

- What do you think about the possibility of finding life on other planets? Have you ever wondered what such life forms might be like?
- Think about how "Stars" adds to what you know about astronomy.
- Add items to the Concept/Question Board about astronomy.

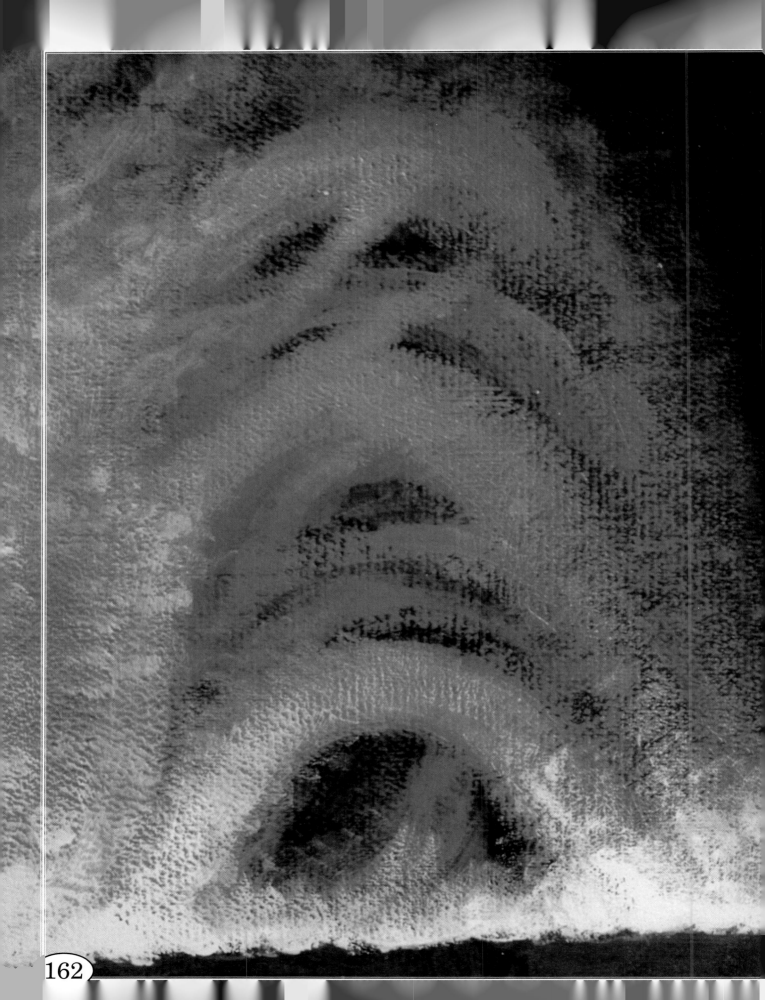

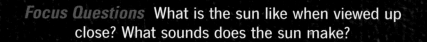

SUN

by Myra Cohn Livingston
illustrated by
Leonard Everett Fisher

Space
is afire
with bursts of bubbling gas,

colliding atoms,
boiling wells
and solar flares

spewing

from a burning star, the sun.

Ninety-three million miles away

this mass,
quaking inferno,
pluming arcs and bridges

roars;

a giant bomb
exploding
hydrogen.

Secrets

by Myra Cohn Livingston
illustrated by Leonard Everett Fisher

Space keeps its secrets
hidden.
It does not tell.
Are black holes time machines?
Where do lost comets go?

Is Pluto moon or planet?

How many, how vast
unknown galaxies beyond us?

Do other creatures
dwell   on distant spheres?

Will we ever know?
Space is silent.
It seldom answers.

But we ask.

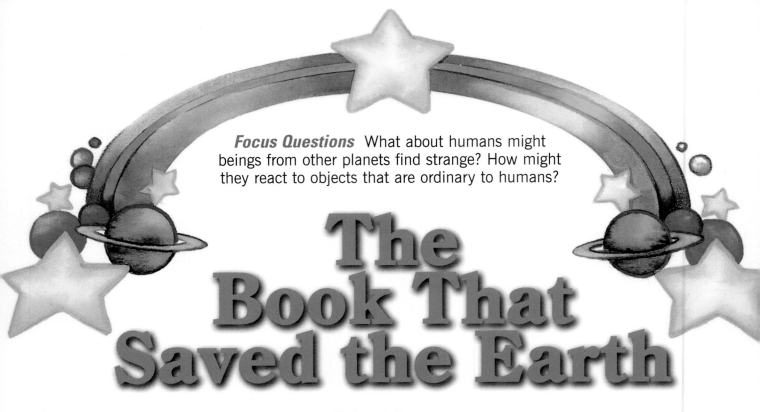

Focus Questions What about humans might beings from other planets find strange? How might they react to objects that are ordinary to humans?

The Book That Saved the Earth

Claire Boiko
illustrated by Dennis Hockerman

Characters

Historian
Great and Mighty Think-Tank
Apprentice Noodle
Captain Omega
Sergeant Oop
Lieutenant Iota
Offstage Voice

Time: 2543 A.D.

Before Rise: *Spotlight shines on* Historian, *who is sitting at table down right, on which there is a movie projector. A sign on an easel beside him reads:* MUSEUM OF ANCIENT HISTORY: DEPARTMENT OF THE TWENTIETH CENTURY. *He stands and bows to audience.*

Historian: Good afternoon. Welcome to our Museum of Ancient History, and to my department—curiosities of the good old, far-off twentieth century. The twentieth century was often called the Era of the Book. In those days, there were books about everything from anteaters to Zulus. Books taught people how to, and when to, and where to, and why to. They illustrated, educated, punctuated and even decorated. But the strangest thing a book ever did was to save the

Earth. You haven't heard about the Macronite invasion of 1988? Tsk, tsk. What *do* they teach children nowadays? Well, you know, the invasion never really happened, because a single book stopped it. What was that book, you ask? A noble encyclopedia? A tome about rockets and missiles? A secret file from outer space? No, it was none of these. It was *(Pauses, then points to projector)*——here, let me turn on the historiscope and show you what happened many, many centuries ago, in 1988. *(He turns on projector, and points it left. Spotlight on* Historian *goes out, and comes up down left on* Think-Tank, *who is seated on raised box, arms folded. He has huge, egg-shaped head, and he wears long robe decorated with stars and circles.* Apprentice Noodle *stands beside him at an elaborate switchboard. A sign on an easel reads:* MACRON SPACE CONTROL. GREAT AND MIGHTY THINK-TANK, COMMANDER-IN-CHIEF. BOW LOW BEFORE ENTERING.*)*

Noodle *(Bowing)*: O Great and Mighty Think-Tank, most powerful and intelligent creature in the whole universe, what are your orders?

Think-Tank *(Peevishly)*: You left out part of my salutation, Apprentice Noodle. Go over the whole thing again.

Noodle: It shall be done, sir. *(In singsong)* O Great and Mighty Think-Tank, Ruler of Macron and her two moons, most powerful and intelligent creature in the whole universe——*(Out of breath)* what-are-your-orders?

Think-Tank: That's better, Noodle. I wish to be placed in communication with our manned space probe to the ridiculous little planet we are going to put under our generous rulership. What do they call it again?

Noodle: Earth, Your Intelligence.

Think-Tank: Earth——of course. You see how insignificant the place is? But first, something important. My mirror. I wish to consult my mirror.

Noodle: It shall be done, sir. *(He hands Think-Tank hand mirror.)*

Think-Tank: Mirror, mirror, in my hand, who is the most fantastically intelligently gifted being in the land?

Offstage Voice *(After a pause)*: You, sir.

Think-Tank *(Striking mirror)*: Quicker. Answer quicker next time. I hate a slow mirror. *(He admires himself.)* Ah, there I am. Are we Macronites not a handsome race? So much more attractive than those ugly earthlings with their tiny heads. Noodle, you keep on exercising your mind, and some day you'll have a balloon brain just like mine.

Noodle: I certainly hope so, Mighty Think-Tank.

Think-Tank: Now, contact the space probe. I want to invade that primitive ball of mud called Earth before lunch.

Noodle: It shall be done, sir. *(He twists knobs and adjusts levers on switchboard. Electronic buzzes and beeps are heard. Noodle and Think-Tank remain at controls, as curtain rises.)*

* * *

Setting: *The Centerville Public Library.*

At Rise: Captain Omega *stands at center, opening and closing card catalogue drawers, looking puzzled. Lieutenant Iota is up left, counting books in bookcase. Sergeant Oop is at right, opening and closing book, turning it upside down, shaking it, and then riffling pages and shaking his head.*

Noodle *(Adjusting knobs)*: I have a close sighting of the space crew, sir. (Think-Tank *puts on pair of huge goggles and turns toward stage to watch.)* They seem to have entered some sort of Earth structure.

Think-Tank: Excellent. Make voice contact.

Noodle *(Speaking into a microphone)*: Macron Space Control calling the crew of Probe One. Macron Space

Control calling the crew of Probe One. Come in, Captain Omega. Give us your location.

Captain Omega *(Speaking into disc which is on chain around his neck)*: Captain Omega to Macron Space Control. Lieutenant Iota, Sergeant Oop and I have landed on Earth without incident. We have taken shelter in this *(Indicates room)*——this square place. Have you any idea where we are, Lieutenant Iota?

Iota: I can't figure it out, Captain. *(Holding up book)* I've counted two thousand of these peculiar things. This place must be some sort of storage barn. What do you think, Sergeant Oop?

Oop: I haven't a clue. I've been to seven galaxies, but I've never seen anything like this. Maybe they're hats. *(He opens book and puts it on his head.)* Say, maybe this is a haberdasher's store!

Omega *(Bowing low)*: Perhaps the Great and Mighty Think-Tank will give us the benefit of his thought on the matter.

Think-Tank: Elementary, my dear Omega. Hold one of the items up so that I may view it closely. (Omega *holds book on palm of his hand.)* Yes, yes, I understand now. Since Earth creatures are always eating, the place in which you find yourselves is undoubtedly a crude refreshment stand.

Omega *(To Iota and Oop)*: He says we're in a refreshment stand.

Oop: The Earthlings certainly do have a strange diet.

Think-Tank: That item in your hand is called a "sandwich."

Omega *(Nodding)*: A sandwich.

Iota *(Nodding)*: A sandwich.

Oop *(Taking book from his head)*: A sandwich?

Think-Tank: Sandwiches are the main staple of Earth diet. Look at it closely. (Omega *squints at book.)* There are two slices of what is called "bread," and between them there is some sort of filling.

Omega: That is correct, sir.

Think-Tank: To confirm my opinion, I order you to eat it.

Omega *(Gulping)*: Eat it?

Think-Tank: Do you doubt the Mighty Think-Tank?

Omega: Oh, no, no. But poor Lieutenant Iota has not had his breakfast. Lieutenant Iota, I order you to eat this—this sandwich.

Iota *(Dubiously)*: Eat it? Oh, Captain! It's a very great honor to be the first Macronite to eat a sandwich, I'm sure, but—but how can I be so impolite as to eat before my Sergeant? *(Handing* Oop *book; brightly)* Sergeant Oop, I order you to eat the sandwich.

Oop *(Making a face)*: Who, sir? Me, sir?

Iota and **Omega** *(Slapping their chests in a salute)*: For the glory of Macron, Oop.

Oop: Yes, sirs. *(Unhappily)* Immediately, sirs. *(He opens his mouth wide. Omega and Iota watch him breathlessly. He bites down on corner of book, and pantomimes chewing and swallowing, while making terrible faces.)*

Omega: Well, Oop?

Iota: Well, Oop? (Oop *coughs.* Omega *and* Iota *pound him on back.)*

Think-Tank: Was it not delicious, Sergeant Oop?

Oop *(Slapping his chest in salute)*: That is correct, sir. It was *not* delicious. I don't know how the Earthlings can get those sandwiches down without water. They're dry as Macron dust.

Noodle: Sir—O Great and Mighty Think-Tank. I beg your pardon, but an

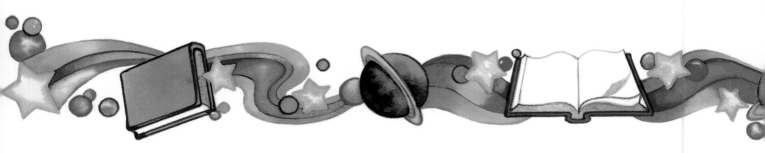

insignificant bit of data floated into my mind about those sandwiches.

Think-Tank: It can't be worth much, but go ahead. Give us your trifling bit of data.

Noodle: Well, sir, I have seen surveyor films of those sandwiches. I noticed that the Earthlings did not *eat* them. They used them as some sort of communication device.

Think-Tank *(Haughtily)*: Naturally. That was my next point. These are actually communication sandwiches. Think-Tank is never wrong. Who is never wrong?

All *(Saluting)*: Great and Mighty Think-Tank is never wrong.

Think-Tank: Therefore, I order you to listen to them.

Omega: Listen to them?

Iota and Oop *(To each other; puzzled)*: Listen to them?

Think-Tank: Do you have marbles in your ears? I said, listen to them. *(Macronites bow very low.)*

Omega: It shall be done, sir. *(They each take two books from case, and hold them to their ears, listening intently.)*

Iota *(Whispering to Omega)*: Do you hear anything?

Omega *(Whispering back)*: Nothing. Do you hear anything, Oop?

Oop *(Loudly)*: Not a thing! (Omega *and* Iota *jump in fright.)*

Omega *and* **Iota:** Sh-h-h! *(They listen intently again.)*

Think-Tank: Well?, Well? Report to me. What do you hear?

Omega: Nothing, sir. Perhaps we are not on the correct frequency.

Iota: Nothing, sir. Perhaps the Earthlings have sharper ears than we do.

Oop: I don't hear a thing. Maybe these sandwiches don't make sounds.

Think-Tank: What? What? Does someone suggest the Mighty Think-Tank has made a mistake?

Omega: Why, no, sir. No, sir. We'll keep listening.

Noodle: Please excuse me, Your Brilliance, but a cloudy piece of information is rolling around in my head.

Think-Tank: Well, roll it out, Noodle, and I will clarify it for you.

Noodle: I seem to recall that the Earthlings did not *listen* to the sandwiches. They opened them, and watched them.

Think-Tank: Yes, that is quite correct. I will clarify that for you, Captain Omega. Those sandwiches are not for ear communication, they are for eye communication. Now, Captain Omega, take that large, bright-colored sandwich over there. It appears to be important. Tell me what you observe.

(Omega *picks up very large copy of "Mother Goose," holding it so that the audience can see title.* Iota *looks over* Omega's *left shoulder, and* Oop *squints over his right shoulder.*)

Omega: It appears to contain pictures of Earthlings.

Iota: There seems to be some sort of code.

Think-Tank *(Sharply interested)*: Code? Code? I told you this was important. Describe the code.

Oop: It's little lines and squiggles and dots. Thousands of them, next to the pictures.

Think-Tank: Code. Perhaps the Earthlings are not so primitive as we have thought. We must break the code. We must.

Noodle: Forgive me, Your Cleverness, but did not the chemical department give our spacemen a supply of Vitamin X to increase their intelligence?

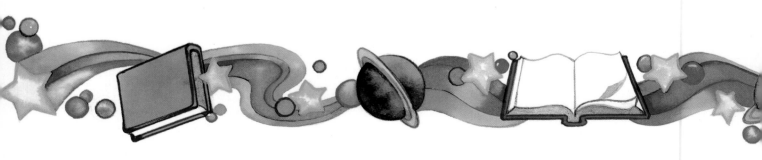

Think-Tank: Stop! A thought of magnificent brilliance has come to me. Spacemen, our chemical department has given you a supply of Vitamin X to increase your intelligence. Take it immediately and then watch the sandwich. The meaning of the code will slowly unfold before you.

Omega: It shall be done, sir. Remove pill. *(Crew take vitamins from boxes on their belts.)* Present Vitamin X. *(They hold vitamins out in front of them, stiffly.)* Swallow. *(They put vitamins into their mouths and gulp simultaneously. They open their eyes wide, shake their heads, and they put their hands to their foreheads.)* The cotangent of a given angle in a right triangle is equal to the adjacent side divided by the hypotenuse.

Iota: *Habeas corpus ad faciendum et recipiendum!*

Oop: There is change of pressure along a radius in curvilinear motion.

Think-Tank: Excellent. Now, decipher that code.

All: It shall be done, sir. *(They frown over book, turning pages.)*

Omega *(Brightly)*: Aha!

Iota *(Brightly)*: Oho!

Oop *(Bursting into laughter)*: Ha, ha, ha!

Think-Tank: What does it say? Tell me this instant. Transcribe, Omega.

Omega: Yes, sir. *(He reads with great seriousness.)*

"Mistress Mary, quite contrary,
How does your garden grow?
With cockle shells and silver bells
And pretty maids all in a row."

Oop: Ha, ha, ha. Imagine that. Pretty maids growing in a garden.

Think-Tank *(Alarmed)*: Stop! This is no time for levity. Don't you realize the seriousness of this discovery? The Earthlings have discovered how to combine agriculture and mining. They

can actually *grow* crops of rare metals such as silver. And cockle shells. They can grow high explosives, too. Noodle, contact our invasion fleet.

Noodle: They are ready to go down and take over Earth, sir.

Think-Tank: Tell them to hold. Tell them new information has come to us about Earth. Iota, continue transcribing.

Iota: Yes, sir. *(He reads very gravely.)*

"Hey diddle diddle! The cat and
the fiddle,
The cow jumped over the moon,
The little dog laughed to see
such sport,
And the dish ran away with
the spoon."

Oop *(Laughing)*: The dish ran away with the spoon!

Think-Tank: Cease laughter. Desist. This is more and more alarming. The Earthlings have reached a high level of civilization. Didn't you hear? They have taught their domesticated animals musical culture and space techniques. Even their dogs have a sense of humor. Why, at this very moment, they may be launching an interplanetary attack of millions of *cows!* Notify the invasion fleet. No invasion today. Oop, transcribe the next code.

Oop: Yes, sir. *(Reading)*

"Humpty Dumpty sat on the wall,
Humpty Dumpty had a great fall;
All the King's horses and all the
King's men,
Couldn't put Humpty Dumpty
together again."

Oh, look, sir. Here's a picture of Humpty Dumpty. Why, sir, he looks like——he looks like——*(Turns large picture of Humpty Dumpty toward Think-Tank and audience)*

Think-Tank *(Screaming and holding his head)*: It's me! It's my Great and Mighty Balloon Brain. The Earthlings have seen me. They're after me. "Had a great fall!" That means they plan to

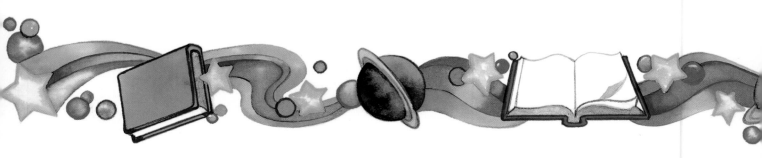

capture Macron Central Control and me! It's an invasion of Macron! Noodle, prepare a space capsule for me. I must escape without delay. Spacemen, you must leave Earth at once, but be sure to remove all traces of your visit. The Earthlings must not know that I know——(Omega, Iota *and* Oop *rush about, putting books back on shelves.)*

Noodle: Where shall we go, sir?

Think-Tank: A hundred million miles away from here. Order the invasion fleet to evacuate the entire planet of Macron. We are heading for Alpha Centauri, a hundred million miles away. (Omega, Iota, *and* Oop *run off right, as* Noodle *helps* Think-Tank *off left and curtain closes. Spotlight shines on* Historian *down right.)*

Historian *(Chuckling)*: And that's how one dusty old book of nursery rhymes saved the world from an invasion from Macron. As you all know, in the twenty-fifth century, five hundred years after all this happened, we Earthlings resumed contact with Macron, and we even became very chummy with the Macronites. By that time, Great and Mighty Think-Tank had been replaced by a very clever Macronite——the Wise and Wonderful Noodle! Oh, yes, we taught the Macronites the difference between sandwiches and books. We taught them how to read, too, and we established a model library in their capital city of Macronopolis. But, as you might expect, there is still one book that the Macronites can never bring themselves to read. You've guessed it——*Mother Goose! (He bows and exits right.)*

The End

The Book That Saved the Earth

Meet the Author

Claire Taylor Boiko has worked at many different jobs in theater ever since she was a young woman. While in her twenties, she worked as an actress in Children's Theater. Later, she worked behind-the-scenes on musical shows for soldiers in the Army. Now she writes plays for children. Her plays are found in books such as *Children's Plays for Creative Actors* and *Plays and Programs for Boys and Girls*. Ms. Boiko writes plays about things that interest her, including science, myths, and folk music.

Meet the Illustrator

Dennis Hockerman has been a freelance designer and illustrator for the last 25 years. Besides illustrating children's books, he has done work for the greeting card, gift wrap, and toy industries. In his spare time, Mr. Hockerman enjoys working at his printing press creating limited edition, hand-colored etchings.

176

Theme Connections

Within the Selection

Record your answers to the questions below in the Response Journal section of your Writer's Notebook. In small groups, report the ideas you wrote. Discuss your ideas with the rest of your group. Then choose a person to report your group's answers to the class.

- Would the play you just read be more realistic if it weren't written as a comedy?
- In what ways do the Macronites remind you of humans?
- Aside from the aliens, what other facts or details about space or space travel does this story contain?

Across Selections

- How does the author's purpose for writing this story differ from the author's purpose for writing "Galileo," "Stars," or "Telescopes"?
- Compare "The Book That Saved the Earth" to "The Heavenly Zoo." What about these selections is the same?

Beyond the Selection

- If intelligent aliens came to Earth, where would you suggest they go to learn the most important information about earthlings and the planet?
- Think about how "The Book That Saved the Earth" adds to what you know about astronomy.
- Add items to the Concept/Question Board about astronomy.

Woven into the fabric of each person's history are stories—personal stories, cultural stories, and family stories—that define that person. These stories can tell us where we came from, who we are, and sometimes, where we are going.

The Land I Lost:

Adventures of a Boy in Vietnam

from the book by Huynh Quang Nhuong
illustrated by Neil Waldman

I was born on the central highlands of Vietnam in a small hamlet on a riverbank that had a deep jungle on one side and a chain of high mountains on the other. Across the river, rice fields stretched to the slopes of another chain of mountains.

There were fifty houses in our hamlet, scattered along the river or propped against the mountainsides. The houses were made of bamboo and covered with coconut leaves, and each was surrounded by a deep trench to protect it from wild animals or thieves. The only way to enter a house was to walk across a "monkey bridge"—a single bamboo stick that spanned the trench. At night we pulled the bridges into our houses and were safe.

There were no shops or marketplaces in our hamlet. If we needed supplies—medicine, cloth, soaps, or candles—we had to cross over the mountains and travel to a town nearby. We used the river mainly for traveling to distant hamlets, but it also provided us with plenty of fish.

During the six-month rainy season, nearly all of us helped plant and cultivate fields of rice, sweet potatoes, Indian mustard, eggplant, tomatoes, hot peppers, and corn. But during the dry season, we became hunters and turned to the jungle.

Wild animals played a very large part in our lives. There were four animals we feared the most: the tiger, the lone wild hog, the crocodile, and the horse snake. Tigers were always trying to steal cattle. Sometimes, however, when a tiger became old and slow it became a maneater. But a lone wild hog was even more dangerous than a tiger. It attacked every creature in sight, even when it had no need for food. Or it did crazy things, such as charging into the hamlet in broad daylight, ready to kill or to be killed.

The river had different dangers: crocodiles. But of all the animals, the most hated and feared was the huge horse snake. It was sneaky and attacked people and cattle just for the joy of killing. It would either crush its victim to death or poison it with a bite.

Like all farmers' children in the hamlet, I started working at the age of six. My seven sisters helped by working in the kitchen, weeding the garden, gathering eggs, or taking water to the cattle. I looked after the family herd of water buffaloes. Someone always had to be with the herd because no matter how carefully a water buffalo was trained, it always was ready to nibble young rice plants when no one was looking. Sometimes, too, I fished for the family while I guarded the herd, for there were plenty of fish in the flooded rice fields during the rainy season.

I was twelve years old when I made my first trip to the jungle with my father. I learned how to track game, how to recognize useful roots, how to distinguish edible mushrooms from poisonous ones. I learned that if birds, raccoons, squirrels, or monkeys had eaten the fruits of certain trees, then those fruits were not poisonous. Often they were not delicious, but they could calm a man's hunger and thirst.

My father, like most of the villagers, was a farmer and a hunter, depending upon the season. But he also had a college education, so in the evenings he helped to teach other children in our hamlet, for it was too small to afford a professional schoolteacher.

My mother managed the house, but during the harvest season she could be found in the fields, helping my father get the crops home; and as the wife of a hunter she knew how to dress and nurse a wound and took good care of her husband and his hunting dogs.

I went to the lowlands to study for a while because I wanted to follow my father as a teacher when I grew up. I always planned to return to my hamlet to live the rest of my life there. But war disrupted my dreams. The land I love was lost to me forever.

These stories are my memories. . . .

When she was eighty years old grandmother was still quite strong. She could use her own teeth to eat corn on the cob or to chew on sugar plants to extract juice from them. Every two days she walked for more than an hour to reach the marketplace, carrying a heavy load of food with her, and then spent another hour walking back home. And even though she was quite old, traces of her beauty still lingered on: Her hands, her feet, her face revealed that she had been an attractive young woman. Nor did time do much damage to the youthful spirit of my grandmother.

One of her great passions was theater, and this passion never diminished with age. No matter how busy she was, she never missed a show when there was a group of actors in town. If no actors visited our hamlet for several months, she would organize her own show in which she was the manager, the producer, and the young leading lady, all at the same time.

My grandmother's own plays were always melodramas inspired by books she had read and by what she had seen on the stage. She always chose her favorite grandson to play the role of the hero, who would, without fail, marry the heroine at the end and live happily ever after. And when my sisters would tell her that she was getting too old to play the role of the young heroine anymore, my grandmother merely replied: "Anybody can play this role if she's young at heart."

When I was a little boy my grandmother often took me to see the opera. She knew Chinese mythology by heart, and the opera was often a dramatization of this mythology. On one special occasion, during the Lunar New Year celebrations—my favorite holiday, because children could do anything they wanted and by tradition no one could scold them—I accompanied my grandmother to the opera.

When we reached the theater I wanted to go in immediately. But my grandmother wanted to linger at the entrance and talk to her friends. She chatted for more than an hour. Finally we entered the theater, and at that moment the "Faithful One" was onstage, singing sadly. The "Faithful One" is a common character in Chinese opera. He could be a good minister, or a valiant general, or someone who loved and served his king faithfully. But in the end he is unjustly persecuted by the king, whose opinion of him has been changed by the lies of the "Flatterer," another standard character.

When my grandmother saw the "Faithful One" onstage she looked upset and gave a great sigh. I was too interested in what was happening to ask her the reason, and we spent the next five hours watching the rest of the opera. Sometimes I cried because my grandmother cried at the pitiful situation of the "Faithful One." Sometimes I became as angry as my grandmother did at the wickedness of the "Flatterer."

When we went home that night my grandmother was quite sad. She told my mother that she would have bad luck in the following year because when we entered the theater, the "Faithful One" was onstage. I was puzzled. I told my grandmother that she was confused. It would be a good year for us because we saw the good guy first. But my mother said, "No, son. The 'Faithful One' always is in trouble and it takes him many years to vindicate himself. Our next year is going to be like one of his bad years."

So, according to my mother's and grandmother's logic, we would have been much better off in the new year if we had been lucky enough to see the villain first!

My grandmother had married a man whom she loved with all her heart, but who was totally different from her. My grandfather was very shy, never laughed loudly, and always spoke very softly. And physically he was not as strong as my grandmother. But he excused his lack of physical strength by saying that he was a "scholar."

About three months after their marriage, my grandparents were in a restaurant and a rascal began to insult my grandfather because he looked weak and had a pretty wife. At first he just made insulting remarks, such as, "Hey! Wet chicken! This is no place for a weakling!"

My grandfather wanted to leave the restaurant even though he and my grandmother had not yet finished their meal. But my grandmother pulled his shirt sleeve and signaled him to remain seated. She continued to eat and looked as if nothing had happened.

Tired of yelling insults without any result, the rascal got up from his table, moved over to my grandparents' table, and grabbed my grandfather's chopsticks. My grandmother immediately wrested the chopsticks from him and struck the rascal on his cheekbone with her elbow. The blow was so quick and powerful that he lost his balance and fell on the floor.

Instead of finishing him off, as any street fighter would do, my grandmother let the rascal recover from the blow. But as soon as he got up again, he kicked over the table between him and my grandmother, making food and drink fly all over the place. Before he could do anything else, my grandmother kicked him on the chin. The kick was so swift that my grandfather didn't even see it. He only heard a heavy thud, and then saw the rascal tumble backward and collapse on the ground.

All the onlookers were surprised and delighted, especially the owner of the restaurant. Apparently the rascal, one of the best karate fighters of our area, came to this restaurant every day and left without paying for his food or drink, but the owner was too afraid to confront him.

While the rascal's friends tried to revive him, everyone else surrounded my grandmother and asked her who had taught her karate. She said, "Who else? My husband!"

After the fight at the restaurant people assumed that my grandfather knew karate very well but refused to use it for fear of killing someone. In reality, my grandmother had received special training in karate from my great-great uncle from the time she was eight years old.

Anyway, after that incident, my grandfather never had to worry again. Anytime he had some business downtown, people treated him very well. And whenever anyone happened to bump into him on the street, they bowed to my grandfather in a very respectful way.

One morning my grandmother wanted me to go outside with her. We climbed a little hill that looked over the whole area, and when we got to the top she looked at the rice field below, the mountain on the horizon, and especially at the river. As a young girl she had often brought her herd of water buffaloes to the river to drink while she swam with the other children of the village. Then we visited the graveyard where her husband and some of her children were buried. She touched her husband's tombstone and said, "Dear, I will join you soon." And then we walked back

to the garden and she gazed at the fruit trees her husband had planted, a new one for each time she had given birth to a child. Finally, before we left the garden my sister joined us, and the two of them fed a few ducks swimming in the pond.

That evening my grandmother did not eat much of her dinner. After dinner she combed her hair and put on her best dress. We thought that she was going to go out again, but instead she went to her bedroom and told us that she didn't want to be disturbed.

The family dog seemed to sense something was amiss, for he kept looking anxiously at everybody and whined from time to time. At midnight my mother went to my grandmother's room and found that she had died, with her eyes shut, as if she were sleeping normally.

It took me a long time to get used to the reality that my grandmother had passed away. Wherever I was, in the house, in the garden, out on the fields, her face always appeared so clearly to me. And even now, many years later, I still have the feeling that my last conversation with her has happened only a few days before.

The Land I Lost:

Adventures of a Boy in Vietnam

Meet the Author

Huynh Quang Nhuong was born in My Tho, Vietnam. He was a first lieutenant in the South Vietnamese Army, and was wounded during the Vietnam War. He came to the United States for medical treatment. Once in the U.S., he became a naturalized citizen. He now makes his home in Columbia, Missouri.

Mr. Nhuong is the first Vietnamese writer to write both fiction and nonfiction in English. He says, *"I hope my books will make people from different countries happy. . . ."* He believes that good literature reaches into the hearts of all those who read it, no matter what country they are from, what age they are, or what they believe.

The Land I Lost: Adventures of a Boy in Vietnam was Mr. Nhuong's first book for children. It was published in five different languages and has received awards worldwide.

Meet the Illustrator

Neil Waldman had a painful childhood and art became his outlet. When he was young, he says, *"I would retreat to my bedroom, close the door, and sit down with crayons and a sketch pad. As I watched amazing shapes and colors pour from my crayons onto the blank sheets of paper, I could feel the fear and tension dissolve."* As an adult, he chose to be a children's book illustrator because it allowed him to earn a living while doing what he loved most. Some of Mr. Waldman's favorite books that he has illustrated are *The Never Ending Greenness, Bayou Lullaby,* and *Quetzal.*

Theme Connections

Within the Selection

Writer's Notebook Record your answers to the questions below in the Response Journal section of your Writer's Notebook. In small groups, report the ideas you wrote. Discuss your ideas with the rest of your group. Then choose a person to report your group's answers to the class.

- How did the author feel about the small hamlet where he was born?
- What were some special memories the author had of his childhood? Why were these memories of the people and land so important to him?
- In what way do the author's memories act as a replacement for the homeland that he lost?

Across Selections

- Think of another story you have read where strong family ties played an important role. How did the support of the family strengthen the character's goals or enrich the character's life?

Beyond the Selection

- Have you ever had to leave a place before you were ready to do so? How did your memories of that place help you deal with the event?
- Think about how "The Land I Lost: Adventures of a Boy in Vietnam" adds to what you know about heritage.
- Add items to the Concept/Question Board about heritage.

Scammon Bay

Anchorage

Focus Questions What was life like for the Yup'ik Eskimos of long ago? What is life like for them in the present day? Why do the Yup'iks continue to teach their children the old ways?

IN TWO WORLDS:

• A Yup'ik Eskimo Family •

from the book by Aylette Jenness and Alice Rivers
photographs by Aylette Jenness

THE PAST

• *Long Ago* •

Alice and Billy Rivers live with their children in the small town of Scammon Bay, Alaska, on the coast of the Bering Sea. They are Yup'ik Eskimos. Their story really begins long, long ago.

Alice and Billy's parents, grandparents, great-grandparents, great-great-grandparents——all their ancestors for several thousand years——have always lived here. They were part of a small group of Yup'ik Eskimos whose home was this vast area of tidal flats bordering the sea, with inland marshes, ponds, creeks, and rivers lacing the flat treeless tundra, broken only by occasional masses of low hills.

Each year, as the northern part of the earth tilted toward the sun, the long hours of sunlight here melted the snow, melted the sea ice, melted the rivers, melted, even, the frozen land down to the depth of a foot or so. Briefly, for a few months, birds came from the south to lay their eggs and raise their young. The fish spawned, plants grew, berries ripened. And then the earth tilted away from the sun. Days grew shorter, the sun weaker, temperatures fell. The rain turned to snow, plants withered, birds flew south. Ponds, creeks, rivers, and finally even the Bering Sea froze, and layers of snow covered the whole landscape. Fish, sea mammals, and land animals all moved beneath thick blankets of ice and snow.

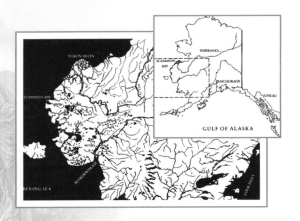

The small, scattered groups of Yup'ik Eskimos knew exactly how to survive here. Living as single families, or in small groups of relatives, they moved with the seasons to catch each kind of fish, bird, or mammal when and where each was most easily available. They harpooned the whales that migrated north along the coast in spring and south in the fall. They shot and snared birds nesting on the tundra, and they gathered the birds' eggs. They netted saltwater fish coming to lay their eggs in the rivers and creeks, and they caught freshwater fish moving beneath the ice of inland creeks. They trapped small mammals on the land for meat and for fur clothing. They knew where to find and how to catch dozens of different fish and animals for food, for clothing, even for light and heat for their small homes.

They had fire, but they didn't know how to use it to make metal. Everything they had they made themselves, with their hands, with stone, bone, or ivory tools—their many intricate snares and nets and traps, their boats and sleds, their homes and their clothing. Life was hard and precarious. Nothing was wasted.

Their mark on the land was light. Today their old sites are nearly part of the earth, not easy to see. These Yup'ik Eskimos didn't build monuments to gods or leaders. They believed that animals had spirits, and that the spirits survived the animals' death to inhabit other animals. After killing a seal, they put water in its mouth to show their caring and respect for it and to ensure that its spirit would return in the form of another seal another time. They made up stories and dances of awe, fear, and pleasure in the animals they knew so well.

They shared with each other, and no one was much better or worse off than anyone else. Families, or groups of families, had rights to certain places for hunting or fishing, but no one owned the land or its resources.

They knew no outsiders, no one different from themselves. During those hundreds and hundreds of years, their way of life changed very little. People followed in the footsteps of their ancestors, children learning from their parents the vast body of knowledge necessary for survival in this environment.

But during the last fifty years, their lives have changed enormously. And these changes are within the memory of the older people living here now.

Listen to Alice Rivers's mother, Mary Ann, describe her childhood. She speaks in Yup'ik, and one of her daughters, Leota, translates into English.

● Mary Ann Remembers ●

"I was born, as I was told, in the late fall. My mother delivered me outside in the tundra, out in the open. My mother told me that after I was born I clutched some tundra moss and grass in my hand. I do not know why I was born outside, but it must have been because my mother was out in the tundra.

"When I was first aware of my surroundings, we lived on the other side of the mountains of Scammon Bay. The name of the place where I was born is called Ingeluk, and I think it's called this name because we are surrounded by small hills. We were the only people living in that area. We were secluded away from other people. There was my father, my mother, my two older sisters, and one older brother, and I am the youngest in the family.

195

"We lived in a sod house. The insides of our house had braided grass hanging on the walls as paneling. We had only one window, which was made out of dried seal guts, and it made a lot of noise when it was windy. Our floor was plain, hard, dried mud. Our beds were dried grass, piled high to keep us warm. We had no blankets. We mostly did with what we had at hand, and we used our parkas to keep us warm. I remember we had one kettle, a small half kerosene tank for our cooking pot, and the plates we had were carved from wood by my father.

"For light, we used seal oil when we had the oil, and it smoked a lot. Other times we had no light because we had no oil. I remember my mother cooked whitefish, and she carefully skimmed off the oil from the pot we had, and what she took out of the cooking pot we used in our oil lamp. The oil from the fish made pretty good light; it never smoked like the seal oil did. There were lots of stories being told, that's what we did during the evenings.

"Our main diet was fish, caught in my father's traps. There were times that we were really hungry. We were very poor. Sometimes when we woke up in the morning, we had nothing at all to eat.

"We didn't have any kind of bread. We did not know what coffee and tea were.

"I saw my first white man when we were traveling by our skin boat. I did not know who he was, but later on I was told that the white man was trading goods for fur or skins. Maybe I was fifteen years old when I saw an airplane.

> *"We lived in a sod house. The insides of our house had braided grass hanging on the walls as paneling. We had only one window, which was made out of dried seal guts, and it made a lot of noise when it was windy."*

196

"I liked the life we used to live a long time ago, but we were always in need of something. I would say we live in comfort now. I don't go in hunger now. I say both lives I led were good, and I like both."

Mary Ann grew up and married a man who lived nearby, Teddy Sundown. They began to raise their family in Keggatmiut, as Scammon Bay is known in Yup'ik. It was a good site, and a number of families settled there. They built their small log houses on the lower slope of a range of hills that rose out of the flat tundra. A clear stream, racing down the hillside, flowed into the river that wound along the base of the hills, and finally emptied into a wide, shallow bay of the Bering Sea. Mary Ann and Teddy still moved to seasonal camps to fish, trap, and hunt, but as the village grew, they began to spend more and more of the year there.

The United States government set up a school in Scammon Bay and hired a Yup'ik teacher. All of the children were expected to attend school.

Missionaries had come to convert the people from their traditional religion, and the village was divided between Catholics and Protestants. Two churches were built.

Alice was the fourth child born to Mary Ann and Teddy. She is shown at the age of ten, standing on the far right of her family. She speaks of growing up in Scammon Bay.

"Our home was a one-room building. Our beds were together——Mom and Dad's bed and our bed. All of us kids slept together in one bed. No table——the tables came later on. We used to eat sitting on the floor, Eskimo way. Mom used to cook bread on top of the stove, 'cause there was no oven. To me it used to be the best bread I've eaten. Then as I grew older, we got a stove and oven, and she started baking bread.

"We ate bread, birds, dried herrings, clams, mussels, fish——boiled and frozen——seals, mink, muskrats. There were two stores. We bought shortening, flour, tea, coffee——just what we needed.

"We were always together. We'd go to church every morning. Mom would wake us up early, we'd go to Mass. We never used to be lazy, we used to just go, get up and go, get up to a real cold morning, and by the time we were home, the house would be nice and warm.

"Right after church we used to go straight to school, all of us. I remember that learning to write my name was the hardest thing. I was maybe about six. We had Eskimo teachers. It was one room, and everything was there.

"After school, we'd have lots of things to do—— bringing some wood in, dishes to wash, house to clean, babies to watch, water to pack. We had aluminum pails with handles. We used to run over to the stream and pack water until we had what we needed. In the winter we had to keep one hole in the ice open the whole winter. This was one of the things I used to do with my sisters, not only me.

"Planes came in maybe once a week with mail. We didn't know about telephones. We had a radio, just for listening. I think we listened to one station all the time. No TV.

"The teachers had a short-wave radio. If someone got sick, they would report us to the hospital. They would give us medication or send us to the hospital in Bethel."

● Alice Grown Up ●

By the time Alice was an adult, Scammon Bay was a village of a hundred and fifty people, with twenty-five log and frame homes. For transportation, each family had a dog sled and team, and a boat for use in summer.

The government began to take a larger role in the Yup'ik villages. A new school was built, with living quarters for non-Eskimo teachers from outside of Alaska. Children were taught a standard public elementary school curriculum, which had little reference either to their own lives or to what they knew and didn't know about life outside Scammon Bay. They were forbidden to speak Yup'ik in school, in the belief that this would help them to learn English, and that learning English was very important.

A postmaster was hired from among the village men, and a custodian for the school. A health aide was trained, and a small clinic built and stocked. More planes came to Scammon Bay, and it became easier to fly someone needing hospital care out——as long as the weather was good.

199

Government money became available for low-income families and for the elderly and disabled. There were few opportunities to earn cash, but almost all of the men in Scammon Bay were able to earn some money by hunting or trapping seals, mink, muskrats, and beaver and selling the skins to be made into luxury fur coats outside of Alaska. In summer they netted salmon in the river mouths north of Scammon Bay and sold this valuable fish to processors, who marketed it throughout the United States as smoked fish, or lox.

Each summer a freighter came up the coast from Seattle, Washington, with supplies for the villages. Everyone began to buy more factory-made goods. Some families bought stoves that burned fuel oil instead of relying on brush wood they cut nearby. Some bought windmills, which produced enough electricity for one or two light bulbs in their homes. Some bought snowmobiles, which enabled them to travel farther than they could by dog team to hunt and trap, but which, unlike dogs, required money for fuel and new parts.

And for the first time in the long history of the Yup'ik Eskimos, some people began to travel away from their homeland. Some teenagers went to boarding school in the state of Washington. Some men went to National Guard training, and some families moved away permanently, settling in Alaskan towns and cities, or even as far away as Oregon and California.

But most remained in Scammon Bay, and some new Yup'ik people came to live there from other towns.

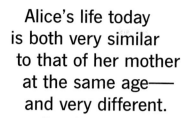

Alice's life today
is both very similar
to that of her mother
at the same age—
and very different.
Scammon Bay has grown
and changed in many ways.

There are three hundred and fifty people in
Scammon Bay now, living in fifty-six houses. Most of the
old log homes are now used for storage, and many
people, like the Riverses, have new houses provided by
the government at low cost. A dish antenna relays
television to all the homes. Satellite transmission enables
families to make telephone calls anywhere in the world.
Huge storage tanks hold fuel to run an electric generator
that provides enough power for each home to have all
the lights that people want. A water and sewage disposal
system required building a water treatment plant and a
lagoon on the tundra for waste water. The dump, full of
cans, plastic, fuel drums, and broken machinery, is a
reminder of the difficulty of disposing of modern trash.

For some years the state government made a great
deal of money from taxes on oil found in Alaska, and this
money paid for many of the modern conveniences in
Scammon Bay and other rural towns. An airstrip was
built so that planes could land more easily at all times of
the year; it is regularly plowed in winter. Three
small planes a day fly into Scammon Bay,
bringing everything from cases of soft drinks
to boxes of disposable diapers and, of course,
the mail. A huge new gym has been built, and

Satellite transmission enables families to make telephone calls anywhere in the world.

a new clinic, a preschool center, town offices, and a post office. The school is now run by the state, not the federal government, and goes all the way through the twelfth grade.

In spite of the changes, the traditional pattern of living from the land is still powerful. This can be seen most clearly as people move to seasonal camps during the summer months.

●   School   ●

During the school year the family's life falls into very different patterns from those of summer. Billy begins his winter rounds of hunting and fishing, going out by snowmobile nearly every day to get food or firewood for the family. Alice goes to work as the school cook, and the Rivers children go to their classrooms each morning.

Billy Junior, in the second grade, is learning to type. He says proudly, "I've already finished typing one book, and now I'm on another. We can read any kind of books. Now I'm on a hard one."

In Sarah and Isaac's combined third and fourth grade class, Clifford Kaganak teaches Yup'ik. Here he writes words in Yup'ik on the chalkboard, and the class practices reading and translating. They want to be fluent in both of their languages——English and Yup'ik.

Down the hall, Jennifer Allison Keim works with the older Rivers boys——Oscar, Jacob and Abraham. Jacob enjoys using the computers, but generally the boys would rather be out hunting and fishing——or using the school skis. Jennifer says, "My goals are for the kids to be educated to the point where they can protect themselves from outsiders, so if something comes their way that they have to deal with, they'll know how to weigh and measure and make decisions."

The teachers all know that the school has a great responsibility to prepare the kids for the outside world, and they also want to encourage a sense of pride in Yup'ik Eskimo culture. Some students want to go on to college after graduating from high school in Scammon Bay, and the teachers work hard to make this happen.

During the school year, traditional ways of life are practiced mostly on the weekends. The end of each school week marks the beginning of two days of hunting and fishing for the whole Rivers family.

Alice says, "On the weekends, we get to go traveling with Billy. Usually we decide what we're going to do ahead of time, what's going to happen. Like if we want to go fishing, we go fishing, or hunting ptarmigans. We're out most of the day Saturday doing this and that."

This is where Billy becomes the teacher, training the kids in both the oldest methods of hunting and fishing, and the newest. Since the children spend so much time in school, this is an important time for them to learn how to survive as Eskimos.

"I teach my boys the way I've been taught, the way my dad taught me. What I think that's wrong, I try to do it better than my dad. And when I make a mistake, I try to correct it to my boys, so they'll do it better than I did.

"I start taking them out as soon as they're old enough——like in the boat, when they're old enough to sit down and take care of themselves. I tell them little things like taking the anchor out, putting the anchor back up. As soon as they understand our words, we teach them from there. If they show you something that they know, you'll know they learned it——and then they can start doing it by themselves.

"Each one of them that goes with me, I talk to them, I tell them about little things——what's dangerous, what's not dangerous. I tell them about melting ice——even though it looks good on the surface, some places you can't see when it's covered with snow, it's thin. That's where they fall through. I teach them what thin ice looks like, and how it looks when it's safe.

"Oscar's been going with me first, 'cause he's the oldest one, then Jacob. One of them will know more, the one that pays attention more, just like in school. The one that doesn't listen, or doesn't pay attention, he'll make more mistakes or get more scolding.

"Oscar was about seven or eight when I first let him shoot a gun. He got his first seal when he was maybe eight or nine. In the boat I did the driving, and I had him do the shooting. He got a young mukluk that was a baby in springtime. He shot it, and after he shot it, he looked at me, looked back, and he smiled. 'I catch it.' "

Oscar remembers this very clearly. He says, "My grandpa divided the seal up in circles and gave it to the old people." This is the traditional Yup'ik way of sharing a boy's first catch with the elders, still carried on, though motorboats have replaced kayaks, and rifles are used in place of thrown harpoons.

THE FUTURE

Alice and Billy know very well that life is changing fast here in Scammon Bay, and they want their children to be prepared for this.

Alice says, "When I was a kid, I used to do things with my mom. I used to watch her sew. Now I try to have Mattie knit, crochet, make things, but she thinks it's too boring. She knows how to do it, but she can't sit and look at one thing for a long time. I can't even teach her how to sew a skin. She doesn't have any patience.

"Now there's so many other things going on. In our time there was no basketball, no Igloo [community center], hardly any dances."

Billy says, "When I was Billy Junior's age, I used to run maybe twenty or thirty times around a pond with my little wooden boat. Just run around, play with it, put mud inside of it, and run around. I'd never think of TV, it wasn't in my mind.

"Everything is not the same here in Alaska, not like before. Things are changing. Things are getting more expensive. Most of the people are depending on more jobs. I mean working, you have to have a job.

"I talk to the kids, I just say what we'd like them to do. I tell them, 'If you go to school, and be smart over there, and try to learn what you're taught, you guys will have good jobs, and good-paying jobs. I want you to have good-paying jobs, so we'll have the things that we need, anything we need'; like this I talk to them.

"I'd be happy to have them travel to see other countries, to have them learning something that's Outside——*if* they have a job. 'Cause Outside there's many people without jobs, no home. Here it's okay, as we help each other here in the villages.

"We get after the kids for not doing their homework. We want them to be more educated, more than us. I mean, learn more. I only went up to the fifth grade."

Alice agrees. She adds "I want them to learn other ways——Outside ways. And I want them to learn our ways, too—hunting for our kind of foods. We can't have store-bought food all the time. I want them to learn both ways."

Looking down on Scammon Bay from the hill, it seems like a very small settlement, nearly lost in the huge expanse of tundra around it. From this distance it doesn't look so different from the Scammon Bay of Alice's childhood. Yet it is invisibly connected to the whole world now. And so is the Rivers family.

> *"Now there's so many other things going on. In our time there was no basketball, no Igloo [community center], hardly any dances."*

IN TWO WORLDS:

● A Yup'ik Eskimo Family ●

Meet the Authors

Aylette Jenness, a writer and photographer, met **Alice Rivers** when they were both young women. At the time, Aylette had moved to Alaska to write books about the people of Scammon Bay. While writing *Gussuk Boy* and *Dwellers of the Tundra*, she met Alice Rivers. After finishing the books, Aylette left Alaska. When she returned to Alaska for a visit more than twenty years later, she met up with her old friend, Alice Rivers. Alice told her about how different things were in Scammon Bay since she had lived there twenty years ago. The two decided to work together on the story of how Alice's family had grown and changed, and how the little community on the Bering Sea had changed as well. Rivers's mother, Mary Ann Sundown, also contributed to the book by telling about the way people lived during the years she herself was growing up near Scammon Bay.

Theme Connections

Within the Selection

Record your answers to the questions below in the Response Journal section of your Writer's Notebook. In small groups, report the ideas you wrote. Discuss your ideas with the rest of your group. Then choose a person to report your group's answers to the class.

- How does the place in which people live affect their culture and way of life?
- In what ways did the family's life change as Scammon Bay changed?
- What traditions did Alice, Billy, and their children continue to practice? Why do you think these things were important to them? What role do you think traditions will play for the Yup'iks of the future?

Across Selections

- Compare the importance of memories and family stories for the Yup'iks of Scammon Bay with their importance for the author of "The Land I Lost: Adventures of a Boy in Vietnam."

Beyond the Selection

- What stories have your older family members and friends told of how life has changed since they were young? Do they feel that these changes were for the better?
- Think about how "In Two Worlds: A Yup'ik Eskimo Family" adds to what you know about heritage.
- Add items to the Concept/Question Board about heritage.

Focus Questions What did the Netsilik people learn from the Tunrit about survival? Why do you think the Netsilik passed down this story?

History *of the* Tunrit

collected by Knud Rasmussen
a traditional Netsilik Eskimo Legend
translated by Edward Field
illustrated by Pudlo

When our Netsilik forefathers came to these hunting grounds
the Tunrit people already lived here.
It was the Tunrit who first learned
how to survive in this difficult country.
They showed us the caribou crossing places
and taught us the special way to fish in the rivers.

Our people came from inland
so we love caribou hunting more than anything else,
but the Tunrit were sea people
and preferred to hunt seal.
They actually went out on the salt sea in their kayaks,
hunting seal in open water. That takes nerve.
We only hunt them through the ice at breathing holes.
They also caught whales and walruses as they swam by:
The bones of these creatures are still lying around
in the wrecks of the Tunrit houses.
And they hunted bear and wore their skins for clothes.
We wear caribou.

The Tunrit were strong, but easily frightened.
In a fight they would rather run than kill. Anyway,
you never heard of them killing anyone.
And we lived among the Tunrit in those days peacefully,
for they let us come and share their land:
Until once by accident some of them killed one of our dogs
and ran away scared, leaving their homeland.

All of the Tunrit fled finally from their villages here,
although we cannot remember why anymore:
They just ran away or the land was taken from them.
And on parting from us they cried:
"We followed the caribou and hunted them down;
now it is your turn to follow them and do the hunting."

And so we do to this day.

Focus Questions Why doesn't Juan feel at home in
New York City? What might make Juan feel better about
living in the United States?

The West Side

from *How Juan Got Home*
by Peggy Mann
illustrated by Bob Dorsey

*Juan Morales has come from Puerto Rico to New York
City to live with his Uncle Esteban. Juan's mother believes
that he will receive a better education in New York than in
Puerto Rico. When the plane lands and his uncle's arrival at
the airport is delayed, Juan is told that the airline will give
him a free flight back to Puerto Rico if his uncle does not
arrive to pick him up. Juan misunderstands and believes he
will be able to return to Puerto Rico any time he decides to
do so. After a few days in his uncle's apartment and some
unsuccessful attempts to make friends with the English-
speaking boys who live on his street, Juan is unhappy and
is determined to return to Puerto Rico. In the meantime,
however, he agrees to go on a shopping expedition for Puerto
Rican food in a neighborhood on the West Side of New York.*

Juan stepped off the bus at Columbus Avenue. It
was as though he had stepped off the bus into
Puerto Rico. The street was alive with children and
Spanish music. Some of the children, barefoot and wet,
played around the water gushing from a fire hydrant,
ran in and out screaming laughter and Spanish words.
Latin music came blaring from radios on
windowsills . . . from a young man who sat on a box in
front of Bodega Rivera strumming a guitar and singing
a Spanish love song . . . from a bongo band on the
corner playing hard rock with a loud Latin beat.

212

Women leaned out of windows shrilling in Spanish to children on the street. A group of men sat around a bridge table on the sidewalk, playing dominoes. Women in bright cotton dresses sat on the front steps gossiping in Spanish. And the stores! At home the stores often had *americano* names: the Blue Moon Bar Restaurant . . . Joe's Shop . . . the Cooperative . . . Mercado's Barbershop . . . . But here: everything Spanish! Farmacia Flores . . . Tienda La Favorita . . . Zapatería El Quijote . . . Repostería Borinquén. . . .

All crowded together like this, the store signs, the music, the look and the sound of the Spanish people, it seemed somehow *more* Puerto Rican than anything he had seen in Puerto Rico. He was no longer a stranger. He didn't even need to ask directions. With a smile on his face he strode into Bodega Rivera.

He *was* home. The small crowded grocery store was just like the one on his street in Barranquitas. The same small, sweet *niños* bananas hung in clumps in the dusty window; and the long, green *plátanos* hung next to them on iron hooks. The same bins of tropical fruits and vegetables. The same cans and bottles on the shelves: guava juice, papaya juice, *asopao de jueyes*, red beans, pink beans, white beans, pinto beans, chick peas, *Doraditos*, *Florecitas*, *coco rico* and *chinita*. Even the same penny candy machine. And the same packets of ladies' panty hose on the rack behind the counter.

The shopkeeper, who wore a large black mustache and a dirty white apron, was arguing with a customer about the price of his *batatas*. Loudly Señor Rivera informed her that he had to import the *batatas* from the island. If she could not pay for special Spanish food she should eat American.

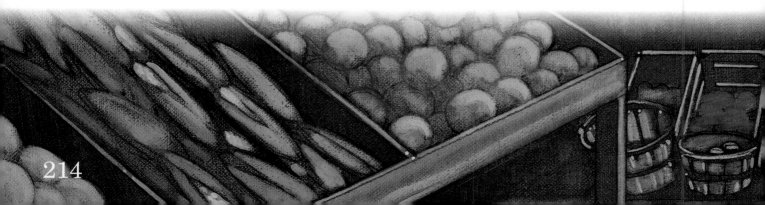

When, grumbling, she counted out her money and left, a boy about Juan's age stood on tiptoe in front of the counter and asked in a loud voice whether Señor Rivera would sell him some boxes.

"Boxes of *what?*" Señor Rivera said.

"Empty boxes," the boy said. "We're having a stickball game on the street tomorrow afternoon and we already sold twenty box seats to people who want to watch from the sidewalk. Now we gotta get the boxes."

"Get out of here, Carlos," Señor Rivera said. "I'm busy."

"But Señor Rivera!" Carlos persisted. "I'm willing to pay for the boxes. Usually you give them out free to customers. I'm going to *pay!*"

"Yes?" Señor Rivera said. "And how are my customers going to carry home their groceries if I got no more boxes?"

"Listen," Carlos said, "I'll make you a deal. If you let us have the boxes, I'll let your son Willie umpire the game."

Señor Rivera said nothing. He scowled.

"As you know," Carlos said, "your boy Willie is kind of a pain-in-the-neck kid. That's why he gets beat up so much. But nobody beats up an umpire. You got to respect an umpire."

"How much did you sell the box seats for?" said Señor Rivera.

"Five cents a box for cardboard, ten cents for wood. I told them they could take the seats home with them."

"And how much are you planning to pay me, Carlos, for every box I give you?"

"Well," Carlos said, "a penny for cardboard. Two cents for wood."

Señor Rivera laughed. "Carlos," he said, "you're going to grow up to be the president of the First National Bank. Listen," he added, "go down in my cellar and haul yourself up twenty boxes. You can have them for free."

Carlos grinned and started for the flight of steps leading down to the cellar.

"Save a box seat for me," Señor Rivera called after him. "I want to come watch my son Willie be umpire."

Juan then stood on tiptoe in front of the greasy glass counter. He ordered twelve *plátanos verdes*, two pounds of *gandules* and one ounce of *ajíes*. But when he paid his money, and held the three paper bags in his hands, he still did not want to leave.

If only his uncle had the job of maintenance engineer on Columbus Avenue! Then he, Juan, might not even want to go home. If he lived over here, then he could go to school over here. Maybe here they even had Spanish schools and he'd never need to learn English at all!

But Uncle Esteban had explained that a boy must go to school in the district where he lived. He would have to go to school on the rich East Side of Manhattan; a school which would, no doubt, be filled up tight with *americanos*.

He noticed the boy called Carlos who came staggering up from the cellar with an armload of cardboard boxes. "Hey!" He walked over to Carlos. "You want me to help you carry those boxes to wherever you're going?"

"Sure," Carlos said in English. "Matter of fact, I was going to ask you to give me a hand." He smiled.

Juan didn't understand the English, but a smile was the same in any language.

He smiled back.

They made two trips from the Bodega Rivera to the basement of the brownstone rooming house where Carlos lived. Juan kept talking almost nonstop all the way. He had so much talk inside him it seemed he just couldn't get it all said.

Carlos spoke very little. When they had finished piling the boxes in a corner of the basement, Carlos explained why he always answered Juan in such short sentences. He knew very little Spanish.

Juan stared at him through the basement gloom, astounded. A *puertorriqueño* who didn't know Spanish?

Carlos shrugged and explained that they'd come from the mainland when he was three years old to live with his grandmother. He'd been brought up on English, in the streets and in school. In fact, the only Spanish he knew came from talking to his grandmother.

Juan nodded. He felt he had found a friend——only to lose him. What was worse, he felt like a fool. Here he'd been jabbering away to this boy all about Barranquitas and his house and his mother and sisters and friends and his miniature car collection and the Piñonas River and his school and the TV programs he watched at home. And all the time Carlos had hardly understood a single word!

"As a matter of fact," Carlos said in English as he started up the basement stairs, "you'll find that most of the Spanish kids on this street don't speak Spanish. At least, their Spanish is nothing to speak of!" Then, having made a kind of pun, Carlos laughed.

But Juan trudging up the stairs behind him did not laugh. He had not understood a word Carlos said.

Carlos turned then and repeated the sentences in a stiff and inaccurate Spanish.

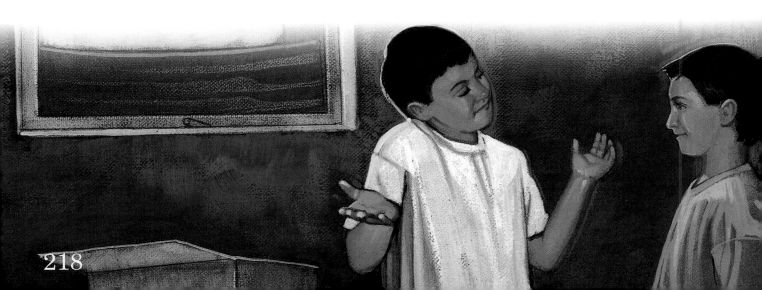

Juan nodded glumly. He felt betrayed. Even if he took the bus over here every day to play with the *puertorriqueño* kids on Columbus Avenue, it would be no good. He would still be a stranger——among his own people. Only they weren't his own people anymore. They were *americanos*.

When they reached the street Carlos said, in Spanish, "Well, thanks for helping me out."

And, in Spanish, Juan replied. "That's okay." Then he added, "I better say good-bye now. I'll be going back home at the end of the week."

"To the island?" Carlos said, in some surprise.

Juan nodded.

"You must be pretty rich," Carlos said, "to come hopping all the way over here just for one week. How much is the plane fare?"

Juan explained that the trip home wouldn't cost him anything. The airline would fly him home free.

Carlos frowned. He did not understand. "Free? How could that be?"

Juan, speaking in slow careful Spanish as though he were addressing a very small child, explained how the airline had promised to send him home free the night he arrived. So since he hadn't taken them up on their offer then, he would do so at the end of the week.

"Listen, you stupid kid," Carlos said. "Sure they were going to send you home free when your uncle didn't show up. I mean they can't let a little kid like you just be hanging around the airport at night all alone. But your uncle *did* show up. So the offer's over. Now you're *his* worry. Not theirs. How could they ever make any money if they kept dealing out free tickets to anyone wanting to make a trip back home?"

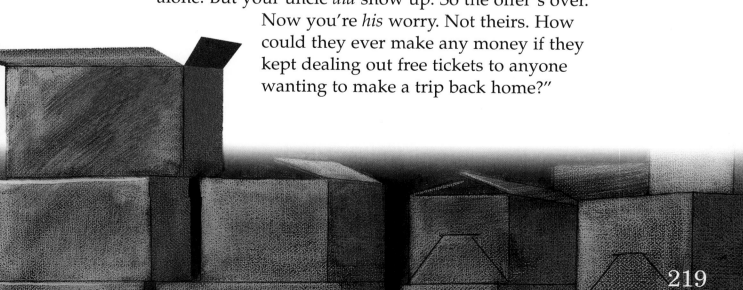

He spoke now in English. Juan kept nodding. Then he said, "*No entiendo.* I not onnerstan'."

So, with some effort, Carlos repeated it all in Spanish. Juan nodded again. This time he understood all too well, and knew with certainty that Carlos was correct. In fact, this very thought had been lurking in the back of his mind. But he hadn't allowed it to come forward before. Because he didn't want to know the truth. The truth that he *could* not go home.

"Listen, kid," Carlos said suddenly, in Spanish, "since you helped me with the boxes, how'd you like a free box seat for the game tomorrow afternoon?"

"What kind of game?" Juan asked.

"Stickball."

"What's stickball?"

"Stickball's what it says it is," Carlos said. "You hit a ball with a stick. Want me to show you?"

Juan nodded.

"C'mon," Carlos said. "I got my equipment upstairs." He shoved open the front door and Juan followed him into the hallway. The place smelled strongly of cats and rancid cooking oil and the garbage which sat outside each doorway in overflowing pails or paper bags.

Juan felt like holding his breath and holding his nose. Who would want to live in such a place when they could be back in the fresh mountain air of Barranquitas where the only smell one noticed was that of flowers?

When they reached the third floor Carlos took a ring of keys from his pocket and started unlocking one of the doors. "We got three different locks," he explained to Juan, "because we have been robbed five times."

Juan was impressed. Carlos must live in a pretty big place with some valuable things in it for anyone to bother robbing his apartment five times. After all, even though the hallways smelled, that didn't mean the apartments weren't beautiful inside.

But inside there was nothing much either. Just one room with a flowered curtain drawn across the middle. The whole place was not much bigger than the bedroom he shared at home with his two sisters. There was a wooden table and four wooden chairs all painted bright green. There was a picture of the Virgin Mary tacked to the wall. And in the corner a small stove and large sink, stacked with dishes. Sunlight fell in through the open window and lay in a long oblong pattern across the worn green linoleum on the floor. There was a flower box on the windowsill with some geraniums in it.

Not a bad place, Juan thought. At least it looked friendly. He'd a lot rather live here than in Uncle Esteban's fine basement apartment where all the windows had bars like a jail.

Carlos meanwhile had gone behind the curtain. He came back with a small rubber ball and a broom. "Of course," he said, "the bat we play with is a mop handle without the mop. But our captain keeps that in his house. I'm the manager of the team," he added, with an edge of pride in his voice. "That means I set up the games and arrange everything. The big game we got on tomorrow is against the Young Princes. Come on. I'll show you how we play."

Juan followed Carlos into the hallway again, waited while his new friend locked the door with three different keys, and went down the stairs after him, taking two at a time as Carlos did.

In the street Carlos waited until a few cars had gone by. Then, when there was a lull in the traffic, he stepped out, threw the ball into the air, swung the broom handle hard. And missed.

Shamefaced, he picked up the ball. "Well, I myself am not so hot at this game," he said in English. "I'm better at organizing than playing. But the idea is, if you hit the ball past the first sewer that's pretty good. If you hit it past the second sewer, that's sensational. And if you hit it past the third sewer, that's impossible. The third sewer's right down at the end of the street. You can hardly even see it from here."

Juan nodded. He had barely understood a word that Carlos said. But he was embarrassed to ask his friend to repeat it all over again in Spanish. So he asked instead, "I try?"

"Sure," Carlos said and threw him the broom which Juan caught in one hand. Then Carlos threw the ball which Juan caught in the other hand. And stepped out into the street.

"Hey! *Watch it!*" Carlos screamed in English.

Juan stepped back just as a yellow taxi sped by his toes. He'd been so intent about showing Carlos that he could hit this ball with the broom that he forgot about everything else——including getting run over. His heart now started thudding with fear at his narrow escape.

"Listen!" Carlos said sternly. "They got such things as cars in this city and don't you ever forget that!"

Juan nodded. He looked carefully up and down the street.

"It's okay now," Carlos said. "Nothing coming."

But still Juan felt afraid.

"Hurry up! *Avanza!*" Carlos said. "Take your chance while you got it."

So Juan, his heart still pounding, stepped out into the street, threw the rubber ball into the air, and hit it with the broom handle. Hard.

He watched the ball proudly as it sped through the air.

Carlos screamed again. And again Juan rushed back to the safety of the sidewalk. But this time there were no cars coming. This time Carlos screamed for another reason. "You hit three sewers!" he kept screaming. "Man, don't you understand, you hit *three sewers!*"

"Yes," said Juan. "I onnerstan'." He did not know what "three sewers" meant. But he did understand that Carlos was impressed at how he had hit the ball.

"Listen," Carlos said. "You must be puttin' me on, man. Telling me you never played stickball before." He repeated the question in Spanish. The words were charged with suspicion. "You sure you never played stickball before?"

Juan shook his head. "No," he said. "I have never played stickball before." He saw no reason to explain that he had been playing stick-stone ever since he was seven years old. Hitting a stone with a stick across the Piñonas River in the Contest game he had invented.

"Listen, kid," Carlos said suddenly. "How'd you like to play on our team tomorrow afternoon?" Then, slowly, carefully he tried the words in Spanish. "*¿Vas a jugar con nosotros mañana?*"

Juan grinned. "Sure, man," he said in English. "Hokay!"

The West Side

Meet the Author

Peggy Mann is a native New Yorker. She has based a lot of her writing on childhood experiences that she had when her family restored a brownstone building on a slum street in Manhattan. Her first book, called *The Street of the Flower Boxes*, was about her years in the brownstone. It was made into a children's television special. Other books in the series include *The Clubhouse, When Carlos Closed the Street, How Juan Got Home*, and *The Secret Dog of Little Luis*.

Today, the slum block she lived on as a little girl is a showplace. Families from the area got together and fixed up all the old brownstones as part of an urban renewal project. Now, that block stands as an example to other urban renewal projects around the country. Peggy Mann started and became the president of one of the committees that makes these projects possible.

Meet the Illustrator

Bob Dorsey has been a professional illustrator for 17 years, working with a wide range of media and a variety of subject matter. Some of his favorite subjects include portraits, wildlife, children, and sports. Mr. Dorsey is well known for the numerous portraits that he has done for the National Baseball Hall of Fame in Cooperstown, New York. His paintings have been exhibited throughout the country.

Theme Connections

Within the Selection

Record your answers to the questions below in the Response Journal section of your Writer's Notebook. In small groups, report the ideas you wrote. Discuss your ideas with the rest of your group. Then choose a person to report your group's answers to the class.

- How did Juan feel the first time he came to the West Side of New York?
- Carlos followed some of the same customs as Juan, but not all of them. Why do you think that was?
- Juan was proud of his culture and language. Why then did he start to speak English with Carlos?

Across Selections

- Compare Juan with the author of "The Land I Lost: Adventures of a Boy in Vietnam." How were their experiences in leaving their homelands similar?

Beyond the Selection

- Think about how "The West Side" adds to what you know about heritage.
- Add items to the Concept/Question Board about heritage.

Family Greeting. 1962. **Eli Tikeayak.** Canadian Inuit, Rankin Inlet. Light green-grey stone. Art Gallery of Ontario, Toronto.

Mother and Child. 1922. **Pablo Picasso.** Oil on canvas. 100 × 81 cm. The Baltimore Museum of Art ©2001 Estate of Pablo Picasso/Artist Rights Society (ARS), New York.

Naranjas (Oranges). 1988. **Carmen Lomas Garza.** Gouache. 20 × 14 in. Collection of Mr. and Mrs. Ira Schneider, Scottsdale, Arizona.

Love As Strong As Ginger

Lenore Look
illustrated by Stephen T. Johnson

GLOSSARY

Chiubungbung (CHEW bung bung): Stinky-stinky. Since Chinese words repeat for emphasis, this means a *very* bad smell.

Chong: A cannery or factory.

Chowing: Frying food quickly in a little fat.

Doong: A sticky rice cake wrapped in bamboo leaves, often filled with pork, salted duck yolk, peanuts, or red-bean paste.

GninGnin (NYIN NYIN): Paternal grandmother. Literally translated means "person-person," or the fullness of two people.

Taishanese: A southern dialect from the western Pearl River delta region of China.

A pair of large rubber gloves that smelled of the sea used to hang in my grandma's kitchen.

"*GninGnin,* may I try those on?" I asked one day.

"*Chiubungbung,*" she replied, meaning stinky-stinky in Taishanese, our Chinese dialect. She broke noodles into a pot of boiling water, and shoved the gloves away from us. Steam rose into her face.

I spent nearly every Saturday with GninGnin in her Chinatown apartment while Mother and Father went to work. She taught me how to make *doong,* sticky rice dumplings wrapped in bamboo leaves, and I taught her how to dress a fashion doll. At lunchtime, she'd make the best meal, clearing room for me in her tiny kitchen where salted butterfish and flounder hung like laundry above our heads.

"I wear my gloves for cracking crabs at the crab *chong*," she explained as she peeled shrimp, my favorite, into the pot, "to keep the jagged shells from cutting my hands." As she reached for some chives to cut into our soup, I looked at her hands. Her skin was baggy around the fingers, and delicate, like the rice paper around candy. Her gloves were the opposite: thick, with patches from a tire repair kit.

"Why do you crack crab?" I asked.

"Only job I could find," she said. "Nobody wants to hire an old woman who can't speak English." She tasted the soup on her dark wooden spoon, then ladled some into bowls. The chives floated like confetti among the shrimp.

"Maybe if I knew English," she said, "I would have become . . . a famous actress!"

"Really?" I stared at my grandma. She posed her head like the movie stars on the calendars the shopkeepers gave her at Christmas. Her eyes twinkled.

"Sure," she said. "Katie, in America, you can become whatever you dream."

"I want to be like you," I said, following her into the next room.

She set our bowls on a table and we sat down on smooth, old stools. "Will you take me to the crab chong?" I asked.

"You want to go there?" She chuckled. "Little dream."

"How do you crack crab?"

"With a mallet." She made a pounding fist. "Then I shake out the meat. They pay me for every pound that I shake out. I can do two hundred pounds a day, enough for bus fare and a fish for dinner . . . and someday, maybe enough to help you go to college."

I slurped my soup. "Is crab tasty?" I asked.

GninGnin picked the shrimp from her bowl and put them in mine. "I don't eat crab. Tastes like hard work."

"Maybe if I'm there, your work will go faster," I said. "I'll crack a hundred crabs for you!"

GninGnin's eyes grew big. "One hundred crabs!" she exclaimed. "This I've got to see."

It was cold the morning my grandma took me to the crab chong. Rain misted our faces and the sky was pebble-dark as we waited, hand in hand, for the bus. When it came, it was crowded with ladies clucking their tongues in singsong languages. They looked like friends on an outing, each sporting rubber gloves, a rubber apron, and tall rubber boots. The bus was chiubungbung. I wrinkled my nose and played a game of holding my breath.

"Where are your gloves?" an old lady in a quilted jacket asked me in our Taishanese.

"No size fits her," GninGnin replied.

"May that always be so," the lady nodded, smiling a gold tooth.

When the bus stopped, I followed GninGnin to a tall building overlooking dark waters. My sneakers turned wet and cold as we passed a man hosing shell and creamy crab guts into the spaces between the planks.

Inside, chiubungbung billowed out from large, hot vats. GninGnin stretched a nylon net over my hair and tied on a bandana to keep me from getting a "crabhead"—a headful of crabmeat. "It's the rules," she whispered. "No one is allowed to look pretty here." Everyone tied on their aprons, and stuffed sponges into the palms of their gloves.

Suddenly, a bell rang and we hurried into a warm room filled with a zillion crabs! The orange hard-shell formed a mountain range that seemed to go on forever. Steam rose from the crabs and covered everything.

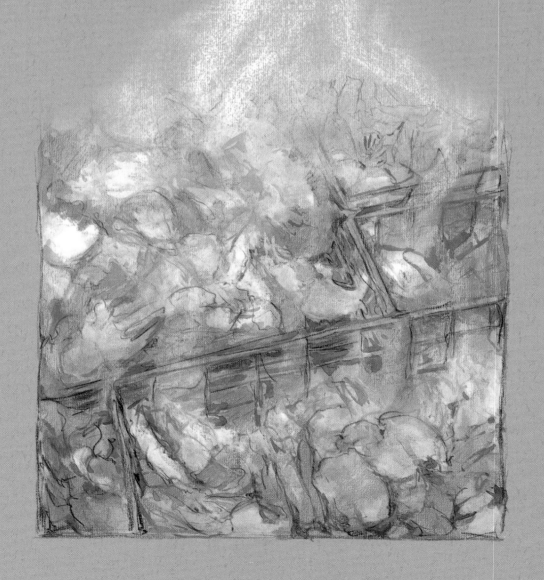

GninGnin disappeared into the fog. Then a terrible deafening noise began. Mallets swung fast and faster. Hands flew, tossing shell and keeping meat. I covered my ears.

I found GninGnin standing behind a crab mountain, moving quickly, forcefully, unlike the way she moved in her kitchen. **Crack!** The tip of a claw came off. GninGnin's whole body shook as she banged her hand on the rim of a small metal box to shake out a few hairs of meat. Then she grabbed another claw. **Crack!** The upper part of the claw split open. **Bang!** Out came a chunk of meat.

Her face grew pink. Crabmeat strands stuck to her cheeks. I moved away. "Don't talk to anyone," she yelled after me. "Every minute is another penny!"

In a corner, one of GninGnin's friends was giving the crabmeat a bath. When she stirred in a shovelful of salt, meat floated and shell pieces sank. She scooped a handful of the meat onto a conveyor belt that moved it under a purple light where others picked out more shell.

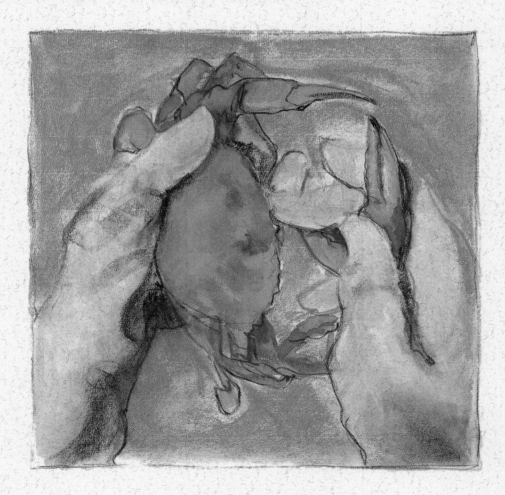

The crabmeat fell into another bath before going to a lady with cans. "Restaurants and stores can't get enough of our crab," said the can lady, popping a small piece into my mouth. It melted like butter. "Good for crab cakes, crab imperial, crabmeat stuffing, crab soup, everything."

I watched until my feet hurt and my stomach growled. Then I wandered back, crunching over empty claws. I found GninGnin standing in the same spot, but now she was covered with tiny, cream-colored hairs. She looked like a strange bird.

"I need to sit down," I moaned.

"There's only one place to sit—on the toilet upstairs," GninGnin replied. She continued to work, but her arms looked heavy; she moved slowly.

The sun had traveled across the windows above her head and the crab chong had grown quiet again.

"How do you keep going?" I asked.

"I don't know . . ." she began.

Then she stopped and lifted her head, blinking away crabmeat. Her face brightened.

"Don't you know that I'm a famous actress making a movie in a crab chong? All around us is the movie set and the other actors. How can I give up when I'm the star?"

Finally, GninGnin reached for the last crab. She turned and held out her mallet. "Would you like to do this one?"

"Yes," I said, eagerly snatching the warm handle. GninGnin tied her apron around me. I put my hands in her roomy gloves and stepped into her place.

With all my strength I hammered at the back of the crab. But nothing happened. I hit it again. Nothing. "It's a bad crab," I complained.

GninGnin laughed. I laughed. Her friends gathered and everyone laughed at my bad crab.

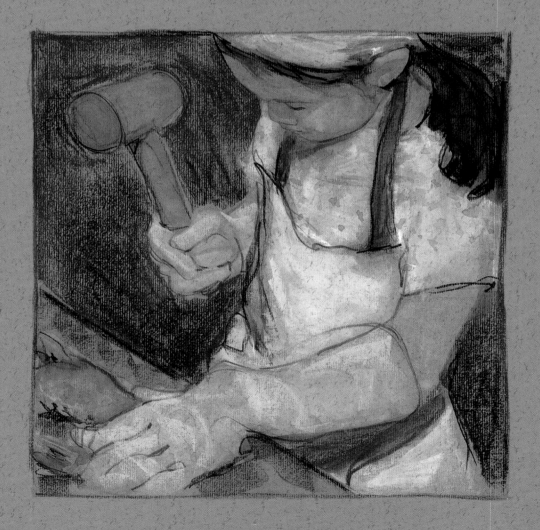

A man with cheeks as orange as cooked crab shell and boots as tall as trees stomped over through the broken shells. "Who have we here?" he boomed. "Are you my newest employee?"

"She's just here to watch her grandma," a lady replied in English for GninGnin.

The man stared at GninGnin. She stared at the crab in front of me. I stared at the gloves hanging on my hands.

"Would you like a job, young lady?" he asked.

I shrugged. "The gloves don't fit."

"How about taking that crab for dinner then?" he said, offering it to me.

I looked at GninGnin. She nodded. "Thanks," I said.

On the ride home, I sat close to GninGnin. Her work done, she was sitting with her eyes closed, her head rocking with the bus. Tears leaked out of the corners of her eyes; she was tired. Her gloves rested on her knees.

That afternoon, GninGnin soaked me in a hot bath to wash the chiubungbung from my hair and skin. Then she prepared my crab.

"You were right, Katie," she said, *chowing* scallions, ginger, and black-bean paste with the crab. "You made my work easier."

"But I forgot to help," I said. "And I'm not strong enough to crack crab!"

She gave me a taste of something delicious on her spoon. "You're strong enough to do other things . . . to become whatever you dream."

I ate GninGnin's words and the wonderful meal she'd prepared for me. Crab chong special, she called it. "Made with love as strong as ginger and dreams as thick as black-bean paste."

And I filled myself with all the flavors of her hard work.

Love As Strong As Ginger

Meet the Author

Lenore Look loves to eat crab, just like her character Katie. Ms. Look also had a grandmother from Southeast Asia who worked in a Seattle cannery. Her grandmother cracked crab all day for three cents a pound. Saturdays, however, she spent with her granddaughter, in the kitchen. Ms. Look remembers those Saturdays and her grandmother's wonderful cooking whenever she eats crabs made with ginger and black bean paste.

Meet the Illustrator

Stephen T. Johnson has illustrated a number of children's books. One of his best-known books is *Alphabet City*, which won the Caldecott Award. For the book, Mr. Johnson created very realistic paintings of city scenes in which the forms of letters can be found. For example, the shape of the letter *P* is found in a subway stair rail.

Like Ms. Look, Mr. Johnson also connects food to some of his favorite memories. For him, it's his grandmother's barbecued chicken that always takes him back to when he was young.

Theme Connections

Within the Selection

Writer's Notebook

Record your answers to the questions below in the Response Journal section of your Writer's Notebook. In small groups, report the ideas you wrote. Discuss your ideas with the rest of your group. Then choose a person to report your group's answers to the class.

- How does Katie feel about her grandmother? How does she feel about her Chinese heritage?
- Why does Katie's grandmother want her granddaughter's life to be different from her own? In what ways do you think she wanted Katie's life to be like hers?
- How does the author use food to tell about the Chinese culture?

Across Selections

- In what other selections in this unit do grandparents play an important role in the story? Why do you think grandparents often play an important role in sharing heritage?
- What did you learn about the food of other groups of people described in the unit stories?

Beyond the Selection

- What foods are part of your heritage? Are there special foods for holidays or celebrations? Describe them.
- Think about how "Love As Strong As Ginger" adds to what you know about heritage.
- Add items to the Concept/Question Board about heritage.

Focus Questions What is it about the women of her heritage that makes the author proud? In what way does she feel indebted to them?

WOMEN

Alice Walker
illustrated by Tyrone Geter

They were women then
My mama's generation
Husky of voice—Stout of
Step
With fists as well as
Hands
How they battered down
Doors
And ironed
Starched white
Shirts

How they led
Armies
Headragged Generals
Across mined
Fields
Booby-trapped
Ditches
To discover books
Desks
A place for us
How they knew what we
Must know
Without knowing a page
Of it
Themselves.

Focus Questions Why is the samovar so important to Nana Sashie?
Why does Rache want to know the story of her grandmother's girlhood?

The Night Journey

from the book by Kathryn Lasky
illustrated by Trina Schart Hyman

Rache lives with her parents, Ed and Leah; her grandmother, Rose; and her great-grandmother, Sashie. Rache's parents and grandmother warn her not to upset Nana Sashie by asking about tsarist Russia and the persecution Jewish people were subjected to there. However, Rache is fascinated by the story Nana Sashie has begun to tell about her family's dangerous escape from that country.

In an old trunk Rache finds a piece of the brass samovar, or tea urn, that figures largely in Nana Sashie's story. The samovar was the one thing that Sashie's mother, Ida, chose to take with her from Russia. The selection begins on the evening when Rache's father surprises the family with a rebuilt samovar. That night, Nana Sashie continues her story for Rache after the others have gone to bed.

"I have one last gift," said Ed.
"Oh, Ed, enough already!"
"This is actually a gift for the whole family."
"Oooooh!" Rache, Leah, and the nanas exclaimed in unison.

"Just one minute while I get it." Ed went to the pantry and returned with something large and fairly tall wrapped in cloth. "It was too big to wrap in paper so I just put this cloth around it." As he set it on the table he asked, "Who wants to unwrap it?"

Rache was puzzled. There were not the usual hesitations, the if-you-don't-like-it statements.

"Rache, why don't you unwrap it?"

"Well, okay," said Rache with slight apprehension. She leaned forwards and gave a light tug. The cloth fell off. There was a sharp gusty sound as each of the women sucked in her breath in shock. Then silence. A samovar——polished and bright——stood before them. Rache heard Nana Sashie whisper something in Yiddish. The top piece——the crown, Ida's crown——flickered unquenchably in the candlelight. The good soldier was back! Rache sat stunned as conversation bubbled up around her.

"It's a samovar!"

Even the babies liked a glass of tea from the samovar.

"Ed, however did you do it?"

From my bed I could see the samovar.

"Well, the part that Rache found started me off."

"Were you here that day?"

Like a polished good soldier.

The words floated back to Rache through the din.

"So I started hunting in antique shops and got some leads from the museum——you know, just to find the other brass parts."

Its brass catching the glow of the gas lamp in the street outside.

"I'll tell you who was really incredibly helpful and who did most of the rebuilding when we got the parts was . . ."

I used to pretend it was a good soldier . . .

"Bo Andersen of Andersen's Jewelry. You know, the son, the kid . . ."

"You mean the one who's about forty?"

"Yes. Well, he just loved working on this."

"Nana Sashie?" Leah suddenly looked worried. "Ed, I hope this doesn't . . . Nana Sashie, are you all right?"

A sentry in the darkness standing watch over us.

There were two small pockets of loud silence in the happy din——one was Nana Sashie, whose face seemed lost in a gentle reverie, and the other was Rache, who, now over her initial astonishment, felt a confusing mixture of emotions. When she had first discovered the samovar part, Rache had been disgusted by Leah's and Nana Rose's ignorance of Sashie's Russia.

251

But now she felt a real apprehension, as if the gulf between the two worlds had closed too quickly and the one world that she had explored with Sashie would no longer be just theirs alone. Sashie! Funny, she had never thought of her as just Sashie before. She had always been Nana Sashie. It was odd. Odder still was her father. Did he know about the meetings with Nana Sashie? Had he seen her go into Nana's room that night?

"Rache! Come back to the world of the living. Thank you."

"Oh, sorry!"

"Nana Sashie asked you a question."

"Oh! What? What, Nana?"

"Would you kindly fetch the toolbox. There are a few bolts that need tightening if we are going to use this for making tea——which we are!"

After tightening several bolts, Nana Sashie declared the samovar fit for a trial run and insisted that they bring it to her bedroom.

"I don't like the idea of her sleeping with that thing burning in her room," said Nana Rose to Ed and Leah.

"What do you mean? I slept with 'that thing' burning every night in my room for my first nine years!"

"Sparks could fly."

"No, it's very well designed," said Ed. "It's probably safer than our electric toaster."

"Well, I don't like the idea."

"Well, I do," Nana Sashie said bluntly.

"I thought it was supposed to be for the whole family?" Nana Rose persisted.

"It is. You can come up to my room for tea any time. It's easier for you to come upstairs than for me to come down."

That seemed to settle it; the samovar went to Nana Sashie's room. If people wanted a cup of tea, they had to go to her bedroom, which consequently became quite socially active.

But that first night the samovar would belong to Nana Sashie and Rache alone. At least, that was the thought in Rache's mind as she moved across the hall carpeting to Sashie's room. It was 2:30 in the morning and Rache had not even needed the alarm to wake her for this short hike toward the long journey through time, through Nana Sashie's time, to the world that might not be strictly their preserve for much longer. She stepped into the bedroom. The polished good soldier loomed before her in the night. The street lights were lawns away in the suburbs, and yet the samovar seemed lambent and luminous, as if catching the reflections from a distant mirror.

"I knew you'd come tonight."

Rache jumped in surprise. The voice sounded so young.

"Nana Sashie!"

"Who else?"

"You're awake?"

"Yes."

"How's your stomach?"

"What about my stomach?"

"The garlic didn't upset it?"

"Of course not! Stop with the stomach already! Come sit down here beside me." She patted the covers. "Quite remarkable, isn't it? With just one piece to start with, your father did an amazing job! And now he's back, the good soldier." Nana Sashie gave Rache's hand a squeeze.

Like iron filings pulled to a magnet, Rache's and Sashie's eyes were drawn to the glow of the samovar. The old eyes flickered with new color. Time melted. A century bent. There was a young voice.

"We're going with him?"

A strange waxy face with dreadful eyes had melted out of the mist of the cobbler's alley. Sashie felt a stinging cuff on her ear as soon as she asked the question.

"Be quiet!" Her father's voice was sharp. He leaned forward and greeted Wolf warmly.

As Sashie saw her father's hand actually touch the other man's flesh, she felt her stomach turn, and she recoiled in horror. She sought her mother's hand, but Ida was like a statue, rigid, her eyes unseeing sockets. Through the fog came the disembodied cluckings of chickens. Sounds, even the strangest ones, took on a peculiar intimacy in the thickness of a fog, and Sashie shivered as she heard these.

"Wolf Levinson," said Joe. "My family——Sashie; my wife, Ida; my sister, Ghisa; and my father, Sol."

Wolf nodded and touched his hand to his hat in his first social gesture in twenty-five years.

"We have no time to waste, Joe." Sashie felt her mother wince at hearing her husband's name spoken by this man. "So if you will follow me, the wagon's right here. I have arranged the coops so you can get in and lie flat. Then I'm afraid after you're settled I must put them back to cover you."

"Yes. Yes, Wolf, we understand," said Joe.

"Well then, this way and we can lay out the bedclothes to make it more comfortable." There was a bustling as bundles were taken off backs and rearranged in the wagon. Sashie was busy untying her own, but she suddenly was aware of a stony, inexorable stillness directly behind her. It was as if Ida were not even breathing. Joe put down his toolbox and moved quickly to her side. He spoke gently. "Come on now, Ida." He began to untie her bundle quickly. "It's going to be all right."

"The chickens are one thing, but the devil is something else!"

"Don't be silly, Ida." But Ida did not answer.

Crawling down a temporary center aisle Wolf had made, Sashie was helping Ghisa spread the bedclothes on the floor of the wagon. As long as she kept helping Ghisa she did not have to look at or really think about the strange face with the awful eyes. But now there was trouble. She could sense it. Ida was not moving and Joe was desperate. Sashie peeked around a coop.

Her mother's bedrock stance shocked her. She felt the real possibility that the escape might never begin, that they were doomed to stand here until morning, when they would be discovered. And then what? She had absolutely no idea how her father could ever move her mother onto the wagon. It would take a miracle. Sashie suddenly thought of Moses standing by the Red Sea before it parted. Next to Ida, the Red Sea was a puddle to jump. Sashie had never seen anything as unmovable as Ida. Partially hidden by the coop, Sashie listened to the drama taking place between her parents.

"Ida, you must!" pleaded Joe.

"Who is this man?"

"Ida, he is our only chance."

"What hell has he been to?"

"Ida!" Joe swallowed hard and brought his face close to hers. "For the love of our children, get in that wagon!" What in the world was he going to do, Sashie wondered. Carry her?

"Ida, say this with me." And Joe began a soft chant: *"She'ma Y'Isoreal! Adonai Aloujanou! Adonai Echod!* Hear, O Israel! The Lord our God! The Lord is One!"

Sashie's eyes widened as she saw her mother lean on her father's arm and begin to move. As she took these first steps on the longest journey, Sashie could hear her mother whispering softly the words of the *Shema*, the Jewish statement of faith.

The blankets had been spread. Ida and Sashie stretched out in the most forward part of the wagon, each with a baby tucked in at her side. The space left between them was for Joe. At their toes were the tops of Ghisa's and Zayde Sol's heads, who were stretched out from the midsection of the wagon to the back end. Ida and Sashie settled in as best they could. With a small pillow under their heads, they had about twelve or fifteen inches clearance between their faces and the chicken coops. This seemed much more ample than Sashie had imagined. There was plenty of room to place a tier of the samovar over her face as a shield.

"This isn't bad, Mama," said Sashie, trying on the samovar face mask. "Here, try it." Sashie turned toward her mother to hand her the brass piece.

"No, I want to see," Ida said emphatically.

"So much for the samovar!" muttered Ghisa, whose voice floated up from Sashie's feet. There was no way that Sashie could see Ghisa's or Zayde Sol's face, and she found that she missed the smirk that must have punctuated her aunt's remark.

She could just see her mother's face by turning her head to the side, and she could see Louie's chubby face, tucked in under her own arm and sleeping for now. Cecile's face was mostly buried under her mother's blouse, but Sashie listened hard and through the clucking gale of the chickens above could hear the deep, throaty sucking noises of the infant as she nursed, a sound she had heard a thousand times but which thrilled her in a new way. Her father had arranged himself between Ida and Sashie. His head was a little forward of theirs, so he did not block their view of each other, and in order to see Joe, Ida and Sashie needed only to crane their necks and look up a bit. He quickly put a hand on each of their shoulders.

"Well, is everything as comfortable as possible here? You know, you don't need to be on your backs; you can turn over on your stomachs. Everyone all right?" Joe asked. "Ida?"

"All right." She replied flatly.

"Sashie?"

"Fine, Papa."

"Ghisa?"

"Lovely!" Darn, Sashie thought. She wished she could see Ghisa's face.

"Papa?" Joe asked.

There was a slight pause, then, "I'm alive?"

"All ready?" Wolf's face loomed at the end of the aisle.

"All set," Joe answered. His voice seemed tinged with excitement that bordered more on joy than fear.

"All right, I'll put on the last coops."

There was a great clatter and clacking as Joe dropped the first coop into the center aisle where it rested on the edges of the flanking coops. A little chunk of white night disappeared, and Sashie felt her heart beat faster. More clatter and clucks, and another piece of the night vanished. One by one the coops were dropped, and piece by piece the world above Sashie and her family was eaten up. The clucking of chickens choked the air around her, and Sashie found herself gulping for breath. Terrified of inhaling one of the white feathers that tumbled crazily through the air, she tried to screen her mouth with her scarf, but then it was harder to breathe.

"Sashie!" Her father's voice came through strong and gentle. "Look at me, Sashela." She craned her neck towards her father. "You breathe like me now. Do just what I do. First in through the nose, not too deep, then out through the mouth blowing softly. Slowly. Take your time, Sashela. There's plenty of air. And you think of nice things, like the smell of bread baking and kites flying and the first leaves of May and lighting Hanukkah candles."

"Harruh!" They heard Wolf grunt and slap the reins on the horse's back. The wagon groaned and lurched forwards, the wheels creaking, and they were on their way. Sashie thought she could count every cobblestone as the wagon rolled down the cobbler's alley. But she kept breathing just as her father had told her to and tried to think of nice things——things that now seemed rare and wondrous, like an open window on a starry summer night, a raindrop's path on glass, April branches with leaves curled tight as babies' fists.

They must be on Vaskeyevka Street. She would try and guess

their route as they went. But she certainly could not see, and at this hour there were no sounds except the blizzard of cluckings that raged inches above them. She wondered if they would go by the park. And then after the park, what? She had never gone beyond the park. The Alexandra Gate of the park was the farthest perimeter of her life. Some chicken droppings splattered on her cheek, but just as disgust welled up inside Sashie a new noise split the cluckings——iron spikes hitting stone. The world above was laced with the rhythmic strikes.

"Whoa! Whoa!" She felt the wagon stop. Ghisa slid forwards a bit, her head pressing on Sashie's feet, and Sashie's head pressed against her father's arm. Louie's eyes flew open. Sashie opened her eyes as wide as she could and, staring directly into the little boy's, commanded his silence with an unblinking and fierce gaze that was intended to freeze his tongue. Quickly she reached up her sleeve for a sugar stick and popped it into his mouth. It worked, this time. Outside she could hear Wolf conversing in Russian with some men. The street was being repaired and impassable for a four-wheel vehicle. They must turn around and take Zolodievka Street. There followed a great deal of jangling and jolting shot through with Wolf's grunts and barks at the horse. Sashie felt the wagon roll backwards a few feet, then forwards. There were more barks. From the noise Sashie thought that Wolf must be off the wagon and guiding the horse around by pushing and pulling on the harness. Louie cried out once, but the sound was drowned by the tumult of the horse whinnying in protest, chickens clucking, harness jangling, wheels creaking, not to mention the string of curses and barks emanating from Wolf.

"Old man!" said one of the street workers jovially. "Watch your tongue. You know there are not just roosters aboard your wagon. I see some hens!"

The swirl of feathers seemed to freeze in the air above Sashie. She felt Ghisa grab her foot and her father's hand bite into her shoulder.

"Just joking!" She heard the man protest innocently. "Can't you take a joke, old man?"

Sashie had not heard Wolf say anything to the street worker, but she had a sense that Wolf need not say much to fill another with dread. The wagon was finally turned around. The street worker stood just by Sashie's side of the wagon now. With only the boards between them, she could hear him mutter nervously to the other, "Queer eyes!" Sashie could feel Wolf climbing into the driver's seat.

"Harruh!" he yelled. The wagon lurched forwards and clattered out of the street.

If they had to take Zolodievka Street instead of this one, it must be fairly near, and if it were fairly near, reasoned Sashie, the Alexandra Gate of the park was not that far away. Approaching the edge of her known world, Sashie felt a ripple of excitement run through her body. She remembered suddenly a book her father had shown her that had a picture of a map from long long ago, from before Columbus had discovered the new world. The map showed a world with the continents and oceans known in the early fifteenth century. At a certain distance from the land, sea serpents were drawn riding through the crests of waves, with the legend HERE BEGINNETH THE REGION OF THE DRAGONS. Except, thought Sashie, in Russia the dragons live everywhere, and she and her family were supposed to be escaping from them to the tsarless region of what angels? She was not sure. Although she herself had not dealt directly with the dragons, Sashie never once doubted their existence. One did not have to have tea with the tsar and tsarina to have his life sabotaged by them, or their ministers, or the notorious Black Hundreds, who were nothing but street thugs glorified by the tsar and given a license to kill Jews. She remembered her father's stories of the army and she had the feeling that that was not the half of it. And she would never forget the night the news came of her grandparents. She had been only three years old at the time, but she would never forget it——the hollow, stunned voice of her mother repeating over and over, "Both of them?" No, Sashie believed in these dragons, and something deep, deep inside told her that the dragon's fire had scorched Wolf. His eyes were queer because he had looked straight down the fiery throat. She wondered what it was he had seen. She would probably never know, Sashie thought, and she could certainly never ask.

Louie had finished his sugar stick and was demanding more. Sashie felt the wagon turn another corner. They must be near the Alexandra Gate. Had Columbus been forced to begin the region of the dragons with a baby wailing for more and twisting his nose, as Louie was now twisting Sashie's? "Hush, hush!" commanded everyone, but Louie would not be quiet.

"Give him another one!" hissed Ghisa from Sashie's feet. Sashie groped up her sleeve for another sugar stick. "Here," she huffed, "what do I care if you grow up to have rotten teeth!"

Ida prayed a strange prayer——that her baby boy would grow old enough to have rotten teeth. And Joe, buoyed by Sashie's relentless optimism, smiled quietly to himself and patted his daughter on the shoulder.

Sashie had fifteen sugar sticks. At this rate, she calculated, they would not last the day. "We might need the b-o-t-t-l-e." Ida and Joe weren't overjoyed at the prospect of drugging babies, but such a possibility had had to be planned for on this trip and a bottle of milk with a light sleeping draught had been prepared. Just then Sashie heard a torrent of water from a slop bucket being thrown out a high window. The chickens on the left side of the wagon forward of her sent up a loud cackle.

They must have caught some of it, and then under the layer of cackles was another noise——a steamy hiss of curses from Ghisa. There seemed to be more street noises now——shutters being opened, dogs barking, more wheels creaking, fragments of early morning talk drifting out of doorways as shopkeepers readied for trade. But where were they? It sounded nothing like the noises one would hear around the Alexandra Gate. There were not any buildings near the gate from whose windows slop buckets would be emptied. They must be beyond the gate and near the outskirts of Nikolayev, Sashie thought. As if to answer her question, there was suddenly a new sound and a new motion as the wheels of the wagon rolled from cobblestones to wood. The bass tones of the wooden planks rumbled beneath the wheels and the rush of coursing spring waters muted the manic cluckings. Even Louie, who had managed to sit up, stopped sucking on his sugar stick.

"What dat?" the baby demanded softly.

"It's the river." Sashie whispered. "We're leaving Nikolayev now."

"Oh."

"Be a good boy, Louie!" Sashie patted his knee. Louie was now starting to crawl around, exploring under the chicken coops. It seemed to keep him quiet and drain off some of his energy, so nobody tried to stop him. There wasn't far he could go.

As the wagon moved from the bridge to the dirt road, the clucks and cackles rolled up once more in a suffocating swarm. Oh, to hear water again! thought Sashie. But the liquid resonance of the flowing river was soon a memory obliterated by the cackles that seemed to bristle right inside Sashie's brain. She would go mad if she listened to the chickens another minute! She would think of a song. But she could not think of one. She would try to hear the road under the wheels. But she could not hear it. The road did, however, feel different from the cobblestone streets. It was softer. The speed seemed slower— not just slower, but thicker, Sashie thought. How can motion feel thick? It was not a bad feeling. And the noise, it wasn't noise. She caught herself. How can I hear noise, Sashie thought, above the cackles? But she did. And it was different. It wasn't noise that was reflected from hard surfaces like cobblestones, wood, and granite. It came from a deep quiet center. They were soft and sucking sounds; the sound of things being absorbed, soaked up. It's mud sounds, thought Sashie, ecstatically. "I am listening to spring mud." It was like beautiful music to Sashie.

Just above the mud but not as high as the wagon top she heard another sound. It was the whispering of a south wind blowing through winter grass. Sashie had never in her life been outside the city. She had never known the sound of the vast quietness of the country, which absorbed noise to make new sound. She lay perfectly still, listening as the country sounds bloomed around her like huge flowers.

Through the minutes and in and out of hours they slept, whispered, ate a hunk of bread or piece of potato. The babies were doing tolerably well and the sleeping draught had not yet been needed. A huge baked potato kept Louie busy for twenty minutes. A medley of whispered nursery rhymes delivered by Sashie and her father averted a near tantrum.

Sashie had just finished drawing tiny faces on both her thumb and index finger for a puppet finger show to entertain Louie when she felt Wolf slow the horse.

"Whoa!" he said.

The horse and the wagon stopped. Just as Wolf had begun to speak to the horse, Sashie had heard distant rapid beats, like small explosions in the earth.

"Trouble!" Wolf's voice was tight with fear. "Everybody must be quiet! It's soldiers." He paused, and Sashie thought she could hear the breath catch in his throat. "My God, it's an imperial regiment!"

Then there was a timpani of cold metal as sabers and spurs jangled in the air. Sashie had managed to grab Louie and press him flat on the floor. Her father lay his leg over the little boy's kicking ones and Sashie clapped her hand over his mouth.

"Hail! In the name of their imperial majesties, the Tsar Nicholas and the Tsarina Alexandra!"

Wolf mumbled something conciliatory, but Sashie could not hear the exact words, for the only noise was that of metal clanging, leather squeaking, hooves striking the ground, animals panting, and occasional coughs. The chickens' clucking was eclipsed by the noises that accompanied the tsar's regiment of twenty on an exercise in the countryside. And beneath the chicken coops the human cargo lay in frozen terror.

"You carry chickens, I see . . ." The commander spoke. "And where are you bound for?"

"Oh, just to Borisov to deliver them for my boss to a client."

"How generous of your boss. I am sure he would not begrudge a few chickens for the tsar's regiment, and the client will never miss them."

"Lieutenant, if you please, two or three coops." Sashie heard a man jump from a horse.

"Aaaaagggg!" screamed Wolf. "Hold it!"

" 'Hold it!' You old Zhidi!" The last word hung in the air like a dagger dripping blood. "Zhidi," the abusive word for "Jew," had become quite popular with the latest wave of pogroms. Sashie trembled all over. She pressed her hand harder on Louie's mouth.

The commander spoke slowly. "You deny one of the tsar's most loyal and favored regiments a few chickens? To deny the tsar's officers is to deny the tsar, and to deny the tsar is to deny God!" the voice thundered.

"No! No! I do not deny anything to you, your . . . your excellency. It's just that the coops are in bad repair and if you carry them with you they are bound to come apart and the chickens escape. Better you take the chickens slaughtered."

"Fine. Lieutenant, skewer a few chickens then, if you will."

There was a bright flash and Sashie's breath suddenly locked in her throat. Her eyes widened in terror as she saw the tip of a thin silver blade slice through the mesh and come within three inches of her face. Time stopped as her eyes focused on the glinting sliver of death that played above her. She could even see the scarlet sleeve of the officer's jacket. The three gold buttons blazed through a small flurry of white feathers, and the black decorative braid at the cuff was like four coiled snakes ready to strike. The silvery death dance went on raging above her face and throat. The moist still air from her half-open mouth fogged the blade tip.

"Here! I find you a fat one. Those are all skinny." The blade stilled. The silver death retreated through the slashed mesh to the world above, and Sashie fainted.

A few seconds later she came to and heard Wolf talking rapidly.

"Those are the scrawny ones. Good breeders, but no good eating. Now over here we have your scratchers."

"Scratchers?" asked the commander.

"Yeah, scratchers. They have to scratch for their food. Makes 'em tough. Stringy. They're big chickens, mind you. Weighty, but quite tough. No flavor. But here. Here in the middle we have our plumpsters——we call them plumpsters." Wolf prattled on faster than a runaway cart down Kliminsky Street on the science and technology of poultry. "With the plumpsters you get more meat per cubic centimeter than any other kind of chicken. Succulent! Juicy! You see, the plumpsters are not required to scratch for their food. And what food it is! Whole-grain bread soaked in gravy, pumpkin seeds, kasha. We Zhidi should only eat like that! The plumpsters' main job in life is eating, with an occasional stroll in a very small area. A chicken, one might say, truly fit for a tsar. Please sire, your sword. I will fetch you the plumpest of the plumpsters. Yes, a rare bird indeed!"

Sashie felt the wagon shake as Wolf pulled himself up on the side. "Kosher is quick!" She heard Wolf mutter to himself in Yiddish. In less than three minutes he had slaughtered ten chickens. Blood dripped down the center aisle onto the bedclothes.

"Your chickens, your excellency. May you and your officers eat them in good health!"

"Your client will never miss them," came the reply.

As the spurs dug into flanks, whinnies mixed with leathery squeaks and metallic janglings filled the air. The command finally came——"Forward!"——and then the rapid explosive noises of eighty hooves striking the earth as they moved off with their imperial load.

Zhidi, Sashie thought, when at last she could think again. Wolf called himself a Zhidi. How very strange that he could do this——abuse himself with this foul word even though it was done to ingratiate himself with the commander. For the first hours after the encounter with the regiment, Sashie lay in a state of total exhaustion. It was as if her nerves, her brain, and each muscle in her body had used every bit of energy available. Gradually, however, she began to realize that she was alive. It was a miracle. It was as if she were a newborn baby with an older mind that could appreciate the wonder of its own birth—— of being born a whole, complete human being. She tingled all over with the sheer excitement of her own living body. She touched her throat and face. She traced the gullies and curves of her ears. She pressed hard through all the layers of clothing and felt a rib. She took a joyous inventory of her body. Then after the miracle of survival was confirmed, she thought of Wolf and the word he had used in reference to himself. How absolutely confounding and unfathomable it was. She could not imagine ever calling herself by this horrible name, no matter what the danger was.

Sashie had stared unblinkingly as Death sliced the air just inches from her face and throat. She was sure Wolf had seen something worse, but what was it? The haunted man contained a death riddle. Sashie had been brought to the edge, but Wolf in some way had crossed over.

The fog had long ago burned off and slants of sunlight had pierced through the mesh and feather storm into the netherworld of the coops. But now the sun was at too low an angle to light the wagon, and Sashie felt a twilight chill. If she could only move more, she would feel warmer. Louie was warm as a puppy from crawling around under the coops, and though he was now sleeping, his short little body could curl up into a nice ball perfect for conserving energy. Sashie tucked him in closer to her own body to steal a little heat. Soon she drifted in and out of a troubled sleep that jolted and lurched and flashed with silver blades dripping blood. Then everything stopped and she woke up into a night-still world with her own hand fast at her throat.

"All right!" Wolf shouted. She felt him jump down from the driver's seat. "We're here."

"My God!"

"Thank God!"

"Am I dead or alive?"

"Or a chicken!"

"It's all right, Ida, we're here!"

"Oh, Joe!"

"Hang on, folks. I'll get the coops off in half a second." Sashie felt Wolf climb on the back end of the wagon. She heard the clatter of the first coop being removed.

"Ah!" exclaimed Ghisa with wonder as she saw the first piece of the world above. Another two coops were removed and Sashie heard Zayde Sol recite a *broche*, a prayer, upon seeing the evening again. Then another coop was removed and a square of night sky reappeared, black velvet chinked with stars. Piece by piece the sky came back and the wind, with the smell of winter grass and earth, blew across Sashie's face.

Each person had to be helped off the wagon by Wolf and, except for Louie, walked around a few feet by him until their legs and back regained their strength. Sashie needed Wolf's arm only for a couple of steps. Almost immediately she was off on her own trying out her new legs. First she tried walking a few meters, but the night was so warm, the air so gentle, and the field so vast that Sashie felt she must dance, leap, fly through this startling country. Under the starry dome of the Russian night Sashie whirled and jumped. Her head thrown back, she watched the stars spin and smelled the thawing earth and listened to the wind songs in the grass.

Ghisa too was soon running and skipping in jerky little circles around a moonlit tree stump. The babies squealed and Ida and Joe said soft prayers of thanksgiving and laughed gently with each other in the night. And Zayde Sol said more *broches*——*broches* for seeing stars again, *broches* for seeing the moon, *broches* for seeing a baby walk, and *broches* for seeing a granddaughter dance.

The Night Journey

Meet the Author

Kathryn Lasky says she has always been a "compulsive story maker" and today writes books for children, teenagers, and adults. She enjoys being her own boss, setting her own hours, and being able to wear anything she wants to work.

Her book *The Night Journey* won the Association of Jewish Libraries Sydney Taylor Book Award and was named a Notable Book by the American Library Association.

Other works by Lasky include *Sugaring Time, The Weaver's Gift, Puppeteer, Beyond the Divide, Prank,* and *Pageant.*

Meet the Illustrator

Trina Schart Hyman started drawing at a very young age but attended five art schools and rode her bike 3,000 miles through the Netherlands and England before she started taking her art portfolio to publishers. They rejected her work for three years, but today she is a Caldecott Award-winning artist for children's books.

Hyman says her illustrations are full of her friends, family, and neighbors. In *Snow White,* some of the dwarfs are people she knows!

Theme Connections

Within the Selection

Record your answers to the questions below in the Response Journal section of your Writer's Notebook. In small groups, report the ideas you wrote. Discuss your ideas with the rest of your group. Then choose a person to report your group's answers to the class.

- Why did Ed have the samovar repaired? What meaning does the samovar hold for Sashie?
- Why was Sashie interested in telling her great-granddaughter about Tsarist Russia?
- How do you think hearing Sashie's frightening story affected Rache's feelings about her heritage?

Across Selections

- Compare Rache's feelings for Sashie with those of Katie toward her grandmother in "Love As Strong As Ginger."
- How is the grandmother in "The Land I Lost: Adventures of a Boy in Vietnam" like Sashie?

Beyond the Selection

- Think about how "The Night Journey" adds to what you know about heritage.
- Add items to the Concept/Question Board about heritage.

Eloise Greenfield stands at the far right of this photograph taken at Parmele in 1941.
With her are her grandfather, her mother, her grandmother, Wilbur, Vedie, and Gerald.

Parmele

from *Childtimes: A Three-Generation Memoir*
by Eloise Greenfield and Lessie Jones Little

Every summer we took a trip down home. Down home was Parmele.

To get ready for our trip, Daddy would spend days working on our old car, putting it in shape to go on the road, and Mama would wash and iron all of our clothes. Then everything would be packed in the tan leather suitcase and the black cardboard suitcase, and we'd be ready to go.

Mama and Daddy would sit in the front with Vedie in Mama's lap, and Wilbur, Gerald, and I sat in the back with our legs on top of the suitcases. This was before cars had trunks. Or radios. Or air conditioners or heaters. And there were no superhighways. The speed limit was forty-five miles an hour, and we went thirty-five to keep from straining the car.

It was an eight-hour trip to Norfolk, Virginia, where we always went first. Grandma Pattie Ridley Jones and Grandpa had moved there by that time, and we'd spend about a week with them, then go on to Parmele for another week.

On the road, I played peek-a-boo with Vedie between her naps. Or my brothers and I would count all the cars on the road. We'd say, "There go one! That's twenty-two. There go another one!" And we'd read out loud the rhymes on the red signs advertising Burma shaving cream, and wave at people sitting on their porches, and argue with each other until one of us got real mad and real loud and Mama told us we were giving her the jimjams and to be quiet.

One thing that we saw on the road frightened me. Chain gangs. We saw them often, the lines of black men in their black-and-white-striped jail suits, chained by their ankles and watched over, as they repaired the roads, by white men with guns.

I wasn't afraid of the men, and I didn't think about maybe getting shot. But for a reason I didn't understand, I was afraid of the whole thing. Those bent-over striped backs, the sharp points of the picks the men swung, the sound of the picks hitting the concrete, the sight of men with long guns, pacing. It scared me.

After a few miles, that scared feeling would fade away, and I'd start to have fun again, or I might take a nap, and it always seemed as if days had passed before we finally crossed the line into Parmele.

By the time of my visits there, only a few trains were still passing through. My Parmele wasn't a train town or a mill town. It was a quiet town. Chinaberry trees and pump water and tree swings and figs and fat, pulpy grapes on the vine. People saying, "hey" instead of "hi," the way they did in Washington, *hey-ey*, sending their voices up, then down, softly, singing it through their noses. Parmele was me running from the chickens when I was little, riding around the yard in a goat-pulled cart, sitting on the porch and letting people going by in their cars wave at me, reading in the rocking chair, taking long walks to the gas station for soda pop with the children of Mama's and Daddy's childtime friends. Parmele was uncles and aunts and cousins. And Granny. And Pa.

Mack and Williamann Little, 1890s.

They were Daddy's parents, Mack and Williamann Little. Black people in Parmele called them Mr. Mack and Miss Williamann. White people called them Uncle Mack and Ain' Williamann.

Granny was thin and whitehaired. She kept snuff tucked inside her bottom lip and wore aprons over her long dresses. I remember her most bending over the collards in her garden or feeding the chickens. She used to sew leftover material from my dresses into her patchwork quilts. She used to make apple jelly and green tomato pickles. Anything her grandchildren wanted, she wanted them to have.

And so did Pa.

"Leave the children alone," he used to tell mamas and daddies. "They ain't doing nothing."

Pa was a sharecropper. He worked in the fields, farming the land for the white man who owned it, and got paid in a share of the crops he raised. Along with that, he had almost always had some kind of little business going, even when Daddy was a boy——a meat market, an icehouse, a cleaner's, a grocery store.

Long before I was born, Pa had been a member of the Marcus Garvey group that used to meet in Parmele on Sunday afternoons. It was one of thousands of branches of the United Negro Improvement Association headed by Marcus Garvey. They met to talk about the beauty and strength of blackness, and to plan the return of black people to Africa.

I didn't think my grandfather was afraid of anything except the frogs that came out of the

Eloise Little, 1932

mud-filled ditches at night and flopped across the yard, and he knew plenty of names to call them. The thumb on his right hand looked like a little baldheaded man. The top joint had been cut off in a farm accident, and he had put it in a jar of preserving liquid that stayed on the front-room mantel. I never got tired of looking at it.

Children hung around Pa, nieces and nephews and neighbors, listening to his stories, giggling at his jokes. Some nights there would be just us——Wilbur, Gerald, and me, with our grandfather——sitting on the porch where the only light was that of the stars and the nearest house was a long way down the road. He'd tell scary stories, and get really tickled when we got scared. He swore his ghost stories were true.

"One night," he'd say, "me and my brother John was coming 'cross that field over yonder." He'd make his arm tremble and point toward the woods across the highway. "And we commence to hearing this strange sound. Ummmmm-*umph!* Ummmmm-*umph!* And we looked up and saw this . . . this *haint!*"

He'd twist his face and narrow his eyes in horror as he stared out into the darkness, and I could just feel all those haints hovering behind us, daring us to turn around and run for the door.

Sometimes Pa would stop right in the middle of a story.

"Then what happened, Pa?" one of us would ask.

"Oh, I left after that," he'd say, and he'd laugh. Then we'd laugh, small nervous laughs, wanting to believe that it had all been just a joke.

Every year when it was time for us to leave, a sudden change would come over Pa. One minute he'd be challenging

Eloise Little and Bobby Greenfield, 1948

Vera and Vedie Little, Langston Terrace, 1949

Daddy to a foot race that never took place, and the next minute he was weak and sick, trying to get us to stay. He didn't think he would live to see us the following summer, he'd say. At breakfast he'd begin the blessing with, "Lord, I sure do thank You for allowing me to see my family one last time before You call me home," and he'd pray a long, sad prayer that brought tears to our eyes.

But finally, when nothing worked, Pa would give up and help Daddy load the car with suitcases and with sacks of fresh corn and peanuts. There'd be hugs and kisses and more tears, and then we'd drive away, leaving him and Granny standing on the side of the road, waving, waving, waving, getting smaller and smaller, until they blended into one and disappeared.

Pa never liked to leave home. Granny came to visit us a few times over the years, but Pa always made an excuse. He couldn't get away right then, he had too much work to do, or something. One year, though, he had to come. He'd had a stroke, and Mama and Daddy brought him to Washington to take care of him. The stroke had damaged his body and his mind, so that he didn't understand much of what was going on around him, but he knew he wasn't where he wanted to be. Mama would take him for a walk and he'd ask people on the street, "Which way is Parmele?"

My grandfather never got back to Parmele. He lived in Washington for eighteen months, and then, in 1951, at the age of seventy-eight, he died.

Parmele

Meet the Authors

Eloise Greenfield was born during the Great
Depression in Parmele, North Carolina. However,
she did most of her growing up in Washington, DC.
Her father used to pile the family into the car once
a week to visit the library for a supply of books.
She says she found far too few books that told the
truth about African-Americans, and she wanted to
change that.

Today she is a member of the African-American
Writers Guild. She uses grant money to teach creative
writing to elementary and junior high students, and has
written many award-winning books.

Lessie Jones Little was born in Parmele,
North Carolina, and spent most of her childhood
there. Like many of the people in her town, she and
her family made their money working on farms.
The work was very hard and tiring, and didn't pay
well. The money she earned went toward buying
schoolbooks and cloth for her dresses.

When she graduated from high school, she was
awarded a pin that signified she had earned the
best grades. She went on to work as a teacher and
then a clerk at the Office of the Surgeon General. It
wasn't until she was sixty-seven years old that she
began writing children's books. She collaborated
on two books with her daughter, Eloise Greenfield,
and also wrote an award-winning book of poems.

Theme Connections

Within the Selection

Record your answers to the questions below in the Response Journal section of your Writer's Notebook. In small groups, report the ideas you wrote. Discuss your ideas with the rest of your group. Then choose a person to report your group's answers to the class.

- What did the author enjoy about visiting her grandparents?
- Why were these yearly visits important for her and other family members?
- How does the author's writing reveal the pride she shows in her history and culture?

Across Selections

- Compare the respect the author has for her grandfather with the respect that Rache has for Nana Sashie in "The Night Journey."
- Which family in the other stories in the unit seems most like this one? Why do you feel that way?

Beyond the Selection

- What do you enjoy about visiting your older family members and friends? What have you learned from them about your heritage?
- Think about how "Parmele" adds to what you know about heritage.
- Add items to the Concept/Question Board about heritage.

Making a New Nation

For over two hundred years, the Constitution has been the guiding force for American government. But where did the ideas for the Constitution come from? And why did American colonists think they needed this new form of government?

...If You Lived at the Time of the American Revolution

Kay Moore

illustrated by Daniel O'Leary

Introduction

Have you ever wondered why the Fourth of July is a holiday? Before that date in 1776, the thirteen American colonies were part of an empire of more than thirty-two lands ruled by the King of England. The Declaration of Independence, which was signed by members of the Continental Congress on July 4, 1776, showed that the colonies wanted to be free. But it took a war for this to actually happen.

This war is called the "American Revolution." Some call it the "War of Independence" or the "Revolutionary War." It is usually viewed as a struggle between the American colonies and King George III of England, who ruled the British Empire.

But it was also a "civil" war, a war that is fought between people of the same country.

There were people from many different backgrounds living in the British American colonies. Not all of them thought it was a good idea to break away from England. If you and your family remained loyal to the king, you were called Loyalists. If you and your family wanted to be free from British rule, you were called Patriots.

What was life like before the Revolution?

All thirteen American colonies ruled by England were along the Atlantic Ocean. About two and a half million people lived in the colonies.

You could travel on the Boston Post Road from Boston to New York, then on to Philadelphia. These were the three largest cities in the colonies. Other roads went south from Pennsylvania to South Carolina. All the roads were narrow and rough. It was better to travel by water if you could.

Mail went by stagecoach between New York and Philadelphia three times a week in spring and summer, and twice a week between Boston and Philadelphia. In fall and winter, service was less often.

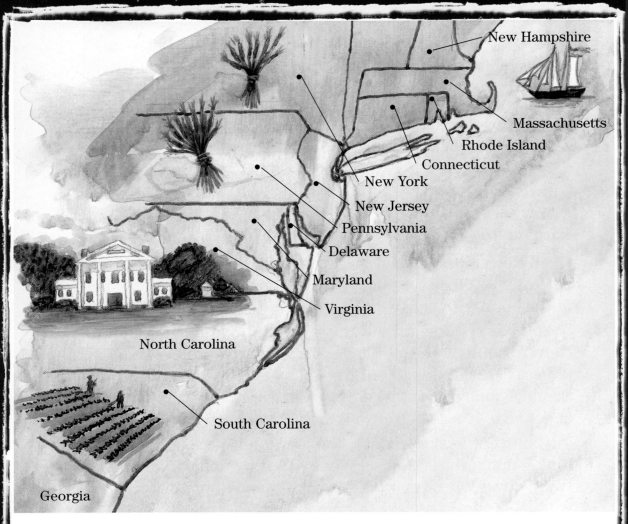

New Hampshire

Massachusetts

Rhode Island

Connecticut

New York

New Jersey

Pennsylvania

Delaware

Maryland

Virginia

North Carolina

South Carolina

Georgia

Each colony was interested in its local problems. The colonies did not work well together.

The area called New England included the colonies of Massachusetts, New Hampshire, Rhode Island, and Connecticut. Shipbuilding, fishing, hunting for whales, and buying, selling, and shipping goods were important to these colonies.

The Middle Colonies of New York, Pennsylvania, New Jersey, and Delaware had soil that was good for growing many different kinds of fruits and vegetables. So much wheat was grown in Pennsylvania and New York that they were called "the bread basket of the empire."

In the South were the colonies of Maryland, Virginia, North Carolina, South Carolina, and Georgia. Here, tobacco was grown on large farms called plantations. In some areas, farmers grew rice, and indigo plants used to make blue dye.

What started the Revolution?

The first settlers in the colonies liked having British help and protection. British soldiers were there to help them fight Native American enemies and to keep other countries, such as France and Spain, from invading. It was like your mother watching over you. However, as you grow older, you will want more freedom to make your own decisions. That is how many of the colonists felt.

The colonists grew tired of following British rules. England controlled trade and told people where they could settle. They forced the colonists to provide housing and food for the British soldiers sent to protect them.

Since 1760, the colonists had also had to pay taxes for various products. Under a law called the Stamp Act (1765), the colonists had to pay extra money for newspapers, land deeds, card games, dice games, and even for graduation diplomas.

The colonists had no direct way to complain, since no one from the colonies was allowed to be a member of the British Parliament, which made the rules. James Otis, a Boston lawyer, stirred up the colonists when he said they should not pay taxes until they could send a person to speak for the colonies in Parliament. "Taxation without representation is tyranny!" he exclaimed.

After years of protest, the British took away all the taxes except the one on tea. This did not satisfy the Patriots. On December 16, 1773, angry Patriots, dressed as Mohawk Indians, dumped 342 crates of tea into Boston Harbor.

King George decided to punish Boston for the "Boston Tea Party" by closing the port. Nothing would go in or out of the city until the tea was paid for, and the city told the king it was sorry that this had happened.

Some people thought it was time for the colonies as a group to protest British taxes. In September 1774, men from the colonies met together in Carpenters' Hall in Philadelphia. Called the "Continental Congress," this group became the informal government of the colonies.

Bad feelings continued. Finally, British soldiers and Patriots fought at Lexington and Concord, Massachusetts, on April 19, 1775. This was the start of the American Revolution.

Who were the Loyalists?

About one-third of the people living in the colonies wanted to remain as citizens of England. They stayed loyal for different reasons:

1. They believed the king had the right to rule the colonies and that his laws were fair.
2. They were afraid of the British soldiers.
3. They had family in England and didn't want to put them in danger.
4. They felt that a government run by rich Patriots would be worse.

These people were known as "Loyalists," "Royalists," "friends of the government," "the King's friends," or "Tories."

Some Loyalists joined the British army and became regular British soldiers (called "Redcoats" or "Lobsterbacks" by the Patriots because of the color of their uniforms).

Others formed Loyalist units that fought with the British. Among these were the Loyal Greens, King's American Regiment, Queen's Loyal Rangers, and Royal American Regiment.

Many Native Americans, including the Iroquois and Seneca nations, joined the British side. So did thousands of African Americans. They had been slaves, brought over to the colonies from Africa against their will to work on plantations in the South, or born in the colonies as slaves. The British gave them their freedom in return for their help.

Soldiers from Germany, called "Hessians," were paid by the British to come and help their troops.

Many people who had recently come to the colonies from England, Scotland, Ireland, and Germany also remained loyal to the King of England.

There were so many Loyalists in New York City that it became known as the Tory capital of America. Delaware and the southern colonies also had a large number of Loyalists. All types of people were Loyalists, including lawyers, merchants, ministers, government officials, farmers, and workers.

LOYALIST SOLDIERS

Redcoat

Freed Slave

Iroquois brave

Member of the Royal American Regiment

Hessian

Who were the Patriots?

In the beginning, the Patriots were the people in the colonies who wanted England to remove taxes. But soon the word "liberty" was being heard. The Patriots no longer wanted to be "British Americans"—they just wanted to be "Americans." They supported the Continental Congress as a way to rule themselves. They started thinking of themselves as the "United Colonies."

Patriots were known by many names including "Rebels," "Liberty Boys," "Sons (or Daughters) of Liberty," "Colonials," and "Whigs." About one-third of the people living in the thirteen colonies were Patriots.

When war broke out, the "Continental Army" was formed with men from the colonies and a few men from Canada. Most Native Americans were on the British side, but some tribes helped the Patriots.

The Patriots enlisted slaves to fight for them after England had already taken on thousands of African-American soldiers.

Although more blacks joined the British army, it is thought that about five thousand fought for the Patriots. Since slaves did not have last names, many gave themselves names such as "Liberty" or "Freedom." One unit from Connecticut included men named Sharp Liberty and Cuff Freedom.

In 1778, France joined the Patriots' side. They sent money, troops, and a navy.

Spain and Holland entered the war in 1779, supplying money to the Patriots.

Did everyone in the colonies take sides?

No. Many people tried to stay neutral (not choose a side) during the war. Some changed sides depending on what was happening.

Many families split because of different views about the war. Benjamin Franklin was a well-known Patriot. His son, William, was the Royal Governor of New Jersey and warned the people in that colony not to act against the king. William became the head of the Board of American Loyalists.

George Washington was the leader of the Continental Army. His older half brother, Lawrence, was a Loyalist.

Some people hoped to stay out of the war entirely. The religion of the Quakers and Mennonites did not allow them to fight, although some did take sides.

Others were not free to express openly their true feelings, but were expected to go along with the view of their households. These included slaves and indentured servants—men and women who had to work for someone else for a number of years to pay off a debt.

You could not always be sure how someone felt about the war. There were no lines dividing each side. Your family might be Patriots and your next-door neighbors Loyalists.

In some families, a couple of family members would travel to Britain and the rest would stay in the colonies. In this way, the family was sure to be on the winning side, no matter which side won.

How would your life have changed after the Declaration of Independence?

The Declaration of Independence was written mainly by Thomas Jefferson and adopted by the Continental Congress in 1776. The Declaration listed twenty-seven ways the king had hurt the colonies.

Patriots agreed with the Declaration. They now viewed the colonies as thirteen states making one nation.

The Declaration divided many families, friends, and neighbors. Some Patriots were against British taxes, but didn't favor a total break with Britain. John Dickinson, a member of Congress from Philadelphia, spoke out strongly, saying, "Declaring our independence at a time like this is like burning down our house before we have another."

Some of these Patriots began siding with the British and even moved to England.

Men who wanted independence went to fight with the Continental Army or with their local militia. In Massachusetts, they were known as "minutemen" because they could get ready to fight in a minute. More soldiers came from Massachusetts and Connecticut than other areas.

With men away from home, family life changed.

Women had to run farms and manage businesses. Children helped harvest crops, and made sure animals were fed and watered. Sometimes, fathers and brothers would return home to help plant or harvest crops and then go back to their units and the fighting.

Money could be scarce for soldiers' families because soldiers often didn't get paid for over a year.

Did any women or children fight in the Continental Army?

Boys often went to war with their fathers or older brothers. At age sixteen, boys could join the army. Younger boys might have played the drum, bugle, or fife for the soldiers.

Nathan Futrell was a drummer boy in the North Carolina Continental Militia when he was seven years old.

At ten, Israel Task left his Massachusetts farm to be a cook and carry messages during battles.

Women and girls took care of the wounded, cooked food, and washed and mended uniforms.

Some women were part of the fighting, too. They carried pitchers of water to cool down the cannons and give the men drinks. These women were called "Molly Pitchers" by the soldiers. When her husband was hurt, Mary Hays stopped carrying water and took over his job loading and firing a cannon. After the war, she was awarded a pension of forty dollars a year for her service.

Families sometimes went with their men and the army. The armies didn't often fight in winter so General George Washington's wife, Martha, spent eight years in winter camp with her husband, returning to Mount Vernon, their Virginia home, each spring.

Was it hard to get money during the war?

Because of the war, gold and silver coins were hard to come by. And the war cost a lot of money! To pay for the war, the Continental Congress asked each state to print its own paper money. At first Patriots used the paper dollars in support of their cause.

However, this kind of money lost value because so much was printed and it was easy to copy. Many people called the paper money "shin plasters," because they felt it was only useful as a bandage for a sore leg. People began to say,

"It's not worth a Continental" when they meant something was not worth very much.

This kind of situation is called inflation. It got so bad that in March of 1780, a paper dollar was worth just a fourth of a cent! And things kept getting worse. In May of 1781, it took 225 paper dollars to equal one gold dollar. A few weeks later, you needed 900 paper dollars to buy one gold dollar's worth of supplies.

It was said that it took a wagon-load of money to buy a wagon-load of food. Some soldiers even refused to be paid in the paper money at all; they wanted hard gold.

How did people get food and clothes?

You didn't need much money to buy food if you lived in the country. Most homes had a vegetable garden. Also, you could pick wild fruits, berries, and nuts. You could catch fish and hunt for deer and wild turkeys.

Nothing was wasted:

- Animal bones were saved and made into buttons.
- Goose feathers were used to stuff pillows.
- Reeds and twigs were woven into baskets.
- Old pieces of cloth and outgrown clothing were cut into squares and sewn into quilts. During the war years, quilt-makers invented patterns they called "Washington's Puzzle" or "Washington's Plumes."

Patriots who lived in cities often received food, clothing, and other necessities from relatives or friends who lived in the country. You could also trade with Patriot neighbors.

Sometimes you just did without.

How did you get news about the war and what was happening in the other colonies?

Getting news was important to the Patriots even before the war began. Each colony had set up a "committee of correspondence," who hired its own riders to carry messages by horseback. (This was long before the telephone, radio, television, or even the telegraph had been invented.)

Messages were delivered from one town to the next until all colonies received the news.

Sometimes, information was sent by ship instead of overland.

After the war began, the committees of correspondence formed "committees of safety." Their riders were constantly in danger of being captured by the British.

Children were sometimes used as messengers. One young messenger was nine-year-old John Quincy Adams, who later became the sixth president of the United States. He took messages from his mother, Abigail, in Braintree, Massachusetts, to his father, John, in Boston.

Another way to find out the news was from a newspaper. The *Boston Gazette* and the *South Carolina Gazette* were two papers that reported news with a Patriot view. The *Royal Gazette* (New York) was the best known of the Loyalist newspapers.

Most newspapers were printed only once a week and had four pages, with three columns on each page.

In small towns a "town crier," sometimes a schoolboy, might share news aloud. As more and more people learned to read, there was less need to have a town crier.

Pamphlets and books were also printed. Thomas Paine's *Common Sense* had sent the idea of freedom throughout the colonies when it was published in January of 1776. It was often re-read and shared during the war. On the last page in bold letters were the words, **"THE FREE AND INDEPENDENT STATES OF AMERICA."**

As thousands of people read the forty-seven pages, they saw themselves as the "United States."

More news could be found on posters, called broadsides, that were nailed to trees, poles, and buildings. Broadsides were used to get men to join the army and for various public announcements.

Who were the famous Patriots?

The most well known were the men who helped promote the idea of freedom.

George Washington

George Washington, a planter and soldier from Virginia, was chosen to be commander of the Continental Army. Called "the Father of Our Country," Washington was a strong leader who held the army together when the soldiers faced many problems.

Patrick Henry

Paul Revere

Patrick Henry from Virginia was known as "the Son of Thunder" because of his patriotic speeches. He started many people thinking about freedom when he said, "Give me liberty or give me death."

Paul Revere was a silversmith in Boston. He was a leader of the Sons of Liberty, a messenger, and a secret agent for the Patriots. On April 18, 1775, Revere made his famous midnight ride from Boston to Lexington, Massachusetts, to warn the citizens that the British army was on its way. Revere was captured, but he escaped safely. The next day, the battle of Lexington and Concord marked the beginning of the American Revolution.

John Adams, **Benjamin Franklin**, and **Thomas Jefferson** were the most well known of the committee who wrote the Declaration of Independence. Jefferson did most of the actual writing.

John Adams

Benjamin Franklin

Thomas Jefferson

Marquis de Lafayette

The **Marquis de Lafayette** was a rich Frenchman who decided to help the Patriots. His full name was Marie Joseph Paul Yves Rich Gilbert de Motier. At nineteen, Lafayette brought a ship and money to the colonies from France. He asked only to serve and would not take any pay. He was an excellent soldier and helped Washington throughout the war in many ways.

A schoolmaster who joined the army at the start of the war, **Nathan Hale** volunteered to spy for the Patriots, but was caught by the British. Before he was hung, he is reported to have said, "I only regret I have but one life to lose for my country."

Crispus Attucks was a black man killed during the "Boston Massacre" in 1770, when five people were shot by British soldiers. This event pushed many people to join the Patriots.

Women were also interested in rights and freedom.

Nathan Hale

Crispus Attucks

Abigail Adams

Mercy Otis Warren

Abigail Adams ran the family farm in Massachusetts while husband John was working in the Continental Congress in Philadelphia. She wrote letters to him, reminding him "not to forget the ladies" as Congress was writing laws for the new government.

Mercy Otis Warren was James Otis's sister. An excellent writer, she wrote plays that made fun of the British. Printed in pamphlets, her plays were very popular. Later, she wrote three books that described the events of the American Revolution.

Phillis Wheatley

Phillis Wheatley was an African girl brought to the colonies as a slave. Bought by the Wheatley family, she learned to read and write, and wrote poetry. Phillis wrote a poem for General Washington and visited him at army headquarters. She is known as the first published black woman poet in America.

Deborah Sampson dressed in men's clothes and joined the Continental Army in 1782 as Robert Shurtleff. She received an honorable discharge for her work as a soldier when her identity was discovered in 1783.

Deborah Sampson

What ended the war?

After over six years of fighting, the British army gave up to the American forces at 2 P.M. on October 19, 1781, at Yorktown, Virginia. General Charles Cornwallis said he was too ill to surrender personally to General Washington. And so British General Charles O'Hara surrendered to American General Benjamin Lincoln at Yorktown. The British officer presented his sword and the American tapped it as an acceptance of surrender. The British fifes played the song, "The World Turned Upside Down." This was a good tune because life in America changed greatly after this day.

News of the surrender spread throughout the states by messengers, newspapers, and broadsides. It reached Philadelphia on October 22 and Boston on October 27. Towns celebrated with cannon salutes, bonfires, and fireworks. People kept the lamps in their houses lit all night. Loyalists had to keep their lights on, too.

It took until September 1783 for the final peace agreement to be written. The Treaty of Paris really ended the American Revolution. In the treaty, the new country was recognized and its boundaries decided. Fishing limits were set along the coast of Canada.

It was also agreed that Congress would recommend to the states that they restore property to any Loyalists who had not fought in the war. In most cases, the states did not do this.

... If You Lived at the Time of the

American Revolution

Meet the Author

Kay Moore is a freelance journalist who has worked as a feature writer and city editor at various newspapers. She also co-writes books with her husband, Louis Moore. She sees newspaper writing as being very different from book writing. Newspaper writing allows her to be in immediate contact with readers about issues that are important to them. Book writing involves a longer process, but she likes its "enduring nature." She says, *"It stimulates me to know that a book preserves for posterity my values and interpretation of life."*

Theme Connections

Within the Selection

Record your answers to the questions below in the Response Journal section of your Writer's Notebook. In small groups, report the ideas you wrote. Discuss your ideas with the rest of your group. Then choose a person to report your group's answers to the class.

- Why did the Loyalists want to remain under the British rule?
- Why did the Patriots want to rule themselves?
- What did the Continental Congress do?

Across Selections

- How are the issues from the American Revolution time period linked to your heritage?

Beyond the Selection

- Think about how "If You Lived at the Time of the American Revolution" adds to what you know about making a new nation.
- Add items to the Concept/Question Board about making a new nation.

Yankee Doodle

*No one knows for sure who was the first
to sing "Yankee Doodle." The story has it
that members of the British army came
up with the lyrics and set them to the
tune of an old folk melody. They wrote the
song to poke fun at the colonial militia,
whose appearance and manners seemed
rather unrefined to the British. Instead of
being offended by the song, colonists
thought it was funny and took the song as
their own. "Yankee Doodle" grew to include
over a hundred verses. The following
lyrics are thought to be two of the song's
original verses.*

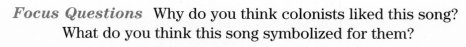

1. Fa-ther and I went down to camp, A-long with Cap-tain Good-in', And there we saw the men and boys As thick as hast-y pud-din.

Chorus
Yan-kee Doo-dle keep it up, Yan-kee Doo-dle, dan-dy.

Mind the mu-sic and the step, And with the girls be han-dy.

There was Captain Washington
Upon a slapping stallion
A-giving orders to his men
I guess there was a million.

Chorus
Yankee doodle, keep it up
Yankee doodle dandy
Mind the music and the step
And with the girls be handy.

The Night the Revolution Began

from *Give Me Liberty!*
by Russell Freedman

William Gray, a master rope maker, knew there was going to be trouble in Boston that night. He wanted no part of it. As dusk fell, he closed the shutters of his house and shop. After supper, he sent his apprentice, fourteen-year-old Peter Slater, upstairs and locked the boy in his room.

Peter waited until the house was quiet. Then he knotted his bedding together, hung it out the window, and slid to freedom. He wasn't a rope maker's apprentice for nothing.

He hurried along dark cobbled streets to a secret meeting place, a blacksmith's shop where a crowd of men and boys seemed to be getting ready for a costume party. They were smearing their faces with coal dust and red paint and wrapping old blankets around their shoulders, disguising themselves as Mohawk Indians.

Carrying hatchets and clubs, the "Indians" emerged from hiding and marched to Griffin's Wharf, where three British merchant ships were tied up at the dock. The ships' holds were filled to bursting with 342 chests of fine blended tea, shipped from England by the East India Company and worth a king's ransom.

Dozens of other men and boys were arriving at Griffin's Wharf from all over Boston. Among them were blacksmiths, masons, shipwrights, shoemakers, farmers, laborers, merchants, and apprentices—even a few well-known citizens, men of prominent families and positions who had come along as lieutenants to direct the action and help keep order. These men had blackened and painted their faces with special care so they could not be recognized. They were running a great risk, for they planned to get rid of every pound of tea in the holds of those British ships. If their names became known, they could be arrested and tried for destroying the East India Company's property.

The Boston Tea Party was an act of defiance, a protest against the policies of the British Parliament and King George III, who ruled England's colonies in North America. The colonists objected to paying King George's taxes without having a voice in Parliament. They called it taxation without representation. And while the tax on tea was a small one, just three cents a pound, it was regarded as a symbol of British tyranny.

The destruction of tea at Boston Harbor

Throughout the thirteen colonies, people had boycotted British tea rather than pay the hated tax. The ports of New York and Philadelphia had refused to accept the East India Company's tea, and the ships had sailed back to London with their cargoes. At Charleston, South Carolina, the tea was unloaded, but then it was stored in damp warehouse vaults and left to rot.

In Boston, the three tea ships had been tied up at Griffin's Wharf for more than two weeks. When the ships refused to depart, a group of men calling themselves the Sons of Liberty hatched their secret plan to destroy the tea. All told, perhaps two hundred men and boys took part in the action. Divided into three groups, they boarded the ships, summoned the mates, demanded lanterns and keys, and went to work.

"Everything was as light as day, by the means of lamps and torches—a pin might be seen lying on the wharf," Robert Sessions recalled. The tea chests were hoisted up from the holds, broken open, and the tea dumped over the side into the moonlit waters of Boston Harbor.

"I never worked harder in my life," remembered Joshua Wyeth, who was fifteen at the time. "Although it was late in the evening when we began, we had discharged the whole three cargoes before the dawn of day."

Several thousand people had gathered to watch in silent approval from the

Dumping the tea overboard

wharf. Aboard the ships, great care was taken that the protest be carried out with discipline. Nothing but the tea was disturbed, and "not the least insult was offered to any person," John Andrews reported. After each hold had been emptied, the deck was swept clean. Everything left was put back in its proper place. Then a ship's officer was asked to come up on deck and see that no damage had been done—except to the tea, emptied from hundreds of chests, which was now floating away with the tide.

When all the tea had been thrown overboard, the "Mohawks" fell into line and marched away to the music of a fife, surprised that they had met no opposition. British warships anchored less than a quarter mile away had not attempted to interfere. In fact, the British admiral in charge of the fleet happened to be spending the night at a friend's house near Griffin's Wharf. He had watched the entire scene from an upstairs window.

As the marchers passed by, Admiral John Montague threw open the window, stuck out his head, and shouted, "Well, boys, you have had a fine, pleasant evening for your Indian caper—haven't you? But mind, you've got to pay the fiddler yet!"

"Oh, never mind!" one of the marchers shouted back. "Never mind, Squire! Just come out here if you please and we'll settle the bill in two minutes."

With that, Admiral Montague slammed the window shut.

Soon afterward, a rollicking new song was heard in the taverns of Boston and about the shops and wharves. It began like this:

Rally, Mohawks! Bring out your axes,
And tell King George we'll pay no taxes
    On his foreign tea. . . .

The Night the Revolution Began

Meet the Author

Russell Freedman grew up in San Francisco. His parents were good friends with several authors. Many of the authors came over to discuss the news of the day with the Freedmans. The ideas that were discussed by these authors in his home helped Russell learn to develop his own thoughts. It was a skill he would use well as an author. The idea for his first book was taken from an article in *The New York Times*. It was about teenagers who had already done amazing things in their lives. He called it *Teenagers Who Made History*.

Theme Connections

Within the Selection

Record the answers to the questions below in the Response Journal section of your Writer's Notebook. In small groups, report the ideas you wrote. Discuss your ideas with the rest of the group. Then choose a person to report your group's answers to the class.

- Who were the Sons of Liberty?
- Why did the colonists object to paying King George's tax on the tea?
- What did people throughout the thirteen colonies do to protest the English tea tax?

Across Selections

- According to the selection "…If You Lived at the Time of the American Revolution," how did the Boston Tea Party lead to the First Continental Congress?

Beyond the Selection

- Think about how "The Night the Revolution Began" adds to what you know about making a new nation.
- Add items to the Concept/Question Board about making a new nation.

Focus Questions Who was Paul Revere?
Why was his midnight ride so important?
Did Revere achieve what he set out to do?

The Midnight Ride of
Paul Revere

Henry Wadsworth Longfellow
illustrated by Jeffrey Thompson

Listen, my children, and you shall hear
Of the midnight ride of Paul Revere,
On the eighteenth of April, in Seventy-five;
Hardly a man is now alive
Who remembers that famous day and year.

He said to his friend, "If the British march
By land or sea from the town to-night,
Hang a lantern aloft in the belfry arch
Of the North Church tower as a signal light,—
One, if by land, and two, if by sea;
And I on the opposite shore will be,
Ready to ride and spread the alarm
Through every Middlesex village and farm,
For the country folk to be up and to arm."

Then he said, "Good Night!" and with muffled oar
Silently rowed to the Charlestown shore,
Just as the moon rose over the bay,
Where swinging wide at her moorings lay
The Somerset, British man-of-war;
A phantom ship, with each mast and spar
Across the moon like a prison bar,
And a huge black hulk, that was magnified
By its own reflection in the tide.

Meanwhile, his friend, through alley and street,
Wanders and watches with eager ears,
Till in the silence around him he hears
The muster of men at the barrack door,
The sound of arms, and the tramp of feet,
And the measured tread of the grenadiers,
Marching down to their boats on the shore.

Then he climbed the tower of the Old North Church,
By the wooden stairs, with stealthy tread,
To the belfry-chamber overhead,
And startled the pigeons from their perch
On the sombre rafters, that round him made
Masses and moving shapes of shade,—
By the trembling ladder, steep and tall,
To the highest window in the wall,
Where he paused to listen and look down
A moment on the roofs of the town,
And the moonlight flowing over all.

Beneath, in the churchyard, lay the dead,
In their night-encampment on the hill,
Wrapped in silence so deep and still
That he could hear, like a sentinel's tread,
The watchful night-wind, as it went
Creeping along from tent to tent,
And seeming to whisper, "All is well!"
A moment only he feels the spell
Of the place and the hour, and the secret dread
Of the lonely belfry and the dead;

For suddenly all his thoughts are bent
On a shadowy something far away,
Where the river widens to meet the bay,—
A line of black that bends and floats
On the rising tide, like a bridge of boats.

Meanwhile, impatient to mount and ride,
Booted and spurred, with a heavy stride
On the opposite shore walked Paul Revere.
Now he patted his horse's side,
Now gazed at the landscape far and near,
Then, impetuous, stamped the earth,
And turned and tightened his saddle girth;
But mostly he watched with eager search
The belfry-tower of the Old North Church,
As it rose above the graves on the hill,
Lonely and spectral and sombre and still.
And lo! As he looks, on the belfry's height
A glimmer, and then a gleam of light!
He springs to the saddle, the bridle he turns,
But lingers and gazes, till full on his sight
A second lamp in the belfry burns!

A hurry of hoofs in a village street,
A shape in the moonlight, a bulk in the dark,
And beneath, from the pebbles, in passing, a spark
Struck out by a steed flying fearless and fleet:
That was all! And yet, through the gloom and the light,
The fate of a nation was riding that night;
And the spark struck out by that steed, in his flight,
Kindled the land into flame with its heat.

He has left the village and mounted the steep,
And beneath him, tranquil and broad and deep,
Is the Mystic, meeting the ocean tides;
And under the alders, that skirt its edge,
Now soft on the sand, now loud on the ledge,
Is heard the tramp of his steed as he rides.

It was twelve by the village clock,
When he crossed the bridge into Medford town.
He heard the crowing of the cock,
And the barking of the farmer's dog,
And felt the damp of the river fog,
That rises after the sun goes down.

It was one by the village clock,
When he galloped into Lexington.
He saw the gilded weathercock
Swim in the moonlight as he passed,
And the meeting-house windows, blank and bare,
Gaze at him with a spectral glare,
As if they already stood aghast
At the bloody work they would look upon.

It was two by the village clock,
When he came to the bridge in Concord town.
He heard the bleating of the flock,
And the twitter of birds among the trees,
And felt the breath of the morning breeze
Blowing over the meadows brown.
And one was safe and asleep in his bed
Who at the bridge would be first to fall,
Who that day would be lying dead,
Pierced by a British musket-ball.

You know the rest. In the books you have read,
How the British Regulars fired and fled,—
How the farmers gave them ball for ball,
From behind each fence and farm-yard wall,
Chasing the red-coats down the lane,
Then crossing the fields to emerge again
Under the trees at the turn of the road,
And only pausing to fire and load.

So through the night rode Paul Revere;
And so through the night went his cry of alarm
To every Middlesex village and farm,—
A cry of defiance and not of fear,
A voice in the darkness, a knock at the door,
And a word that shall echo forevermore!
For, borne on the night-wind of the Past,
Through all our history, to the last,
In the hour of darkness and peril and need,
The people will waken and listen to hear
The hurrying hoof-beats of that steed,
And the midnight message of Paul Revere.

Historical Note

Henry Wadsworth Longfellow's stirring poem of the events leading up to the battle of Lexington and Concord made Paul Revere a folk hero for generations of Americans. But Longfellow's poem is not an actual historical account. In fact, Paul Revere never even made it to Concord. What was the true story of Paul Revere's ride? It goes like this:

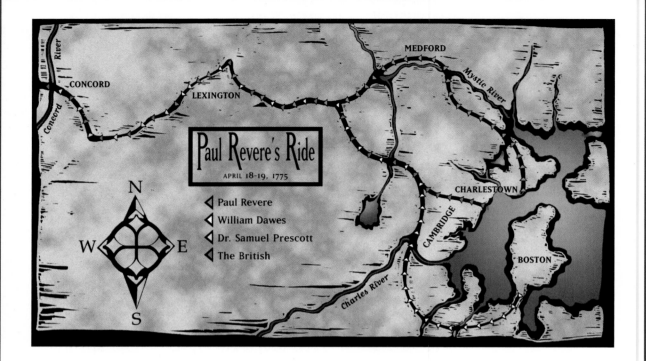

The American Revolution had not yet started on the 18th of April in 1775. So far, the colonists had only been protesting and arguing to try to get England to treat them more fairly. But there were many who thought that the colonies should break away from England, and some had started to collect guns and ammunition so that they would be ready to fight if necessary. The British knew the rebels were preparing for war and were worried. Whenever they could, they seized guns and ammunition from the rebels to keep them from growing too strong.

On the night of April 18, a British force of about 700 men left Boston. They were planning to surprise the town of Concord and seize colonial ammunition stored there.

But patriots had been spying on the British troops for some time and had caught wind of the plan. That night silversmith Paul Revere and shoemaker William Dawes set off to sound the alarm. Besides alerting the countryside, they also hoped to warn two rebel leaders in Lexington: Samuel Adams and John Hancock.

Revere had been an active revolutionary for some time. He had helped plan the Boston Tea Party, and some think that he participated in it as well; he had spied on British troop movements around Boston; and he had ridden back and forth to Philadelphia several times, carrying news to and from the Continental Congress.

The weekend before, Doctor Joseph Warren, one of the last leaders of the independence movement still in Boston, had assigned Revere and Dawes to spread the news of the British troop movements. Worried that he might not get out of Boston safely, Revere asked a friend to hang signal lanterns in the tower of Christ Church in Boston. The signals would let patriots across the river know whether the British were marching out of Boston by land or rowing across the Charles River "by sea." That way, even if Revere was stopped from leaving Boston, others could carry the news to Lexington and Concord.

But in the end the signals weren't necessary. Revere avoided capture, and was rowed across the river by two friends. In Charlestown he borrowed a horse and set off for Lexington, stopping at each house to call the patriots to arms.

Arriving at Lexington at about midnight, Revere alerted Adams and Hancock and then was joined by Dawes, who had taken another route from Boston. They started for Concord. Just outside Lexington, another patriot, Dr. Samuel Prescott, joined them. The three men continued toward Concord, stopping at every house to spread the alarm.

On the way, a British patrol stopped the men and tried to arrest them. Prescott knew the area well and escaped immediately by jumping his horse over a stone wall. He galloped on to Concord. A little later, Dawes fled back to Lexington on foot. Revere was not so lucky. The British held him for a couple of hours and then let him go without his horse. He never got to Concord but did return to Lexington in time to witness the battle there.

The redcoats arrived in Lexington on the morning of April 19. About 70 patriots were ready, lined up on the village green, and the first battle of the Revolution began. No one knows who fired the first shot, but when the fighting stopped, eight patriots lay dead, and the redcoats had won.

The British marched on to Concord, sure that the militia there could be defeated as easily as the one at Lexington. But Prescott had arrived with his warning, and more than 300 patriots lay in wait at North Bridge. In the fighting, three redcoats and two rebels were killed. With more patriots arriving, the British turned around and retreated to Boston.

As the British marched back to Boston, they were met by patriots who had been roused by Revere, Dawes, and Prescott and were on their way to join the battle in Concord. When these patriots saw the British marching away from Concord, they attacked. By the time they reached Boston, the British had lost 200 men, and the Revolutionary War had begun.

The Midnight Ride of Paul Revere

Meet the Author

Henry Wadsworth Longfellow was
the most popular and widely read American poet
of the world during his lifetime. He was also a
college professor, a writer of textbooks, and a
translator (he learned 11 languages). This poem
is one of his most famous. Other poems of his
include "Evangeline, A Tale of Arcadia," "The
Courtship of Miles Standish," "The Song of
Hiawatha," and "The Village Blacksmith." All of his
poems are known for having truly American themes.

Meet the Illustrator

Jeffrey Thompson likes to borrow from both
old and new techniques when creating his illustrations.
His artwork takes on the traditional look of being created
with watercolors, woodcuts, and scratch boards, but
he enhances their color using a computer program.
Mr. Thompson's dream is to become a full-time author
and illustrator of children's books.

Theme Connections

Within the Selection

Record the answers to the questions below in the Response Journal section of your Writer's Notebook. In small groups, report the ideas you wrote. Discuss your ideas with the rest of the group. Then choose a person to report your group's answers to the class.

- What was the purpose of Paul Revere's ride?
- What did the lanterns in the North Church tower mean?
- How did Longfellow's account of Paul Revere's ride differ from the event as it actually occurred?

Across Selections

- The Historical Note for this selection mentions that Paul Revere helped plan the Boston Tea Party. According to "The Night the Revolution Began," what was the name of the group of people responsible for this act of protest?

Beyond the Selection

- Have you read or heard any other poems based on people or events from the time period of the American Revolution? If so, what were their titles, and what stories did they tell?
- Think about how "The Midnight Ride of Paul Revere" adds to what you know about making a new nation.
- Add items to the Concept/Question Board about making a new nation.

Focus Questions Who were the people who drafted and signed the Declaration of Independence? What was the significance of this document? How did it influence people around the world?

The Declaration of Independence

by R. Conrad Stein

It was a rainy, forbidding night in July 1776 when Caesar Rodney of the Delaware Colony received an urgent message: COME AT ONCE. YOUR VOTE IS URGENTLY NEEDED. Rodney saddled his horse and began a treacherous, eighty-mile ride to Philadelphia. Caesar Rodney headed to Philadelphia for the most important decision of his life: to vote yes or no for independence.

By the summer of 1776, the colonies were in an all-out war with their mother country, England. The road to Philadelphia took Rodney past lonely farms and cut through untamed woods. He was forty-eight years old and weakened by a prolonged illness. Still, he urged on his horse and forged toward Philadelphia, where he knew he would witness history. It was mid-afternoon of the following day when he galloped up to Philadelphia's State House (later named Independence Hall). Without removing his spurs or brushing the mud off his clothes, Rodney took his seat with the Delaware delegation. The voting process had already begun. When the question of independence—aye or nay—was posed to Delaware, Rodney shouted out, "Aye!"

The Delaware vote helped to sway other delegations. By the end of the session, twelve of the thirteen English colonies had chosen to walk the dangerous path of independence. Only New York, whose delegates were locked in arguments, failed to vote. The date of this historic meeting was July 2, 1776. Some historians believe the second of July ought to be celebrated as American Independence Day. But at another meeting held two days later, the delegates approved the most famous document in American history, the Declaration of Independence. Like a trumpet blast, the Declaration told the world that a new nation had been born.

In the months leading up to this historic event, Americans had divided into roughly three opinion groups: one-third favored independence; one-third wanted reconciliation with England; and still another third were fence-sitters, undecided about a course of action. Caesar Rodney's Delaware delegation was a good example. Of the three Delaware representatives, Rodney supported independence, another man opposed it, and a third made up his mind only after Rodney's dramatic entrance into the hall.

Caesar Rodney was called to Philadelphia, which was the capital of the American colonies in the 1770s.

The colonists' hesitancy to declare independence was understandable. England was the most powerful country in the world. Never before had a British colony broken away from the mother country. Writing the Declaration of Independence was the same as drafting a declaration of war. If the war were lost, those who had signed the independence document would likely be hung for treason by vengeful English leaders.

These dire consequences mattered little to American radicals—those colonists who urged independence at any price. The radicals argued that the fighting had already begun. Now it was only right and proper to prepare a formal paper recognizing a state of war with England and telling the world that America was free from British rule. In June 1776, Congress had decided that it would write this declaration.

The task of writing the document was given to a committee of five men. Three of these five would grow to be some of the most revered names in American history: Benjamin Franklin, John Adams, and Thomas Jefferson. The other two authors were Roger Sherman of Connecticut and Robert Livingston of New York.

(Above) The Philadelphia State House, where the Second Continental Congress met. Today, this historic building is called Independence Hall.
(Right) The Second Continental Congress meets.

Benjamin Franklin, one of the most respected and influential Americans of the colonial era.

John Adams played a key role in drafting the Declaration of Independence. He went on to be the nation's first vice president under George Washington. He was then elected president and served from 1797 to 1801.

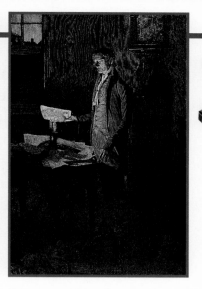

Thomas Jefferson wrote the Declaration of Independence in the Philadelphia house. Jefferson went on to become the governor of Virginia in 1779, served as vice president under John Adams, and was the third president of the United States (1801–1809).

At seventy years of age, Benjamin Franklin was the oldest signer of the Declaration. His countrymen hailed him as a scientist, scholar, inventor, and a wise political adviser. He had chosen the path of independence only two years earlier. Franklin's son, William, remained loyal to Britain, and political arguments between the father and son split the family. Benjamin Franklin was considerably depressed over the situation, but he remained on the side of independence.

John Adams, from Massachusetts, was a radical who had dedicated his life to the cause. Adams was fearless in debate and often made bitter enemies of those colonists who were fence-sitters or who were still loyal to England.

Thomas Jefferson was the man who actually wrote the document. The committee realized that a document written by five different men might be difficult to understand. Hoping to produce a convincing document, the committee gave Jefferson the task. John Adams told Jefferson there were three important reasons why Jefferson should do the writing: "Reason first— you are a Virginian, and a Virginian ought to appear at the head of this business. Reason second—I am obnoxious, suspected, and unpopular. You are very much otherwise. Reason third—you can write ten times better than I can."

Jefferson was more than just a gifted writer. He was a genius in many fields, the type of glorious star who rises only once in a generation. The thirty-three-year-old Jefferson was one of the youngest members of Congress, yet he could read, write, and speak four foreign languages: Greek, Latin, French, and Italian. He designed buildings, composed music, and experimented in science. A voracious reader, he pored through all of the major classics while he was still in his teens.

For most of his life, Jefferson had been a loyal subject of England. He once wrote, "There is not in the British Empire a man who more cordially loves a union with Great Britain than I do." But by 1776, even Jefferson was convinced that separation from Great Britain was the only course open to the colonies.

Jefferson wrote the Declaration of Independence on the second floor of a house at Seventh and Market Streets in Philadelphia. He was renting the house from a bricklayer named Jacob Graff. Jefferson worked standing up, not sitting down, at a writing table that is still preserved. He kept long hours, sometimes writing well past midnight. He wrote with the point of a goose quill dipped in ink. It was the common pen of the time, but it was a devilish instrument to use.

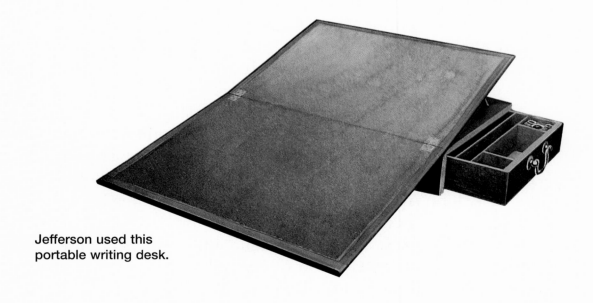

Jefferson used this
portable writing desk.

It scratched, it smeared, and it held so little ink it had to be dipped in the inkwell following every word.

To break his tiresome routine, Jefferson took long walks. He was an athletic man who stood six-feet, two-inches tall in an age when the average man's height was five-feet, five-inches.

Sometimes John Adams or the aging Ben Franklin accompanied Jefferson on his hikes, but they were unable to keep up with the taller man's brisk pace. His walks took him to the countryside or to Philadelphia's waterfront, where ships crowded at the docks. All the time, his head buzzed with thoughts of the project—words to add here, sentences to change there.

Thomas Jefferson began the Declaration with words that have thrilled students of history for more than two hundred years:

> *When in the Course of human events, it becomes necessary for one people to dissolve the political bands which have connected them with another, and to assume among the powers of the earth, the separate and equal station to which the Laws of Nature and of Nature's God entitle them, a decent respect to the opinions of mankind requires that they should declare the causes which impel them to the separation.*

In the first half of this powerful sentence, Jefferson announced that the colonies had separated from England. In the second half of the same sentence, he promised to state the reasons, or the "truths," behind the decision to separate.

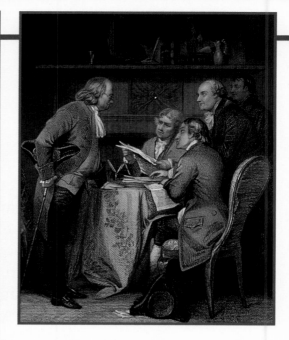

(Left) Jefferson's handwritten draft of the opening section of the Declaration of Independence. (Above) Franklin, Jefferson, Adams, Livingston, and Sherman (left to right) debate the Declaration.

He continued:

We hold these truths to be self-evident, that all men are created equal, that they are endowed by their Creator with certain unalienable Rights, that among these are Life, Liberty and the pursuit of Happiness. That to secure these rights, Governments are instituted among Men, deriving their just powers from the consent of the governed. . . .

These celebrated words state the belief that the king and the common person are equal in the eyes of God. Therefore, governments can exist only with the consent of the people they govern. This was an idea that was born in England and was nurtured in the frontier of America.

The next clause contained the Declaration's real fire:

That whenever any Form of Government becomes destructive of these ends, it is the Right of the People to alter and abolish it. . . .

This right of a people to "alter or abolish" a government was a revolutionary concept. It would shake the earth for centuries.

The Declaration of Independence laid out the reasons why the Americans were rebelling against England. According to British thinking, this American rebellion violated the law. Jefferson forcefully rejected this idea—he explained that the Americans were justified in their actions. He claimed that the British treatment of the colonies was itself a breach of the law. But to what law did Jefferson refer? Certainly not the laws in the colonial statute books, most of which were written by British lawmakers. Instead, Jefferson cited a higher law, a natural law—"the Laws of Nature and of Nature's God."

The belief in a natural law, one more powerful even than the decrees of a king, had been developed by British and French philosophers more than one hundred years earlier. John Locke was a prominent British philosopher who lived in the 1600s. Locke argued that God created divine laws at the dawn of time. People naturally obey these laws as they pursue liberty and happiness. When kings and governments set up laws that interfere with this natural pursuit, they—the rulers—disrupt divine law.

Thomas Jefferson

The philosopher John Locke

In a letter written in 1823, Jefferson looked back and claimed the words of the Declaration came purely from his own heart. "I turned to neither book nor pamphlet when writing it," he said. But Jefferson's mind was a storehouse of ideas. He had read Locke, as he had read all of the important philosophers. Today, most scholars conclude the democratic ideas of Locke are wondrously expressed in Jefferson's Declaration of Independence.

The longest section of the Declaration lists twenty-seven grievances the American colonists claimed against the British government. Jefferson's main complaints had to do with the king's taxes on Americans and the presence of British troops in the colonies.

After the list of grievances, Jefferson wrote a strong statement of independence: ". . . That these United Colonies are, and of Right ought to be Free and Independent States . . ." And the very last sentence of the Declaration was intended to rally the delegates into a firm and unwavering stand for revolution: "And for the support of this declaration . . . we mutually pledge to each other our Lives, our Fortunes, and our sacred Honor."

It took Jefferson seventeen days to write the Declaration of Independence. Occasionally, he showed samples of the unfinished manuscript to John Adams and Benjamin Franklin. In an early version, Jefferson had written,

"We hold these Truths to be sacred and undeniable, that all men are created equal . . ." Franklin saw this, crossed out "sacred and undeniable," and inserted the now-famous phrase "self-evident." Franklin thought the change would make the writing stronger, and scholars today agree he was correct. Jefferson also laboriously rewrote many of his own passages.

On July 2, 1776, the same day Congress voted for independence, the membership began debating the merits of Jefferson's Declaration. Delegates bickered with each other, and many changes were made to the exact wording Jefferson had worked so hard to perfect. Jefferson later called these changes "mutilations."

Most of the arguments were minor, but one paragraph severely divided the membership. This paragraph dealt with slavery. Included in Jefferson's list of grievances against the king was a long, angry argument against slavery.

Jefferson (right) discusses a passage of the Declaration with Benjamin Franklin (left).

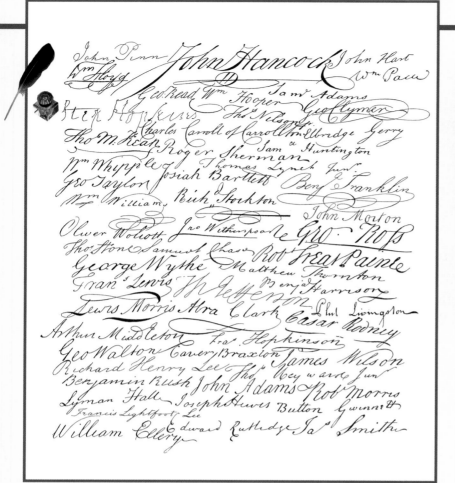

This illustration (left) shows all the signatures on the Declaration of Independence; John Hancock (above) signed first and with the most elegant penmanship.

Jefferson equated the slave trade with the work of evil pirates, and he denounced the idea of slavery as an "assemblage of horrors." It is curious that Jefferson would blame the British king for slavery since the colonists, themselves, held about half a million slaves. These slaves did not work for King George III, but rather for the profit of their American masters. Even Jefferson, who claimed to despise slavery, owned 150 slaves, who worked on his Virginia plantation.

Jefferson's denouncement of slavery disturbed the delegates from the South, where plantation owners relied on slaves to work their fields. At the urging of South Carolina and Georgia, the antislavery paragraph was excluded from the Declaration. As glorious as the document was, the phrase "all men are created equal" remained somewhat empty. It certainly did not apply to the thousands of slaves in the American colonies.

After two days of debate, the Declaration of Independence was approved by Congress on July 4, 1776. It was, in effect, the birth certificate of the United States of America. Congress decided that an official copy of the Declaration should be printed in ornamental script on parchment paper. After this copy was completed, the actual signing of the document occurred on August 2. John Hancock, president of the Congress, was the first to sign, and his signature is the boldest. Most of the signers were present on August 2, and the rest later added their autographs. Included among the signers were two future presidents (John Adams and Thomas Jefferson), three vice presidents, sixteen state governors, and ten members of the United States Congress. Signing as part of the Delaware delegation was Caesar Rodney, who died of cancer eight years later. He was suffering from the disease even while making his famous eighty-mile race to Philadelphia. The best British doctors surely could have eased his pain, but Rodney was a rebel who backed independence. He was therefore denied the assistance of British medical experts.

Copies of the Declaration were printed in Philadelphia and sent to cities and villages in all the colonies. Excited crowds gathered at town squares to hear local officials read the document. When the Declaration was read in Philadelphia, John Adams reported, "Three cheers rendered.

In the days after the Declaration of Independence was signed (left), copies were printed, and it was read to joyous crowds throughout the colonies (above).

The bells rang all day and almost all night." After a reading in Savannah, Georgia, the townspeople held a mock funeral procession, and symbolically "buried" King George III.

The Declaration of Independence helped to unite what had been a divided land. Pro-British and fence-sitting colonists lost their influence under the power of Jefferson's words. Radicals now became the patriots; the timid were thought of as traitors.

After the Revolutionary War ended in 1783, the spirit of the Declaration of Independence marched outward to foreign lands. Just six years later, the people of France rose up against their king, using the American document as their guiding light. In the early 1800s, Latin American countries began breaking away from three centuries of Spanish rule. Leaders of those Latin American revolutions had studied the American Declaration. Probably no single document has had such an impact on the modern world as the one written in 1776 by Thomas Jefferson.

The announcement of the Declaration of Independence touched off celebrations in which American patriots destroyed symbols of Great Britain's rule. Here, people tear down a statue of the king of England.

The king's coat of arms is removed from the Philadelphia State House, signifying that England no longer rules the colonies.

The United States was an established nation in 1826, when John Adams, age ninety-one, lay dying in his house at Quincy, Massachusetts. He struggled to stay alive until July 4 so he could mark one more anniversary of the Declaration, one more birthday of the nation. His last words reflected thoughts of an old friend: "Thomas Jefferson still survives."

Some five hundred miles away, in Monticello, Virginia, eighty-three-year-old Thomas Jefferson was also near death. Shortly after midnight of July 3, 1826, Jefferson asked his granddaughter, who stood at his bedside, "This is the fourth?" She told him it was, and then perhaps he smiled. In one of the most remarkable coincidences in history, Thomas Jefferson and John Adams—the two great architects of the American Revolution—died within hours of each other on July 4, 1826. It was the fiftieth anniversary of the Declaration of Independence.

John Adams

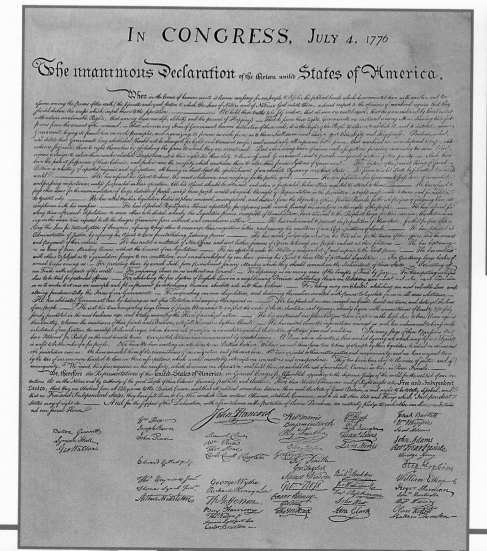

The Declaration of Independence

Meet the Author

R. Conrad Stein has written over fifty children's books. Many of his books for young readers are about historical events. His goal is to present the complex issues that surround these events in a way that is interesting and easily understood. Some of his other works are *The Story of the Great Depression*, *The Story of the San Francisco Earthquake*, and *The Story of the Flight at Kitty Hawk.*

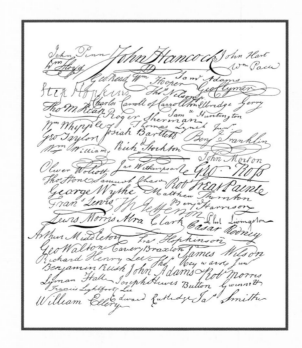

Theme Connections

Within the Selection

Record the answers to the questions below in the Response Journal section of your Writer's Notebook. In small groups, report the ideas you wrote. Discuss your ideas with the rest of the group. Then choose a person to report your group's answers to the class.

- Why were the colonists hesitant to declare independence?
- Who were the members of the committee responsible for drafting the Declaration of Independence? Who wrote most of the document?
- How did the Declaration of Independence change the way the colonists viewed themselves?

Across Selections

- In what ways was cooperation involved in the writing and the approval of the Declaration of Independence?

Beyond the Selection

- Think about how "The Declaration of Independence" adds to what you know about making a new nation.
- Add items to the Concept/Question Board about making a new nation.

Midnight Ride of Paul Revere. 1931. **Grant Wood.** Oil on composition board. 30 × 40 inches. Metropolitan Museum of Art, New York.

The Birth of Our Nation's Flag. 1893. **Charles H. Weisgerber.** Betsy Ross House.

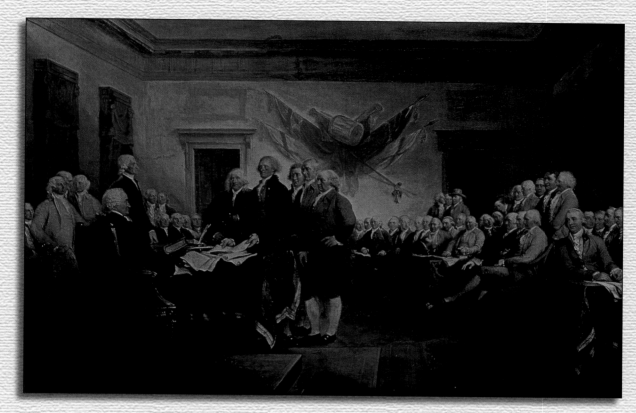

Signing the Declaration of Independence, July 4th, 1776. 18th Century.
John Trumbull. Oil on Canvas. Yale University Art Gallery, New Haven, CT.

Siege of Yorktown, October 17, 1781. 1836. **Louis-Charles Couder.**
Chateaux de versailles et de Trianon Versailles, France.

Focus Questions Who was James Armistead? What was his connection to the Marquis de Lafayette and Lord Charles Cornwallis?

THE MASTER SPY OF YORKTOWN

Burke Davis
illustrated by Stephen Snider

George Washington

In the spring of 1781, General Washington rushed a band of 1,200 men southward to meet British raiders who were looting and burning their way through Virginia. The commander chosen for this tiny force was the Marquis de Lafayette, one of the youngest major generals in history. The Frenchman was determined to halt the invaders, who were led by the newest of British generals, the American traitor Benedict Arnold.

Lafayette, who was only twenty-three years old, had come to America four years earlier as a volunteer, sailing in a ship he had bought for the voyage. As one of the richest men in France, Lafayette had done much to bring help from King Louis XVI to the American rebels—troops, ships, guns, money, and uniforms. And in Virginia, at last, his dream had come true, a chance to command an American army, however small.

The Marquis de Lafayette

The young Frenchman soon found that his task was not easy. Virginia farmers hid their horses and wagons so that Lafayette's soldiers could not seize them for use against the enemy. The little army was often hungry, for people of the countryside refused to sell their meat and grain in exchange for the almost worthless American paper money. It was just as Governor Thomas Jefferson had warned Lafayette; Virginia was a state of "mild laws and a people not used to prompt obedience."

Lafayette also found that the enemy was too strong for him, since there were two British armies in Virginia, one under Benedict Arnold and another under Lord Charles Cornwallis. With better trained troops and thousands of horses stolen from Virginia plantations, the redcoats moved swiftly. The British burned the capital at Richmond, many warehouses full of valuable tobacco and supplies of rebel arms and food, and chased the Virginia legislature across the state. Governor Jefferson narrowly escaped capture and resigned his office. Lafayette complained to Washington, "I am not strong enough to get beaten. Government in this state has no energy and laws have no force. . . . The enemy can overrun the country."

Lord Charles Cornwallis

Still, the Frenchman refused to give up. His troops hung about the British, as closely as they dared without risking battle. And since he could not hope to defeat the enemy openly, Lafayette began sending spies into the enemy camps.

The most important of the American spies was a black man, JAMES ARMISTEAD, the slave of William Armistead, a farmer who lived near the town of Williamsburg. He was only twenty-one, even younger than Lafayette, but the Frenchman saw that his volunteer was brave as well as bright and felt that he would be loyal to the American rebels—even though he had not been promised his freedom for risking his life as a spy.

James Armistead went at once to the camp of Benedict Arnold, made his way to headquarters, and sent Lafayette word of everything he saw. The British were not suspicious of the smiling young black man who had come as a volunteer and was so willing to serve officers in camp and to guide them on the roads. But messengers went out to Lafayette almost daily, reporting what Armistead had seen.

Making use of these secret reports, a band of Virginia soldiers sneaked into the British camp one night and almost captured Benedict Arnold himself. Still the redcoats did not suspect young James Armistead. Arnold and his officers felt sure that the black man would remain loyal to them because he wanted most of all freedom from his life as a slave.

When Benedict Arnold left Virginia and returned to the war in the north, James Armistead went into the camp of Lord Cornwallis, where he served as a waiter at headquarters. He continued to report to Lafayette almost daily, though the risk of death was now greater and his work was much harder. Cornwallis was a good general who was careful to see that his enemies had little chance to learn his plans.

As Lafayette reported, "His Lordship is so shy of his papers that my honest friend says he cannot get at them." The Frenchman further complained to Washington that he was forced "to guess at every possible whim of an enemy that flies with the wind and is not within the reach of spies." But though Lafayette admitted that he was "devilishly afraid" of Cornwallis and was worried because his spies could not steal British maps and orders, he continued to camp very near the enemy, warned of every redcoat move by messengers from James Armistead. The armies trailed west through Virginia, and then back to the coast from the Blue Ridge Mountains, the British raiders leading, the Americans following stubbornly, a few miles in the rear. Cornwallis seldom realized that he was being followed, but Lafayette pretended that his tiny force was driving the British before it, in hopes of keeping up the morale of Virginia civilians.

James Armistead left no record of his life in the enemy camp during these weeks, but since he spent much time in the tent of Lord Cornwallis, he was certainly a trusted servant. He probably stood near the general during meals, serving food and drink and listening to the talk of officers, pretending that he did not understand their plans, and certainly did not dream of revealing them to Lafayette and the Americans. But often, by day and night, James Armistead whispered what he had overheard to other black men in the camp, and within a few hours Lafayette had word of British plans.

In July, when Cornwallis's army had moved to the east and was camped in the small city of Portsmouth, near Chesapeake Bay, James Armistead reported that a fleet of sailing ships had come to anchor in the harbor, ready to carry British troops to a new post. Lafayette expected news that Cornwallis had sailed, but for weeks there was no change. The ships lay idle at anchor day after day, and enemy troops remained in their camp at Portsmouth. At last, in early August, there was a warning from James Armistead: Cornwallis had sailed, no one knew where. The army of redcoats had disappeared from Portsmouth.

Within a few days, Lafayette's scouts learned the enemy's secret. Cornwallis was unloading his troops at Yorktown, a small tobacco port on the York River, within sight of the broad Chesapeake. Lafayette and his Americans moved nearer, to Williamsburg, where they could keep watch. They saw that Cornwallis was in no hurry to build defenses about the village. The weather was hot, and only a few men worked at digging trenches. Lafayette reported the news to Washington, who was still in the north.

Sometime during these days James Armistead returned to Lafayette's camp and no doubt told the French officer that he had been sent there by Cornwallis himself—as a spy for the British!

There was soon exciting word from headquarters. General Washington wrote Lafayette that "news of very great importance" was on its way. The commander urged the Frenchman to hold Lord Cornwallis in Yorktown and to prevent his army from escaping. Lafayette guessed the truth: Washington and the French commander in America, Count Rochambeau, were marching south with their troops, and at the same time French fleets were sailing for the Chesapeake. Cornwallis was to be cut off by land and sea.

Meantime, only Lafayette's small army could hold Cornwallis in place.

Lafayette reported to Washington, "I hope you will find we have taken the best precautions to lessen his Lordship's chances to escape."

By early September the trap was closing on Cornwallis. A French fleet defeated British warships at sea just outside the Chesapeake, drove them back to their port in New York, and anchored in the bay. By the middle of the month, Washington and Rochambeau and the first of their soldiers reached Williamsburg, where Lafayette welcomed them. Two weeks later the American and French armies, led by Lafayette's small force, marched the few miles to Yorktown and surrounded the village.

The allied soldiers dug trenches, ever closer to the enemy. Huge French cannon were hauled into place and began firing in early October. By October 19, after only ten days of shelling, Cornwallis surrendered. His army marched out from the battered lines of Yorktown and laid down its arms.

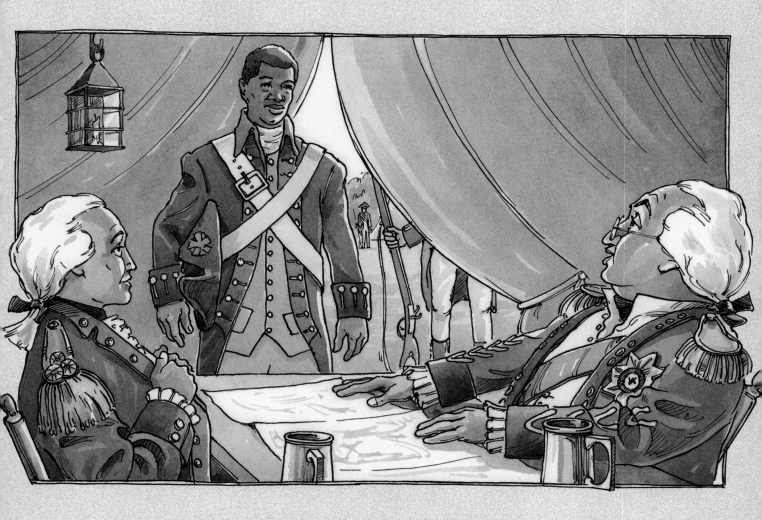

The battles of the Revolution were over. The broken-hearted Cornwallis himself did not ride out with his troops on the day of surrender, but remained in his headquarters in a cave beside the York River.

It was only two days later, when he had recovered, that Cornwallis left the village. In defeat he went to the headquarters of young Lafayette. The two generals were talking of the campaign, looking over the maps, when Cornwallis looked up to see the familiar face of James Armistead. The black spy wore an American uniform. The British general shook his head grimly, for it was only then that he realized that the volunteer who had served him so faithfully was in truth an American counterspy. The cunning and devotion of this young slave had played an important part in winning the final battle of the war.

One year after a treaty of peace had ended the war, Lafayette wrote a certificate praising the work of James Armistead as a spy:

This is to Certify that the Bearer By the Name of James Has done Essential Services to me While I Had the Honour to Command in this State. His Intelligences from the Enemy's Camp were Industriously Collected and More Faithfully deliver'd. He properly Acquitted Himself with Some important Commissions I Gave Him and Appears to me Entitled to Every Reward his Situation Can Admit of. Done Under my Hand, Richmond November 21st 1784

Lafayette

Soon afterward, James Armistead sent this certificate to the General Assembly of Virginia and asked that he be declared a free man. In his petition he said that he had volunteered to help against the British: ". . . during the time of his serving the Marquis Lafayette he often at the peril of his life found means to frequent the British camp, by which means he kept open a channel of the most useful communications to the army of the state . . . of the most secret & important kind; the possession of which if discovered on him would have most certainly endangered the life of your petitioner . . ."

Even now Armistead said he would not demand his freedom unless his master, William Armistead, could be paid a reasonable price "for the loss of so valuable a workman."

The Virginia General Assembly agreed. The state paid Armistead a fair price, and James Armistead became a free man. From that time onward, he called himself James Lafayette.

By the year 1819, when he was growing old, James Lafayette had become "poor and unable to help himself." Once more he turned for help to the assembly, which voted him $60, a large sum for those days. He was also granted $40 a year for the rest of his life, a pension such as those paid to privates who had served in the army during the Revolution.

One of the great days in James Lafayette's life came in 1824, when he was sixty-four years old, and the aging Lafayette visited Richmond on his final tour of America. Great crowds lined the streets to see the French hero who had made possible American independence, and thousands watched as the Marquis greeted James Lafayette as an old comrade.

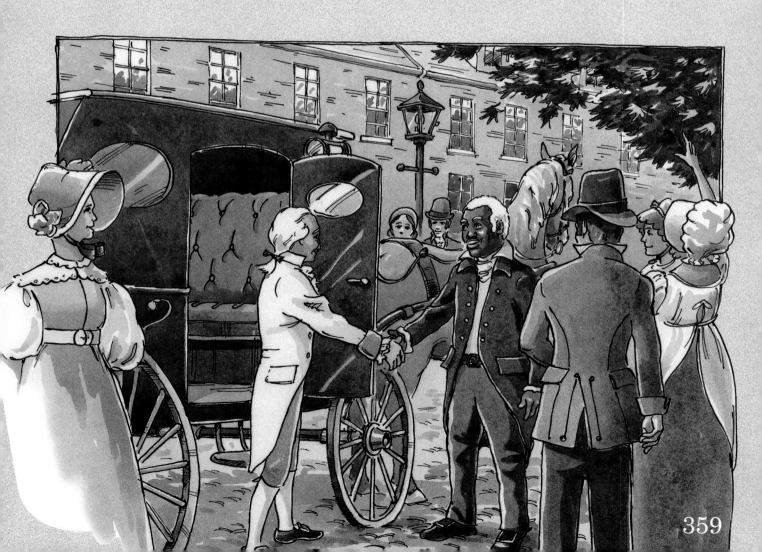

It was during this visit to Richmond that James Lafayette sat for his portrait, painted by the well-known artist John B. Martin. The portrait still hangs in a Virginia museum, showing the lean, erect black spy, dressed in a handsome military coat as a reminder of the days when he had won his own freedom and helped to win that of his country as well.

It is thought that the friendship and faithful service of James Armistead Lafayette caused the Marquis to become a leader in the movement to end slavery and to extend help to the black people of many nations.

At the close of the Revolution, Lafayette suggested to Washington a plan "which might greatly benefit the black part of mankind." He suggested that they purchase "a small estate where we may try the experiment to free the Negroes and use them only as tenants."

This led Lafayette to other efforts to outlaw slavery. In Paris, five years later, he helped to found a society of The Friends of the Blacks, and for the rest of his life he supported efforts to give equal rights to men of all races.

James Armistead Lafayette was the best-known black spy in the American army, but he was by no means the only one.

A slave by the name of SAUL MATTHEWS served also as a spy and guide in the British camp at Portsmouth. The white colonel Josiah Parker said of him that he "deserved the applause of his country" for his bravery. A Virginia historian reported that this slave of Thomas Matthews "brought back military secrets of such value to Colonel Parker that on the same night, serving as a guide, he led a party of Americans to the British garrison . . ." At another time, when Saul Matthews's master and other white Virginia soldiers had fled across the state border into North Carolina, Matthews was once more sent to spy on the enemy and returned with plans of British movements. Such distinguished officers as Baron von Steuben, Peter Muhlenberg, and General Nathanael Greene praised Matthews highly for his services.

Like James Armistead, he continued to work as a slave
after the war, but at last he too asked the legislature for help
and was granted his "full liberty" for his "very many essential
services . . . during the late war."

Others served in the same way, among them two slaves
whose records included only their first names:

"*Antigua*: In March 1783 a slave by this name was lauded
by the General Assembly of South Carolina for his skill in
'procuring information of the enemy's movements and
designs.' He 'always executed the commissions with which he
was entrusted with diligence and fidelity, and obtained very
considerable and important information, from within the
enemy's lines, frequently at the risk of his life.' To reward him,
the assembly liberated his 'wife named Hagar, and her child.'"
Antigua seems to have remained a slave all his life.

"*Quaco*: During the British occupation of Newport, Rhode Island, Quaco's Tory master sold him to a colonel in the king's army. Quaco fled to the Patriot lines with valuable information. In January 1782, the General Assembly of Rhode Island, saying 'the information he then gave rendered great and essential service to this state and the public in general,' declared Quaco free."

We will probably never learn more of the work of black spies during the Revolution, but it is certain that these secret services were so valuable that without them the struggle for the country's independence might have been lost.

THE MASTER SPY OF YORKTOWN

Meet the Author

Burke Davis's talent for writing led him to work as a newspaper editor, a reporter, and a columnist over a span of 25 years. He then wrote for Colonial Williamsburg for the next 18 years. During this time he also wrote numerous novels, biographies, history books, and children's books. Much of his writing focuses on the history of the United States. Some of his titles include *Getting to Know Thomas Jefferson's Virginia, Heroes of the American Revolution, Appomattox: Closing Struggle of the Civil War*, and *Gray Fox: Robert E. Lee and the Civil War.*

Meet the Illustrator

Stephen Snider has been a freelance illustrator for twenty years. He and his wife Jackie, who is also an illustrator, live and work out of their country home in southern Ontario. There they enjoy their six indoor cats, one barn cat, two dogs, two horses, and hundreds of birds.

Theme Connections

Within the Selection

Record the answers to the questions below in the Response Journal section of your Writer's Notebook. In small groups, report the ideas you wrote. Discuss your ideas with the rest of the group. Then choose a person to report your group's answers to the class.

- How did the Marquis de Lafayette, a Frenchman, come to be involved in the American Revolution?
- What kinds of information did James Armistead obtain for Lafayette from the British?
- What are the names of some other African-American spies whose service during the American Revolution was recorded?

Across Selections

- James Armistead was able to ride into British camps easily as a volunteer. Based on what you read about the Loyalists in "...If You Lived at the Time of the American Revolution," why do you think this was?
- Compare and contrast the Marquis de Lafayette's efforts to end slavery in the colonies to those of Thomas Jefferson, in "The Declaration of Independence."

Beyond the Selection

- Think about how "The Master Spy of Yorktown" adds to what you know about making a new nation.
- Add items to the Concept/Question Board about making a new nation.

Focus Questions Why did people living in the states not want a national constitution? Why did they come to need one? What system of government did the framers of the national constitution create? How is democracy important to this system of government?

Shh! We're Writing the Constitution

Jean Fritz
illustrated by Tomie dePaola

After the Revolutionary War most people in America were glad that they were no longer British. Still, they were not ready to call themselves Americans. The last thing they wanted was to become a nation. They were citizens of their own separate states, just as they had always been: each state different, each state proud of its own character, each state quick to poke fun at other states. To Southerners, New Englanders might be "no-account Yankees." To New Englanders, Pennsylvanians might be "lousy Buckskins." But to everyone the states themselves were all important. "Sovereign states," they called them. They loved the sound of "sovereign" because it meant that they were their own bosses.

George Washington, however, scoffed at the idea of "sovereign states." He knew that the states could not be truly independent for long and survive. Ever since the Declaration of Independence had been signed, people had referred to the country as the United States of America. It was about time, he thought, for them to act and feel united.

Once during the war Washington had decided it would be a good idea if his troops swore allegiance to the United States. As a start he lined up some troops from New Jersey and asked them to take such an oath. They looked at Washington as if he'd taken leave of his senses. How could they do that? they cried. New Jersey was their country!

So Washington dropped the idea. In time, he hoped, the states would see that they needed to become one nation, united under a strong central government.

But that time would be long in coming. For now, as they started out on their independence, the thirteen states were satisfied to be what they called a federation, a kind of voluntary league of states. In other words, each state legislature sent delegates to a Continental Congress which was supposed to act on matters of common concern.

In September 1774, when the First Continental Congress met, the common concern was Great Britain. Two years later, after the Declaration of Independence had been signed, the concern was that the country needed some kind of government. Not a fully developed government because of course they had their states. All they wanted were some basic rules to hold them together to do whatever needed to be done. So the Congress wrote the Articles of Confederation which outlined rules for a "firm league of friendship." In practice, however, the states did not always feel a firm need to follow any rules.

The Congress, for instance, could ask the states to contribute money to pay the country's debts, but if the states didn't feel like contributing, no one could make them. Congress could declare war but it couldn't fight unless the states felt like supplying soldiers. The trouble was that their president had no definite powers and the country had no overall legal system. So although the Congress could make all the rules it wanted, it couldn't enforce any of them. Much of the time the states didn't even bother to send delegates to the meetings.

By 1786, it was becoming obvious that changes were needed. People were in debt, a few states were printing paper money that was all but worthless, and in the midst of this disorder some people could see that America would fall apart if it didn't have a sound central government with power to act for all the states. George Washington, of course, was one who had felt strongly about this for a long time. Alexander Hamilton was another. Born and brought up in the Caribbean Islands, he had no patience with the idea of state loyalty. America was nothing but a monster with thirteen heads, he said. James Madison from Virginia wanted a strong America too. He was a little man, described as being "no bigger than half a piece of soap," but he had big ideas for his country.

In 1786 these men, among others, suggested to the Congress that all the states send delegates to a Grand Convention in Philadelphia to improve the existing form of government. It sounded innocent. Just a matter of revising the old Articles of Confederation to make the government work better. No one would quarrel with that.

But they did.

Rhode Island refused to have anything to do with the convention. Patrick Henry, when asked to be a delegate from Virginia, said he "smelt a rat" and wouldn't go. Willie Jones of North Carolina didn't say what he smelled, but he wouldn't go either.

But in the end the convention was scheduled to meet in the State House in Philadelphia on May 14, 1787.

James (or "Jemmy") Madison was so worked up about it that he arrived from Virginia eleven days early. George Washington left his home, Mount Vernon, on May 9 with a headache and an upset stomach, but he arrived in Philadelphia on the night of May 13th. The next morning a few delegates from Pennsylvania and a few from Virginia came to the meeting but there needed to be seven states present to conduct business. Since there were only two, the meeting was adjourned.

It was May 25th before delegates from enough states showed up. They blamed their delays on the weather, muddy roads, personal business, lack of money. Delegates from New Hampshire couldn't scrape up enough money to come until late July, but even so, they beat John Francis Mercer of Maryland. He sauntered into the State House on August 6th.

The most colorful arrival was that of Benjamin Franklin who at eighty-one was the oldest of the delegates. Because he experienced so much pain when he was bounced about in a carriage, Franklin came to the convention in a Chinese sedan chair carried by four prisoners from the Philadelphia jail. (He lived in the city so they didn't have far to carry him.)

In all, there would be fifty-five delegates, although coming and going as they did, there were seldom more than thirty there at the same time. The first thing the delegates did was to elect George Washington president of the convention. They escorted him to his official chair on a raised platform. Then the other members of the convention took their seats at tables draped with green woolen cloth.

James Madison sat in the front of the room and as soon as the talking began, he began writing. Never absent for a single day, he kept a record of all that was said during the next four months, stopping only when he, himself, wanted to speak.

They knew that there would be many arguments in this room, but they agreed that they didn't want the whole country listening in and taking sides. They would keep the proceedings a secret. So before every meeting the door was locked. Sentries were stationed in the hall. And even though it turned out to be a hot summer, the windows were kept closed. Why should they risk eavesdroppers? Members were not supposed to write gossipy letters home.

Nor to answer nosy questions. Nor to discuss their business with outsiders. Benjamin Franklin was the one who had to be watched. He meant no harm but he did love to talk, especially at parties, so if he seemed to spill the beans, another delegate was ready to leap into the conversation and change the subject.

For fifty-five men to keep a secret for four months was an accomplishment in itself. But they did. Of course this didn't prevent rumors from starting. Once it was rumored that the convention was planning to invite the second son of George the Third to become King of America. The delegates were furious. They might not be able to say what they were going to do, but they had no trouble saying what they were *not* going to do. And they were not inviting the second or third son of George the Third or of anyone else to be King of America.

If the people of the country were afraid of what might happen in the convention, so were the delegates themselves. They didn't call the document they were working on a "constitution"; they referred to it as "the plan." Because they knew that the country was sensitive to the word "national," they tried to stick to "federal," a word they were used to and one which didn't reduce the power of the states. But after Edmund Randolph, Governor of Virginia, had presented what came to be called the Virginia Plan, he spoke right out.

In the Virginia Plan, Randolph explained, there would be three branches of government. The executive branch would have a head who would be responsible for running the government. The legislative branch would be made up of

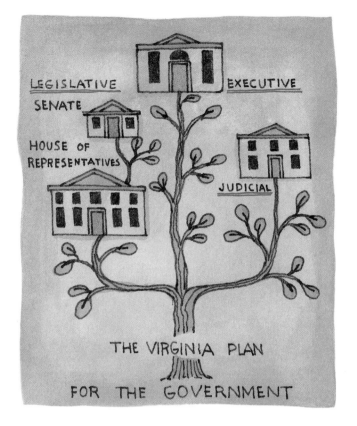

LEGISLATIVE

SENATE

HOUSE OF
REPRESENTATIVES

EXECUTIVE

JUDICIAL

THE VIRGINIA PLAN

FOR THE GOVERNMENT

two houses which would make laws. The House of
Representatives would be elected directly by the people;
the Senate, the smaller and supposedly more coolheaded
body, would be elected by the House. Together they would
be called the Congress. The third branch would be the
judiciary headed by a Supreme Court, which would make
sure that laws were constitutional and were properly obeyed.

Edmund Randolph was a tall, handsome, likable man and
nothing he said at first seemed alarming. Some of the states
had constitutions that were similar to the one he described.
Besides, the members knew that after Randolph's plan had
been discussed, other members would have a chance to
present their plans. But at the end of his speech Randolph
did arouse his audience. It should be clear, he said that his
resolutions were not merely for a federal government but
for a national government that would be supreme over
the states.

There was a dead silence.

Pierce Butler of South Carolina was one of the first to recover. He jumped down hard on the word "national" but John Dickinson of Delaware said there was nothing wrong with the word. "We *are* a nation!" he declared.

No! For Elbridge Gerry of Massachusetts this kind of talk was scary. He was a thin, worrying sort of man who was sometimes called "Grumbletonian" behind his back. National? he sputtered. How could they think national? They had been sent here to revise the Articles of Confederation, not to destroy them.

As the meetings went on, all kinds of fear surfaced. The smaller states with fewer people were afraid of the larger states which had more people. In the past the votes of all states, no matter what their population, had counted the same. But a national government would be more concerned with individual people than with the states themselves.

So what would happen to the small states now? And what kind of government were they forming? Some people were afraid of a "high-toned" or aristocratic government run by a small, privileged, wealthy group, the way a monarchy was usually run. Others were just as afraid of the common people having too much power. They weren't capable of governing, it was said.

Eventually the convention did agree on a national legislature to consist of two houses but before final acceptance, the word "national" was crossed out.

Still, there were so many questions to decide. What about the person who was to be the executive or head of the government? Should there be just one person? If so, would he seem like a king? Why not three people, each representing a different part of the country? But what if they fought among themselves? What if they couldn't reach an agreement? Should the executive be paid a salary? (Yes, said Madison. Don't count on patriotism.) But who should pay the salary—the states or the government of the United States? How should the executive be chosen? By the people? By the states? By a branch of the United States legislature? By electors? By lot? (They had to vote sixty times before they could settle this question.) And how long should the executive serve? If he were thought to be guilty of misconduct, could they impeach him? Could they remove him from office?

Alexander Hamilton was one of the few who wanted the president to serve a long term, perhaps even for life.

He thought it would be embarrassing to watch a lot of ex-presidents wandering around like ghosts. But suppose you had a long-term president, Franklin pointed out. And suppose he turned out to be a bad president. What then? Out of simple kindness they ought to provide some way to get rid of him. Otherwise, Franklin chuckled, the only thing they could do would be to shoot him.

In the end it was decided that there should be a single executive who would be paid out of the Treasury of the new government. He would be chosen by electors from each state, and he would serve four years. And yes, if it was necessary, he could be impeached.

But what if he should die while in office? Or be impeached? Who would take his place? So there had to be a vice president, the one who came in second in the presidential election. And since the vice president should do more than just wait around to see if the president would make it through his term, he was given the job of presiding over the Senate.

Mr. Randolph finished presenting his plan on May 29 and for the next two weeks—until June 13—the convention went over it. Some measures were voted on, some would be revised, and all would be discussed again and again. But there was also the chance that the whole plan would be scrapped for something else. After a day's recess, on June 15, William Paterson of New Jersey stood up. Only five feet two, he wasn't as impressive a figure as Mr. Randolph, but he was a cheerful, modest, likable man. Still, he didn't approve of a single idea of Mr. Randolph's. The government should be a federation of states as it was now, with each state having an equal vote, he said. It should consist of one legislative body with several executives at its head. According to Mr. Paterson, the Virginia Plan was impractical, illegal, and expensive. How could so many members of Congress, he asked, find the money to travel from all over the country to attend meetings?

When James Madison answered Mr. Paterson, it was as if he were fencing. Madison danced all around Mr. Paterson's arguments, thrusting at first one point, then another until it seemed as if there were nothing left of William Paterson's plan. And there wasn't. When the delegates were asked to vote in favor of one of the two plans, Mr. Randolph's won. Seven states against three. (Maryland's delegation was divided.) Randolph's plan still had to be thrashed out, but the idea of a federation was dead. With this vote the delegates committed themselves to write a constitution for a new nation, whether all of them were willing to call it that or not.

Shh! We're Writing the Constitution

Meet the Author

Jean Fritz's fascination with historical figures began at a young age. Her father used to tell her tales about American heroes. She was so intrigued by these tales that she made it her hobby to find out everything she could about the famous people in them. She then turned her findings into stories. She now has many books filled with fascinating details about American historical figures.

Meet the Illustrator

Tomie dePaola's true love is writing and illustrating books for children. He has illustrated over 80 children's books. More than 60 of these books also were written by him. Some of the titles for which he is most well known include *Tomie dePaola's Mother Goose*, *Tomie dePaola's Favorite Nursery Tales*, and *Watch Out for the Chicken Feet in Your Soup*. The last story was based on his Italian grandmother who really did put chicken feet in her chicken soup!

Theme Connections

Within the Selection

Record the answers to the questions below in the Response Journal section of your Writer's Notebook. In small groups, report the ideas you wrote. Discuss your ideas with the rest of the group. Then choose a person to report your group's answers to the class.

- What was the original purpose of the Grand Convention? How did this purpose change?
- Why did the delegates keep the contents of their meetings a secret for four months?
- What were the three branches of government in the Virginia plan? What were the responsibilities of each branch?

Across Selections

- George Washington and Benjamin Franklin both participated in the Grand Convention. In what previous selections from this unit have you read about these people, and what did you learn about them?

Beyond the Selection

- Think of the last time you worked on a project with a group of people. What kinds of problems did you have with decision making and coordinating schedules, and how did your group solve these problems?
- Think about how "Shh! We're Writing the Constitution" adds to what you know about making a new nation.
- Add items to the Concept/Question Board about making a new nation.

Focus Questions Why did Benjamin Franklin urge delegates to sign the Constitution? Why did he believe that the Constitution was as close to being perfect as it could be? Why did he think that the Constitution might not work without every delegate's support?

We, the People of the United States

from *The American Revolutionaries: A History in Their Own Words, 1750–1800*

by Milton Meltzer

How would the new nation be governed? During the Revolutionary War the thirteen sovereign states had come together for joint defense and to conduct a common foreign policy. But each insisted on the right to rule itself and refused to surrender its sovereignty to the Confederation. That government had been set up by the Articles of Confederation, adopted in 1781. It rapidly proved too weak and inadequate. The states quarreled among themselves over boundary lines, over tariffs, over court decisions; and hard times deepened the bitterness. A strong central authority was badly needed to coordinate interest and ensure order.

Something had to be done, and quickly. The states agreed that a national convention should meet in Philadelphia to strengthen the federal government so it could better meet the needs of the union. In May, 1787, fifty-five delegates from all the states met, with George Washington presiding. Over half the men were under forty; Benjamin Franklin, at eighty-two, was by far the oldest.

The delegates threw aside the old articles and wrote a completely new Constitution during sixteen weeks of a hot summer. Out of their deliberations came a document whose wisdom, practical ingenuity, and vitality armed the new nation for a turbulent future.

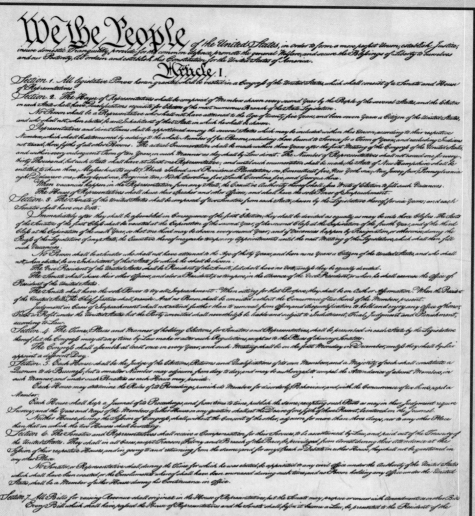

Here is the preamble, which consists of two brief parts. The first defines the source of authority from which the Constitution is derived. The second defines the objects for which the Constitution and the government based upon it are created. The concept of "the people" as the source of power would undergo broader definition as time passed, giving new life to the Constitution in every generation:

WE, THE PEOPLE of the United States, in order to form a more perfect union, establish justice, insure domestic tranquility, provide for the common defence, promote the general welfare, and secure the blessings of liberty to ourselves and our posterity, do ordain and establish this Constitution for the United States of America.

Benjamin Franklin
The American Museum,
Philadelphia, December,
1787

The diversity of opinions and prejudices, the clash of regional and economic interests, the varying philosophical views, made agreement on this basic document almost impossible. Luckily, Benjamin Franklin shared with Washington the task of conciliating the delegates, holding them together to complete the great work. As Franklin was too infirm to take the floor, his few speeches were read by James Wilson. But on the floor and off, he stressed the need for compassion and humility with that homely charm and wit that had made him so great an asset in diplomacy.

When the delegates reached a final draft, Franklin spoke to them, urging all to sign it. On September 17, 1787, the day of the signing of the Constitution, the old man rose and asked the convention to listen while Wilson read these words that would be reprinted in more than fifty newspapers. They would exert the most decisive influence during the intense ratification debate in the states:

I CONFESS that I do not entirely approve of this Constitution at present, but, Sir, I am not sure I shall never approve it: For having lived long, I have experienced many instances of being obliged, by better information or fuller consideration, to change opinions even on important subjects, which I once thought right, but found to be otherwise. It is therefore that the older I grow the more apt I am to doubt my own judgment, and to pay more respect to the judgment of others. Most men, indeed, as well as most sects in religion, think themselves in possession of all truth, and that wherever others differ from them it is so far error. . . . But though many private persons think almost as highly of their own infallibility as of that of their sect, few express it so naturally as a certain French lady who, in a little dispute with her sister, said, I don't know how it happens, sister, but I meet with nobody but myself that's always in the right.

In these sentiments, Sir, I agree to this Constitution, with all its faults, if they are such; because I think a general government necessary for us, and there is no form of government but what may be a blessing to the people if well administered; and I believe further that this is likely to be well administered for a course of years, and can only end in despotism, as other forms have done before it, when the people shall become so corrupted as to need despotic government, being incapable of any other.

I doubt, too, whether any other convention we can obtain may be able to make a better Constitution: for when you assemble a number of men to have the advantage of their joint wisdom, you inevitably assemble with those men all their prejudices, their passions, their errors of opinion, their local interests, and their selfish views. From such an assembly can a perfect production be expected? It therefore astonishes me, Sir, to find this system approaching so near to perfection as it does; and I think it will astonish our enemies, who are waiting with confidence to hear that our councils are confounded, like those of the builders of Babel, and that our states are on the point of separation, only to meet hereafter for the purpose of cutting one another's throats.

Thus I consent, Sir, to this Constitution because I expect no better, and because I am not sure that it is not the best. The opinions I have had of its errors I sacrifice to the public good. I have never whispered a syllable of them abroad. Within these walls they were born, and here they shall die. If every one of us in returning to our constituents were to report the objections he has had to it, and use his influence to gain partisans in support of them, we might prevent its being generally received, and thereby lose all the salutary effects and great advantages resulting naturally in our favor among foreign nations, as well as among ourselves, from our real or apparent unanimity.

Washington presiding over the Constitutional Convention in the earliest known engraving of the meeting.

Much of the strength and efficiency of any government, in procuring and securing happiness to the people depends on opinion, on the general opinion of the goodness of that government as well as of the wisdom and integrity of its governors. I hope, therefore, that for our own sakes, as a part of the people, and for the sake of our posterity, we shall act heartily and unanimously in recommending this Constitution, wherever our influence may extend, and turn our future thoughts and endeavors to the means of having it well administered.

On the whole, Sir, I cannot help expressing a wish that every member of the convention, who may still have objections to it, would with me on this occasion doubt a little of his own infallibility, and to make manifest our unanimity, put his name to this instrument.

The American Museum, Philadelphia, December, 1787

We, the People of the United States

Meet the Author

Milton Meltzer grew up in a neighborhood of immigrant families. As a young man he got his first writing job on a state-funded theater project. From there, he went on to have many jobs that involved writing. He was an editor, a journalist, a speechwriter, and the author of scripts for radio documentaries. However, he did not write his first book until he was forty years old.

His books were inspired by the many important historical events he had lived through. He was an infant during World War I, a young man during the Great Depression, and an air traffic controller during World War II. Because of this, he has used writing to search for connections between the past and the present. It was also his goal to help young people learn about the struggles of the many different cultural groups that make up America.

Theme Connections

Within the Selection

Record the answers to the questions below in the Response Journal section of your Writer's Notebook. In small groups, report the ideas you wrote. Discuss your ideas with the rest of the group. Then choose a person to report your group's answers to the class.

- Why was there so much disagreement over what the Constitution should say?
- Why did Benjamin Franklin urge delegates to sign the Constitution even though he did not agree with every part of it?
- Why did Franklin think it was impossible for those assembled at the Grand Convention to create a "perfect" constitution?

Across Selections

- How does what you learned from this selection about the writing of the Constitution compare and contrast with what you learned in "Shh! We're Writing the Constitution"?
- In what ways were cooperation and competition involved in the writing and approval of the Constitution?

Beyond the Selection

- Think of a time in your life when you were involved in making a group decision. Was everyone in the group able to get exactly what he or she wanted? If you had had only yourself to consider in the decision, would you have decided differently? Why?
- Think about how "We, the People of the United States" adds to what you know about making a new nation.
- Add items to the Concept/Question Board about making a new nation.

Some familiar images connected with the American West are of wagon trains crossing its wide prairies, seemingly endless deserts, and rugged mountains. Who were the people who made these grueling trips to find new land and new lives? Who were the people who already lived here, and what was their history? How has the West changed over the years?

Focus Questions Why did Lewis and Clark explore the West?
How was Sacagawea important to the expedition?
What were her reasons for making the trip?

Sacagawea's Journey

from *Sacagawea*
by Betty Westrom Skold
illustrated by Craig Spearing

In 1803, President Thomas Jefferson purchased the Louisiana Territory, an area that extended from the Mississippi River to the Rocky Mountains and that doubled the size of the United States. In 1804, he sent an expedition headed by Meriwether Lewis and William Clark to explore this region and to find a route through it to the Pacific Ocean. About forty-five men set off from St. Louis and traveled up the Missouri River to the territory of the Mandan Indians. There they met a French fur trader, Toussaint Charbonneau, and his wife, Sacagawea. Sacagawea was not a Mandan. She was a Shoshone, a member of a group living in the Rocky Mountains. Sacagawea had been captured as a young girl and brought east. At the time she met Lewis and Clark she was sixteen or seventeen years old and had recently given birth to a son that the men nicknamed Pompy. She and her husband were hired to go with the expedition as interpreters and guides.

Sacagawea stuffed a little more soft, dry grass into Pompy's cradleboard, put the child into it, and tied the rawhide thongs. Her eyes swept the room that had sheltered her through the winter, now stripped of the buffalo robes and the hunting and cooking gear. The last fire was dying on the hearth as she stepped outside.

The ground under her moccasins was spongy and damp from the melting snow. Tender new buds dotted the cottonwoods. For several days Lewis and Clark had seen swans and wild geese flying northeastward in the evening. The Hidatsas had been leaping across the ice cakes to catch the buffalo floating downstream. Soon the river would be ice-free and ready. The captains had taken charge of the final packing, carefully separating the maps, papers, and wildlife specimens that would be sent back to President Jefferson from the provisions that would go farther up the Missouri with their Corps of Discovery.

Now it was April 7, 1805. Today they would say good-bye to the Mandans and Hidatsas, who watched from the banks of the river. It would also be a day of parting for six American soldiers and two French traders, who would return to St. Louis with the keelboat and two canoes. The main part of the Corps of Discovery——Captains Lewis and Clark, Sacagawea, Pompy, Charbonneau and another interpreter, three sergeants, twenty-three privates, and a black slave named York——would follow the Missouri westward in the two long pirogues and six dugout canoes.

Shadows were lengthening into late afternoon when the big keelboat and two canoes began to move back down the Missouri toward St. Louis. Almost at the same time, the six dugout canoes and two pirogues of the westbound party pushed away from the shoreline and started up the river.

The men were in good spirits——talking, laughing, waving at the Indians along the banks. Sacagawea began the journey more quietly. No sign of excitement showed on her face, and her voice was calm. Only months later would the others realize the depth of her feeling as she started the journey.

Sacagawea took her turn with the others, sometimes paddling in one of the boats, often walking along the shore. The world of the plains seemed to flow by. Flocks of geese fed in the young grass, while sparrow hawks wheeled across the sky. Patches of juniper spread along the sides of the hills. Maple trees were budding and plum bushes were in bloom, but winter was not quite over. Once in a while snow would sift down briefly on a land that had already felt the touch of spring.

At Fort Mandan Sacagawea had become acquainted with the military life of the Americans. She had grown used to the uniforms, the salutes, the sentinels, the commands, and had learned the names of the thirty men whom her family had joined. As the real work of the expedition began, she came to know each person as an individual. Each one had been chosen for the skills that would help the Corps of Discovery as a whole.

Captain Lewis was a brave and thoughtful leader who enjoyed walking alone out on the prairie, studying the animals or gathering bits of plant life. It was he who learned to chart their route by the stars. Captain Lewis also served as doctor for the expedition, giving out medicines from his small leather bag. Sacagawea learned that Captain Clark's talents as mapmaker and peacemaker were equaled by his leadership skills.

Private Cruzatte, whose violin music had delighted her at Fort Mandan parties, was experienced in river travel. Sergeant Gass was a carpenter, and Private Shields was an expert gunsmith. Drewyer served as an interpreter, but he was also an able hunter. The black man, York, worked as Captain Clark's personal servant, and he provided entertainment for the whole Corps with his story-telling. Sergeant Ordway became a capable commander whenever the captains were not around. John Colter, from the Kentucky woods, had been chosen for hunting skills, and in a single day he bagged an elk, three deer, a wolf, and five turkeys. Charbonneau proved to be a surprisingly good trail cook.

Even Scannon, Captain Clark's big, black, Newfoundland dog, had his chores. An alert watchdog, he frightened away animals who wandered into camp during the night. He also helped with Pompy, lying like a faithful guardian beside the baby's cradleboard.

Sacagawea cheerfully kept pace along the trail, moving with a light, firm step. Food-gathering skills from her Shoshone childhood proved useful again and again. Just two days from Fort Mandan, when they had halted for dinner, she sharpened a digger stick and began to poke around in small piles of driftwood. She uncovered a good supply of wild artichokes, buried there by mice.

Day after day Sacagawea walked along the shore or rode in a canoe with the others, but in a sense she made the journey alone. Not even the child on her shoulders shared her experience. No one else could share her dream of homecoming.

Evenings around the campfire were a pleasant time. After supper the men would often throw quoits, a game in which they tossed rope rings at stakes. Sometimes they danced to the music of violin and mouth harp. The captains and several of the others faithfully wrote down each day's events in their journals by the dim light of the fire. Sacagawea sat cross-legged on the ground, mending buckskins and watching over Pompy.

For several days they passed through prairie country like one large grassy pasture. Gentle herds of buffalo, elk, and antelope gazed at them curiously, sometimes following the men who walked on shore. Deer peered shyly from the brush.

By late April they had reached the woodlands at the mouth of the Yellowstone River. Happy to have arrived at this first important landmark, they celebrated with music, dancing, and a small ration of spirits.

May 14 brought troubles to the expedition. Six of the hunters wounded a brown grizzly. Crazed by pain, the bear charged and chased them along the bank. The men plunged into the river, and others in the party were able to kill the bear with eight shots.

After sunset that evening the white pirogue was almost destroyed. The sail had been raised to take advantage of a brisk wind. Steering was Charbonneau, a timid and clumsy river pilot. A sudden squall struck the boat at an angle, ripping the brace of the sail from the man who held it, and the boat tipped over on its side. Charbonneau had never learned to swim. He cried out to God in terror and dropped the rudder. Cruzatte, in the bow, threatened to shoot him if he did not take hold of the rudder and do his duty. A trembling Charbonneau obeyed.

Meanwhile Sacagawea, balancing the baby on her back, calmly reached far out over the side and grabbed the valuable cargo that had fallen overboard. After the pirogue had been dragged to shore and bailed out with kettles, the rescued articles were spread out on the ground to dry. By her quick thinking Sacagawea had saved many things of value to the expedition. She had rescued instruments for navigation, scientific books needed by the captains for their work, and trading goods needed to make peaceful contact with Indians they would meet along the way.

Almost every day the travelers reached some new tributary of the Missouri. They remembered maps drawn on skins or in the earth by Hidatsa warriors back at Fort Mandan. As each river was identified by its Hidatsa name, they could feel confident that they were on the right track. When they came to a river with water the tan color of milky tea, they named it the Milk River. This was the river known to the Hidatsas as "The River Which Scolds At All Others." Small, unnamed streams were given new names by Lewis and Clark. When a lively, clear-running river was named for Sacagawea, she accepted the honor with shy pleasure. Another stream was called Blowing Fly Creek for the hordes of flies that swarmed over their meat. Judith's River was named for a friend of Captain Clark's from Virginia.

In the high country near the mouth of Judith's River, they found the remains of a large Indian camp that had been deserted a short time before. All over the hills were the scattered ashes of cooking fires where tipis had stood. A child's ball and a moccasin found on the site were brought to Sacagawea. She looked at them carefully, then shook her head. They were not Shoshones.

In early June the party came to a branching of the river that gave them a problem. Which of the branches was the "true Missouri"? Was it the one that seemed to come from the north, or was it the branch that flowed from the southwest? Most of the Corps were sure that the northern branch was the Missouri. It looked like the river they had followed all the way from the Mississippi, broad and thick with mud. The captains, on the other hand, wanted to follow the southern branch, a clear, swift-running stream with a rock and gravel bed. They reasoned that the Missouri had its source in the mountains and that a mountain stream would be swift and clear.

A wrong decision could be a costly mistake. Already they could see snow-topped mountains in the distance. Even if they should find the "Northwest Passage," crossing the mountains in winter would be a risky business. If they should turn up the wrong river, it could waste precious weeks of summer travel time. The captains decided that a camp should be set up for a few days at the fork of the rivers. Small exploring parties would go up each of the branches and decide which fork led to the Great Falls described by the Hidatsas, and from there to Shoshone country.

Clearly it was a good time to pause. Those not in the exploring parties could spend their time dressing skins for clothing. Uniforms had fallen to shreds, and buckskin clothing had to be made to replace them. Moccasins had been so cut by the rocky trails that they had been thrown away, and the men could barely walk on their bruised feet. Many of them were exhausted from towing the boats free from sandbars or sloshing through cold water up to their armpits. Poor diet and muddy water caused diarrhea and nausea, while chilling rains brought raging fever.

Lewis was so sure that the muddy northern branch could not be the Missouri that he named it Maria's River, after his cousin, Maria Wood. Nevertheless, he agreed to take a party up this river while Captain Clark explored the southern branch. The Lewis party found out that the northern branch flowed through a picture book country of beautiful birds, wild roses, and herds of game animals, but both he and Clark were still convinced that the southern branch was the Missouri. To find out for sure, they decided that Lewis would take four men and follow the southern branch on foot in search of the Great Falls.

Lewis and a small land party pushed up into the rolling hills and across a level plain. Suddenly he heard the distant sound of falling water and saw spray rising above the horizon. He followed the sound of roaring water until he stood on a pile of rocks and looked in wonder at the water cascading over huge bluffs, nine hundred feet wide and eighty feet high. In some places the water fell in great sheets, while at other points it was broken by rocks into glittering spray. He had reached the Great Falls of the Missouri River. Back at camp, he reported that there was no way to pass this point by water. They would have to organize a portage around the falls, but they had followed the "true Missouri."

Captain Lewis learned that Sacagawea had become ill during his absence. The young woman who had met all the hardships of the journey now lay sick in the covered part of the white pirogue, shaded from the July heat. She was gripped by many pains, weak, and exhausted. Her pulse was irregular, and her fingers twitched. Captain Clark had tried medicines and had bled her, but she was no better.

The white explorers were worried. They had grown fond of this brave Shoshone woman, and she had been useful to them in finding roots, sewing buckskin, and pointing out the landmarks along the way. Now, just when they needed her most, on the very edge of Shoshone country, she lay close to death.

Finally, in desperation, Captain Lewis had mineral water brought from a nearby sulfur spring and poured it down her throat. Within minutes Sacagawea began to perspire, and her pulse grew stronger. The crisis had passed.

The captains decided that the Maria's River camp would be a good place to leave the large red pirogue and some of the provisions to lighten the load for the portage around the falls and for travel through the mountains. The men dug deep, bottle-shaped holes called caches in the ground and filled them with salt, tools, powder, and lead. Signs of the digging were removed. They dragged the pirogue up on an island, tied it to trees, and covered it with brush.

To move the six dugouts around the falls, they built makeshift wagons. The mast of the white pirogue was cut up for axles and rounds were sliced from a huge cottonwood tree to form wheels.

The eighteen-mile portage around the Great Falls was an eleven-day struggle. The explorers limped in thin moccasins over needle-sharp ground covered with buffalo tracks and prickly pear cactus, shoving the two heavy, clumsy carts. Axles cracked and wagon tongues broke, so new ones had to be made from willow trees. In a stiff breeze the men hoisted a sail on one of the canoes and the wind helped carry it along on the wagon wheels.

One day a sudden storm pelted the party with huge, bouncing hailstones. Water filled runoff channels, almost sweeping Captain Clark, Sacagawea, and Pompy away in a flash flood. They found shelter under a rock shelf and watched a wall of water moving down the creek. Pushing the mother and baby ahead of him, Captain Clark scrambled up the hill to safety just before they would have been swept away.

After they had completed the exhausting portage, they built two canoes and moved up the river, which was narrow and crowded with islands. At a place where the Missouri loops like a rattlesnake, huge rocks hung out over the

banks and pressed the river into a narrow channel. Captain Lewis marveled at the scene and called it the "Gates of the Rocky Mountains."

Time had been lost in the portage, and the explorers were impatient to find the Shoshones. Each day they found new signs that the Shoshones were near, including many small, deserted camps among the hills. Sacagawea pointed out remains of willow shelters and trees that had been stripped of bark, explaining that the Shoshones used the soft underpart of the wood for food. One morning they saw smoke rising in the distance. They guessed that the Shoshones might have seen their party and set the prairie afire to warn other families that Blackfeet or Hidatsa warriors might be near.

In a green valley Sacagawea identified White Earth Creek, where her people used to gather earth for their paint. The Three Forks of the Missouri were near. For Sacagawea and for the Corps of Discovery, it was a time of hope. Soon they would set foot in the land of her people, the Land of the Shining Mountains.

Every day brought fresh signs that the Shoshones were near, creating new hope that contact could be made. Sacagawea rode in the river party with Lewis, while Captain Clark and a few others moved ahead by land, scouting for signs of the Shoshones. The Rocky Mountains crowded in close to the river like tall, rugged giants, and Captain Lewis was worried. They might be headed toward savage rapids or waterfalls. Could the river possibly run through these mountains without suddenly tossing their canoes into some wild, unexpected danger? Sacagawea assured him that the river would not suddenly change. There would be a strong and rapid flow, but no waterfalls that could wreck the canoes.

Misery followed them up the river. Shoulders ached from poling canoes between rocks. Cactus needles pierced their feet, and barbed seeds poked through their leggings. Each evening Sacagawea huddled close to the fire, protecting

Pompy from the mosquitoes and gnats that swarmed around his head. They slept under mosquito biers, gauzy netting stretched over wooden frames.

On the morning of July 27, the river route opened suddenly on a beautiful stretch of plains and meadows surrounded by distant high mountains. Sacagawea grew silent and her body became tense. Her eyes moved quickly from water to shore, and then off to the forest that covered the mountain slopes. Quietly she identified this as the place of the Hidatsa raid five summers before. She pointed to the rocky shoals in the middle of the river where she had been pulled up on the horse of the Hidatsa warrior. No word from her could possibly explain the mixture of feelings that almost overwhelmed her. No word from these white men could take away the painful memory of violence. No word from them could possibly add to the joy of her return.

Sacagawea's Journey

Meet the Author

Betty Westrom Skold's four-and-a-half year battle with tuberculosis made her childhood dream of becoming a teacher impossible. During her sickness, however, she spent a lot of time reading and writing. So, she became a writer on a small town newspaper instead.

Skold met an educational publisher who asked her to write a children's biography of Sacagawea. It became her first book as a professional writer. Today, Skold writes for a variety of age groups and tries new kinds of writing all the time. She has been a journalist, a poet, an essayist, a biographer, and a fiction writer.

Meet the Illustrator

Craig Spearing has a degree in illustration and printmaking. The first trade book he illustrated was *Prairie Dog Pioneers* by Jo and Josephine Harper. Since, he has created many illustrations for children's educational books and magazines.

His father was a geologist and his mother was a historian. He admires that his father was an eternal "Boy Scout" and his mother always valued careful research. He says that both his parents played an important part in shaping the way he does illustrations.

Theme Connections

Within the Selection

Record your answers to the questions below in the Response Journal section of your Writer's Notebook. In small groups, report the ideas you wrote. Discuss your ideas with the rest of your group. Then choose a person to report your group's answers to the class.

- What new frontier did the expedition of Meriwether Lewis and William Clark set out to explore? What was the primary goal for their expedition?
- What aspects of the journey were new for Sacagawea? What parts of the trip were not?
- In what ways were Sacagawea's leadership and resourcefulness necessary to Lewis and Clark and other members of their expedition?

Across Selections

- What role did cooperation play in the success of the Lewis and Clark expedition? How might the trip have been different without it?
- Compare "Sacagawea's Journey" to the selection "Parmele" in Unit 3. In what way was Sacagawea's trip similar to the summer visits the author of that selection made to Parmele?

Beyond the Selection

- Think about how "Sacagawea's Journey" adds to what you know about the American West.
- Add items to the Concept/Question Board about the American West.

Buffalo Hunter. c.1844. **Artist Unknown.**
Oil on canvas. Santa Barbara Museum of Art.

Focus Questions In what ways were the buffalo important to the Native Americans of the Great Plains? How did the building of the Transcontinental Railroad affect the buffalo?

Buffalo Hunt

from the book by Russell Freedman

A Gift from the Great Spirit

Over blazing campfires on winter nights, Indian storytellers spoke of the buffalo. They told tales of buffalo giants and buffalo ghosts, of buffalo that changed magically into men, of children who were raised by buffalo and understood their language.

In olden times, it was said, buffalo used to eat Indians. They ate so many Indians that a legendary figure called Old Man had to put a stop to it. He organized a race between the buffalo and the Indians to decide who should eat whom. The Indians won.

On the Great Plains of North America, every Indian tribe had a rich and ready store of buffalo tales and legends. According to the Comanche, buffalo came from gigantic caves somewhere on the windswept ranges of the Texas Panhandle. Each spring, the Great Spirit sent throngs of buffalo from those hidden caves onto the open plains, as a gift to the Indian people.

Up North, the Blackfoot said that a lake in Canada was the place where the buffalo began. They were born beneath the water, in the darkest depths of the lake. If you could visit that sacred spot on the right night, at exactly the right time, you would hear an eerie rumbling coming from the middle of the lake. Then you would see the buffalo rise out of the water and crowd onto the shore, their shaggy fur wet and dripping, their curved horns gleaming in the moonlight.

To the Plains Indians, the buffalo, or American bison, was the most important animal on Earth. This snorting, lumbering beast provided almost everything the Indians needed to stay alive. The buffalo kept their bellies full and their bodies warm. It supplied raw materials for their weapons, tools, ornaments, and toys. The rhythm of their daily lives was ruled by the comings and goings of the great buffalo herds.

It is little wonder that the Indians worshipped the buffalo as a sacred animal. Before and after every hunt, they praised the spirit of the buffalo and thanked him for giving his meat. Men, women, and children carried buffalo-shaped rocks and fossils for good luck. They believed in the powerful magic of buffalo dreams. When they died, they hoped to go to a happy hunting ground in the sky where buffalo flourished. Looking into the night sky, the Pawnee believed that the Milky Way was formed by dust left behind by the spirit-buffalo.

As recently as 150 years ago, countless millions of buffalo still roamed the prairies and plains. They ranged from the Mississippi River westward to the Rockies, and from Canada down to the Rio Grande. Native American hunters had been stalking the animals for many thousands of years. During most of that time, the Indians had neither horses nor guns. They hunted on foot, and they killed their prey with stone-tipped arrows and spears. They knew how to creep up on a grazing herd, how to surround the buffalo, and how to drive them into corrals or stampede them over cliffs.

Without horses, the Indians had to travel on foot whenever they moved their encampments. Back then, they used big shaggy dogs as pack animals to help carry their tipis and other belongings. Sometimes on a long journey the dogs would grow tired and begin to droop and lag and hang their tongues. Then someone would cry, "Buffalo ahead! Fresh meat in plenty!" And the dogs would bound forward as though they had just set out. Later, the Indians would remember that era as their Dog Days.

The first horses were brought to North America by Spanish explorers in the 1500s. Within a century or so, runaway horses had drifted northward from Spanish settlements in Mexico and were roaming the plains in wild herds. The Indians learned to capture and tame those wild horses, and the horses changed their lives.

Now they could travel long distances to find the buffalo. They could chase the herds and kill the choicest animals. And with pack horses, they could

Catching the Wild Horse. **George Catlin.** The Thomas Gilcrease Institute of American History and Art, Tulsa, Oklahoma.

carry bigger tipis and more possessions with them as they traveled across the plains. In time, the Indians became some of the world's finest horsemen, experts at hunting and fighting on horseback.

When white trappers and traders began to visit the Great Plains in the early 1800s, about 250,000 Indians were living in the region. They belonged to some two dozen distinct tribes, each with its own language and customs. Many of these tribes had migrated from the woodlands of the East, but only a few, like the Pawnee of Kansas and Nebraska, still practiced the old arts of farming and fishing.

Most of the Plains Indians had given up the settled life of farmers and fishermen to follow the buffalo herds. They spent the winter in sheltered camps. But in spring they folded their tipis and roamed the plains. They hunted other animals besides the buffalo, of course—deer, antelope, elk, and an occasional bear. But buffalo meat was their staple food, buffalo hunting their main occupation.

Painted elkskin robe.
Late 19th Century. Crow.
The National Museum of
the American Indian,
Smithsonian Institution.

A Plains tribe was made up of many small, independent bands. Once or twice a year, all the bands belonging to a tribe would assemble for a great religious ceremony, a tribal council, or a communal hunt. But mostly, the bands moved about on their own. Each band had its own encampments, or villages. And each band hunted in a different part of the tribal territory.

Hunting was a man's responsibility. Every able-bodied boy was taught that he should become a fearless hunter and warrior. Small boys ran about yip-yapping in play hunts, dreaming of the day when they would be big enough to ride after a herd of stampeding buffalo. A successful hunter could provide for many people. He became a man of influence, entitled to honors and privileges.

Women were responsible for putting the buffalo and other game to good use. It was a woman's job to skin and butcher the buffalo, to preserve the meat and tan the hides. As Indian girls grew up, they learned from their mothers and grandmothers the art of transforming a dead buffalo into a thousand practical and useful objects.

The buffalo was the biggest animal on the plains. A full-grown bull stood six feet tall at the humped shoulders and weighed a ton or more. An angry bull could stab a bear to death. He could toss a wolf so high into the air that the wolf would be killed by the fall.

While buffalo were somewhat dim-sighted, they could hear the faintest sounds and smell enemies from three miles away. And when they sensed danger, they moved fast. A bull or cow could wheel about on its slim hind legs and run as fast as a horse. When a whole herd stampeded, the earth trembled.

White explorers were astonished at the size of the herds they saw as they crossed the Great Plains. There were times when buffalo stretched endlessly across the countryside as far as the eye could see. Artist George Catlin described these herds when he traveled west during the 1830s to study and paint the Indians. "Buffalo graze in immense herds and almost incredible numbers," he wrote. "And they roam over vast tracts of country."

No one really knows how many buffalo roamed the prairies and plains before the white man came. The Indians thought there were enough buffalo to last forever. It seemed impossible that they could ever disappear.

The Hunt

On the day set for starting a hunt, everyone was up at sunrise. The women went right to work, packing their household belongings and getting everything ready for the move. Youngsters rounded up the horses and dogs. The men gathered in small groups to discuss the day's plans.

After a quick morning meal, the leaders of the hunt, the marshals, assembled. They took their feathered banners in their hands, mounted their horses, and gave the signal to break camp.

With that, the Indian village disappeared almost like a puff of smoke. Tipis dropped to the ground as the women removed the buffalo-skin walls and took down the long poles that held the tipis erect.

The poles were now put to a different use. Lashed to the sides of a horse so they trailed behind on the ground, the poles supported a sturdy rawhide platform called a travois (tra-VOY). This platform held the folded tipi walls and the family's household goods. Sometimes

Band of Sioux Moving Camp with Dogs and Horses. 1837–39. **George Catlin.** Oil on canvas. National Museum of American Art, Smithsonian Institution.

small children or sick people sat on top of the pile to be hauled along by a strong packhorse. Dogs also worked as pack animals, pulling travois designed to fit their size and strength.

When the horses and dogs were harnessed and loaded and ready to go, the people and their animals moved out across the plains. The warriors, mounted on the best hunting horses, rode along in front. They were followed by boys and girls driving the herd of extra horses. Behind them came the women leading the packhorses, along with the small children and the old folks, some riding, some walking, and some being carried on the travois. Every woman had a heavy pack on her back. The men never carried packs. They kept their arms free to use their weapons in case of a surprise attack.

Scouts rode far ahead of the marching people, and far to either side, watching for signs of buffalo or lurking enemies. Other warriors acted as a rear guard. They followed the group at a distance, seeing that no one lagged behind.

Strung out across the prairie, the Indians formed a grand procession. People sang as they marched along, dogs barked, horses whinnied, bells jingled. They moved forward each day by easy stages, so their horses would be in good condition when they found the buffalo.

At the end of a day's march, the marshals picked the spot where they would pitch camp. The women quickly put up the tipis and prepared the evening meal as the men gathered to chat and smoke. On the open plains, the Indians usually camped in a circle, with the doorway of each tipi facing east to catch the morning sun.

When they reached the territory where they expected to hunt, the scouts fanned out across the countryside, looking for buffalo. Everyone else waited in the hushed camp. Marshals moved quietly from one tipi to the next. They reminded people in low tones not to sing or shout or make any loud noise that might scare off the buffalo, which could hear weak and distant sounds.

The scouts, meanwhile, searched for buffalo signs. Sometimes they relied on animal helpers. The Comanche watched for ravens. They thought that if a raven circled four times overhead and cawed, it would then fly off toward the buffalo. A Cheyenne hunter would find a cricket, hold it in his hand, and wait to see which way its antennae pointed. The buffalo, he believed, would be found in that direction.

When a herd was sighted, the successful scout rushed back to camp. As he arrived, people crowded around, greeting him with congratulations and thanks. First he smoked a ceremonial pipe with one of the band's elders. Then he reported what he had seen.

The chase usually started the next morning. As soon as it was light enough to see, the hunters mounted their horses. Riding close together, they stayed downwind from the herd, so the buffalo would not catch their scent.

When they were as close as they could get without disturbing the buffalo, they paused and waited. The marshals looked over the area and selected the best spot to launch the attack. Silently, they led the hunters forward and spaced them evenly, so that each would have a fair start. Then one of the marshals rode out in view of both hunters and buffalo. He waved his hand above his head, and the chase began.

Bending low over their horses, the Indians galloped toward the grazing herd. At first the buffalo paid little attention. Often the hunters would almost reach the herd before the buffalo became alarmed and started to run.

Each man acted on his own now. Holding his bow in his left hand, urging his horse on with the whip strapped to his right wrist, a hunter picked his target and went after it at full speed. His horse was trained to approach the buffalo from the right, so the rider could shoot his arrow to the left, toward the animal. As he closed in, he aimed for a spot just behind the buffalo's last rib, where the arrow would pierce the animal's lungs. A single well-aimed arrow could kill the biggest buffalo.

Buffalo Chase with Bows and Lances. 1832–33. **George Catlin.** Oil on canvas. National Museum of American Art, Smithsonian Institution.

Sometimes an arrow would strike with such force that it would be completely buried. It might pass all the way through the animal, come out the other side, and drop to the ground. If an arrow failed to go deep enough, the hunter might reach over, pull it out of the buffalo, and use it again.

Once an arrow hit its mark, the hunter instantly took off after another buffalo. His horse understood exactly what to do. Running free, guided only by words or knee pressure, a trained hunting pony would leap away from a buffalo's horns as soon as it heard the twang of the bowstring.

Some men found the bow and arrow too tame. They preferred to use spears, for it took more strength and courage to spear a buffalo. To carry only a spear on the hunt was a mark of daring and pride.

With any weapon, the chase was risky. Horses stumbled in prairie-dog holes. Wounded buffalo lashed out with their horns. Sometimes an enraged bull crashed headlong into a horse and rider. The buffalo claimed many victims as hunters were trampled in the dust or died of broken bones.

While the chase was thrilling, it wasn't always the best way to hunt. During a typical chase on horseback, each hunter might bring down two or three buffalo. Under the right conditions, the Indians could get better results with less danger by hunting in the old way——on foot.

In that case, they would stake their horses and creep up on the buffalo, crawling on hands and knees through tall grass. As long as the Indians were hidden, the buffalo would go right on grazing, even as arrows flew silently around them. Each man might shoot several buffalo in quick succession before the others became frightened and ran off.

In winter, when the grass offered little cover, a hunter might sneak up on a herd disguised in a buffalo robe. Or he could drape himself in the skin of a white wolf. Healthy buffalo in herds did not fear wolves and didn't run when they saw one.

If a herd was small enough, the Indians sometimes surrounded the buffalo on foot. Approaching downwind, they fanned out, moved in from all sides, and formed a tight ring. Then they ran in circles around the herd, whooping and yelling and waving their arms as the terrified animals milled about in confusion. Slowly the Indians closed the circle until they were close enough to let go with their arrows and spears.

The first buffalo to be hit would fall near the outside of the circle, blocking the path of those inside the ring. As more buffalo fell, their bodies trapped the others. Sometimes not a single animal escaped alive.

On horseback, the Indians could surround bigger herds, galloping around them in a circle. One afternoon in 1832, the artist George Catlin, armed with his pencil and sketchbook, watched from a distance as 500 Sioux horseman surrounded a herd near the present site of Pierre, South Dakota. By sundown, the hunters had killed 1,400 buffalo.

The Buffalo Hunt No. 39. 1919.
Charles M. Russell.
Oil on canvas. Amon Carter Museum, Fort Worth, Texas.

The Silk Robe. c. 1890. **Charles M. Russell.** Oil on canvas. Amon Carter Museum, Fort Worth, Texas.

From the Brains to the Tail

A successful hunt called for a feast. Beside the campfire that evening, a medicine man offered prayers of thanksgiving. He thanked the spirits for their aid during the chase, and he thanked the buffalo for giving his meat to the people. Choice bits of meat were sliced off, held up for the spirits to see, then buried as an offering.

There was plenty for everyone to eat. A single fat buffalo cow supplied enough meat to feed a hundred hungry people. They gorged themselves on fresh tongue roasted over the open fire, on tasty morsels cut from the buffalo's hump. They ate hot, dripping ribs and steaks. And they feasted on yards of roasted gut, turned inside out, stuffed with chunks of meat, and seared over glowing coals. The sweet, nutritious bone marrow was saved for the old folks. It was the only meat their toothless gums could chew.

Most of the meat taken during a big hunt was preserved for the future. The women cut the meat into strips and hung it over high poles to dry. After several days, this sun-dried meat, called jerky, was so well preserved that it would last for months. It could be carried anywhere and would not spoil, even during the hottest months.

Some of the dried meat was pounded to a pulp, mixed with buffalo fat, and flavored with crushed nuts, berries, and fruit. This was called pemmican. Packed in buffalo-skin bags, pemmican would last for years without spoiling. Sliced and dipped in wild honey, it was nourishing and delicious, a favorite food among the Indians, and later the white fur traders as well.

Every part of the buffalo that could be chewed, swallowed, and digested was used for food. And every other part was put to some use.

Indian women spent a great deal of time and effort tanning buffalo hides. After a hunt, the fresh hides were spread out on the ground, hairy side down, and pegged in place. Using scrapers made of buffalo bone, the women scraped all the flesh, fat, and blood from the hides. They cured and bleached the hides in the sun, and soaked them in a tanning fluid of buffalo brains, liver, and fat mixed with water. Then they worked the hides for several days——rubbing, kneading, squeezing, stretching——to make them soft and supple. A good hunter might have several wives working on hides taken from the animals he had killed.

If the hides were to be used as winter robes, the hair was left in place. Thick-furred buffalo robes made warm and comfortable cloaks and bedding. They could be cut and stitched into caps, earmuffs, leggings, and mittens. The finest robes came from buffalo killed during the winter, when nature gave the animal a full coat to protect it from snow and cold.

With the hair scraped off, the hides were smoked over fires to make them waterproof. They could then be fashioned into dozens of useful articles. They were used for the walls of tipis, for clothing and moccasins, for pouches, purses, and saddlebags. Babies were carried in

Comanche Village in Texas, Women Dressing Robes and Drying Meat. 1834–35.
George Catlin. Oil on canvas. National Museum of Art, Smithsonian Institution.

cradleboards lined with the softest buffalo calfskin. The dead were laid to rest wrapped in buffalo-hide winding sheets.

Thick rawhide from the necks of old bulls was stretched to make tough war shields and the soles of winter moccasins. Strong sinews from the neck and back of the buffalo provided bowstrings and thread. The buffalo's hair was twisted into ropes and bridles, woven into ornaments, stuffed into leather balls. Its stomach became a water jug, its tail a flyswatter.

Buffalo horns were used for cups, ladles, and spoons, and to carry hot coals to the next campground. The hooves produced glue; the fat, soap. The bones were shaped into knives, spears, and tools of many kinds. On the northern plains, the backbone with ribs attached made a toboggan for children in winter.

Even the buffalo's droppings were valuable. On the treeless plains, firewood was scarce. But there was an endless supply of sundried buffalo dung left behind by the grazing herds. These prized "buffalo chips" burned slowly, produced a hot fire, and were ideal for cooking. They were used for that purpose by the Indians, and later by white settlers too.

A fall buffalo hunt would continue until the band had all the hides and meat it needed for the winter. Then the Indians would settle down in their winter camps. Every band had its favorite winter camping sites near woods, in a sheltered canyon, or along a river bottom. Instead of camping in a circle, as they did on the open plains, the Indians pitched their winter tipis in a line that sometimes stretched for miles along the canyon floor or the river's banks.

A tipi provided a warm and cozy winter home. Because it was shaped like a cone, it could withstand the most violent winds and blizzards. Its walls were waterproof. An open fire in the center of the tipi furnished heat, light, and a stove for indoor cooking. The smoke spiraled up through an adjustable smoke hole at the top of the tipi. At night, firelight would shine through the translucent buffalo-skin walls, and from the outside, the tipi glowed like a lantern.

Tipis were usually owned by the women who made them. A typical tipi measured perhaps fifteen feet across at the base, allowing sufficient living space for the family and its possessions. It could be put up in fifteen minutes by the women of the household. It could be taken down in five minutes. And it could be packed on a horse travois and carried anywhere.

When the hunting was good, the Indians went into winter camp with tons of sun-dried buffalo meat. They didn't have to hunt day after day, all winter long, for fear of starving. Between hunts, they were free to do as they wished. "It was a great life," said Tom Le Forge, a white man who lived several years with the Crows. "At all times I had ample leisure for lazy loafing and dreaming and visiting."

With the Buffalo Gone

Year after year without fail, the buffalo drifted back and forth across the plains in tune with the seasons. Usually they traveled in small bands. But during the late summer rutting season, they gathered in enormous herds that numbered hundreds of thousands of animals. A truly great herd might be fifty miles long and take days to pass by.

Buffalo Chase, A Single Death. 1832-33. **George Catlin.** National Museum of American Art, Smithsonian Institution, Washington, DC.

Indians had hunted the buffalo for thousands of years without making much of a dent in the herds. Sometimes they killed more animals than they could use. When they drove a herd over a cliff, they could not always carry away all the meat. But for the most part, the Indians were not wasteful. They hunted when they needed meat and hides.

As white people came to the plains, the buffalo herds began to dwindle. By the early 1800s, trading posts were springing up all over the West. White traders wanted buffalo robes and tongues for profitable markets in the East. In exchange, they offered guns, tools, tobacco, whiskey, and trinkets. The Indians had always hunted for their own needs. Now, by killing a few more buffalo, they could obtain the white man's goods.

Soon the Indians were killing buffalo for their hides and tongues alone. Tongues packed in salt were shipped in barges down the Missouri River, to be sent to the cities of the East, where they were sold as an expensive delicacy. Buffalo robes became fashionable as lap robes and blankets. White people had them made into fur coats. During the 1830s and 1840s, hundreds of thousands of robes were shipped east.

By then, white hunters were beginning to kill more buffalo than the Indians. Pioneers traveling westward in covered wagons shot the animals for food along the way, scaring off entire herds. Before long, few buffalo could be found along the great trails leading west. Then the United States Army hired professional hunters to supply buffalo meat to western military posts. And as railroads were built across the prairies and plains, white hunters furnished buffalo meat for the railroad construction crews.

The Herd on the Move. 1862.
William J. Hays.
Toned lithograph.
Amon Carter
Museum, Fort
Worth, Texas.

Buffalo hunting became a popular sport. Many travelers felt that a trip west wasn't complete unless they had shot themselves a buffalo. American millionaires and European noblemen toured the West in style, with servants to hand them their guns and champagne to drink after the hunt. Railroads began to feature special excursion trains through buffalo country. As the trains chugged along, passengers could poke their guns through the open windows and fire away at the grazing herds.

By the 1860s, Indian tribes found that the buffalo were disappearing from their traditional hunting grounds. When they went elsewhere to hunt, they were followed almost immediately by white hunters, soldiers, and settlers. "Wherever the whites are established, the buffalo is gone," complained the Sioux Chief White Cloud, "and the red hunters must die of hunger."

Indians who once had been friendly to white people vowed to go on the warpath. Alarmed by the large-scale slaughter of their herds, angry warriors from many tribes banded together. They began to attack wagon trains, ranch houses, and railroad construction crews.

There were still about eight million buffalo left on the plains in 1870, when a newly invented tanning process sealed the fate of the remaining herds. For the first time, commercial tanneries in the East could turn buffalo hides into expensive leather. A single hide now brought as much as $3—more than a factory worker earned in a week in those days. A professional hide hunter could bag as many as two hundred buffalo in one day.

Organized bands of hide hunters shot their way south from Kansas to Texas. Armed with powerful long-range rifles with telescopic sights, they began to slaughter buffalo at the rate of a million a year. As the animals fell, gangs of skinners stripped them of their valuable hides and left the carcasses to rot on the prairie.

Indian war parties attacked the hide hunters wherever they found them, but the hunters could not be stopped. Within a few years, the Indians saw their main source of food, clothing, and shelter vanish.

At one time, perhaps sixty or seventy million buffalo had roamed the plains. By the early 1880s, the endless herds had been wiped out. Only a few hundred wild buffalo were still hiding out in remote mountain valleys.

With the buffalo gone, the proud and independent Plains Indians became a conquered people. Their way of life was destroyed, their hunting grounds taken over by white ranchers and settlers. Swept by starvation and disease, the great hunting tribes were confined to reservations, where they depended on government food rations. Their children were sent to boarding schools to learn the language and customs of the white man.

The days of the buffalo hunters had faded like a dream. But Indian storytellers still gather on winter nights to keep the old tales alive. They speak of a time when buffalo ruled the plains, and Indian warriors rode out to meet them.

> I go to kill the buffalo.
> The Great Spirit sent the buffalo.
> On hills, in plains and woods.
> So give me my bow; give me my bow;
> I go to kill the buffalo.
>
> ——SIOUX SONG

Buffalo Hunt

Meet the Author

Russell Freedman seemed destined to be a writer. He grew up in a home frequently visited by authors. He later became a reporter and stumbled across a story about a sixteen-year-old boy who invented the braille typewriter. The story inspired his first book, *Teenagers Who Made History*.

Mr. Freedman travels widely to do the research for his books. When he is not writing, he enjoys attending films, concerts, and plays.

Meet the Illustrators

George Catlin made a series of journeys into unmapped Native American territory, visiting most of the major tribes from the Upper Missouri River to the Mexican Territory in the far Southwest. He wandered alone from tribe to tribe, fearlessly entering their villages, where he was greeted with courtesy and friendship. From these visits, he created hundreds of paintings and drawings, giving most of the outside world its first glimpse at Native American life.

Charles M. Russell visited the Montana Territory when he was sixteen and soon made that part of the country his home. He worked as a hunter and as a cowboy, while painting and sculpting in his spare time. He later became a full-time artist, famous for his paintings and sculptures of cowboy life.

Theme Connections

Within the Selection

Record your answers to the questions below in the Response Journal section of your Writer's Notebook. In small groups, report the ideas you wrote. Discuss your ideas with the rest of your group. Then choose a person to report your group's answers to the class.

- In what ways were the lives of Plains Indians dependent upon the buffalo?
- How did conflicts over resources destroy the buffalo and the traditional way of life for Plains Indians?
- How did life change for Plains Indians after the destruction of the great buffalo herds?

Across Selections

- In what way is the Pawnee story about the origin of the Milky Way similar to the ancient Greek and Indian stories in "The Heavenly Zoo"?
- Native Americans and the government disagreed about the right of the government to force a way of life on others. What does this issue have in common with the disputes that led to the American Revolution?

Beyond the Selection

- How do you think conflicts over land should be handled today? If a valuable resource, such as a plant that cures a disease, is found on land owned by others, should the government have the right to claim that land? Why or why not?
- Think about how "Buffalo Hunt" adds to what you know about The American West.
- Add items to the Concept/Question Board about the American West.

The Whole World Is Coming

a Sioux Indian poem
illustrated by Stella Ormai

The whole world is coming,
A nation is coming, a nation is coming,
the eagle has brought the message to the tribe.
Over the whole earth they are coming;
the buffalo are coming, the buffalo are coming,
the crow has brought the message to the tribe.

428

The Flower-Fed Buffaloes

Vachel Lindsay
illustrated by Stella Ormai

The flower-fed buffaloes of the spring
In the days of long ago,
Ranged where the locomotives sing
And the prairie flowers lie low:
The tossing, blooming, perfumed grass
Is swept away by the wheat,
Wheels and wheels and wheels spin by
In the spring that still is sweet.
But the flower-fed buffaloes of the spring
Left us, long ago.
They gore no more, they bellow no more,
They trundle around the hills no more:
With the Blackfeet, lying low,
With the Pawnees, lying low,
Lying low.

The Journal of Wong Ming-Chung

Laurence Yep
illustrated by Karen Jerome

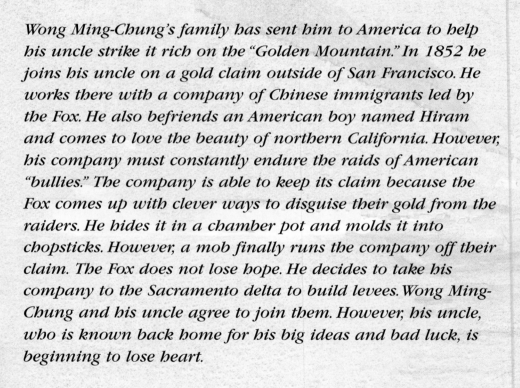

Wong Ming-Chung's family has sent him to America to help his uncle strike it rich on the "Golden Mountain." In 1852 he joins his uncle on a gold claim outside of San Francisco. He works there with a company of Chinese immigrants led by the Fox. He also befriends an American boy named Hiram and comes to love the beauty of northern California. However, his company must constantly endure the raids of American "bullies." The company is able to keep its claim because the Fox comes up with clever ways to disguise their gold from the raiders. He hides it in a chamber pot and molds it into chopsticks. However, a mob finally runs the company off their claim. The Fox does not lose hope. He decides to take his company to the Sacramento delta to build levees. Wong Ming-Chung and his uncle agree to join them. However, his uncle, who is known back home for his big ideas and bad luck, is beginning to lose heart.

April 23

We followed the river all day without seeing anyone else.

It's like the end of the world. The only signs that humans had been here were the rotting rockers and ruined shacks.

We've camped for the night on an abandoned claim. The shack's roof is gone. A broken rocker sits beside the bank. Holes dot the banks. It looks like a battlefield.

430

The bank juts out like a finger, forming a breakwater. The river forms a lazy eddy behind it, which the Fox said would be a good spot for gold to drop out.

It's a good thing we've stopped, too. My feet are so sore that I soaked them in the river. For once, I'm grateful the water is icy cold.

Uncle sat like a lump beside me. He said he didn't see how we'd ever get really rich piling up dirt for levees. It's like we're in prison and every day we have to do hard work.

I reminded him of what the Fox said—that we'll still be sending home something. It might be less but it will still be a lot by Chinese standards. But Uncle just kept staring at the river.

The cook fixed a quick meal. Since we can eat only what we could carry away, everything's rationed. The meals are small—about what they'd be back in China.

But we're alive. That's the important thing.

April 24

I can hardly write these words. Uncle's left me.

This morning he told the Fox that he was going to stay and prospect. He bought his own ticket here, so he was free to leave like any employee. The Fox didn't need a carpenter anymore.

The Fox thought he'd lost his senses. After all, we'd just gotten chased off our claim by a mob. Uncle might not survive the next mob.

Uncle said he would search around here for a new claim. The Fox had said it was safe enough.

The Fox tapped his nose and said, "That's because there's no gold, or this would have told me."

Uncle has plans for home. He can't carry them out piling up dirt.

The Fox shook his head but suggested that I go with him.

I was scared at the idea of staying in the gold country. However, I thought of Uncle left alone in the mountains with his bad luck. He wouldn't last a week.

So I said I was going to help Uncle.

Uncle tried to use his authority as the head of the family and tell me to go with the Fox.

I refused.

Uncle said I was useless to him. He didn't want me hanging around his neck anymore like a stone.

I started to cry. Even if Father and Mother didn't need me, I had been sure Uncle did.

Uncle kept saying a lot of hurtful things. I tried to remind him that he had been glad when I came.

He insisted that had been a lie and said I was nothing but a burden on him.

The Fox came over and put his hands on my shoulders. As we walked away, he told the cook to leave some supplies and a few tools with Uncle.

The others made their farewells to Uncle, but I stood by the path ready to go. When we left Uncle, I didn't even look back.

We've made camp for our noon meal. However, I've had no appetite. I have to talk to someone, even if it's only my diary.

How could Uncle say those things? How?

Evening

I am writing this quickly by moonlight. I tossed and turned for hours. I can't let Uncle die in the mountains. Even if he doesn't love me, he is still family.

Everyone is asleep. I'm going to leave a note for the Fox and then sneak away and find Uncle.

April 25

About an hour after midnight last night, I reached the shack where we had left Uncle.

Uncle was sitting by the river. His shoulders were silvery in the moonlight.

I hesitated, expecting him to say more hurtful things. However, I'd had time to rehearse a speech. So I told him I'd try my best not to be a burden.

Uncle came rushing toward me before I could finish. He gave me a big hug. He told me he hadn't meant what he said.

I asked him why he had said it then.

Uncle thought I would be safer with the Fox. Those hurtful words were maybe the hardest things he'd ever had to say.

I'm not ashamed to say that we both wept. When we finished, we decided to look for gold in the morning.

434

To change our luck, I spun on my heel and recited, "Spin around, turn around, luck changes."

With a chuckle, Uncle copied me.

When we entered the shack to go to sleep, I had to laugh. There isn't any roof. We might just as well sleep outside.

However, the shack does have a fireplace. After we had gathered branches, I got a good fire roaring in the fireplace. Then we lay down in our blankets.

As I stared at the flickering flames, I thought of Mother. I used to squat by the front of the stove feeding the fire while she cooked. She used to like to hum, and the flames seemed to dance to her tune.

When will I see her again?

Later

Just had the worst nightmare. The mob was chasing me. I tried to run, but there was mud all around. I kept slipping and sliding and the mob kept gaining.

I must not have slept for very long, though, because the fire is just now dying. There are little dots of light all over the dirt floor of the cabin. They look like the torches the mob carried.

We're safe. We're safe. For now.

Still later

I'm trembling so badly I can barely write these words.

As I stared at the glittering floor, my curiosity got the better of my fear. What was reflecting the light?

So I crawled out of my blanket and crept across the floor with my nose almost touching the dirt.

I smelled gold. After spending all that time drying it and weighing it with the Fox, I know its smell by now.

That's it. Drying it!

The owner of the claim probably got the gold from the river. That means he had to dry it at night just as the Fox did with his gold.

There is gold dust scattered all around us.

I've got to wake Uncle and tell him.

Night

When I first told Uncle my theory, he didn't get excited.

Instead, he said it was an interesting idea, but why didn't the owner pick up the gold?

I said that maybe the light had to be just right from the fireplace.

Uncle looked thoughtful. He admitted that he hadn't noticed it when he first came in here. And it had still been day then.

I tried another explanation. The Fox had said this area had been worked in the early months of the gold rush. There was still plenty of easy gold then.

Uncle eagerly agreed. He said that maybe the owner thought the floor wasn't worth the time.

I said that the owner had probably thought there would be nuggets just waiting to be picked upriver.

"Maybe even big as melons," Uncle had to laugh.

His boast in the village seems so long ago now.

We'll wait until sunrise. One of the walls should give us the lumber to build a rocker. Then we'll know.

I don't know how much sleep I'll get, though.

April 26

It took half the day to build the rocker. Then Uncle dug up a shovelful of soil by the fireplace. Carefully he carried it over to the rocker. I used my hat to pour water in.

Gently we began to make the rocker sway. Water ran through the holes at the bottom.

Then we held our breaths as the water poured out.

Uncle got discouraged right away when he didn't see anything.

I leaned my head this way and that, studying the wooden cleats from all angles. "Wait," I said. There was a faint gleam of light.

I ran my fingertips along the edge and held it up. Bits of gold clung to it.

April 27
Evening

We're rich!

It took only one and a half days to get a small pouch of gold! Uncle says we'll make our melon-sized nuggets the hard way, one flake at a time.

April 29

We went into town to buy supplies and tools like pails and things, but we were careful not to bring too much gold with us. Uncle let me do the talking since I've learned more American than he has.

The Americans laughed at us when we registered our claim. Then they told us there is no gold up there.

Uncle was curious when I insisted on buying a big chamber pot but he gave in.

Later, when I told him what the Fox used his chamber pot for, Uncle had a good chuckle.

May 4

We've cleaned out the cabin floor.

Uncle says our method of mining is worth more than the gold itself. We have to protect it.

I agree, so we've filled in the holes and smoothed over the dirt floor with branches. When we were finished, it looked just as we had first seen it.

Now it's on to the next abandoned claim.

May 24

We stop only at abandoned claims where there was likely to have been gold at one time. Uncle and I have picked up a lot from the Fox and his nose for gold. We look for spots where the river widens and the water slows, or behind breakwaters like our first claim. Sometimes we look inside the bends of the river or in the pool of slow water that forms just before the rapids.

So far we've tried ten more abandoned claims on this side of the river. Not every miner was careless, but two more have paid off. One of them was the richest of all.

Every time we file a new claim in town, they laugh at us some more. We're just the crazy Chinese to them.

We just smile.

While we work, I tell Uncle about some of the investment schemes I heard from my friends and some of the miners' letters. Uncle agrees with me that a store might be a good idea sometime in the future.

Uncle says that maybe once we have the store, we'll bring some of our cousins over from China.

May 26

We're going to take our gold into Sacramento. It's time to bank it.

May 27
En route to Sacramento

It's so strange to be riding a wagon back to Sacramento. The wagon's going directly there, so the trip is much shorter than when I first went into the gold fields.

Our gold is in a basket that I'm sitting on. No one looks twice at two dirty, raggedy guests. And we muddied up our basket to look just as run-down as us.

The hills are green from the winter rains. In the dells where the water gathers, flowers are blooming. I think you could grow anything here.

Hiram's right. It's the soil here that's the real gold in America. Once the metal's gone, it's gone. The earth will keep bringing up new crops each year.

I wonder what happened to Hiram and his dream of a farm?

May 31
Sacramento

I am writing this while the clerk in the American bank finishes weighing and recording our deposits.

When we arrived on the wagon in Sacramento, I saw that it was all new. About a month after I came through here, a terrible fire burned down everything.

When we opened our basket in the American bank, the bank clerk was very curious. He kept wanting to know if we had made a big strike. On the way down here, though, Uncle and I had already decided to just smile and say as little as possible.

Once we get our bank draft, we'll go over to Chinatown to the headquarters of our district back in China.

Then we can send some of the money in the American bank back to China. I wish I could hear the clan when our money gets there. They'll say Uncle must have luck as big as a mountain.

The Journal of Wong Ming-Chung

Meet the Author

Laurence Yep was born in San Francisco, California. His Chinese-American family lived in an African-American section of the city, so he had to commute to a bilingual school in Chinatown. Yep says he never encountered white culture in America until high school, and always felt like an outsider. Growing up, he found few books that dealt with being a Chinese-American. Because of this, he uses his own writing to fight racial stereotypes. He likes to write about this feeling of being an outsider and believes this is the reason he is so popular with young adult readers.

Meet the Illustrator

Karen Jerome teaches drawing and painting to children when she is not illustrating books. *"We draw from photographs, famous painters' artwork, stuffed animals, horse statues, mirrors and much more. That's how I learned to improve my skills as an artist, and that's how my students are improving theirs."* Karen also likes to fish, ski, play tennis, take photographs, paint landscapes, and write children's stories.

Theme Connections

Within the Selection

Record your answers to the questions below in the Response Journal section of your Writer's Notebook. In small groups, report the ideas you wrote. Discuss your ideas with the rest of your group. Then choose a person to report your group's answers to the class.

- Why did Uncle and Wong Ming-Chung care about finding gold? What did they hope to do with the money?
- What dangers and struggles did gold miners of the time face? How did Uncle and Wong Ming-Chung protect themselves and their gold?
- Why are some people willing to leave their families, friends, and homes to move to a new place?

Across Selections

- Compare the gold miners' view of the land to the white traders' view of the buffalo.
- How does a sense of family responsibility tie this story to "Juggling" in Unit 1?

Beyond the Selection

- Have you ever left something you cared about for the possibility of future rewards? What did you leave? What did you gain? What did you learn along the way?
- Think about how "The Journal of Wong Ming-Chung" adds to what you know about the American West.
- Add items to the Concept/Question Board about the American West.

Buckskin Ghost Dance Arapaho Dress.
Buckskin. Courtesy of the National
Museum of the American Indian.
Smithsonian Institution.

***Among the Sierra
Nevada in California.***
1868. **Albert Bierstadt.**
Oil on canvas.
183 × 305 cm. National
Museum of American Art,
Smithsonian Institution,
Washington, DC.

Advice on the Prairie. **William T. Ranney.** Oil on canvas.
14 × 20 in. From the Collection of Gilcrease Museum, Tulsa.

Vaqueros in a Horse Corral. 1877. **James Walker.** Oil on canvas.
24 × 40 in. From the Collection of Gilcrease Museum, Tulsa.

Focus Questions What are the characteristics of the
Navaho settlement in this story? How do the soldiers force
the Navaho to leave the canyon?

The Coming of the Long Knives

from *Sing Down the Moon*
by Scott O'Dell
illustrated by Den Schofield

*The year is 1864. Bright Morning, a fourteen-year-old
Navaho girl, lives with her family in what is now Arizona. Bright
Morning, her family, and her friend Tall Boy, who was crippled
saving Bright Morning from Spanish slave traders, have no idea that
an encounter with the United States soldiers they call the Long
Knives will change their lives forever.*

The pinto beans pushed up through the earth and the
peaches began to swell. Wool from the shearing was stored
away for the winter weaving. My father and brother went
into the mountains and brought back deer meat which we cut
into strips and dried. It was a good summer and a good autumn.

Then early one winter morning three Long Knives came. They
were from the white man's fort and they brought a message from
their chief. When all of our people were gathered in the meadow
one of the soldiers read the message, using Navaho words. He
read fast and did not speak clearly, but this is what I remember.

> People of the Navaho Tribe are commanded
> to take their goods and leave Canyon de Chelly.

The Long Knife read more from the paper which I do not
remember. Then he fastened the paper to a tree where all in the
village could see it and the three soldiers rode away.

There was silence after the soldiers left. Everyone was too
stunned to speak or move. We had been threatened before by the
Long Knives, but we lived at peace in our canyon, so why should
they wish to harm us?

446

Everyone stared at the yellow paper fastened to the cottonwood tree, as if it were alive and had some evil power. Then, after a long time, Tall Boy walked to the tree. Grasping the paper, he tore it into many pieces and threw them into the river. We watched the pieces float away, thinking as they disappeared that so had the threat of the white men. But we were wrong. At night, in the dark of the moon, the Long Knives came.

The morning of that day we knew they were coming. Little Beaver, who was tending his mother's sheep, saw them from the high mesa. He left his flock and ran across the mesa and down the trail, never stopping.

He fell in front of his mother's hogan and lay there like a stone until someone threw a gourd of water in his face. By that time all the people in the village stood waiting for him to speak. He jumped to his feet and pointed into the south.

"The white men come," he cried. "The sun glints on their knives. They are near."

447

"How many?" Tall Boy said.

"Many," cried Little Beaver, "too many."

My father said, "We will take our goods and go into the high country. We will return when they are gone."

"We will go," said the other men.

But Tall Boy held up his hand and shouted, facing the elder Indians, "If we flee they will follow. If we flee, our goods will remain to be captured. It is better to stay and fight the Long Knives."

"It is not wise to fight," my father said.

"No, it is not," my uncle said, and all the older men repeated what he said.

It was decided then that we should go. But Tall Boy still would not yield. He called to five of the young men to join him in the fight. They went and stood by him.

"We will need you," my father said to the six young men. "We will have to go into high country. Your strength will help us there."

Tall Boy was unbending. My father looked at him, at his arm held helplessly at his side.

"How is it, Tall Boy, that you will fight?" he said. "You cannot string a bow or send a lance. Tell me, I am listening."

I watched Tall Boy's face darken.

"If you stay and cannot fight, what will happen?" my father asked him. "You will be killed. Others will be killed."

Tall Boy said nothing. It hurt me to watch his face as he listened to words that he knew were true. I left them talking and went down to the river. When I came back Tall Boy had gathered his band of warriors and gone.

We began to pack at once. Each family took what it could carry. There were five horses in the village and they were driven up the mesa trail and left there. The sheep and goats were driven a league away into a secret canyon where they could graze. My flock, my thirty sheep, went too, with the rest. I would have gone with them if I had not thought that in a few days the Long Knives would leave and we could come back to our village. I would never have abandoned them.

When the sun was high we filed out of the village and followed the river north, walking through the shallow water. At dusk we reached the trail that led upward to the south mesa. Before we went up the trail the jars were filled with water. We took enough to last us for a week and five sheep to slaughter. The cornmeal we carried would last that long. By that time the soldiers would be gone.

The soldiers could not follow our path from the village because the flowing water covered our footsteps as fast as they were made. But when we moved out of the river our steps showed clear in the sand. After we were all on the trail some of the men broke branches from a tree and went back and swept away the marks we had left. There was no sign for the soldiers to see. They could not tell whether we had gone up the river or down.

The trail was narrow and steep. It was mostly slabs of stone which we scrambled over, lifting ourselves from one to the other. We crawled as much as we walked. In places the sheep had to be carried and two of them slipped and fell into a ravine. The trail upward was less than half a mile long, but night was falling before we reached the end.

We made camp on the rim of the mesa, among rocks and stunted piñon trees. We did not think that the soldiers would come until morning, but we lighted no fires and ate a cold supper of corncakes. The moon rose and in a short time shone down into the canyon. It showed the river winding toward the south, past our peach orchards and corrals and hogans. Where the tall cliffs ended, where the river wound out of the canyon into the flatlands, the moon shone on white tents and tethered horses.

"The soldiers have come," my uncle said. "They will not look for us until morning. Lie down and sleep."

We made our beds among the rocks but few of us slept. At dawn we did not light fires, for fear the soldiers would see the rising smoke, and ate a cold breakfast. My father ordered everyone to gather stones and pile them where the trail entered the mesa. He posted a guard of young men at the trail head to use the stones if the soldiers came to attack us. He then sent three of the fastest runners to keep watch on the army below.

I was one of the three sent. We crawled south along the rim of the mesa and hid among the rocks, within sight of each other. From where I crouched behind a piñon tree, I had a clear view of the soldiers' camp.

As the sun rose and shone down into the narrow canyon I could see the Long Knives watering their horses. They were so far below me that the horses seemed no larger than dogs. Soon afterward six of the soldiers rode northward. They were riding along the banks of the river in search of our tracks. Once they got off their horses and two of them climbed up to Rainbow Cave where cliff dwellers had lived long ago. But they found the houses deserted.

The soldiers went up the river, past the trail that led to the place where we were hidden. They did not return until the sun was low. As they rode slowly along, they scanned the cliff that soared above them, their eyes sweeping the rocks and trees, but they did not halt. They rode down the river to their tents and unsaddled the horses. We watched until they lighted their supper fires, then we went back to our camp.

Tall Boy was sitting on a rock near the top of the trail, at work on a lance. He held the shaft between his knees, using his teeth and a hand to wrap it with a split reed.

I was surprised to see him sitting there, for he and the other young warriors had ridden out of the canyon on the morning the Long Knives came. No one had heard from them since that day. Even his mother and father and sisters, who were hiding with us on the mesa, did not know where he was. At first I thought that he had changed his mind and come back to help protect them. But this was not the reason for his return.

Mumbling something that I could not understand, he went on with his work. I stood above him and as I looked down I noticed a deep scratch across his forehead and that a loop of his braided hair had pulled loose.

"Did you hurt yourself climbing the trail?" I said.

He knotted the reed around the shaft and bit the ends off with his teeth. His right arm hung useless at his side.

"The climb is not difficult," he said.

It was a very difficult climb, but I did not say so, since he wanted me to think otherwise. "Where are the warriors?" I asked him. "Are they coming to help us?"

"They have left the canyon," he said.

"But you did not go," I said, noticing now that he had lost one of his moccasins.

For an instant he glanced up at me. In his eyes I saw a look of shame, or was it anger? I saw that the young warriors had left him behind with the women and old men and children. He was no longer of any use to them.

He held up the lance and sighted along the shaft. "It has an iron point," he said. "I found it in the west country."

"It will be a mighty weapon against the Long Knives," I said.

"It is a weapon that does not require two hands."

"One hand or the other," I said, "it does not matter."

That night we ate another cold supper, yet everyone was in good spirits. The white soldiers had searched the canyon and found no trace of us. We felt secure. We felt that in the morning they would ride away, leaving us in peace.

In the morning guards were set again at the head of the trail. Running Bird and I crawled to our places near the piñon tree and crouched there as the sun rose and shone down on the camp of the Long Knives. Other lookouts hid themselves along the rim of the mesa, among the rocks and brush.

Nothing had changed in the night. There were the same number of tents among the trees and the same number of horses tethered on the riverbank. Our hogans were deserted. No smoke rose from the ovens or the fire pits. There was no sound of sheep bells.

The camp of the Long Knives was quiet until the sun was halfway up the morning sky. Men strolled about as if they had nothing to do. Two were even fishing in the river with long willow poles. Then——while Running Bird and I watched a squirrel in the piñon tree, trying to coax him down with a nut——I saw from the corner of an eye a puff of smoke rise slowly from our village. It seemed no larger than my hand. A second puff rose in the windless air and a third.

"Our homes are burning!"

The word came from the lookout who was far out on the mesa rim, closest to the village. It was passed from one lookout to the other, at last to me, and I ran with it back to our camp and told the news to my father.

"We will build new homes," he said. "When the Long Knives leave we will go into the forest and cut timber. We will build hogans that are better than those the soldiers burned."

"Yes," people said when they heard the news, "we will build a new village."

Tall Boy said nothing. He sat working on his lance, using his teeth and one hand, and did not look up.

I went back to the piñon and my father went with me. All our homes had burned to the ground. Only gray ashes and a mound of earth marked the place where each had stood. The Long Knives were sitting under a tree eating, and their horses cropped the meadow grass.

My father said, "They will ride away now that they have destroyed our village."

But they did not ride away. While we watched, ten soldiers with hatchets went into our peach orchard, which still held its summer leaves. Their blades glinted in the sunlight. Their voices drifted up to us where we were huddled among the rocks.

Swinging the hatchets as they sang, the soldiers began to cut the limbs from the peach trees. The blows echoed through the canyon. They did not stop until every branch lay on the ground and only bare stumps, which looked like a line of scarecrows, were left.

Then, at the last, the Long Knives stripped all the bark from the stumps, so that we would not have this to eat when we were starving.

"Now they will go," my father said, "and leave us in peace."

But the soldiers laid their axes aside. They spurred their horses into a gallop and rode through the cornfield, trampling the green corn. Then they rode through the field of ripening beans and the melon patch, until the fields were no longer green but the color of the red earth.

"We will plant more melons and corn and beans," my father said.

"There are no seeds left," I said. "And if we had seeds and planted them they would not bear before next summer."

We watched while the soldiers rode back to their camp. We waited for them to fold their tents and leave. All that day and the next we watched from the rim of the mesa. On the third day the soldiers cut alder poles and made a large lean-to, which they roofed over with the branches. They also dug a fire pit and started to build an oven of mud and stones.

It was then we knew that the Long Knives did not plan to leave the canyon.

"They have learned that we are camped here," my father said. "They do not want to climb the cliff and attack us. It is easier to wait there by the river until we starve."

Clouds blew up next morning and it began to rain. We cut brush and limbs from the piñon pines and made shelters. That night, after the rain stopped, we went to the far side of the mesa where our fires could not be seen by the soldiers and cooked supper. Though there was little danger that the soldiers would attack us, my father set guards to watch the trail.

We were very careful with our jars of water, but on the sixth day the jars were empty. That night my father sent three of us down the trail to fill the jars at the river. We left soon after dark. There was no moon to see by so we were a long time getting to the river. When we started back up the trail we covered our tracks as carefully as we could. But the next day the soldiers found that we had been there. After that there were always two soldiers at the bottom of the trail, at night and during the day.

The water we carried back lasted longer than the first. When the jars were nearly empty it rained hard for two days and we caught water in our blankets and stored it. We also discovered a deep stone crevice filled with rainwater, enough for the rest of the summer. But the food we had brought with us, though we ate only half as much as we did when we were home in the village, ran low. We ate all of the corn and slaughtered the sheep we had brought. Then we ground up the sheep bones and made a broth, which was hard to swallow. We lived on this for two days and when it was gone we had nothing to eat.

Old Bear, who had been sick since we came to the mesa, died on the third day. And that night the baby of Shining Tree died. The next night was the first night of the full moon. It was then that my father said that we must leave.

Dawn was breaking high over the mesa when we reached the bottom of the trail. There was no sign of the soldiers.

My father led us northward through the trees, away from our old village and the soldiers' camp. It would have been wiser if we had traveled in the riverbed, but there were many who were so weak they could not walk against the current.

455

As soon as it grew light we found patches of wild berries
among the trees and ate them while we walked. The berries
were ripe and sweet and gave us strength. We walked until
the sun was overhead. Then, because four of the women could
go no farther, we stopped and rested in a cave.

We gathered more berries and some roots and stayed there
until the moon came up. Then we started off again, following
the river northward, traveling by the moon's white glow. When
it swung westward and left the canyon in darkness we lay
down among the trees. We had gone no more than two leagues
in a day and part of a night, but we were hopeful that the
soldiers would not follow us.

456

In the morning we built a small fire and roasted a basket of roots. Afterward the men held council to decide whether to go on or to stay where we were camped.

"They have burned our homes," my father said. "They have cut down the trees of our orchard. They have trampled our gardens into the earth. What else can the soldiers do to us that they have not already done?"

"The Long Knives can drive us out of the canyon," my uncle said, "and leave us to walk the wilderness."

At last it was decided that we stay.

We set about the cutting of brush and poles to make shelters. About mid-morning, while we were still working on the lean-tos, the sound of hoofs striking stone came from the direction of the river.

Taking up his lance, Tall Boy stepped behind a tree. The rest of us stood in silence. Even the children were silent. We were like animals who hear the hunter approach but from terror cannot flee.

The Long Knives came out of the trees in single file. They were joking among themselves and at first did not see us. The leader was a young man with a red cloth knotted around his neck. He was looking back, talking to someone, as he came near the place where Tall Boy stood hidden.

Tall Boy stepped from behind the tree, squarely in his path. Still the leader did not see him.

Raising the lance, Tall Boy quickly took aim and drew back, ready to send it toward the leader of the Long Knives. He had

practiced with the lance before we came down the mesa, time after time during all of one day, trying to get used to throwing it with his left hand. With his right hand he had been the best of all the warriors. It was with a lance that he had killed the brown bear beyond Rainbow Mountain, a feat of great skill.

But now, as the iron-tipped weapon sped from his grasp, it did not fly straight. It wobbled and then curved upward, struck the branch of a tree, and fell broken at the feet of the soldier's horse.

The horse suddenly stopped, tossing its head. Only then did the soldier turn to see the broken lance lying in front of him. He looked around, searching for the enemy who had thrown it. He looked at my father, at my uncle, at me. His eyes swept the small open space where we stood, the women, the children, the old people, all of us still too frightened to move or speak.

Tall Boy, as soon as he had thrown the lance, dodged behind the tree where he had hidden before, backed away into the brush and quietly disappeared. I saw his face as he went past me. He no longer looked like a warrior. He looked like a boy, crushed and beaten, who flees for his life.

The rest of the Long Knives rode up and surrounded us. They searched us one by one, making certain that no one carried a weapon, then they headed us down the canyon.

We passed the ruined fields of beans and corn and melons, the peach trees stripped of their bark and branches, our burned-out homes. We turned our eyes away from them and set our faces. Our tears were unshed.

Soon we were to learn that others bore the same fate, that the whole nation of the Navahos was on the march. With the Long Knives at their backs, the clans were moving——the Bitter-Water, Under-His-Cover, Red-House, Trail-to-the-Garden, Standing-House, Red-Forehead, Poles-Strung-Out——all the Navahos were marching into captivity.

The Coming of the Long Knives

Meet the Author

Scott O'Dell was born in Los Angeles. At that time, California was still frontier country. *"That is why,"* he told one interviewer, *"I suppose, the feel of the frontier and the sound of the sea are in my books."*

O'Dell was a cameraman on the original motion picture of *Ben Hur,* carrying the first Technicolor camera. It wasn't until after serving in the Air Force during WWII that he became involved with books. He was an editor and an author of books for adult readers before finding his true calling, writing for children. He once said, *"Writing for children is more fun than writing for adults and more rewarding."* He believed in children's special ability to live through the people they read about in stories.

Meet the Illustrator

Den Schofield was always reading as a child and the artwork in the stories captured his attention. His parents encouraged his interest in drawing and history. He pursued a degree in illustration but immediately joined the military after college. Mr. Schofield finally started working for the publishing industry after being released from active duty. He now makes an effort to obtain work relating to his favorite subjects: history, the outdoors, and western or adventure themes.

Theme Connections

Within the Selection

Record your answers to the questions below in the Response Journal section of your Writer's Notebook. In small groups, report the ideas you wrote. Discuss your ideas with the rest of your group. Then choose a person to report your group's answers to the class.

- Why do you think the soldiers were told to move the Navaho from their homes in Canyon de Chelly?
- How do you think the soldiers felt about having to force the Native Americans from their homes?
- Again and again Bright Morning's father predicted that the Long Knives would leave the Navaho village and return to their fort. Why was it so surprising to him that the Long Knives did not leave?

Across Selections

- Compare what happened to the Navaho with what happened to the Plains Indians in "Buffalo Hunt." Discuss the similarities and differences in the ways that Native Americans were forced to change their ways of life.

Beyond the Selection

- Think about how "The Coming of the Long Knives" adds to what you know about the American West.
- Add items to the Concept/Question Board about the American West.

Focus Questions What kinds of animals does Arliss encounter on the frontier? How does he get himself into trouble with the bear? Who will rescue Arliss?

Old Yeller & the Bear

from **Old Yeller**
by Fred Gipson
illustrated by Jennifer Heyd Wharton

Fourteen-year-old Travis lives with his family in Texas during the 1860s. Travis feels responsible for his mother and brother while his father is away on a long cattle drive. Travis thinks the big yellow dog that adopts his family is a useless nuisance until a bear shows him how wrong he is.

That Little Arliss! If he wasn't a mess! From the time he'd grown up big enough to get out of the cabin, he'd made a practice of trying to catch and keep every living thing that ran, flew, jumped, or crawled.

Every night before Mama let him go to bed, she'd make Arliss empty his pockets of whatever he'd captured during the day. Generally, it would be a tangled-up mess of grasshoppers and worms and praying bugs and little rusty tree lizards. One time he brought in a horned toad that got so mad he swelled out round and flat as a Mexican tortilla and bled at the eyes. Sometimes it was stuff like a young bird that had fallen out of its nest before it could fly, or a green-speckled spring frog or a striped water snake. And once he turned out of his pocket a wadded-up baby copperhead that nearly threw Mama into spasms. We never did figure out why the snake hadn't bitten him, but Mama took no more chances on snakes. She switched Arliss hard for catching that snake. Then she made me spend better than a week, taking him out and teaching him to throw rocks and kill snakes.

That was all right with Little Arliss. If Mama wanted him to kill his snakes first, he'd kill them. But that still didn't keep him from sticking them in his pockets along with everything else he'd captured that day. The snakes might be stinking by the time Mama called on him to empty his pockets, but they'd be dead.

Then, after the yeller dog came, Little Arliss started catching even bigger game. Like cottontail rabbits and chaparral birds and a baby possum that sulled and lay like dead for the first several hours until he finally decided that Arliss wasn't going to hurt him.

Of course, it was Old Yeller that was doing the catching. He'd run the game down and turn it over to Little Arliss. Then Little Arliss could come in and tell Mama a big fib about how he caught it himself.

I watched them one day when they caught a blue catfish out of Birdsong Creek. The fish had fed out into water so shallow that his top fin was sticking out. About the time I saw it, Old Yeller and Little Arliss did, too. They made a run at it. The fish went scooting away toward deeper water, only Yeller was too fast for him. He pounced on the fish and shut his big mouth down over it and went romping to the bank, where he dropped it down on the grass and let it flop. And here came Little Arliss to fall on it like I guess he'd been doing everything else. The minute he got his hands on it, the fish finned him and he went to crying.

But he wouldn't turn the fish loose. He just grabbed it up and went running and squawling toward the house, where he gave the fish to Mama. His hands were all bloody by then, where the fish had finned him. They swelled up and got mighty sore; not even a mesquite thorn hurts as bad as a sharp fish fin when it's run deep into your hand.

But as soon as Mama had wrapped his hands in a poultice of mashed-up prickly-pear root to draw out the poison, Little Arliss forgot all about his hurt. And that night when we ate the fish for supper, he told the biggest windy I ever heard about how he'd dived 'way down into a deep hole under the rocks and dragged that fish out and nearly got drowned before he could swim to the bank with it.

But when I tried to tell Mama what really happened, she wouldn't let me. "Now, this is Arliss's story," she said. "You let him tell it the way he wants to."

I told Mama then, I said: "Mama, that old yeller dog is going to make the biggest liar in Texas out of Little Arliss."

But Mama just laughed at me, like she always laughed at Little Arliss's big windies after she'd gotten off where he couldn't hear her. She said for me to let Little Arliss alone. She said that if he ever told a bigger whopper than the ones I used to tell, she had yet to hear it.

Well, I hushed then. If Mama wanted Little Arliss to grow up to be the biggest liar in Texas, I guessed it wasn't any of my business.

All of which, I figure, is what led up to Little Arliss's catching the bear.

I think Mama had let him tell so many big yarns about his catching live game that he'd begun to believe them himself.

When it happened, I was down the creek a ways, splitting rails to fix up the yard fence where the bulls had torn it down. I'd been down there since dinner, working in a stand of tall slim post oaks. I'd chop down a tree, trim off the branches as far up as I wanted, then cut away the rest of the top. After that I'd start splitting the log.

I'd split the log by driving steel wedges into the wood. I'd start at the big end and hammer in a wedge with the back side of my axe. This would start a little split running lengthways of the log. Then I'd take a second wedge and drive it into this split. This would split the log further along and, at the same time, loosen the first wedge. I'd then knock the first wedge loose and move it up in front of the second one.

Driving one wedge ahead of the other like that, I could finally split a log in two halves. Then I'd go to work on the halves, splitting them apart. That way, from each log, I'd come out with four rails.

Swinging that chopping axe was sure hard work. The sweat poured off me. My back muscles ached. The axe got so heavy I could hardly swing it. My breath got harder and harder to breathe.

An hour before sundown, I was worn down to a nub. It seemed like I couldn't hit another lick. Papa could have lasted till past sundown, but I didn't see how I could. I shouldered my axe and started toward the cabin, trying to think up some excuse to tell Mama to keep her from knowing I was played clear out.

That's when I heard Little Arliss scream.

Well, Little Arliss was a screamer by nature. He'd scream when he was happy and scream when he was mad and a lot of times he'd scream just to hear himself make a noise. Generally, we paid no more mind to his screaming than we did to the gobble of a wild turkey.

But this time was different. The second I heard his screaming, I felt my heart flop clear over. This time I knew Little Arliss was in real trouble.

I tore out up the trail leading toward the cabin. A minute before, I'd been so tired out with my rail splitting that I couldn't have struck a trot. But now I raced through the tall trees in that creek bottom, covering ground like a scared wolf.

Little Arliss's second scream, when it came, was louder and shriller and more frantic-sounding than the first. Mixed with it was a whimpering crying sound that I knew didn't come from him. It was a sound I'd heard before and seemed like I ought to know what it was, but right then I couldn't place it.

Then, from way off to one side came a sound that I would have recognized anywhere. It was the coughing roar of a charging bear. I'd just heard it once in my life. That was the time Mama had shot and wounded a hog-killing bear and Papa had had to finish it off with a knife to keep it from getting her.

My heart went to pushing up into my throat, nearly choking off my wind. I strained for every lick of speed I could get out of my running legs. I didn't know what sort of fix Little Arliss had got himself into, but I knew that it had to do with a mad bear, which was enough.

The way the late sun slanted through the trees had the trail all cross-banded with streaks of bright light and dark shade. I ran through these bright and dark patches so fast that the changing light nearly blinded me. Then suddenly, I raced out into the open where I could see ahead. And what I saw sent a chill clear through to the marrow of my bones.

There was Little Arliss, down in that spring hole again. He was lying half in and half out of the water, holding onto the hind leg of a little black bear cub no bigger than a small coon. The bear cub was out on the bank, whimpering and crying and clawing the rocks with all three of his other feet, trying to pull away. But Little Arliss was holding on for all he was worth, scared now and screaming his head off. Too scared to let go.

How the bear cub ever came to prowl close enough for Little Arliss to grab him, I don't know. And why he didn't turn on him and bite loose, I couldn't figure out, either. Unless he was like Little Arliss, too scared to think.

468

But all of that didn't matter now. What mattered was the bear cub's mama. She'd heard the cries of her baby and was coming to save him. She was coming so fast that she had the brush popping and breaking as she crashed through and over it. I could see her black heavy figure piling off down the slant on the far side of Birdsong Creek. She was roaring mad and ready to kill.

And worst of all, I could see that I'd never get there in time!

Mama couldn't either. She'd heard Arliss, too, and here she came from the cabin, running down the slant toward the spring, screaming at Arliss, telling him to turn the bear cub loose. But Little Arliss wouldn't do it. All he'd do was hang with that hind leg and let out one shrill shriek after another as fast as he could suck in a breath.

Now the she bear was charging across the shallows in the creek. She was knocking sheets of water high in the bright sun, charging with her fur up and her long teeth bared, filling the canyon with that awful coughing roar. And no matter how fast Mama ran or how fast I ran, the she bear was going to get there first!

I think I nearly went blind then, picturing what was going to happen to Little Arliss. I know that I opened my mouth to scream and not any sound came out.

Then, just as the bear went lunging up the creek bank toward Little Arliss and her cub, a flash of yellow came streaking out of the brush.

It was that big yeller dog. He was roaring like a
mad bull. He wasn't one-third as big and heavy as the
she bear, but when he piled into her from one side, he
rolled her clear off her feet. They went down in a wild,
roaring tangle of twisting bodies and scrambling feet
and slashing fangs.

As I raced past them, I saw the bear lunge up to
stand on her hind feet like a man while she clawed
at the body of the yeller dog hanging to her throat.
I didn't wait to see more. Without ever checking my
stride, I ran in and jerked Little Arliss loose from the
cub. I grabbed him by the wrist and yanked him up
out of that water and slung him toward Mama like he
was a half-empty sack of corn. I screamed at Mama.
"Grab him, Mama! Grab him and run!" Then I swung
my chopping axe high and wheeled, aiming to cave in
the she bear's head with the first lick.

But I never did strike. I didn't need to. Old Yeller
hadn't let the bear get close enough. He couldn't handle
her; she was too big and strong for that. She'd stand
there on her hind feet, hunched over, and take a roaring
swing at him with one of those big front claws. She'd
slap him head over heels. She'd knock him so far that
it didn't look like he could possibly get back there before
she charged again, but he always did. He'd hit the
ground rolling, yelling his head off with the pain of the
blow; but somehow he'd always roll to his feet. And here
he'd come again, ready to tie into her for another round.

I stood there with my axe raised, watching them for a long moment. Then from up toward the house, I heard Mama calling: "Come away from there, Travis. Hurry, son! Run!"

That spooked me. Up till then, I'd been ready to tie into that bear myself. Now, suddenly, I was scared out of my wits again. I ran toward the cabin.

But like it was, Old Yeller nearly beat me there. I didn't see it, of course; but Mama said that the minute Old Yeller saw we were all in the clear and out of danger, he threw the fight to that she bear and lit out for the house. The bear chased him for a little piece, but at the rate Old Yeller was leaving her behind, Mama said it looked like the bear was backing up.

But if the big yeller dog was scared or hurt in any way when he came dashing into the house, he didn't show it. He sure didn't show it like we all did. Little Arliss had hushed his screaming, but he was trembling all over and clinging to Mama like he'd never let her go. And Mama was sitting in the middle of the floor, holding him up close and crying like she'd never stop. And me, I was close to crying, myself.

Old Yeller, though, all he did was come bounding in to jump on us and lick us in the face and bark so loud that there, inside the cabin, the noise nearly made us deaf.

The way he acted, you might have thought that bear fight hadn't been anything more than a rowdy romp that we'd all taken part in for the fun of it.

Old Yeller & the Bear

Meet the Author

Fred Gipson wrote adventure novels for children and adults. These stories usually featured animals. His first big success was *Hound-Dog Man*, which was later made into a film. He is best known, however, for *Old Yeller* and its sequel, *Savage Sam*, both of which were produced as movies.

A lover of animals, Mr. Gipson raised cattle and hogs on his own farm. He enjoyed fly fishing and hunting deer, wild turkey, quail, and doves. Of his work he said, *"I've always liked true adventure tales and have always felt I learned more history of my country from these tales than I ever did from history books."*

Meet the Illustrator

Jennifer Heyd Wharton's illustrations are often seen in children's books, newspapers, and magazines. She uses her skillful blending of hue and light to capture and share the joyful moments that weave the fabric of our lives. Ms. Wharton says, *"I use my art to sing what my voice cannot. And the song I strive to share is that of praise for the wonder and joy of life always present in the harmony of shapes and colors that surround us."* She currently operates her own studio in Annapolis, Maryland.

Theme Connections

Within the Selection

Record your answers to the questions below in the Response Journal section of your Writer's Notebook. In small groups, report the ideas you wrote. Discuss your ideas with the rest of your group. Then choose a person to report your group's answers to the class.

- What responsibilities did women and children have when men were away on cattle drives?
- What dangers and struggles were part of life on the Texas frontier? How did the settlers handle these challenges?
- Why did the Texas settlers choose to stay in a land where they faced attacks by ferocious animals?

Across Selections

- Compare "Old Yeller and the Bear" with "Buffalo Hunt." What role did animals play in the lives of both Texas settlers and Native Americans?
- What do Mama in "Old Yeller and the Bear" and Sacagawea have in common?

Beyond the Selection

- How would you feel about a life like Travis's in frontier Texas? What parts of frontier life sound fun or rewarding? What parts would be more difficult for you?
- Think about how "Old Yeller and the Bear" adds to what you know about the American West.
- Add items to the Concept/Question Board about the American West.

Bill Pickett
Rodeo-Ridin' Cowboy

Andrea D. Pinkney

illustrated by Brian Pinkney

Folks been tellin' the tale
since way back when.

*They been talkin' 'bout
that Pickett boy.*

Growed up to be a rodeo-ridin' man.

*His story keeps spreadin' on
like swollen waters in the wide Red River.*

*Yeah, folks been tellin' the tale
since way back when.*

*And they'll keep on tellin' it
till time's time ends.*

—A.D.P.

Long before Bill Pickett was born, a wagon train traveled west, all the way from South Carolina. It was 1854. Eager Americans were packing up their belongings and wheeling on to the Great Plains. Some of these pioneers were white folks, looking for a new life in a new land. The rest were black——enslaved people forced to follow their masters.

The men, women, and children loaded everything they owned into those covered wagons: croaker-sacks, homespun duds, and bedclothes bundled tight. To pass the time on the slow, steady trek, the southerners sang traveling songs:

Westward ho, where the gettin's good.
On to the land of opportunity.
Westward ho, gonna stake my claim.
On to Texas, the Lone Star State.

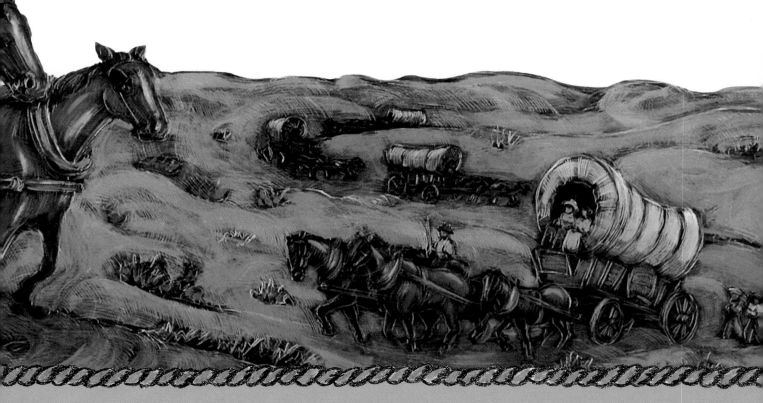

During this long journey a baby boy was born. His name was Thomas Jefferson Pickett. He was a free-spirited young'un. But he wasn't free. Born into slavery, he had to wake when his master said *wake*, work when his master said *work*, sleep when his master said *sleep*.

On the Texas plains Thomas grew up learning to brand cattle and swing a lariat. He and his family worked for the white folks, helping them tame the parched soil into prospering feed crops.

Then the Civil War ravaged the United States. And when the war ended, all enslaved people were declared free——as free as the bluebonnet blossoms that covered the Texas prairie.

Thomas married a woman named Mary Virginia Elizabeth Gilbert. They settled with other freed slaves at Jenks-Branch, a small community just north of Austin, Texas. Heaven blessed Thomas and Mary with thirteen children.

Their second-born child was Willie M. Pickett, but folks called him Bill. A young'un who took after his father, Bill was the feistiest boy south of Abilene. He was quick as a jackrabbit, more wide-eyed than a hooty owl——and curious.

Bill's parents now owned a small plot of land, where they raised chickens and pigs and grew sweet corn, tomatoes, and collards. They sold the vegetables and fruits in town to earn their living.

Bill's brothers and sisters helped tend the crops. But Bill was always wandering off. Most days he straddled the rickety corral gate to watch cattle drives tramp along the Chisholm Trail, a gritty stretch of road that snaked from the Rio Grande to the heart of Kansas.

Bill watched as the cowboys drove thousands of ornery longhorn steers past his parents' farm to stockyards in Kansas. Each trail crew had a trail boss, a cook, and a slew of cowboys. Bill always offered them a friendly "How do?" Some cowboys tipped their hats to signal hello. But they hardly ever stopped. And behind them they left hoof-beaten dirt and the smell of adventure.

In the evenings, after the last batch of corn pone had been eaten, Bill and his family would gather round the stove fire for a night of story swapping.

Bill had two cousins, Anderson Pickett and Jerry Barton, who were trail-driving horsemen. When they came to visit, they bragged about roping steer, breaking ponies, and protecting their trail crews against buffalo stampedes. Bill and his family loved to learn their campfire songs about nights on the trail, when Anderson and Jerry slept under the black western sky with nobody watching them but the stars.

All these songs and stories sparked Bill's imagination. They made him more up-jumpy than ever. He would lie in his bed and dream of the day when he'd be old enough to rope mossback cattle and help stray dogies keep up with the herd.

One afternoon Bill was straddling the gate as usual when he spotted an eye-popping sight. A bulldog was holding a restless cow's lower lip with its fangs. Bill moved closer to get a good look at how the dog's bite kept the squirming cow down. Soon Bill got to wondering: *If a small bulldog can bite-hold a big-lipped cow, why can't I do the same?*

Days later, on his way to school, Bill passed a band of cowboys from the Littlefield Cattle Company. The men were having a hard time branding their calves.

"Want some help?" Bill called to them. The cowboys looked at this brazen boy and went back to their work.

"I can hold one of them calves by the lip with my teeth, just like a bulldog," Bill went on. "I can do it sure as my name's Bill Pickett."

The cowboys turned out a rip-roarin' laugh.

But one of them put forth a challenge: "Let the boy go 'head and try it, if he dares."

The men roped the calf and threw it to the ground. Bill put his face down and sunk his teeth into the animal's lip. Then Bill held the calf firm while the cowboys pressed a hot branding iron into its side.

"Bulldoggin'——done by a young'un!" The cowboys cheered. Invented there and then by feisty Bill Pickett, that was bulldogging, bite-'em style.

When he was no more than fifteen and still itching for adventure, Bill set out to find his own way. Like many young'uns who came from large families, Bill had to go out and earn a living to help make ends meet.

Bill found work as a cowhand on ranches all over Texas. He spent long days saddling horses and mucking out their stalls. During the winter it was Bill's job to watch for wolves that crept up to the henhouses.

Bill learned to lasso and ride like the cowboys he'd seen pass by on the Chisholm Trail. He practiced bulldogging by catching steers that charged off into the mesquite brush. Soon Bill could tame broncs better than almost any other ranch hand. And every now and then, when work was slow, Bill went home to his mama and daddy's farm. Each time he had a new story of his own to tell his family.

Word of Bill's fearless riding spread from ranch to ranch. On Sundays folks gathered at local barnyards to watch Bill snatch a fire-eyed steer by the horns. Men, women, and young'uns rode on horseback and in their buggies to admire Bill's skill. They dropped coins in his hat to show how much they liked his horsemanship.

One morning, while he was working at a ranch in Taylor, Texas, Bill heard that the Williamson County Livestock Association had brought a fair to town. The fair included a full-scale rodeo. Men from the association had parked their wagons on a hill a few miles south of Taylor. Their rodeo was going to be a big event. Bill was determined to compete.

For the first time Bill performed his bulldogging stunt before a large rodeo crowd. As the steer thundered into the arena, Bill jumped from the back of his horse and grabbed it by the horns. Then, before the beast knew what was coming, Bill dug his teeth into the animal's tender upper lip. He raised his hands in victory as the grizzly critter went down without a fight.

Somebody let out a holler. *"Hooeee! Hooeee-hi-ooooh!"* All the folks watching the rodeo clapped and stomped.

"He threw that beast but good!"

"That cowboy's brave clear down to his gizzards!"

"Hot-diggity-dewlap!"

After that Bill bulldogged at rodeos throughout the West. When he wasn't bulldogging for show, he still worked on ranches to make ends meet. But stories about Bill's rodeo ridin' kept on keeping on——from Texas to Arkansas to Oklahoma to Kansas to Colorado and on up through the hills of Wyoming. Now everybody wanted to see Bill perform his special bulldogging feat.

Two years later, in 1890, Bill married Maggie Turner. Bill and Maggie made Taylor, Texas, their home, and together they birthed two boys and seven girls. Sometimes Maggie and the young'uns came to watch Bill perform when he bulldogged at rodeos near their small farm. They cheered the loudest of all.

Finally Bill decided to trade ranch work for rodeo. At first it wasn't easy. He had to leave Maggie and his children for weeks at a time. And some rodeos turned Bill away. Many rodeo owners believed black cowboys should ride with their own kind.

But the newspapers didn't seem to care if Bill was black or white——Bill's *bulldogging* was news! The *Wyoming Tribune* and the *Denver Post* printed stories about the wild-riding South Texas brushpopper who could tackle a steer with his bare hands, and his bite. Slowly Bill began to earn his living as a bulldogger.

Whenever Bill came home after time on the road, he would sit his family down and let loose his tales of the rodeo. He told Maggie and their children how, everywhere he went, folks called him the Dusky Demon on account of the dusty dirt cloud that billowed behind him whenever he performed his fearless riding. All his young'uns listened close, the same way their daddy had done to his cousins' stories when he was a boy.

In 1905, when Bill was performing in the Texas Fort Worth Fat Stock Show, he was taken by surprise. After the rodeo a fine-talkin' man named Zack Miller approached Bill and shook his hand.

Zack Miller and his brothers, Joe and George, owned one of the biggest ranches in the West. Their 101 Ranch spread over three towns——White Eagle, Red Rock, and Bliss——in Oklahoma. The Miller brothers also owned a traveling Wild West show, a spectacle greater than the small-time rodeos where Bill usually performed. The 101 Ranch Wild West Show had ninety cowboys and cowgirls, three hundred animals, and sixteen acts.

The Millers' show was famous. But to make it the best, they had to have a cowboy who could draw crowds and keep folks yip-yapping for more. The Millers had heard about Bill Pickett. After seeing Bill perform that day, Zack knew Bill was just the cowboy they needed. He asked Bill to join the 101 Ranch Wild West Show. He even told Bill that Maggie and their children would be welcome to live at the 101 Ranch while Bill traveled.

Bill didn't have to think twice. Zack's offer was the best he'd ever got. It wasn't long before Bill and his show horse, Spradley, became the 101's star attraction.

Soon Bill began to take his bulldogging to the far corners of the world. Crowds stood up and cheered when Bill bulldogged at Madison Square Garden in New York City.

In Mexico City townspeople filled the stands at El Toro, the national building, to watch the Dusky Demon face a fighting bull that was meaner than ten bulls in one.

Bill bulldogged in Canada and in South America, too. And in 1914 he performed in England for King George V and Queen Mary!

Bill's bulldog act helped turn the 101 Ranch Wild West Show into a high-falutin' wonder. Even more important, Bill helped make rodeo one of the best-loved sports of his time.

After years of bulldogging with the 101 show, Bill decided to give traveling a rest. He wanted to spend more time with Maggie and their children. So he returned to the 101 Ranch, where he lived and worked as a cowhand. To keep his skills strong, he bulldogged in rodeos closer to home.

Bulldogging lived on long after Bill died in 1932. But nobody could snatch a steer the way Bill did. When Bill's children were grown, they gathered up their own young'uns and told them about their grandfather, Bill Pickett——the feisty cowboy-child from south of Abilene who grew up to be the Dusky Demon.

More About Black Cowboys

America's history is rich with heroes. Cowboys——the men who tamed the Wild West during the late 1800s——are perhaps the most celebrated of all American legends. Nearly thirty-five thousand cowboys drove cattle when the Old West was in its prime. About one in four of these pioneers was African American.

While many enslaved black people migrated west with their masters before the Civil War, others came after the war ended in 1865 to take advantage of the work opportunities they hoped would come with their newly gained freedom. With their families these courageous people sometimes built self-sufficient, all-black towns. They became cavalrymen, trail bosses, barbers, trappers, nurses, state legislators——and cowboys.

When black men and women arrived on the western plains, they brought with them their own tradition of working with livestock and tending the land. Under the lash of slavery they had cultivated the skills of branding cattle and rounding up and taming horses. They'd worked long hours in plantation fields and had made an art of growing crops from seed to stalk under the harshest conditions.

Their knowledge——along with the care and dignity with which they performed their work——was well suited to the needs of the growing cattle business in the western states from 1865 to the turn of the century.

When the Civil War ransacked the nation, many Texans went off to fight, leaving their ranches to ruin. After the war, longhorn steers wandered wild throughout Texas, while in the northern and eastern states a demand for beef grew. During the Reconstruction period, some Texans saw a business opportunity to turn the Southwest into what came to be called the Cattle Kingdom. To make this empire grow, these businessmen needed strong, capable cowboys to work on their ranches. Black cowboys were willing and eager to take on the challenge.

In the Cattle Kingdom, skill, not skin color, was the primary concern. Along with white cowboys African Americans drove longhorn cattle for hundreds of miles to railroad cars stationed in Abilene, Kansas. Once the steers reached the Kansas railroad, they were shipped to stockyards in Chicago, Illinois, and Kansas City, Missouri.

Cowboys paid tribute to their workaday world by competing in rodeos. Rodeos began as small contests among cowboys to see who could rope and ride the best. By 1870 rodeo competitions were common and popular throughout the Southwest. They eventually became large spectator events that charged admission and paid cash prizes to participants.

Today seven standard contest events make up a rodeo: saddle bronc riding, bareback riding, bull riding, calf roping, team roping, barrel racing, and steer wrestling, which is also called bulldogging.

Bill Pickett's one-of-a-kind bulldogging established steer wrestling as a rodeo event. Today's "doggers" don't sink their teeth into a steer's lip like Bill did in his heyday. But they do try——with all the might and muscle they can muster——to wrestle the snorting beast to the dirt.

In 1971 Bill Pickett became the first African American inducted into the National Cowboy Hall of Fame and Western Heritage Center in Oklahoma City, Oklahoma. A bronze statue that depicts Bill bulldogging was unveiled in 1987 at the Fort Worth Cowtown Coliseum in Fort Worth, Texas. Today folks still praise Bill as Zack Miller, owner of the 101 Ranch, once did: "Bill Pickett was the greatest sweat-and-dirt cowhand that ever lived——bar none."

——Andrea Davis Pinkney

Bill Pickett
Rodeo-Ridin' Cowboy

Meet the Author and Illustrator

Andrea and Brian Pinkney are the husband-and-wife team that worked together to publish "Bill Pickett: Rodeo-Ridin' Cowboy." Andrea did the writing and Brian did the illustrating. Andrea has a degree in journalism. She has been a novelist, a picture-book writer, and the author of articles for *The New York Times* and *Highlights for Children.*

Brian always wanted to be an illustrator because his father, Jerry Pinkney, is a children's book illustrator, and his mother, Gloria Jean Pinkney, is a children's book writer. He earned two degrees in art, and today he works on books both with his wife and on his own. He has taught at the Children's Art Carnival in Harlem and at the School of Visual Arts.

Andrea and Brian Pinkney have worked together on other books including *Alvin Ailey* and *Duke Ellington: The Piano Prince and His Orchestra.*

Theme Connections

Within the Selection

Record your answers to the questions below in the Response Journal section of your Writer's Notebook. In small groups, report the ideas you wrote. Discuss your ideas with the rest of your group. Then choose a person to report your group's answers to the class.

- What were some of the reasons that African-Americans moved west to Texas?
- The height of the cowboy period lasted only 20 years. Why do you think so many books and movies have been created about such a brief period of time?
- What personality traits helped Bill become a successful rodeo star?

Across Selections

- Compare this story with "Old Yeller and the Bear." What characteristics does young Bill Pickett share with Little Arliss?
- What role does storytelling play in the lives of the characters in this story? How does this relate to the stories about heritage that you read in Unit 3?

Beyond the Selection

- Think about how "Bill Pickett: Rodeo-Ridin' Cowboy" adds to what you know about the American West.
- Add items to the Concept/Question Board about the American West.

McBroom the Rainmaker

Sid Fleischman
illustrated by Bill Ogden

I dislike to tell you this, but some folks have no regard for
the truth. A stranger claims he was riding a mule past our
wonderful one-acre farm and was attacked by woodpeckers.

Well, there's no truth to that. No, indeed! Those weren't
woodpeckers. They were common prairie mosquitoes.

Small ones.

Why, skeeters grow so large out here that everybody uses
chicken wire for mosquito netting. But I'm not going to say
an unkind word about those zing-zanging, hot-tempered,
needle-nosed creatures. They rescued our farm from ruin.
That was during the Big Drought we had last year.

Dry? Merciful powers! Our young'uns found some tadpoles
and had to teach them to swim. It hadn't rained in so long
those tadpoles had never seen water.

That's the sworn truth——certain as my name's Josh
McBroom. Why, I'd as soon grab a skunk by the tail as tell
a falsehood.

Now, I'd best creep up on the Big Drought the way it
crept up on us. I remember we did our spring plowing, as
usual, and the skeeters hatched out, as usual. The
bloodsucking rapscallions could be mighty pesky, but we'd
learned to distract them.

"Will*jill*hester*chester*peter*polly*tim*tom*mary*larry*and-
little*clarinda!*" I called out. "I hear the whine of gallinippers.
We'd better put in a patch of beets."

496

Once the beets were up, the thirsty skeeters stuck in their long beaks like straws. Didn't they feast though! They drained out the red juice, the beets turned white, and we harvested them as turnips.

The first sign of a dry spell was when our clocks began running slow. I don't mean the store-bought kind——no one can predict the weather with a tin timepiece. We grew our own clocks on the farm.

Vegetable clocks.

Now, I'll admit that may be hard to believe, but not if you understand the remarkable nature of our topsoil. Rich? Glory be! Anything would grow in it——lickety-bang. Three or four crops a day until the confounded Big Dry came along.

Of course, we didn't grow clocks with gears and springs and a name on the dial. Came close once, though. I dropped my dollar pocket watch one day, and before I could find it, the thing had put down roots and grown into a three-dollar alarm clock. But it never kept accurate time after that.

It was our young'uns who discovered they could tell time by vegetable. They planted a cucumber seed, and once the vine leaped out of the ground, it traveled along steady as a clock.

"An inch a second," Will said. "Kind of like a second hand."

"Blossoms come out on the minute," Jill said. "Kind of like a minute hand."

They tried other vegetable timepieces, but pole beans had a way of running a mite fast and squash a mite slow.

As I say, those homegrown clocks began running down. I remember my dear wife, Melissa, was boiling three-and-a-half-minute eggs for breakfast. Little Clarinda planted a cucumber seed, and before it grew three blossoms and thirty inches, those eggs were hard-boiled.

"Mercy!" I declared. "Topsoil must be drying out."

Well, the days turned drier and drier. No doubt about it—— our wonderful topsoil was losing some of its get-up-and-go. Why, it took almost a whole day to raise a crop of corn. The young'uns had planted a plum tree, but all it would grow was prunes. Dogs would fight over a dry bone——for the moisture in it.

"Will*jill*hester*chester*peter*polly*tim*tom*mary*larry*and-little*clarinda!*" I called. "Keep your eyes peeled for rain."

They took turns in the tree house scanning the skies, and one night Chester said, "Pa, what if it doesn't rain by Fourth of July? How'll we shoot off firecrackers?"

MILK

"Be patient, my lambs," I said. We used to grow our own firecrackers, too. Don't let me forget to tell you about it. "Why, it's a long spell to Fourth of July."

My, wasn't the next morning a scorcher! The sun came out so hot that our hens laid fried eggs. But no, that wasn't the Big Dry. The young'uns planted watermelons to cool off and beets to keep the mosquitoes away.

"Look!" Polly exclaimed, pointing to the watermelons. "Pa, they're rising off the ground!"

Rising? They began to float in the air like balloons! We could hardly believe our eyes. And gracious me! When we cut those melons open, it turned out they were full of hot air.

Well, I was getting a mite worried myself. Our beets were growing smaller and smaller, and the skeeters were growing larger and larger. Many a time, before dawn, a rapping at the windows would wake us out of a sound sleep. It was those confounded, needle-nosed gallinippers pecking away, demanding breakfast.

Then it came——the Big Dry.

Mercy! Our cow began giving powdered milk. We pumped away on our water pump, but all it brought up was dry steam. The oldest boys went fishing and caught six dried catfish.

"Not a rain cloud in sight, Pa," Mary called from the tree house.

"Watch out for gallinippers!" Larry shouted, as a mosquito made a dive at him. The earth was so parched, we couldn't raise a crop of beets and the varmints were getting downright ornery. Then, as I stood there, I felt my shoes getting tighter and tighter.

"Thunderation!" I exclaimed. "Our topsoil's so dry it's gone in reverse. It's *shrinking* things."

Didn't I lay awake most of the night! Our wonderful one-acre farm might shrink to a square foot. And all night long the skeeters rattled the windows and hammered at the door. Big? The *smallest* ones must have weighed three pounds. In the moonlight I saw them chase a yellow-billed cuckoo.

Didn't that make me sit up in a hurry! An idea struck me. Glory be! I'd break that drought.

First thing in the morning I took Will and Chester to town with me and rented three wagons and a birdcage. We drove straight home, and I called everyone together.

"Shovels, my lambs! Heap these wagons full of topsoil!"

But Larry and little Clarinda were still worried about Fourth of July. "We won't be able to grow fireworks, Pa!"

"You have my word," I declared firmly.

Before long, we were on our way. I drove the first wagon, with the young'uns following along behind in the other two. It might be a longish trip, and we had loaded up with picnic hampers of food. We also brought along rolls of chicken wire and our raincoats.

"Where are we going, Pa?" Jill called from the wagon behind.

"Hunting."

"Hunting?" Tom said.

"Exactly, my lambs. We're going to track down a rain cloud and wet down this topsoil."

"But how, Pa?" asked Tim.

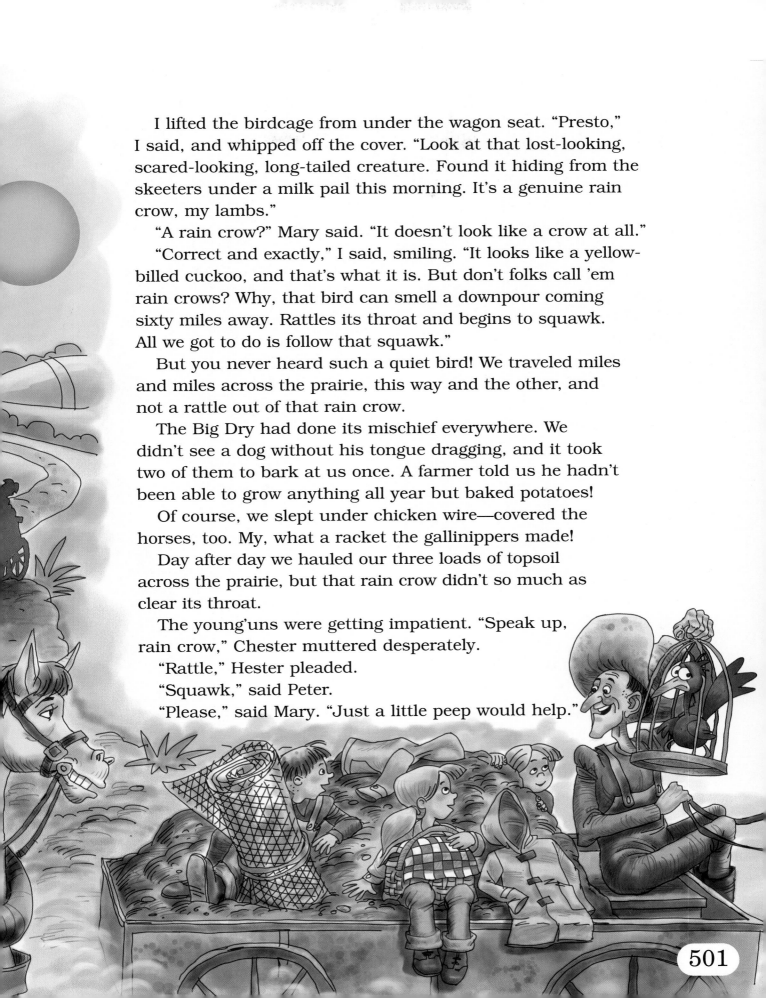

I lifted the birdcage from under the wagon seat. "Presto," I said, and whipped off the cover. "Look at that lost-looking, scared-looking, long-tailed creature. Found it hiding from the skeeters under a milk pail this morning. It's a genuine rain crow, my lambs."

"A rain crow?" Mary said. "It doesn't look like a crow at all."

"Correct and exactly," I said, smiling. "It looks like a yellow-billed cuckoo, and that's what it is. But don't folks call 'em rain crows? Why, that bird can smell a downpour coming sixty miles away. Rattles its throat and begins to squawk. All we got to do is follow that squawk."

But you never heard such a quiet bird! We traveled miles and miles across the prairie, this way and the other, and not a rattle out of that rain crow.

The Big Dry had done its mischief everywhere. We didn't see a dog without his tongue dragging, and it took two of them to bark at us once. A farmer told us he hadn't been able to grow anything all year but baked potatoes!

Of course, we slept under chicken wire—covered the horses, too. My, what a racket the gallinippers made!

Day after day we hauled our three loads of topsoil across the prairie, but that rain crow didn't so much as clear its throat.

The young'uns were getting impatient. "Speak up, rain crow," Chester muttered desperately.

"Rattle," Hester pleaded.

"Squawk," said Peter.

"Please," said Mary. "Just a little peep would help."

Not a cloud appeared in the sky. I'll confess I was getting a mite discouraged. And the Fourth of July not another two weeks off!

We curled up under chicken wire that night, as usual, and the big skeeters kept banging into it, so you could hardly sleep. Rattled like a hailstorm. And suddenly, at daybreak, I rose up laughing.

"Hear that?"

The young'uns crowded around the rain crow. We hadn't been able to hear its voice rattle for the mosquitoes. Now it turned in its cage, gazed off to the northwest, opened its yellow beak, and let out a real, ear-busting rain cry.

"K-*kawk*! K-*kawk*! K-*kawk*!"

"Put on your raincoats, my lambs!" I said, and we rushed to the wagons.

"K-*kawk*! K-*kawk*! K-*kawk*!"

Didn't we raise dust! That bird faced northwest like a dog on point. There was a rain cloud out there and before long Jill gave a shout.

"I see it!"

And the others chimed in one after the other. "Me, too!"

"K-*kawk*! K-*kawk*! K-*kawk*!"

We headed directly for that lone cloud, the young'uns yelling, the horses snorting, and the bird squawking.

Glory be! The first raindrops spattered as large as quarters. And my, didn't the young'uns frolic in that cloudburst! They lifted their faces and opened their mouths and drank right out of the sky. They splashed about and felt mud between their toes for the first time in ages. We all forgot to put on our raincoats and got wet as fish.

Our dried-up topsoil soaked up raindrops like a sponge. It was a joy to behold! But if we stayed longer, we'd get stuck in the mud.

"Back in the wagons!" I shouted. "Home, my lambs, and not a moment to lose."

Well, home was right where we left it.

I got a pinch of onion seeds and went from wagon to wagon, sowing a few seeds in each load of moist earth. I didn't want to crowd those onions.

Now, that rich topsoil of ours had been idle a long time——it was rarin' to go. Before I could run back to the house, the greens were up. By the time I could get down my shotgun, the tops had grown four or five feet tall—— onions are terrible slow growers. Before I could load my shotgun, the bulbs were finally bursting up through the soil.

We stood at the windows watching. Those onion roots were having a great feast. The wagons heaved and creaked as the onions swelled and lifted themselves——they were already the size of pumpkins. But that wasn't near big enough. Soon they were larger'n washtubs and began to shoulder the smaller ones off the wagons.

Suddenly we heard a distant roaring in the air. Those zing-zanging, hot-tempered, blood-sucking prairie mosquitoes were returning from town with their stingers freshly sharpened. The Big Dry hadn't done their dispositions any good——their tempers were at a boil.

"You going to shoot them down, Pa?" Will asked.

"Too many for that," I answered.

"How big do those onions have to grow?" Chester asked.

"How big are they now?"

"A little smaller'n a cow shed."

"That's big enough," I nodded, lifting the window just enough to poke the shotgun through.

Well, the gallinippers spied the onions——I had planted red onions, you know——and came swarming over our farm. I let go at the bulbs with a double charge of buckshot and slammed the window.

"Handkerchiefs, everyone!" I called out. The odor of fresh-cut onion shot through the air, under the door, and through the cracks. Cry? In no time our handkerchiefs were wet as dishrags.

"Well! You never saw such surprised gallinippers. They zing-zanged every which way, most of them backwards. And weep? Their eyes began to flow like sprinkling cans. Onion tears! The roof began to leak. Mud puddles formed everywhere. Before long, the downpour was equal to any cloudburst I ever saw. Near flooded our farm!

The skeeters kept their distance after that. But they'd been mighty helpful.

With our farm freshly watered we grew tons of great onions——three or four crops a day. Gave them away to farmers all over the country.

The newspaper ran a picture of the whole family——the rain crow, too.

The young'uns had a splendid Fourth of July. Grew all the fireworks they wanted. They'd dash about with bean shooters——shooting radish seeds. You know how fast radishes come up. In our rich topsoil they grew quicker'n the eye. The seeds hardly touched the ground before they took root and swelled up and exploded. They'd go off like strings of firecrackers.

And, mercy, what a racket! Didn't I say I'd rather catch a skunk by the tail than tell a fib? Well, at nightfall a scared cat ran up a tree, and I went up a ladder to get it down. Reached in the branches and caught it by the tail.

I'd be lying if I didn't admit the truth. It was a skunk.

McBroom the Rainmaker

Meet the Author

Sid Fleischman was fascinated with sleight of hand performers during his school years. After graduating at the age of seventeen, he had a traveling act of his own, performing tricks countrywide. He later went to college, after which he became a reporter and writer for the San Diego paper. He started writing for young readers by making up stories for his own children. He writes at a huge table stacked with story ideas, library books, research, letters, notes, pens, pencils, and a typewriter. His cat, Nora, sits close by to help him when he needs it. One of his most popular book characters is McBroom, who is the star of several tall tales.

Meet the Illustrator

Bill Ogden lives on five acres of land in New Hampshire, with his wife and his son. He is a true nature lover, who shares his land with a wide variety of animals, such as deer, foxes, beavers, coyotes, hawks, mice, ducks, geese, raccoons, otters, owls, giant blue herons, crows, and *"extremely large tomato horn worms."* When he's not drawing, he says he can be found in the great outdoors, *"stalking the wild mushroom, catching the wily bass, and chasing the dreaded, garden-eating woodchuck."*

Theme Connections

Within the Selection

Record your answers to the questions below in the Response Journal section of your Writer's Notebook. In small groups, report the ideas you wrote. Discuss your ideas with the rest of your group. Then choose a person to report your group's answers to the class.

- What were some of the challenges settlers faced from natural phenomena such as droughts?
- Why do you think families such as the McBrooms moved to the American West?
- In tall tales the truth is exaggerated. What truths about the American West are represented in this story?

Across Selections

- How is the use of humor in this tall tale similar to the way the team members of the S.O.R. Losers used humor?
- Compare the farm life of the settlers in "Old Yeller and the Bear" with the farm life of McBroom and his family.

Beyond the Selection

- Have you ever used humor to make the most of a difficult situation? Describe the problem and tell how humor helped you work through it.
- Think about how "McBroom the Rainmaker" adds to what you know about the American West.
- Add items to the Concept/Question Board about the American West.

Some people spend their lives searching for something—freedom, adventure, excitement, and knowledge. Sometimes their search takes them on fantastic journeys and quests. What motivates these searchers? What makes them keep going, always searching?

509

Focus Questions Where does Jumping Mouse want to go?
Will he be able to reach his destination? What character trait
helps him most on his journey?

The Story of Jumping Mouse

retold and illustrated by
John Steptoe

O nce there was a young mouse who lived in the brush near a great river. During the day he and the other mice hunted for food. At night they gathered to hear the old ones tell stories. The young mouse liked to hear about the desert beyond the river, and he got shivers from the stories about the dangerous shadows that lived in the sky. But his favorite was the tale of the far-off land.

The far-off land sounded so wonderful the young mouse began to dream about it. He knew he would never be content until he had been there. The old ones warned that the journey would be long and perilous, but the young mouse would not be swayed. He set off one morning before the sun had risen.

It was evening before he reached the edge of the brush. Before him was the river; on the other side was the desert. The young mouse peered into the deep water. "How will I ever get across?" he said in dismay.

"Don't you know how to swim?" called a gravelly voice.

The young mouse looked around and saw a small green frog.

"Hello," he said. "What is swim?"

"This is swimming," said the frog, and she jumped into the river.

"Oh," said the young mouse, "I don't think I can do that."

"Why do you need to cross the river?" asked the frog, hopping back up the bank.

"I want to go to the far-off land," said the young mouse.
"It sounds too beautiful to live a lifetime and not see it."

"In that case, you need my help. I'm Magic Frog. Who
are you?"

"I'm a mouse," said the young mouse.

Magic Frog laughed. "That's not a name. I'll give you
a name that will help you on your journey. I name you
Jumping Mouse."

As soon as Magic Frog said this, the young mouse felt a
strange tingling in his hind legs. He hopped a small hop and,
to his surprise, jumped twice as high as he'd ever jumped
before. "Thank you," he said, admiring his powerful new legs.

"You're welcome," said Magic Frog. "Now step onto this leaf
and we'll cross the river together."

When they were safely on the other side, Magic Frog said,
"You will encounter hardships on your way, but don't despair.
You will reach the far-off land if you keep hope alive within you."

Jumping Mouse set off at once, hopping quickly from bush to bush. The shadows circled above, but he avoided being seen. He ate berries when he could find them and slept only when he was exhausted. Days passed. Though he was able to travel quickly, he began to wonder if he'd ever reach the other side of the desert. He then came upon a stream that coursed through the dry land. Under a large berry bush he met a fat old mouse.

"What strange hind legs you have," said the fat mouse.

"They were a gift from Magic Frog when she named me," said Jumping Mouse proudly.

"Humpf," snorted the fat mouse. "What good are they?"

"They've helped me come this far across the desert, and with luck they'll carry me to the far-off land," said Jumping Mouse. "But now I'm very tired. May I rest here a while?"

"Indeed you may," said the fat mouse. "In fact, you can stay forever."

"Thank you, but I'll stay only until I'm rested. I've seen the far-off land in my dreams and I must be on my way as soon as I'm able."

"Dreams," said the fat mouse scornfully. "I used to have such dreams, but all I ever found was desert. Why go jumping about the desert when everything anyone needs is right here?"

Jumping Mouse tried to explain that it wasn't a question of need, but something he felt he had to do. But the fat mouse only snorted again. Finally Jumping Mouse dug a hole and curled up for the night.

The next day the fat mouse warned him to stay on this side of the stream. "A snake lives on the other side," he said. "But don't worry. He's afraid of water, so he'll never cross the stream."

Life was easy beneath the berry bush, and Jumping Mouse was soon rested and strong. He and the fat mouse ate and slept and then slept and ate. Then one morning, when he went to the stream for a drink, he caught sight of his reflection. He was almost as fat as the fat old mouse!

"It's time for me to go on," thought Jumping Mouse. "I didn't come all this way to settle down under a berry bush."

Just then he noticed that a branch had gotten caught in the narrow of the stream. It spanned the water like a bridge——now the snake could cross! Jumping Mouse hurried back to warn the fat mouse. But the mousehole was empty, and there was a strange smell in the air. Snake. Jumping Mouse was too late. "Poor old friend," he thought as he hurried away. "He lost hope of finding his dream and now his life is over."

Jumping Mouse traveled throughout the night, and the next morning he saw that he had reached a grassy plain. Exhausted, he hopped toward a large boulder where he could rest in safety. But as he got closer, he realized the boulder was an enormous, shaggy bison lying in the grass. Every once in a while it groaned.

514

Jumping Mouse shivered at the terrible sound. "Hello, great one," he said bravely. "I'm Jumping Mouse and I'm traveling to the far-off land. Why do you lie here as if you were dying?"

"Because I *am* dying," said the bison. "I drank from a poisoned stream, and it blinded me. I can't see to find tender grass to eat or sweet water to drink. I'll surely die."

Jumping Mouse was sad to see so wondrous a beast so helpless. "When I began my journey," he said, "Magic Frog gave me a name and strong legs to carry me to the far-off land. My magic is not as powerful as hers, but I'll do what I can to help you. I name you Eyes-of-a-Mouse."

As soon as he had spoken Jumping Mouse heard the bison snort with joy. He heard but he could no longer see, for he had given the bison his own sight.

"Thank you," said Eyes-of-a-Mouse. "You are small, but you have done a great thing. If you will hop along beneath me, the shadows of the sky won't see you, and I will guide you to the mountains."

515

Jumping Mouse did as he was told. He hopped to the rhythm of the bison's hooves, and in this way he reached the foot of the mountains.

"I am an animal of the plains, so I must stop here," said Eyes-of-a-Mouse. "How will you cross the mountains when you can't see?"

"There will be a way," said Jumping Mouse. "Hope is alive within me." He said good-bye to his friend; then he dug a hole and went to sleep.

The next morning Jumping Mouse woke to cool breezes that blew down from the mountain peaks. Cautiously he set out in the direction of the coolness. He had not gone far when he felt fur beneath his paws. He jumped back in alarm and sniffed the air. Wolf! He froze in terror, but when nothing happened he gathered up his courage and said, "Excuse me. I'm Jumping Mouse, and I'm traveling to the far-off land. Can you tell me the way?"

"I would if I could," said the wolf, "but a wolf finds his way with his nose, and mine will no longer smell for me."

"What happened?" asked Jumping Mouse.

"I was once a proud and lazy creature," replied the wolf. "I misused the gift of smell, and so I lost it. I have learned not to be proud, but without my nose to tell me where I am and where I am going, I cannot survive. I am lying here waiting for the end."

Jumping Mouse was saddened by the wolf's story. He told him about Magic Frog and Eyes-of-a-Mouse. "I have a little magic left," he said. "I'll be happy to help you. I name you Nose-of-a-Mouse."

The wolf howled for joy. Jumping Mouse could hear him sniffing the air, taking in the mountain fragrances. But Jumping Mouse could no longer smell the pine-scented breezes. He no longer had the use of his nose or his eyes. "You are but a small creature," said Nose-of-a-Mouse, "but you have given me a great gift. You must let me thank you. Come, hop along beneath where the shadows of the sky won't see you. I will guide you through the mountains to the far-off land."

517

So Jumping Mouse hopped to the rhythm of the wolf's padding paws, and in this way he reached the far-off land.

"I am an animal of the mountains, so I must stop here," said Nose-of-a-Mouse. "How will you manage if you can no longer see or smell?"

"There will be a way," said Jumping Mouse. He then said good-bye to his friend and dug a hole and went to sleep.

The next morning Jumping Mouse woke up and crawled from his hole. "I am here," he said. "I feel the earth beneath my paws. I hear the wind rustling leaves on the trees. The sun warms my bones. All is not lost, but I'll never be as I was. How will I ever manage?" Then Jumping Mouse began to cry.

"Jumping Mouse," he heard a gravelly voice say.

"Magic Frog, is that you?" Jumping Mouse asked, swallowing his tears.

"Yes," said Magic Frog. "Don't cry, Jumping Mouse. Your unselfish spirit has brought you great hardship, but it is that same spirit of hope and compassion that has brought you to the far-off land. You have nothing to fear, Jumping Mouse. Jump high, Jumping Mouse," commanded Magic Frog.

Jumping Mouse did as he was told and jumped as high as he could. Then he felt the air lifting him higher still into the sky. He stretched out his paws in the sun and felt strangely powerful. To his joy he began to see the wondrous beauty of the world above and below and to smell the scent of earth and sky and living things.

"Jumping Mouse," he heard Magic Frog call. "I give you a new name. You are now called Eagle, and you will live in the far-off land forever."

519

The Story of Jumping Mouse

Meet the Author and Illustrator

John Steptoe grew up in the Bedford-Stuyvesant section of Brooklyn, New York. As a teenager, he was sent to a special art school in Manhattan. While still in high school, he took his portfolio of artwork to the editors of *Harper's Magazine*. They suggested that he use his artwork for a children's book. *Stevie* became his first children's book and was published by the time he was 19 years old. By the age of 20, the John Steptoe Library in Brooklyn was dedicated to him.

Over the next two decades, Mr. Steptoe illustrated over a dozen books. His first goal was to create books that could be enjoyed especially by African-American children. However, he said later in his career, *"I hope I have made a statement that is even greater than my discovery of reasons to be proud of African ancestors. I hope my writing is also a statement of brotherhood in the wide world into which I was born."*

Theme Connections

Within the Selection

Record your answers to the questions below in the Response Journal section of your Writer's Notebook. In small groups, report the ideas you wrote. Discuss your ideas with the rest of your group. Then choose a person to report your group's answers to the class.

- How and why did Jumping Mouse choose to share his strengths with all the animals he met?
- What did this story teach about obstacles that get in the way of goals?
- What did the Magic Frog mean when he said that Jumping Mouse would reach the far-off land if he kept his hopes alive?

Across Selections

- Choose a character from another story you have read. What goals did the character set? What obstacles did that character encounter? How did the character overcome those challenges?
- What role does cooperation play in helping Jumping Mouse and the other animals in this story overcome difficulties?

Beyond the Selection

- What obstacles have you overcome to reach your goals? What kept you going when times got tough?
- Think about how "The Story of Jumping Mouse" adds to what you know about journeys and quests.
- Add items to the Concept/Question Board about journeys and quests.

Focus Questions In this selection, what quest motivates
Shackleton's journey? What new quest arises from the journey?
How are the two quests different in nature?

Trapped by the Ice!

by Michael McCurdy

October 27, 1915

The *Endurance* was trapped. Giant blocks of ice were
slowly crushing her sides. From the deck, Sir Ernest
Shackleton looked at the snow and ice that spread to the
horizon. Ten months before, all he had wanted was to be the
first person to cross the South Pole's ice cap. Now his only
concern was for his men. What would happen to them—and
how much longer did the ship have before it broke apart?
The *Endurance* was leaking badly. Shack could not delay.

Shack ordered his crew off the *Endurance* and camp was set up on the frozen Weddell Sea. Tools, tents, scrap lumber for firewood, sleeping bags, and what little food rations and clothing the men had left were saved from their ship, along with three lifeboats in case they ever reached open water. The *Endurance* was a sad sight now, a useless hulk lying on its side. For months she had been the crew's home. Now they would have to get used to life on the ice—stranded hundreds of miles from the nearest land.

November 21, 1915

Almost one month later, the sound of crushing wood startled the men. It was what they had feared. Turning toward the ship's wreckage, they saw her stern rise slowly in the air, tremble, and slip quickly beneath the ice. Minutes later, the hole had frozen up over the ship. She was gone forever, swallowed by the Weddell Sea. Shack talked with the ship's skipper, Frank Worsley, and his next-in-command, Frankie Wild. Among them, they would have to decide what to do next.

December 23, 1915

Executing their plan would be difficult. By pulling the lifeboats, loaded with supplies, they would try to cross the barren ice to open water. If they made it, they would use the three boats to reach the nearest land. Shack studied the unending snow and ice ahead of him. Was it possible? Each boat was mounted on a sledge. Harnessed like horses, the men pulled, one boat at a time. Pulling 2,000-pound loads was hard work. Soon everybody was so tired and sore that no one could pull anymore. The crew would have to wait for the ice, moved by the sea's current, to carry them north to open water.

April 8, 1916

The men smelled terrible. During their five and a half months on the ice they hadn't had a bath. Clothes were greasy and worn thin, and they rubbed against the men's skin, causing painful sores. Hands were cracked from the cold and wind, and hunger sapped everyone's strength. By now, the ice floes were breaking up into smaller and smaller pieces all around the men as they drifted closer to the edge of the polar sea. Shack thought it was a good time to launch the lifeboats, rigged with small canvas sails. He knew his men could not all survive the grueling 700-mile open-boat journey to the whaling station on South Georgia Island. So he decided to try to reach Elephant Island first.

11 p.m. April 8, 1916

Steering around the blocks of ice was hard. The boats bumped into ice floes—or crashed into icebergs. As night fell, the boats were pulled up onto a big floe and the tents were raised. But sleeping was difficult with damp bags and blankets, and with noisy killer whales circling around.

One night, Shack suddenly felt something was wrong. He shook Frankie, and they crawled out of their tent for a look. A huge wave smacked headlong into the floe with a great thud, and the floe began to split into two pieces. The crack was headed straight toward Tent Number 4! Then Shack heard a splash. Looking into the crevasse, he saw a wriggling shape below in the dark water. It was a sleeping bag—with Ernie Holness inside! Shack acted quickly. Reaching down, he pulled the soggy bag out of the water with one mighty jerk. And just in time, too—within seconds the two great blocks of ice crashed back together.

April 13, 1916

Finally, the men reached open water. The savage sea slammed furiously into the three little boats—called the *James Caird*, the *Dudley Docker*, and the *Stancomb Wills*. Tall waves lifted them up and down like a roller coaster. Blinding sea spray blew into the men's faces. Most of them became seasick. Worst of all, they were very thirsty, because seawater had spoiled the freshwater. The men's tongues had swelled so much from dehydration they could hardly swallow. Shack had his men suck on frozen seal meat to quench their thirst. They *had* to make land. They had to get to Elephant Island!

April 15, 1916

After an exhausting week battling the sea, the men nearly lost all hope. Big Tom Crean tried to cheer the men with a song, but nothing worked. Finally, something appeared in the distance. Shack called across to Frank Worsley in the *Dudley Docker*, "There she is, Skipper!" It was land. It was Elephant Island at last. It looked terribly barren, with jagged 3,500-foot peaks rising right up out of the sea, yet it was the only choice the men had.

April 24, 1916

Elephant Island was nothing but rock, ice, snow—and wind. Tents were pitched but quickly blew away. Without resting, Shack planned his departure for South Georgia Island. There he would try to get help. Twenty-two men would stay behind while Shack and a crew braved the 700-mile journey in the worst winter seas on earth. The five ablest men were picked: Frank Worsley; Big Tom Crean; the carpenter, Chippy McNeish; and two seamen, Tim McCarthy and John Vincent. With frozen fingers and a few tools, Chippy prepared the *Caird* for the rough journey ahead. Only nine days after the men had first sighted the deserted island, Shack and his crew of five were on open water once again.

For the men who stayed behind, permanent shelter was now needed or they would freeze to death. Frankie Wild had the men turn the two remaining boats upside down, side by side. Then the boats were covered with canvas and a cookstove was put inside. The hut was dark and cramped, lit only by a burning wick. And something happened that the men had not expected: heat from their bodies and the stove melted the ice under them as well as piles of frozen bird droppings left for years by the frigate birds and penguins. The smell was terrible! Day after day the men looked toward the sea, wondering if Shack would make it back to rescue them. How long would they be left here? Was Shack all right?

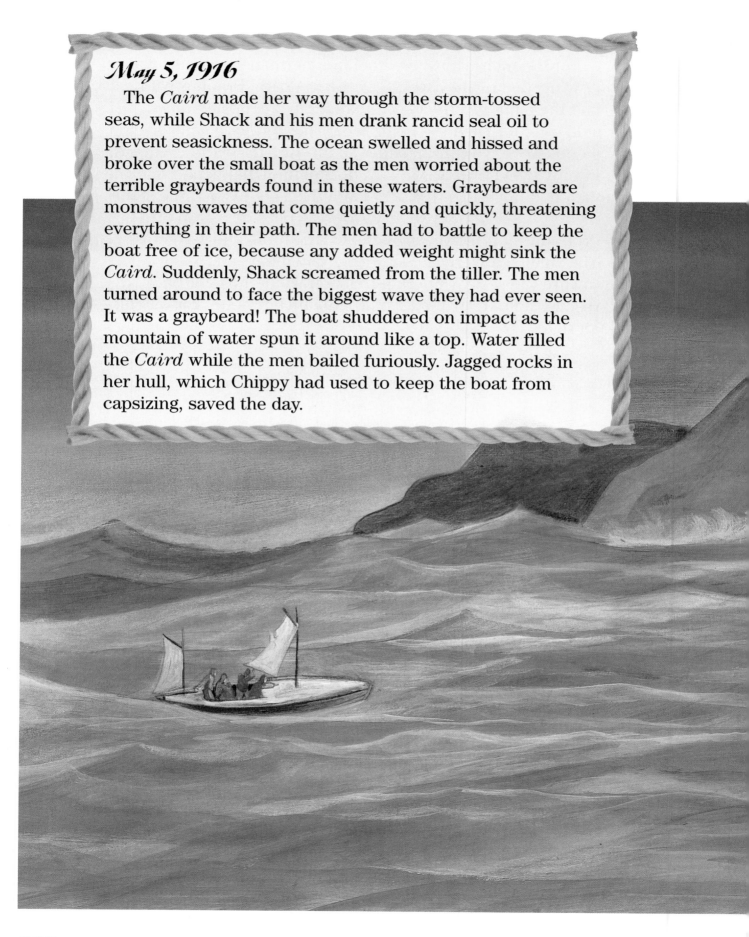

May 5, 1916

The *Caird* made her way through the storm-tossed seas, while Shack and his men drank rancid seal oil to prevent seasickness. The ocean swelled and hissed and broke over the small boat as the men worried about the terrible graybeards found in these waters. Graybeards are monstrous waves that come quietly and quickly, threatening everything in their path. The men had to battle to keep the boat free of ice, because any added weight might sink the *Caird*. Suddenly, Shack screamed from the tiller. The men turned around to face the biggest wave they had ever seen. It was a graybeard! The boat shuddered on impact as the mountain of water spun it around like a top. Water filled the *Caird* while the men bailed furiously. Jagged rocks in her hull, which Chippy had used to keep the boat from capsizing, saved the day.

May 10, 1916

Finally, after seventeen grueling days at sea, young McCarthy shouted, "Land ho!" South Georgia Island lay dimly ahead. The whaling station was on the other side of the island, but the men had to land *now* or die. Their freshwater was gone, and they were too weak to battle the sea to the other side of the island. While the men planned their landing attempt, they were hit by the worst hurricane they had ever encountered. For nine terrible hours they fought to keep afloat. Miraculously, just as things looked hopeless, the sea calmed enough to allow the *Caird* to land safely on the rocky beach of Haakon Bay.

The men landed near a small cave with a freshwater spring nearby. The cave would become a temporary home for John Vincent and Chippy McNeish. Both had suffered too much on the voyage and could not survive the long hike across the island to the whaling station. Tim McCarthy stayed behind to take care of the two sick men. Fortunately, water for drinking, wood from old shipwrecks for fire, and albatross eggs and seals to eat meant those who stayed behind would be all right while waiting for their rescue. But Shack, Big Tom, and Skipper Worsley would have to climb over a series of jagged ridges that cut the island in half like a saw blade. All they could carry was a little Primus stove, fuel for six meals, fifty feet of rope, and an ice ax. Their only food consisted of biscuits and light rations that hung in socks around their necks. On their eighth day ashore, May 18, it was time to set off on the most dangerous climb they had ever attempted.

May 19, 1916

Three times the men struggle up mountains, only to find that the terrain was impassable on the other side. The men stopped only to eat a soup called "hoosh," to nibble on stale biscuits, or to nap five minutes, with each man taking a turn awake so that there would be someone to wake the others. On and on the exhausted men hiked. From one mountain summit they saw that night was coming fast. Being caught on a peak at night meant certain death. They had to make a dangerous gamble. Shack assembled a makeshift toboggan from the coiled-up rope and the men slid 1,500 feet down the mountain in one big slide. Despite the perilous landing, they couldn't help but laugh with relief after they had crashed, unhurt, into a large snowbank.

The men had survived the long slide, but danger still lay ahead. They had been hiking for more than thirty hours now without sleep. Finally, all three heard the sound of a far-off whistle. Was it the whaling station? They climbed a ridge and looked down. Yes, there it was! Two whale-catchers were docked at the pier. From this distance, the men at the station were the size of insects. Shack fought against being too reckless. The three still had to lower themselves down a thirty-foot waterfall by hanging on to their rope and swinging through the icy torrents. At last, the ragged explorers stumbled toward the station. They had done it!

4 p.m. May 20, 1916

Thoralf Sørrle, the manager of the whaling station, heard a knock outside his office and opened the door. He looked hard at the ragged clothes and blackened faces of the men who stood before him. "Do I know you?" he asked.

"I'm Shackleton," came the reply. Tears welled up in Sørrle's eyes as he recognized his old friend's voice.

The three explorers received a hero's welcome from the whaling crew. The whalers knew that no one had ever done what Shack had accomplished. The next day, Skipper Worsley took a boat and picked up McCarthy, Vincent, and McNeish while Shack began preparations for the Elephant Island rescue. It would take more than three months—and four attempts—to break through the winter pack ice and save the stranded men. But Shack finally did it—and without any loss of life. The men were glad to have a ship's deck once again under their feet. Finally, they were going home!

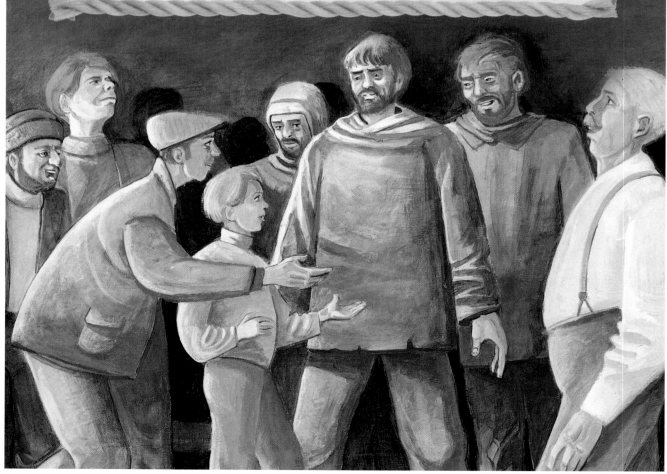

Trapped by the Ice!

Meet the Author and Illustrator

Michael McCurdy had plenty of inspiration to be an artist as he was growing up. Both his father and grandmother were artists, too. Mr. McCurdy went on to become an illustrator and designer for book publishers, magazines, and corporations. His illustration work is greatly inspired by words and text. He gains the most satisfaction from his work when he can participate in all aspects of creating a book.

Theme Connections

Within the Selection

Record your answers to the questions below in the Response Journal section of your Writer's Notebook. In small groups, report the ideas you wrote. Discuss your ideas with the rest of your group. Then choose a person to report your group's answers to the class.

- How did Shackleton's journey change from that which he originally planned? How did his goals change?
- What risks did Shackleton take to meet his goals? Were the risks worth the reward?
- How did courage, determination, and sacrifice help the team reach the safety of the whaling station?

Across Selections

- What role did competition play in Shackleton's initial goal? How did cooperation help the team overcome obstacles and survive their ordeal?
- In what way does Shackleton remind you of Jumping Mouse?

Beyond the Selection

- What risks are you willing to take to meet a goal? How can you tell whether the risks are justified?
- Think about how "Trapped by the Ice!" adds to what you know about journeys and quests.
- Add items to the Concept/Question Board about journeys and quests.

Maps

by Dorothy Brown Thompson

High adventure
And bright dream——
Maps are mightier
Than they seem:

Ships that follow
Leaning stars——
Red and gold of
Strange bazaars——

Ice floes hid
Beyond all knowing——
Planes that ride where
Winds are blowing!

Train maps, maps of
Wind and weather,
Road maps——taken
Altogether

Maps are really
Magic wands
For home-staying
Vagabonds!

Focus Questions What do you think the train symbolizes for the narrator? Would you be willing to leave your friends and family to go to an unknown place?

Travel

Edna St. Vincent Millay
illustrated by Doug Knutson

The railroad track is miles away,
And the day is loud with voices speaking,
Yet there isn't a train goes by all day
But I hear its whistle shrieking.

All night there isn't a train goes by,
Though the night is still for sleep and dreaming,
But I see its cinders red on the sky,
And hear its engine steaming.

My heart is warm with the friends I make,
And better friends I'll not be knowing,
Yet there isn't a train I wouldn't take,
No matter where it's going.

Focus Questions How do the preparations for space travel and land journeys differ? How are astronauts similar to the early land and sea explorers? What makes a quest for humanity different from a personal quest?

APOLLO 11
First Moon Landing

by Michael D. Cole

It was warm on the morning of July 16, 1969, at Cape Kennedy in Florida. On launchpad 39A sat the mighty Saturn V rocket—the most powerful machine ever built. At the top of the towering rocket— 363 feet above the ground— three men waited to begin mankind's most historic journey.

In the right couch was Michael Collins. He was the command module pilot. He would not land on the Moon, but he would orbit the Moon in the command module. The other two astronauts would make the landing on the Moon in the lunar module.

Awaiting liftoff, the Saturn V rocket sits on the launchpad.

Collins was born in Rome, Italy, in 1930 while his father was stationed there with the U.S. Army. Collins had been an air force test pilot and had already been in space before. He flew in the *Gemini 10* mission, and he had walked in space. He was married and had two daughters and a son. Collins liked to joke that because there was no TV set on the command module, he would be one of the few Americans who would not see the Moon landing.[1]

In the middle couch was Edwin E. Aldrin. He would co-pilot the lunar module, which was named *Eagle*. Everyone called him "Buzz." It had been his nickname since his childhood in Montclair, New Jersey. He was thirty-nine years old, and he also had been an air force pilot.

Aviation was in Aldrin's blood. His father had been a colonel in the U.S. Army Air Corps and was a friend of Orville Wright and Charles Lindbergh. His mother's maiden name was Marian Moon. Aldrin had been in space on *Gemini 12*. He held the record for the longest spacewalk. He was an intelligent and serious man who spoke in the precise manner of an engineer. He was married, with two sons and a daughter.

[1] John Barbour, *Footprints on the Moon* (New York: The Associated Press, 1969), p. 184.

Armstrong, Collins, and Aldrin pose for a picture in front of the mighty Apollo/ Saturn V rocket which would carry them to the Moon.

Neil Armstrong, Michael Collins, and Buzz Aldrin will always be remembered for their heroic and historic flight aboard *Apollo 11*.

In the left couch was mission commander Neil A. Armstrong. He was from Wapakoneta, Ohio, where he had earned a pilot's license before he was old enough to drive a car. After flying as a Navy pilot he became an astronaut. He commanded the *Gemini 8* mission. Armstrong was probably the best pilot among all the astronauts. He was married and the father of two sons. His boyish smile made him look much younger than his thirty-eight years. Because he was mission commander, he would be the first person to walk upon the Moon.

These three men were about to experience an extraordinary adventure. All three had been in space before. All had been proud to serve their country in the space program. But they knew this mission was different.

People all over the world were waiting for the launch. They hoped *Apollo 11*'s historic mission to land on the Moon would be a success. People everywhere felt that a part of themselves was going with those three astronauts. Armstrong, Aldrin, and Collins could not escape the fact that this time they did not just represent their country. This time they represented the human race.

The three astronauts suited up in their bulky spacesuits. Then they made the five-mile trip to the launching pad in a large van. It went over a special remote route to avoid the incredible traffic jam that had been building around the Cape for days. Beaches and parks were full of camper trailers. Lakes and waterways were full of boats anchored where they could watch the launch. All of them, and the nearly one billion people around the world who were watching the exciting countdown on television, waited to witness the historic moment when *Apollo 11* began its journey to the Moon.

"Two minutes and ten seconds and counting, and the Moon at this precise second is 218,986 miles away," the announcer said over the Cape loudspeaker.[2] The countdown was going smoothly. Armstrong, Aldrin, and Collins had trained for over a year for this mission. Now it was about to begin. Collins thought they had about a fifty-fifty chance of completing the mission successfully. Armstrong and Aldrin thought their chances were a little better. The three had never discussed the subject with each other.[3]

[2] *Apollo 11, Technical Air-to-Ground Voice Transcription,* Manned Spacecraft Center, Houston, Texas, July 1969. All in-flight communications which follow come from this source.
[3] "Spaceflight Part 3: One Giant Leap," narrated by Martin Sheen, PBS Video (1985).

Apollo 11 Commander Neil A. Armstrong leads astronauts Michael Collins and Edwin E. Aldrin to the van that will take them to the launchpad.

Spectators witness the blast off of the Saturn V rocket.

The countdown swept toward the final minute, then the final seconds. Armstrong wrapped his gloved hand around the abort handle in case the launch went badly. Aldrin looked at Armstrong and then turned to grin at Collins. They were finally going!

Collins remembered walking to the pad just a while ago. He had watched the frosty steam rolling off the rocket's sides when the warm air met the rocket filled with super-cooled liquid oxygen and hydrogen. He remembered thinking the rocket almost seemed *alive*.[4] Seconds from now, it would indeed rumble to life.

The loudspeaker at the Cape kept the thousands of onlookers counting toward the launch. "We are still go with *Apollo 11*. Thirty seconds and counting. Astronauts reported, feel good . . . T minus twenty seconds and counting. T minus fifteen seconds, guidance is internal."

All power was now on in the *Apollo 11* spacecraft. Armstrong, Aldrin, and Collins were excited, but their minds were focused on the many tasks that had to be done.[5]

[4] Michael Collins, *Carrying the Fire: An Astronaut's Journey* (New York: Farrar, Straus & Giroux, 1974), p. 418.
[5] Ibid., p. 419.

"Twelve, eleven, ten, nine, ignition sequence starts." Flame and smoke gushed from the five main engines of the Saturn V rocket. "Six, five, four, three, two, one, zero, all engines running." The controllers at the Cape pushed the engines to the proper thrust of 7.5 million pounds, equal to the power of more than 92,000 locomotives. Then they released the pad's hold-down clamps.

The mighty Saturn V, all 3,000 tons of it, rose from the launchpad.

"LIFT-OFF! We have a lift-off! Thirty-two minutes past the hour. Lift-off on Apollo 11." It was 9:32 A.M. The rocket's deafening rise through the sky could be seen and heard for miles around the Cape. The huge flaming thrust of the engines created a shock wave that could be *felt* for just as far. The powerful Saturn V climbed

At 9:32 A.M. on July 16, 1969, the three astronauts aboard the *Apollo 11* launched into their history-making flight.

through the sky, pushing the three astronauts toward space while the whole world watched.

The exciting launch was a great success. Still, it was hard to believe what was about to happen. In four days, the men of *Apollo 11* would try to land on the Moon.

By Day Four of the mission the Moon's appearance had changed dramatically in the astronauts' eyes. Armstrong, Aldrin, and Collins saw the Moon as a three-dimensional thing for the first time. It was the most awesome sphere they had ever seen. It completely filled their window. Armstrong tried to describe what they were seeing.

"The view of the Moon . . . is really spectacular," he said. "We can see the entire circumference even though part of it is in complete shadow and part of it is in Earthshine (sunlight reflected off the Earth). It's a view worth the price of the trip."

"We're able to see stars again and recognize constellations for the first time on the trip," Collins added. "The Earthshine coming through the window is so bright you can read a book by it."

They could not linger by the windows for long. They were about to pass behind the dark side of the Moon. They would lose contact with Earth for more than thirty minutes. During that time they would fire *Columbia*'s engines to slow themselves down and get into lunar orbit. If it worked, their next step would be to prepare *Eagle* for its descent to the Moon.

The Moon as viewed from *Apollo 11*.

Apollo 11 swung around the dark side of the Moon, losing radio contact with Mission Control. During this first radio blackout the three astronauts and their spacecraft were now in orbit around the Moon.

Coming around on their first orbit, Apollo 11 regained radio contact. The astronauts got their first view of some important sights on the Moon's surface. "We're getting our first view of the landing site approach," Armstrong said. "The pictures brought back by Apollos 8 and 10 have given us a pretty good preview of what to look at here. It looks very much like the pictures, but . . . there's no substitute for actually being here."[6]

[6] Apollo 11, Technical Air-to-Ground Voice Transcription, Manned Spacecraft Center, Houston, Texas, July 1969. All in-flight communications which follow come from this source.

"The *Eagle* has wings" announced Armstrong as the lunar module separated from the command module.

So far the mission was going incredibly well. Armstrong, Aldrin, and Collins settled down to rest before the big day tomorrow. They slept only five or six hours, the shortest rest period of the flight. When they awoke on Sunday, it was time to do what they had been practicing to do for over a year. But this time it would be for real.

Aldrin crawled down the tunnel and through the hatch into *Eagle*. He powered up the spacecraft and ran through a series of systems checks. Armstrong joined him a short time later. The checks continued and everything was go.

"*Apollo*, Houston. We're go for undocking," reported Mission Control. The radio again blacked out, and they swung around the Moon's dark side on their thirteenth orbit. Armstrong and Aldrin extended the landing legs on *Eagle*. After nearly ten years of hard work, the goal of the manned space program was about to be realized. They were ready to go for the landing.

Collins pressed a button in the command module. Latches clicked open, and *Eagle* floated gently away from *Columbia*. Mission Control waited for the signal to come through again. As *Eagle* again came into radio contact, Armstrong announced through the static, "The *Eagle* has wings."

The two ships flew in formation while Collins inspected the lunar module for any problems or damage. "Looks like you've got a mighty good-looking flying machine there, *Eagle*," he said, "despite the fact that you're upside down." Collins later gave *Columbia* a burst from its engine. This boosted him ahead to give *Eagle* some flying room. "OK *Eagle* . . . you guys take care."

"See you later," Armstrong said.

Eagle was again on the dark side, in radio blackout. It began its long arcing descent toward the landing site. The site was in an area on the Moon called the Sea of Tranquility. This place was chosen as a landing site because the area was wide-open and very flat. If all went well, Armstrong and Aldrin would land there in about seventeen minutes. They came out of the radio blackout with everything going fine. *Eagle* had now descended to about ten miles above the lunar surface.

"You are go to continue powered descent," Mission Control said. "You're looking good."

"Got the Earth right out our front window," Aldrin said. Armstrong had turned *Eagle* into position; its landing legs were pointed toward the lunar surface. This enabled the landing radar to lock on and feed altitude and velocity data to the onboard computer. The landing proceeded perfectly as Armstrong and Aldrin descended to 3,000 and then 2,000 feet from the surface. Then things got very tense. An alarm light flashed on their instrument panels.

"Twelve alarm," Aldrin said, "1201." This meant that one of the landing computers was overloaded with data. It was feeding Armstrong and Aldrin faulty information about their descent.

The controllers at Mission Control in Houston were anxiously awaiting the lunar landing.

"Roger," said Mission Control, "1201 alarm." The controllers at Houston assured them the computer would reset. They were to continue the descent despite the alarm.

"We're go," Aldrin replied. "Hang tight. We're go. Two thousand feet." Aldrin continued to read out the data. Armstrong watched out his left window as they approached the landing site. "Seven hundred feet, 21 down," Aldrin said. This meant *Eagle* was seven hundred feet above the Moon and was descending at twenty-one feet per second. "Four hundred feet, down at 9. We're pegged on horizontal velocity. Three hundred feet, down 3 and a half."

The *Eagle* in landing configuration, as photographed from *Columbia*.

The controllers in Houston were on the edge of their seats. Nearly every astronaut in the astronaut program was gathered behind the viewing window in the control room. They were all nervously watching the television screen and listening to Aldrin call out the landing data.[7]

"Altitude-velocity lights. Three and a half down, 220 feet. Thirteen forward, 11 forward, coming down nicely. Two hundred feet, 4 and a half down, 5 and half down."

[7] John Barbour, *Footprints on the Moon* (New York: The Associated Press, 1969), p. 205.

The landing site came into view outside *Eagle*'s two windows. As Armstrong looked, he saw something that made his heartbeat begin to race.[8] The computer was leading *Eagle* to the intended landing site. But that site was littered with boulders the size of automobiles! There was no way they could make a safe landing among those boulders.

Armstrong grasped the rocket control handle with his right hand and overrode the automatic landing system. *Eagle* skimmed over the large field of boulders as Armstrong searched the lunar surface for a smoother landing area. He knew he had to find it in a hurry. *Eagle* was now only one hundred feet above the Moon, and its landing engine was running very close to the end of its fuel.

[8] Peter Bond, *Heroes in Space: From Gagarin to Challenger* (New York: Basil Blackwell, Inc., 1987), p. 191.

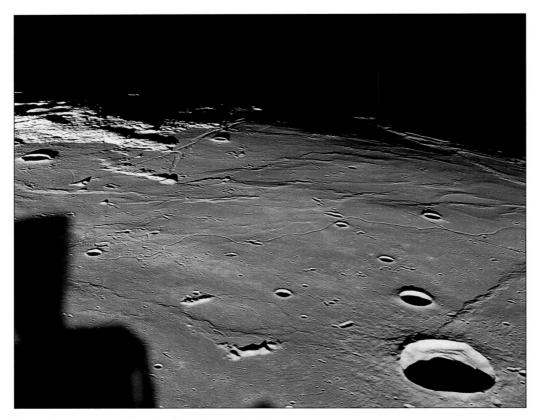

View of the approaching landing site on the Moon, as seen by the astronauts aboard *Apollo 11*.

"Seventy-five feet," Aldrin continued. "Down a half, 6 forward."

"Sixty seconds," Mission Control said, meaning there was only one minute of fuel left in *Eagle*'s landing engine. The controllers in Houston were unaware of the boulders Armstrong had seen. They were anxious for Armstrong to set *Eagle* down.[9]

"Forty feet, down 2 and a half," Aldrin read out to Armstrong, who was flying Eagle toward a spot he saw several hundred yards to the right of his window. Getting there would be cutting it very close. "Picking up some dust. Thirty feet . . . faint shadow. Four forward, drifting to the right a little."

"Thirty seconds," said Mission Control.

"Six forward. Drifting right." *Eagle* was now kicking up a lot of dust on the surface. "Contact light." This meant that one of the feelers on the legs of the lunar module had touched the Moon. The cloud of dust moved away from them. Armstrong and Aldrin sensed that they and *Eagle* had come to a complete stop. They were motionless.

Almost out of habit, Aldrin continued to read out the information from his panel. "Okay, engine stop. . . . descent engine command override, off. Engine arm, off."

All of Mission Control's instruments told the controllers that the lunar module was down. "We copy you down, *Eagle*," came the communicator's voice.

[9] Barbour, p. 206.

A manager at Mission Control studies his console during the *Apollo 11* landing mission.

"Houston," Armstrong replied, hesitating for a moment, "Tranquility Base here. The *Eagle* has landed."

Mission Control erupted in cheers. "Roger Tranquility," the communicator said through the noise, "we copy you on the ground. You've got a bunch of guys about to turn blue. We're breathing again. Thanks a lot."

Aldrin reached across his instrument panel and he and Armstrong shook hands firmly. They had done it! Looking out their windows, they stared with awe at the stark and lonely alien landscape.[10] It was hard to believe they were really on the Moon.

A quarter of a million miles away, people all over the Earth were slowly realizing what had just happened. Human beings had for the first time landed upon another world.

[10] Harry Hurt, III, *For All Mankind* (New York: Atlantic Monthly Press, 1988), p. 169.

Mission Control was still loud with the excitement of the landing. "Be advised there are lots of smiling faces in this room and all over the world. Over," the communicator told the astronauts.[11]

"There are two of them up here," Armstrong replied.

"And don't forget one in the command module," Collins broke in on the circuit. "Tranquility Base, it sure sounded good from here. You guys did a fantastic job."

"Thank you," Armstrong replied. "Just keep that orbiting base ready for us up there now."

Armstrong and Aldrin were scheduled for a four-hour rest period after the landing systems check. They were simply too excited. They requested to go ahead with preparations for the Moon walks now.[12] Houston agreed. The two astronauts ate their first meal on the Moon. Then they spent the next two hours getting suited up for the Moon walks.

The suits Armstrong and Aldrin wore included a backpack that would keep a person alive on the Moon for four hours. It carried oxygen for them to breathe, water to cool the special garment they wore beneath the suit, and communications equipment. As soon as Armstrong and Aldrin sealed their helmets and gloves, they depressurized the cabin. Armstrong dropped to his hands and knees and began to back out of the open hatch. He stepped onto the ladder on one of *Eagle*'s landing legs.

[11] *Apollo 11, Technical Air-to-Ground Voice Transcription,* Manned Spacecraft Center, Houston, Texas, July 1969. All in-flight communications which follow come from this source.
[12] Edwin E. "Buzz" Aldrin, Jr., with Wayne Warga, Return to Earth (New York: Random House, 1973), pp. 232–233.

Back on Earth, millions breathlessly watched their televisions. A camera placed near the base of the lunar module brought them live pictures of Armstrong's ghostly image coming down the ladder. People all over the world were amazed that astronauts were on the Moon. And most of them found it just as amazing that they were able to watch live television pictures of it.

"Okay Neil, we can see you coming down the ladder now," Mission Control said.

Armstrong carefully stepped down each rung of the ladder. It was tricky. He was still getting used to the bulky suit and the Moon's gravity, which is one-sixth the gravity of Earth. "I'm at the foot of the ladder," Armstrong reported. "The LM footpads are only depressed in the surface about one or two inches. Although the surface appears to be very, very fine grained, as you get close to it. It's almost like a powder."

The Mission Control room was completely silent. They were fascinated by every word of Armstrong's description of the Moon's landscape around him. They knew they were witnessing history.

"I'm going to step off the LM now." Armstrong moved his left leg away from *Eagle*'s footpad and planted his boot in the lunar soil—the first human step on another world. "That's one small step for a man . . . one giant leap for mankind."

Millions of people on Earth witnessed this moment of history. It was a moment unlike any other. It gave many people a sense of awe and a feeling of pride that humanity had accomplished such a feat. It left many people, including the famous CBS television news anchor Walter Cronkite, completely speechless.

Armstrong walked around the landing area. His walk looked more like a bouncy skip or a hop. The Moon's gravity allowed him to bound lightly from one foot to the other. He took out a scoop with a long handle to collect the first sample of Moon soil. He collected some soil and rocks in a bag and placed it in a pocket just above his left knee. Then he looked out across the lunar landscape.

Stepping down from the lunar module to the Moon was tricky. Featured on these two pages is Buzz Aldrin descending the ladder.

Aldrin poses near the special American flag which the astronauts put on the Moon. Since there is no wind on the Moon, the flag was stiffened to look as if it was blowing. The lunar module is seen on the left.

"It has a stark beauty all its own," he said. "It's different, but it's very pretty out here."

A few minutes later, Aldrin joined Armstrong on the surface. "Beautiful view!" Aldrin said when he stepped away from the ladder.

"Isn't that something?" Armstrong said. "Magnificent sight out here."

"Magnificent desolation," Aldrin added.

They practiced different methods of walking in Moon's gravity and reported their sensations to Mission Control. Then they unveiled a plaque attached to *Eagle*'s landing leg. Armstrong read it for the viewers back on Earth.

"'Here Men from the planet Earth first set foot upon the Moon, July 1969 A.D. We came in peace for all mankind.' It has the crewmembers' signatures and the signature of the President of the United States."

Next they planted the United States flag near *Eagle* and received a special telephone call from President Richard Nixon.

"For one priceless moment, in the whole history of man," Nixon said, "all the people of Earth are truly one. One in their pride in what you have done. And one in our prayers that you will return safely to Earth."

Two and a half days later, on Thursday, July 24, 1969, *Apollo 11* reentered the Earth's atmosphere. After the fiery reentry, huge red and white parachutes sprang from the nose of the capsule. Neil Armstrong, Edwin E. "Buzz" Aldrin, and Mike Collins came to a soft splashdown in the Pacific Ocean. *Apollo 11* had returned.

They were recovered by the aircraft carrier U.S.S. *Hornet*. President Nixon was waiting to welcome them. Scientists were afraid that the astronauts might have brought dangerous organisms back from the Moon. So the men had to wear strange airtight overalls with headgear that looked like gas masks.

The *Apollo 11* crew awaits pickup by a helicopter from the U.S.S. *Hornet*.

As soon as a helicopter landed them on the carrier, they entered a large van that looked like a camper trailer. It was a comfortable quarantine facility. They took off the suits and looked out a window to participate in a welcoming ceremony with President Nixon. They stayed in the trailerlike facility for three days. Then it was flown by cargo plane to Houston. There it was pulled into the Lunar Receiving Laboratory (LRL). There the astronauts were let out of the trailer and scientists checked them out thoroughly.

For the next three weeks, Armstrong, Aldrin, and Collins lived in the LRL. They debriefed NASA people about the flight and were continually examined for the effects of any possible alien organisms. After three weeks, on August 10, 1969, the quarantine was over. The astronauts were released to the outside world.

For the next two months, Neil Armstrong, Buzz Aldrin, and Mike Collins rode in parades and gave speeches to hundreds of thousands of people on a tour that took them to six continents. They were heroes, and now an important part of history. Eventually the celebrations died down and plans for the next trip to the Moon, *Apollo 12,* continued. But there would never be another Moon mission like *Apollo 11.*

President Richard M. Nixon proudly greets the three astronauts who were being quarantined aboard the U.S.S. *Hornet*.

It is difficult to know the true meaning or importance of humanity's first voyage to another world. Perhaps Buzz Aldrin stated it best in his words to a joint session of Congress, fifty-four days after *Apollo 11* had returned from the Moon:

I say to you today what no men have been privileged to say before: We walked on the Moon. But the footprints at Tranquility Base belong to more than the crew of Apollo 11. . . . *Those footprints belong to the American people . . . who accepted and supported the inevitable challenge of the Moon. And, since we came in peace for all mankind, those footprints belong also to all the people of the world.*

The first step on the Moon was a step toward our sister planets and ultimately the stars. 'A small step for a man' was a statement of fact, 'a giant leap for mankind' is a hope for the future.[13]

[13] Douglas MacKinnon and Joseph Baldanza, *Footprints* (Washington, D.C.: Acropolis Books Ltd., 1989), p. 21.

The city of Chicago welcomes Armstrong, Collins, and Aldrin home with a ticker tape parade.

Meet the Author

Michael D. Cole dreamed of being an astronaut as a child. His fascination with outer space has continued into his adult life. He has written many books about the exploration of space, including *Vostok 1: First Human in Space*, *Columbia: First Flight of the Space Shuttle*, and other books about Apollo and space shuttle missions. His books give readers a window into the technology and people involved in these amazing space adventures.

Theme Connections

Within the Selection

Record your answers to the questions below in the Response Journal section of your Writer's Notebook. In small groups, report the ideas you wrote. Discuss your ideas with the rest of your group. Then choose a person to report your group's answers to the class.

- How was the *Apollo 11* mission different from any of the three astronauts' previous undertakings?
- All three of the astronauts admitted to thinking the *Apollo 11* mission had about as much chance for failure as it did for success. Why did they embark on the mission in spite of this? Do you think they would have felt the mission was worthwhile if they had not accomplished their goal? Explain your answer.
- What did Buzz Aldrin mean when he said that the footprints at Tranquility Base belonged to "all the people of the world"?

Across Selections

- Compare the journeys taken by the three astronauts and by Ernest Shackleton in "Trapped by the Ice!" Which journey required more courage? Why do you think so?
- How is the *Apollo 11* mission similar to the Lewis and Clark expedition in "Sacagawea's Journey"?

Beyond the Selection

- Think about how "*Apollo 11*: First Moon Landing" adds to what you know about journeys and quests.
- Add items to the Concept/Question Board about journeys and quests.

When Shlemiel Went to Warsaw

from the book by Isaac Bashevis Singer
illustrated by Krystyna Stasiak

Though Shlemiel was a lazybones and a sleepyhead and hated to move, he always daydreamed of taking a trip. He had heard many stories about faraway countries, huge deserts, deep oceans, and high mountains, and often discussed with Mrs. Shlemiel his great wish to go on a long journey. Mrs. Shlemiel would reply: "Long journeys are not for a Shlemiel. You better stay home and mind the children while I go to market to sell my vegetables." Yet Shlemiel could not bring himself to give up his dream of seeing the world and its wonders.

A recent visitor to Chelm had told Shlemiel marvelous things about the city of Warsaw. How beautiful the streets were, how high the buildings and luxurious the stores. Shlemiel decided once and for all that he must see this great city for himself.

He knew that one had to prepare for a journey. But what was there for him to take? He had nothing but the old clothes he wore. One morning, after Mrs. Shlemiel left for the market, he told the older boys to stay home from cheder and mind the younger children. Then he took a few slices of bread, an onion, and a clove of garlic, put them in a kerchief, tied it into a bundle, and started for Warsaw on foot.

There was a street in Chelm called Warsaw Street and Shlemiel believed that it led directly to Warsaw. While still in the village, he was stopped by several neighbors who asked him where he was going. Shlemiel told them that he was on his way to Warsaw.

"What will you do in Warsaw?" they asked him.

Shlemiel replied: "What do I do in Chelm? Nothing."

He soon reached the outskirts of town. He walked slowly because the soles of his boots were worn through. Soon the houses and stores gave way to pastures and fields. He passed a peasant driving an ox-drawn plow. After several hours of walking, Shlemiel grew tired. He was so weary that he wasn't even hungry. He lay down on the grass near the roadside for a nap, but before he fell asleep he thought: "When I wake up, I may not remember which is the way to Warsaw and which leads back to Chelm." After pondering a moment, he removed his boots and set them down beside him with the toes pointing toward Warsaw and the heels toward Chelm. He soon fell asleep and dreamed that he was a baker baking onion rolls with poppy seeds. Customers came to buy them and Shlemiel said: "These onion rolls are not for sale."

"Then why do you bake them?"

"They are for my wife, for my children, and for me."

Later he dreamed that he was the King of Chelm. Once a year, instead of taxes, each citizen brought him a pot of strawberry jam. Shlemiel sat on a golden throne and nearby sat Mrs. Shlemiel, the queen, and his children, the princes and princesses. They were all eating onion rolls and spooning up big portions of strawberry jam. A carriage arrived and took the royal family to Warsaw, America, and to the river Sambation, which spurts out stones the week long and rests on the Sabbath.

Near the road, a short distance from where Shlemiel slept, was a smithy. The blacksmith happened to come out just in time to see Shlemiel carefully placing his boots at his side with the toes facing in the direction of Warsaw. The blacksmith was a prankster and as soon as Shlemiel was sound asleep he tiptoed over and turned the boots around. When Shlemiel awoke, he felt rested but hungry. He got out a slice of bread, rubbed it with garlic, and took a bite of onion. Then he pulled his boots on and continued on his way.

He walked along and everything looked strangely familiar. He recognized houses that he had seen before. It seemed to him that he knew the people he met. Could it be that he had already reached another town, Shlemiel wondered. And why was it so similar to Chelm? He stopped a passerby and asked the name of the town. "Chelm," the man replied.

Shlemiel was astonished. How was this possible? He had walked away from Chelm. How could he have arrived back there? He began to rub his forehead and soon found the answer to the riddle. There were two Chelms and he had reached the second one.

Still, it seemed very odd that the streets, the houses, the people were so similar to those in the Chelm he had left behind. Shlemiel puzzled over this fact until he suddenly remembered something he had learned in cheder: "The earth is the same everywhere." And so why shouldn't the second Chelm be exactly like the first one? This discovery gave Shlemiel great satisfaction. He wondered if there was a street here like his street and a house on it like the one he lived in. And indeed, he soon arrived at an identical street and house. Evening had fallen. He opened the door and to his amazement saw a second Mrs. Shlemiel with children just like his. Everything was exactly the same as in his own household. Even the cat seemed the same. Mrs. Shlemiel at once began to scold him.

"Shlemiel, where did you go? You left the house alone. And what have you there in that bundle?"

The children all ran to him and cried: "Papa, where have you been?"

Shlemiel paused a moment and then he said: "Mrs. Shlemiel, I'm not your husband. Children, I'm not your papa."

"Have you lost your mind?" Mrs. Shlemiel screamed.

"I am Shlemiel of Chelm One and this is Chelm Two."

Mrs. Shlemiel clapped her hands so hard that the chickens sleeping under the stove awoke in fright and flew out all over the room.

"Children, your father has gone crazy," she wailed. She immediately sent one of the boys for Gimpel the healer. All the neighbors came crowding in. Shlemiel stood in the middle of the room and proclaimed:

"It's true, you all look like the people in my town, but you are not the same. I came from Chelm One and you live in Chelm Two."

"Shlemiel, what's the matter with you?" someone cried. "You're in your own house, with your own wife and children, your own neighbors and friends."

"No, you don't understand. I come from Chelm One. I was on my way to Warsaw, and between Chelm One and Warsaw there is a Chelm Two. And that is where I am."

"What are you talking about. We all know you and you know all of us. Don't you recognize your chickens?"

"No, I'm not in my town," Shlemiel insisted. "But," he continued, "Chelm Two does have the same people and the same houses as Chelm One, and that is why you are mistaken. Tomorrow I will continue on to Warsaw."

"In that case, where is my husband?" Mrs. Shlemiel inquired in a rage, and she proceeded to berate Shlemiel with all the curses she could think of.

"How should I know where your husband is?" Shlemiel replied.

Some of the neighbors could not help laughing; others pitied the family. Gimpel the healer announced that he knew of no remedy for such an illness. After some time, everybody went home.

Mrs. Shlemiel had cooked noodles and beans that evening, a dish that Shlemiel liked especially. She said to him: "You may be mad, but even a madman has to eat."

"Why should you feed a stranger?" Shlemiel asked.

"As a matter of fact, an ox like you should eat straw, not noodles and beans. Sit down and be quiet. Maybe some food and rest will bring you back to your senses."

"Mrs. Shlemiel, you're a good woman. My wife wouldn't feed a stranger. It would seem that there is some small difference between the two Chelms."

The noodles and beans smelled so good that Shlemiel needed no further coaxing. He sat down, and as he ate he spoke to the children:

"My dear children, I live in a house that looks exactly like this one. I have a wife and she is as like your mother as two peas are like each other. My children resemble you as drops of water resemble one another."

The younger children laughed; the older ones began to cry. Mrs. Shlemiel said: "As if being a Shlemiel wasn't enough, he had to go crazy in addition. What am I going to do now? I won't be able to leave the children with him when I go to market. Who knows what a madman may do?" She clasped her head in her hands and cried out, "God in heaven, what have I done to deserve this?"

Nevertheless, she made up a fresh bed for Shlemiel; and even though he had napped during the day, near the smithy, the moment his head touched the pillow he fell fast asleep and was soon snoring loudly. He again dreamed that he was the King of Chelm and that his wife, the queen, had fried for him a huge panful of blintzes. Some were filled with cheese, others with blueberries or cherries, and all were sprinkled with sugar and cinnamon and were drowning in sour cream.

Shlemiel ate twenty blintzes all at once and hid the remainder in his crown for later.

In the morning, when Shlemiel awoke, the house was filled with townspeople. Mrs. Shlemiel stood in their midst, her eyes red with weeping. Shlemiel was about to scold his wife for letting so many strangers into the house, but then he remembered that he himself was a stranger here. At home he would have gotten up, washed, and dressed. Now in front of all these people he was at a loss as to what to do. As always when he was embarrassed, he began to scratch his head and pull at his beard. Finally, overcoming his bashfulness, he decided to get up. He threw off the covers and put his bare feet on the floor. "Don't let him run away," Mrs. Shlemiel screamed. "He'll disappear and I'll be a deserted wife, without a Shlemiel."

At this point Baruch the baker interrupted. "Let's take him to the Elders. They'll know what to do."

"That's right! Let's take him to the Elders," everybody agreed.

Although Shlemiel insisted that since he lived in Chelm One, the local Elders had no power over him, several of the strong young men helped him into his pants, his boots, his coat and cap and escorted him to the house of Gronam Ox. The Elders, who had already heard of the matter, had gathered early in the morning to consider what was to be done.

As the crowd came in, one of the Elders, Dopey Lekisch, was saying, "Maybe there really are two Chelms."

"If there are two, then why can't there be three, four, or even a hundred Chelms?" Sender Donkey interrupted.

"And even if there are a hundred Chelms, must there be a Shlemiel in each one of them?" argued Shmendrick Numskull.

Gronam Ox, the head Elder, listened to all the arguments but was not yet prepared to express an opinion. However, his wrinkled, bulging forehead indicated that he was deep in thought. It was Gronam Ox who questioned Shlemiel. Shlemiel related everything that had happened to him, and when he finished, Gronam asked, "Do you recognize me?"

"Surely. You are wise Gronam Ox."

"And in your Chelm is there also a Gronam Ox?"

"Yes, there is a Gronam Ox and he looks exactly like you."

"Isn't it possible that you turned around and came back to Chelm?" Gronam inquired.

"Why should I turn around? I'm not a windmill," Shlemiel replied.

"In that case, you are not this Mrs. Shlemiel's husband."

"No, I'm not."

"Then Mrs. Shlemiel's husband, the real Shlemiel, must have left the day you came."

"It would seem so."

"Then he'll probably come back."

"Probably."

"In that case, you must wait until he returns. Then we'll know who is who."

"Dear Elders, my Shlemiel has come back," screamed Mrs. Shlemiel. "I don't need two Shlemiels. One is more than enough."

"Whoever he is, he may not live in your house until everything is made clear," Gronam insisted.

"Where shall I live?" Shlemiel asked.

"In the poorhouse."

"What will I do in the poorhouse?"

"What do you do at home?"

"Good God, who will take care of my children when I go to market?" moaned Mrs. Shlemiel. "Besides, I want a husband. Even a Shlemiel is better than no husband at all."

"Are we to blame that your husband left you and went to Warsaw?" Gronam asked. "Wait until he comes home."

Mrs. Shlemiel wept bitterly and the children cried, too. Shlemiel said: "How strange. My own wife always scolded me. My children talked back to me. And here a strange woman and strange children want me to live with them. It looks to me as if Chelm Two is actually better than Chelm One."

"Just a moment. I think I have an idea," interrupted Gronam.

"What is your idea?" Zeinvel Ninny inquired.

"Since we decided to send Shlemiel to the poorhouse, the town will have to hire someone to take care of Mrs. Shlemiel's children so she can go to market. Why not hire Shlemiel for that? It's true, he is not Mrs. Shlemiel's husband or the children's father.

But he is so much like the real Shlemiel that the children will feel at home with him."

"What a wonderful idea!" cried Feyvel Thickwit.

"Only King Solomon could have thought of such a wise solution," agreed Treitel the Fool.

"Such a clever way out of this dilemma could only have been thought of in our Chelm," chimed in Shmendrick Numskull.

"How much do you want to be paid to take care of Mrs. Shlemiel's children?" asked Gronam.

For a moment Shlemiel stood there completely bewildered. Then he said, "Three groschen a day."

"Idiot, moron, donkey!" screamed Mrs. Shlemiel. "What are three groschen nowadays? You shouldn't do it for less than six a day." She ran over to Shlemiel and pinched him on the arm. Shlemiel winced and cried out, "She pinches just like my wife."

The Elders held a consultation among themselves. The town budget was very limited. Finally Gronam announced: "Three groschen may be too little, but six groschen a day is definitely too much, especially for a stranger. We will compromise and pay you five groschen a day. Shlemiel, do you accept?"

"Yes, but how long am I to keep this job?"

"Until the real Shlemiel comes home."

Gronam's decision was soon known throughout Chelm, and the town admired his great wisdom and that of all the Elders of Chelm.

At first, Shlemiel tried to keep the five groschen that the town paid him for himself. "If I'm not your husband, I don't have to support you," he told Mrs. Shlemiel.

"In that case, since I'm not your wife, I don't have to cook for you, darn your socks, or patch your clothes."

And so, of course, Shlemiel turned over his pay to her. It was the first time that Mrs. Shlemiel had ever gotten any money for the household from Shlemiel. Now when she was in a good mood, she would say to him, "What a pity you didn't decide to go to Warsaw ten years ago."

"Don't you ever miss your husband?" Shlemiel would ask.

"And what about you? Don't you miss your wife?" Mrs. Shlemiel would ask. And both would admit that they were quite happy with matters as they stood.

Years passed and no Shlemiel returned to Chelm. The Elders had many explanations for this. Zeinvel Ninny believed that Shlemiel had crossed the black mountains and had been eaten alive by the cannibals who live there. Dopey Lekisch thought that Schlemiel most probably had come to the Castle of Asmodeus, where he had been forced to marry a demon princess. Shmendrick Numskull came to the conclusion that Shlemiel had reached the edge of the world and had fallen off. There were many other theories. For example, that the real Shlemiel had lost his memory and had simply forgotten that he was Shlemiel. Such things do happen.

Gronam did not like to impose his theories on other people; however, he was convinced that Shlemiel had gone to the other Chelm, where he had had exactly the same experience as the Shlemiel in this Chelm. He had been hired by the local community and was taking care of the other Mrs. Shlemiel's children for a wage of five groschen a day.

As for Schlemiel himself, he no longer knew what to think. The children were growing up and soon would be able to take care of themselves. Sometimes Shlemiel would sit and ponder. Where is the other Shlemiel? When will he come home? What is my real wife doing? Is she waiting for me, or has she got herself another Shlemiel? These were questions that he could not answer.

Every now and then Shlemiel would still get the desire to go traveling, but he could not bring himself to start out. What was the point of going on a trip if it led nowhere? Often, as he sat alone puzzling over the strange ways of the world, he would become more and more confused and begin humming to himself:

> *"Those who leave Chelm*
> *End up in Chelm.*
> *Those who remain in Chelm*
> *Are certainly in Chelm.*
> *All roads lead to Chelm.*
> *All the world is one big Chelm."*

When Shlemiel Went to Warsaw

Meet the Author

Isaac Bashevis Singer was born in Poland in 1904 and grew up in Warsaw. He said of his childhood home, *"My father was an orthodox rabbi, and our house was a house of holy books and learning. Other children had toys. I played with the books in my father's library."*

Singer and his brother came to the United States in 1935. Isaac learned English but wrote all of his books first in Yiddish. He then translated them into his new language. He said of his writing for children, *"Children are the best readers of genuine literature. . . . The young reader demands a real story, with a beginning, a middle, and an end, the way stories have been told for thousands of years."*

Meet the Illustrator

Krystyna Stasiak was born in Poland, but she became a permanent resident of the United States in 1969. As a child, her parents tried to guide her into the world of music. However, she naturally gravitated toward the world of art. She received her art degree from the Academy of Fine Arts in Warsaw, Poland. Today she is a free-lance artist. She exhibits her art in museums and illustrates books for both children and adults.

She loves animals and believes they have their own distinct personalities. She also loves to travel and has visited Italy, Switzerland, and Austria. Her other hobbies include skiing, tennis, literature, languages, and music.

Theme Connections

Within the Selection

Record your answers to the questions below in the Response Journal section of your Writer's Notebook. In small groups, report the ideas you wrote. Discuss your ideas with the rest of your group. Then choose a person to report your group's answers to the class.

- What might have happened to Shlemiel if he had continued his journey?
- What did Shlemiel learn from his journey? Was Shlemiel sorry that he never reached Warsaw?
- How is it possible to have journeys in one's own mind, rather than physically?

Across Selections

- Compare this story with "The Story of Jumping Mouse." Discuss the purpose of each story.

Beyond the Selection

- Shlemiel wanted to travel to a place he had heard was grand. Where do you want to travel, and why do you want to go there?
- Think about how "When Shlemiel Went to Warsaw" adds to what you know about journeys and quests.
- Add items to the Concept/Question Board about journeys and quests.

May, from Les Tres Riches Heures de Duc de Berry.
1413–1416. **Limbourg Brothers.** Ink, tempera, and gold on
parchment. $8\frac{1}{2} \times 5\frac{1}{2}$ in. Musée Conde, Chantilly, France.

Landscape with a Solitary Traveler.
c.1780. **Yosa Buson.** Hanging scroll. Ink
and light colors on silk. 101.5×36.4 cm.
Courtesy of the Kimbell Art Museum,
Fort Worth, Texas.

Don Quixote. 1955. **Pablo Picasso.**
Drawing. Musée d'Art et d'Histoire,
St. Denis, France. ©2001 Estate of Pablo
Picasso/Artist Rights Society (ARS),
New York.

The Return of Ulysses.
1976. **Romare Bearden.**
Silkscreen. Philadelphia
Museum of Art. ©Romare
Bearden Foundation/
Licensed by VAGA,
New York, NY.

Focus Questions What does Miguel think he will earn by finding the sheep? How does Miguel's search become an inner journey? What does he prove to himself?

The Search

from . . . *And Now Miguel*
by Joseph Krumgold
illustrated by Antonio Castro

Miguel Chavez's great wish is to be allowed to accompany his father, uncles, and older brothers on their annual move to the Sangre de Cristo Mountains with the family's sheep herds. Miguel feels that at twelve he is old enough to spend the summer with the men of the family in the mountains rather than stay at home with his mother and younger brother and sister. When some of the family's sheep are lost as the result of a spring storm, Miguel thinks that his chance has come to prove his worth as a shepherd. He intends to find the sheep. However, fearing that Miguel will only get in the way, his father will not allow him to join the search.

My friend Juby was playing basketball when I came to the yard of the schoolhouse. That is, Juby and some of the others were playing just shooting for baskets, and as soon as he saw me, he waved his hand and quit, and came over.

"How're you doing?" he asked me.

I said, "Pretty good," because what's the use telling everybody your troubles?

"D'you folks lose any sheep?" he asked me.

"What?" I made one grab at his arm and held tight.

"Sheep," he said. "What's the matter?"

"Now look, Juby," I said. "What's the use talking you and me? How do you know we got missing sheep? What about them?"

"I saw them."

"What?"

"At least I think they're yours. From the shape of the numbers they look like yours." We don't put our brand on the sheep until after we shear them. But our numbers had a different shape to them than any of the others in the neighborhood.

"Where?"

"Then you did lose some sheep?"

"Juby!" I was a little excited. "What's the use, Juby? Just to talk? Where did you see them?"

"Well——you know Carlotta?"

"Who?"

"Our milk cow."

"Cows? What about the sheep?"

"I'm telling you. She got loose last night, Carlotta, and when I went to herd her back I saw those sheep."

"Where? Where? Where?"

"What's the matter with you, Mike? Something wrong?"

"Juby," I said. "You and me, you're my oldest friend, aren't you?"

"Sure."

"Then tell me, where are the sheep?"

"Give me a chance. I saw them across the river. Maybe fifteen, ewes and lambs. They looked like they were heading straight for Arroyo Hondo." It was just in the opposite direction from where my older brother Blasito and the sheep wagon was, from where he looked this morning. "Were they yours?"

"You don't know what this could mean, Juby. That is for me."

But just then the bell started to ring, and Mrs. Mertian, who is the teacher of our school over there in Los Cordovas, she came to the door and told everybody to come in.

"Let's go." Juby went with the others into the class.

And that's the way things stood.

On one side, Mrs. Mertian with the bell ringing. And on the other side the big mountains, looking very dark and a little mad, if you can think of mountains like they were mad. But that was the way they looked, and at that moment there came thunder from behind them.

And in the middle, I stood. If it ever happened that I came home with the missing sheep? Could anything ever be better?

Mrs. Mertian said, "Miguel."

From the Sangre de Cristo there came thunder, very low.

I did not stand too long. Because there was no question about it! Nothing, that is to say, nothing at all could ever be better.

I headed straight for the *Boys* on the other side of the yard.

"Miguel!" It was Mrs. Mertian yelling. I didn't even look back. I jumped into this whole bunch of bushes and started down the hill.

Big champion jumps, every one breaking a world's record, that's the way I came down that hill. With each jump, everything went flying. My books banging at the end of the rope in my hand, swinging all around. My arms, like I had a dozen of them, each one going off by itself. My feet, like I was on a bike, working away to keep my balance. But I couldn't balance. Except by jumping. I couldn't stop. Each jump bigger than the last. I cleared a bush, then a big cracked rock. Then, I wasn't going to make it but I did, a high cactus. Each jump I thought was the last. Each jump was going to end with a cracked head, a split rib, or maybe two broken legs. But it didn't. I don't know why. There was nothing I could do. I came down that hill, like a boulder bumping in bigger and bigger bumps, bumping its way down a cliff. Straight for the river. Until I wasn't scared of falling anymore. I had to fall! Or land in the river. But how? I grabbed a bush. That didn't stop me. And then my books caught, between a couple of rocks. I slipped, grabbed at another bush. Slid a couple of feet, and then took off again. And then I landed. On my face. I landed in a whole piled up bunch of mesquite. No one, I'm sure ever since that hill was first there, ever came down it so fast.

I wasn't hurt. Except for a scratch stinging near my eye, I was all right. It didn't even bleed. All I needed was to catch my breath. I lay there in the bushes until I did. Breathing and listening for Mrs. Mertian, in case she came to the top of the hill and was yelling down at me. But I didn't hear any yelling. When I looked she wasn't there. The school bell stopped, too. All there was to hear was the thunder, now and then, far off, and the wind blowing quiet.

I got up thinking, I'd done it. After what Juby told me there was only one thing to do, and now I'd done it. Here I was, just me, Miguel, getting the sheep that were lost, all alone. And there would be no one bringing them home but me. All I had to do was to get up there, on the mesa across the river, round up the bunch and march them back to where everyone could see. It would be something worth watching, me herding the ewes and lambs that were lost back into the corral at home. My father would tell me how sorry he was about what happened at breakfast, the way he wouldn't let me go help. And I would tell my father, it was nothing, he didn't have to feel sorry.

I felt good. Looking at the mountains, and the mountains looking down at me as if to see what I was going to do next.

I hopped across the river. The easy place to cross was downstream a way, where there were more rocks to jump on. I didn't bother to go to the easy place. I could have made it even if the rocks were twice as far from each other, feeling good like I was, and all in practice from the way I'd come jumping down the hill. I only slipped into the water twice, without much water getting into my shoes at all.

To get up the cliff on the other side was not easy. It was steep in this place and wet and slippery with the rain, the stones high and smooth with nothing to grab on to except sometimes a juniper bush. And besides having the books in one hand. It would be better without the books. But I couldn't leave them around or hide them, seeing they might get wet. I made it all right, pulling and crawling my way up. Steep places and books, that wasn't too hard. Not to find a bunch of lost sheep, it wasn't.

When I got up to the top and looked, I didn't see them. I guess I did expect a little bit they'd be up there waiting for me. But they weren't. I didn't mind too much. The kind of thing I was doing had to be hard. Such a big thing couldn't be too easy. It'd be like cheating. I set out, walking to the north.

Up on the mesa, it looked empty. Like one of those pictures that my little brother Pedro draws. One straight line across the middle of the page and big zigzags off to one side which is the mountains. Then dark on top for the clouds, which he makes by smudging up all the pencil lines. And dark on the bottom for the mesa, which he makes with a special black crayon. That's all there is in the picture. And that's why it's a good picture. Because that's all there is. Except for some little bushes, juniper and chaparral and sagebrush. With nothing sticking up, only a high soapweed or a crooked-looking cactus. Nothing else.

Especially, no sheep.

I walked from one rise to the next. Every three or four steps turning all around as I walked. And when I got near to the top of each rise I had to run. Because I thought in the next ten, fifteen steps up top there, sure, I'd see them. The first few times I saw nothing, which I didn't mind too much. And the next few times, I saw nothing, too. Pretty soon I was getting ready to see them, because after an hour or so of walking and turning around and running I figured it was hard enough. Even for something big.

Besides I had a pebble in my left shoe. I felt it down there coming up the cliff. I didn't mind then, because it only made everything even harder. And that was all right with me. But now it was getting to hurt good. And I couldn't sit down and take it out. That would be like giving up.

Besides, I didn't have any time to waste. The mesa spread out, as far as you could see, with many breaks——everywhere little canyons and washes. And it was sure that on top of the next canyon, maybe, I was going to see them, those sheep. If I didn't waste time getting up there. Which I didn't. But all I saw was the same kind of nothing that I saw from the last high place, just this wide straight line stretching right across the middle.

Walking down was harder than walking up. For one thing, walking down on my left heel made the pebble bigger. It was getting to feel like a rock. And for another, walking down, you've already seen what there is to see all around, and there's nothing to look forward to until you start to walk up again. It got so I was running more than I was walking. Running downhill because I wanted to get that part over with, and running up because I couldn't wait to get to the top. And all the time, turning around. I got pretty good at being able to turn around and keep running at the same time.

Except what good was it, getting pretty good at anything? When the only thing that counted was to get one look, one quick look at those sheep.

All the turning around did was to get me so mixed up I didn't know whether I was going north, south, east or west. Not that it made any difference, I guess. The sheep weren't particular which direction you went to find them. They weren't in any direction. There were just no sheep. There was all the dark sky, and all this straight flat plain you'd ever want to see. But, no sheep.

And after a couple of hours of seeing no sheep, I would've been glad to see any sheep, even if they weren't ours. I kept trying to see sheep so hard, it was like my eyes got dry and thirsty just to see sheep. To see nothing for two, three hours, especially sheep, it gets hard on your eyes.

It was getting hard on my left foot, too, with that big rock pressing in.

And it wasn't so easy on my hands, either, on account of the books. The books weren't heavy, but when you keep that rope wrapped around your hand it can pinch. And even if you take it off one hand and put it on the other, it don't take long before it's pinching that hand, too.

Another thing was it got to be hard breathing. Because there was no time to stop and get a good breath. There was always somewhere to go take a look, and you couldn't stop because maybe that very second the sheep were moving away out of sight, and that very second if you were up on a top you'd see them.

After so many hours of it being so hard, I figured it was hard enough by then. It was getting long past the time I ought to find our sheep. Only it didn't make any difference how I figured. They weren't there to be found. Not anywhere.

And after a while, walking, walking, every place started to look like you'd been there before. You'd see a piece of tumble weed. And you were sure it was one you saw an hour before. It didn't help to think that maybe you were just walking up and around the same hill all the time.

Then looking, looking, I thought I heard a bell. I listened hard in the wind. One of the ewes that was lost might have a bell. In the flock there are ten or a dozen sheep with bells. Each one is like the leader of a bunch. I stood still, listening. Then I heard it again, and it was for sure a bell. But it was the school bell, far away, back in Los Cordovas. It must've already become noon, and that was the bell for noontime. Soon the ringing far away stopped. And there was nothing to listen to again, except the quiet wind.

It was never the same, after I heard that bell. It made me feel hungry. Because the bell meant going home to eat. And feeling hungry, I got to feel not so good in the other parts of me. Like lonely. At the beginning being alone was the best part of it, going off by myself to bring home the sheep. But now it was getting to look like I wasn't bringing home any sheep. And that made a lot of difference about being alone, while everybody else was back there going home to eat. The only way I could go home was to find them. It wasn't only so I could bring the sheep back. I had to find them so I could go back, too.

From then on, I got very busy. I didn't stop to walk any more. I ran. Everywhere I went I kept up running, and I did most of my breathing going downhill when I didn't have to try so hard to keep running. There was hardly any breath left over to keep looking with. And that was the hardest part of all, the looking. Because there was never anything to see.

And after a long while, I heard the bell again. School was out for the day.

It was hard to figure out what to do next.

I could leave home. That's about all there was left. I couldn't go back without the sheep. Not after what my father said at breakfast, and especially not after the way he looked. And it was clear enough that in all this whole empty place I was never going to find them, those sheep. I could just as well stop, that's all. I could take some time and do a lot of breathing. I could bury my books under a bush. I could sit down and take off my shoe and get rid of that rock with all the sharp edges on it. Then I could go somewhere until I saw a lot of sheep and sit down and look at them, till I got enough again of looking at sheep. And then I could decide where I was leaving home to go to.

Maybe even to the Sangre de Cristo Mountains. On my own, by myself.

But when I looked at the mountains, I knew that was no good. It was impossible. There was only one way to go up into the Mountains of the Sangre de Cristo. And that was to make everyone see you were ready, and then you would go.

Indeed, in order that I should go this way, that's why I was looking for the sheep right now. And if I gave up looking for the sheep, then the idea of going up into the Mountains, I had to give that up, too. I guess if you are going to leave home you just left home, that's all, everything.

Except, it wasn't up to me anymore. It wasn't a question that I should give up looking for the sheep.

It was just no use.

I could keep running from the top of one rise up to the next, looking, looking with my eyes getting drier and drier, without any breath, and the bones in my hands like they were cracking, and the heel of my left foot like it was getting torn away, listening to nothing but the wind——I could keep on doing that forever. It wasn't a question of me giving up, it was a question that just everything had given up, me and everything.

So I sat down. I took a deep breath. And I started to untie the laces from my left shoe. And then——what do you think?

I smelled them.

It is not hard to know that what you're smelling is sheep. If only there are some sheep around to smell. They smell a little sweet and a little old, like coffee that's left over in a cup on the table with maybe used-up cigarettes in it. That's sort of what they smell like.

So when there was this smell, I looked around. I found out from which direction was the wind. And in that direction I went to the top of the next rise, a dozen steps. And no farther away than you could throw a rock, there they were coming up the hill toward me, about fifteen ewes and their lambs, ambling along, having a good time eating, just taking a walk like there was no trouble anywhere in all the world.

"Wahoo!" I took off. Around my head in a big circle I swung my books. Like it was a rope, and I was going to throw a loop on all fifteen at once. "Wahoo!" I took off down that hill as if I were a whole tribe of Indians and the sheep was somebody's chuck wagon that was going to get raided. "Wahoo!"

The sheep looked up, a little like they were a bunch of ladies in church and they were interested to see who was coming through the door.

I showed them who was coming through the door. Before they knew what was happening they were moving. *Whoosh*—— I let my books swing out, and I hit one right in the rump. *Whish*——I kicked another one with my foot that had the rock, so that it hurt me more, I think, than the sheep. I picked up a stone and——*wango*——I let a third one have it in the rear. I got them running right in the opposite direction than they were going.

I kept them going at a gallop. Running first to the one side, then to the other, swinging the books around my head all the time. Yelling and hollering so they wouldn't even dare slow down. They looked scared, but I didn't care. I had waited too long for this. And now I wanted them to know that I was here.

I ran them down the hill fast enough to be a stampede. And whichever one ran last, he was the unlucky one. There were a lot of rocks around, and I throw rocks good.

At the bottom of the hill I quieted down. Why was I acting like I was so mad? I had no reason to be mad at the sheep. It wasn't as if they started out to get me in trouble. Indeed, because of them, here I was doing a great thing. I was finding them and bringing them home. If they didn't take it into their heads to go out and get lost, I never would have this big chance.

I quieted down. I stopped and I breathed. The air was good. After the rain it was clean and it smelled sweet, like a vanilla soda in Schaeffer's Drugstore in Taos before you start to drink it with the straw. I took in the air with deep breaths. I sat down and took off my shoe. I found the rock down near the heel. But my goodness, it wasn't any kind of rock at all. Just a little bit of a chip off a stone. In my foot it felt like a boulder. But in my hand it didn't look like anything at all.

I was quieted down. We started off. It was going to be a long drive home. I didn't mind. There were so many good things to think about. What my father would say to me and my grandfather.

It is no great trouble to drive a small bunch of sheep. You just walk behind them, and if one begins to separate you start in the same direction that it starts and that makes it turn back and bunch up again. It was very little work. So there was much time to think what my uncles would say, and my big brothers. And how Pedro would watch me.

There was much time to look around. At the mountains, not so dark now and not so mad. There was much to see, walking along thinking, breathing, and looking around. How the clouds now were taking on new shapes, the dark ones separating and new big white ones coming up. And on the mesa everything looked fine. I saw flowers. Before when I was looking there were no flowers. Now, there they were. The little pink ones of the peyote plants. And there were flowers on the hedgehog cactus, too, kind of pinkish purple some, and others a real red.

I remembered my brother Gabriel's song about the little red flower. And walking along, thinking, breathing, looking around, I began to sing the song. Only the first words over and over again because I didn't remember the rest, which made no difference, because who was listening anyway? It was just I wanted something to sing.

The Search

Meet the Author

Joseph Krumgold was born into a family that was very involved with the early motion picture industry. By the time he was twelve, he also had decided on a career in the movies. After college, he went to Hollywood. He became a writer and producer of screenplays for the first "talkies." During World War II, he worked for the Office of War Information, where he became interested in people and places. This interest led him to begin making documentary films after the war was over. He traveled all over the United States, Europe, and the Middle East making movies about the lives of interesting people and places. One of his films was about the life of sheepherders in the American Southwest. It was adapted into an award-winning children's book. This is how Mr. Krumgold became a children's book author. He continued writing books for children for the rest of his life.

Meet the Illustrator

Antonio Castro has been working as a freelance artist for the last twenty years, during which time he has achieved much recognition for his art. His work has been exhibited at galleries and museums in El Paso, Texas, and Juarez, Mexico. He has illustrated dozens of children's books and created designs for magazines and album covers. In addition, Mr. Castro teaches advanced illustration for the University of Texas in El Paso.

Theme Connections

Within the Selection

Record your answers to the questions below in the Response Journal section of your Writer's Notebook. In small groups, report the ideas you wrote. Discuss your ideas with the rest of your group. Then choose a person to report your group's answers to the class.

- Why was it so important to Miguel that he find the sheep on his own?
- Why did Miguel think his search for the sheep needed to be difficult?
- In what way does the journey accomplish more than Miguel thought it would?

Across Selections

- Compare Miguel's expectations for his journey with those of Sacagawea in "Sacagawea's Journey." In what way could both Sacagawea's and Miguel's journeys be considered successful?

Beyond the Selection

- Have you ever felt like you needed to prove something to someone else? What did you do about it? How did the experience change you?
- Think about how "The Search" adds to what you know about journeys and quests.
- Add items to the Concept/Question Board about journeys and quests.

Alberic the Wise

Norton Juster
illustrated by Leonard Baskin

More than many years ago when fewer things had
happened in the world and there was less to know,
there lived a young man named Alberic who knew
nothing at all. Well, almost nothing, or depending on your
generosity of spirit, hardly anything, for he could hitch an ox
and plow a furrow straight or thatch a roof or hone his scythe
until the edge was bright and sharp or tell by a sniff of the
breeze what the day would bring or with a glance when a
grape was sweet and ready. But these were only the things he
had to know to live or couldn't help knowing by living and
are, as you may have discovered, rarely accounted as
knowledge.

Of the world and its problems, however, he knew little, and
indeed was even less aware of their existence. In all his life he
had been nowhere and seen nothing beyond the remote estate
on which he lived and to whose lands he and his family had
been bound back beyond the edge of memory. He planted and

harvested, threshed and winnowed, tended the hives and the pigs, breathed the country air, and stopped now and again to listen to the birds or puzzle at the wind. There were no mysteries, hopes or dreams other than those that could be encompassed by his often aching back or impatient stomach. This was the sum of his existence and with it he was neither happy nor sad. He simply could not conceive of anything else.

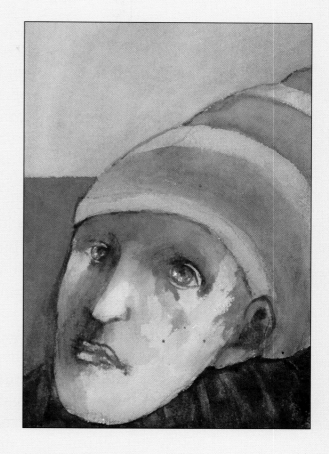

Since the days were much alike he measured his life by the more discernible seasons——yet they too slipped easily by, and would have continued to do so, I'm sure, had it not been for the lone traveler who appeared unaccountably one chill morning at the close of winter. Alberic watched him make his weary way along the road until, when they stood no more than a glance apart, he paused to rest before continuing on his journey. A curious old man——his tattered tunic was patched on patches and his worn shoes left hardly a suggestion of leather between himself and the cold ground. He carried a massive bundle on his back and sighed with the pleasure of letting it slide gently from his shoulder to the ground——then just as gently let himself down upon it. He nodded and smiled, mopped his face carefully with a handkerchief easily as old as himself, then acknowledged Alberic's timid greeting and finally began to speak, and when he did it was of many, many things. Where he had come from and where he was bound, what he had seen and what there was yet to discover——commonwealths, kingdoms, empires, counties and dukedoms——fortresses, bastions and great solitary castles that dug their fingers into the mountain passes and dared the world to pass——royal courts whose monarchs dressed in pheasant skins and silks and rich brocades of purple and lemon and crimson and bice all interlaced with figures of beasts and blossoms and strange geometric devices——and mountains that had no tops and oceans that had no bottoms.

There seemed no end to what he knew or what he cared to speak about, and speak he did, on and on through the day. His voice was soft and easy but his manner such that even his pauses commanded attention. And as he spoke his eyes sparkled and his words were like maps of unknown lands. He told of caravans that made their way across continents and back with perfumes and oils and dark red wines, sandalwood and lynx hides and ermine and carved sycamore chests, with cloves and cinnamon, precious stones and iron pots and ebony and amber and objects of pure tooled gold——of tall cathedral spires and cities full of life and craft and industry——of ships that sailed in every sea, and of art and science and learned speculation hardly even dreamed of by most people——and of armies and battles and magic and much, much more.

Alberic stood entranced, trying desperately to imagine all these wonderful things, but his mind could wander no further than the fields that he could see and the images soon would fade or cloud.

"The world is full of wonders," he sighed forlornly, for he realized that he could not even imagine what a wonder was.

"It is everything I've said and even more," the stranger replied, and since it was by now late afternoon he scrambled to his feet and once more took up his heavy bundle. "And remember," he said with a sweep of his arm, "it is all out there, just waiting." Then down the road and across the stubble fields he went.

For weeks after the old man had gone Alberic brooded, for now he knew that there were things he didn't know, and what magic and exciting things they were! Warm wet breezes had begun to blow across the land and the frozen fields had yielded first to mud and then to early blossoms.

But now this quiet hillside was not enough to hold his rushing thoughts. "It is all out there, just waiting," he said to himself again and again, repeating the old man's words. When he had repeated them often enough, they became a decision. He secretly packed his few belongings and in the early morning's mist left his home and started down into the world to seek its wonders and its wisdom.

For two days and nights and half another day again he walked— through lonely forests and down along the rushing mountain streams that seemed to know their destination far better than he knew his.

Mile after mile he walked until at last the trees and vines gave way to sweeps of easy meadowland and in the distance, barely visible, the towers of a city reflected back the sun's bright rays. As he approached, the hazy form became a jumble of roofs and chimney pots spread out below, and each step closer embellished them with windows, carved gables, domes and graceful spires. All this in turn was circled by a high wall which seemed to grow higher and wider as he descended towards it until at last it filled his vision and hid all else behind it. The stream which only days before had been so gay and playful now broadened and as if aware of its new importance assumed a slow and dignified pace as it passed through the city. Alberic paused for a moment to catch his breath, then, with a slight shiver of anticipation, passed beneath the cool dark gates and entered the city too.

What a teeming, busy place! Houses and shops, music and movement, all kinds of noises, signs and smells, and more people than he ever knew existed. He wandered along the cobbled streets delighted by each new discovery and noting with care the strange new sights and sounds so unfamiliar to his country senses. He soon learned too that he had come to a city famous above all others for the beautiful stained glass manufactured in its workshops.

"A noble and important profession," he decided soberly, "for surely beauty is the true aim of wisdom!" Without delay he went off to apprentice himself to the greatest of the master glassmakers.

"Well, well," growled the old craftsman after examining Alberic carefully, "so you want to make glass. Very well, we shall see. Your duties will be few and simple. Each morning you'll rise before the birds and with the other apprentices fetch sixty barrows of firewood from the forest. Then in each furnace bank a fire precisely hot enough to melt the lead and fuse the glass, and keep them tended constantly so that none goes out or varies even slightly in its heat. Then, of course, work the bellows, fetch the ingots from the foundry, run errands, assist the journeymen as they need, sharpen and repair all the chisels, files, knives, scrapers, shears, mallets and grozing irons so that each is in perfect order, make deliveries quickly and courteously, grind and mix the pigments, work the forge, sweep out the shop, fetch, carry, stoop, haul and bend, and in your spare time help with the household chores. You can of course eat your fill of the table scraps and sleep on the nice warm floor. Well, don't just stand there, you've only started and you're already hours behind in your work." When he finished he smiled a benevolent smile, for he was known for his generous nature.

Alberic applied himself to his new tasks with diligence, working from early morning until late at night when he would curl up in one corner of the shop to dream happily of the day's accomplishments and carefully sort and pack into his memory everything he'd learned. For some time he did only the menial jobs, but soon under the watchful eye of the master he began taking part in more important and exacting procedures. He learned to chip and shape the glass into pieces often no larger than the palm of his hand and then apply the colors mixed in gum or oil with a delicate badger brush and fire these to permanence in the glowing kilns. Then from measurements and patterns he learned to set each piece in the grooved strips of lead and solder them carefully at each joint.

For almost two years he worked and watched as all these small and painstaking operations took form in great windows and medallions of saintly lives or tales of moral instruction which glowed in deep splendid blues and vivid rubies.

Finally the time came for Alberic to prove his skill and take his place among the glassmakers——to create a work entirely on his own. He was determined that it would be a rare and lovely thing and he set about it with quiet intensity.

"What will it be, Alberic?" they all asked eagerly.

"Beautiful," he replied with never a moment's doubt, and that was all he'd say.

And for weeks he worked secretly in one corner of the shop until the day came when his work was to be judged. Everyone gathered to see it. The master looked long and carefully. He stood back to view it in the light and squinted close at matters of fine detail, and then he rubbed his chin and then he tapped his finger and then he swayed and then he sighed and then he frowned.

"No," he said sadly and slowly, "certainly not. You will never be a glassmaker." And everyone agreed, for despite the best of intentions Alberic's work was poor indeed.

How miserable he was! How thoroughly miserable! Why wasn't it beautiful when he had tried so hard? How could he have learned so much and yet still fail? No one knew the answer. "There is no reason now for me to stay," he said quietly, gathering up his bundle, and without even as much as a last look back he walked out into the lonely countryside.

For several days he wandered aimlessly, seeing nothing, heading nowhere, his thoughts turned inward to his unhappy failure. But it was spring and no one who has ever worked the land can long ignore the signs this season brings. Sweet promising smells hung gently in the warm air, and all around the oxlips, daisies and celandine splashed the fields in lively yellow. A graceful bird and then another caught Alberic's eye. The busy buzz and click of small things were reassuring to his ear and even the bullfrogs' heavy thump set his heart beating once again. His spirits and then his hope revived. The world seemed large and inviting once again.

"There are other places and other things to learn," he thought. "Beauty isn't everything. The true measure of wisdom is utility. I'll do something useful." He hurried now and before long came to a city whose stonecutters and masons were renowned throughout the world for the excellence of their work. His thoughts turned to castles and cloisters, massive walls, towering vaults and steeples which only miracles of skill could hold suspended in the air.

"Everything of use and value is made of stone," he concluded and rushed to seek employment with the master stonecutter.

And for two more years he busied himself learning the secrets of this new vocation——selecting and cutting only the finest stone from the quarry——matching, marking and extracting the giant blocks to be moved on heavy wheeled carts to each new building——and then noting carefully how each shaped stone was fitted in its place so that walls and buttresses grew and arches sprang from pier to pier with such precision that no blade however sharp could slip between the joints.

Soon he learned to mix and measure mortar and operate the windlasses whose ingenious ropes and pulleys allowed one man to lift for fifty. Then to make his first careful cuts with bolster and chisel and then stop and watch again as surer hands than his cut and shaped the graceful moldings and intricate tracery which brought the stone to life. As he worked he questioned and remembered everything he saw and heard, and as each day passed, his confidence and his knowledge grew and he began to think of his future life as a great and skillful stonecutter.

When the time came for him to prove his skill to the masons and sculptors of the guild, Alberic chose a piece of specially fine, delicately veined marble and set to work. It was to be the finest carving they had ever seen. With great care he studied and restudied the block and planned his form, then cut into the stone in search of it. He worked in a fever of excitement, his sharp chisels biting off the unwanted material in large chips and pieces. But the image he saw so clearly in his mind seemed always to be just out of sight, a little deeper in the stone. The block grew smaller and the mound of dust and chips larger, and still, like a phantom, the form seemed to recede and still he chased it. Soon there was

nothing left at all. The great block of stone had disappeared and soon afterwards, the stonecutter too. For again, without a word, Alberic gathered up his belongings and passed through the city gate. He had failed once more.

"Usefulness isn't everything," he decided after roaming about disconsolately for several days. "Innovation is surely a measure of wisdom. I'll do something original."

The opportunity presented itself in the very next town, where the goldsmiths, it was said, produced objects of unsurpassed excellence and fancy. Bowls and magic boxes, mirrors, shields and scepters, crowns, rings, enchanted buckles and clasps, and candlesticks and vases of incredible grace and intricacy spilled from these workshops and found their way to every royal court and market in the land. It was here that Alberic learned to draw and shape the fine gold wire and work the thin sheets of metal into patterns and textures of light and shape and then inlay these with delicate enamels and precious stones. It was here also that he worked and hoped for the next two years of his life and it was here that for the third time he failed and for the third time took his disappointment to the lonely countryside.

And so it went, from town to town, from city to city, each noted for its own particular craft or enterprise. There were potters who turned and shaped their wet clay into graceful bowls and tall jugs fire-glazed with brilliant cobalt, manganese and copper oxides. Leather finishers who transformed smooth soft skins into shoes and boots, gloves, tunics, bombards, bottles and buckets. There were weavers and spinners who worked in wools and silks, carpenters and cabinetmakers,

glassblowers, armorers and tinkers. There were scholars who spent their days searching out the secrets of ancient books, and chemists and physicians, and astronomers determining the precise distances between places that no one had ever seen. And busy ports which offered men the sea and all it touched, and smiths and scribes and makers of fine musical instruments, for anyone with such a bent. Alberic tried them all——and watched and learned and practiced and failed and then moved on again. Yet he kept searching and searching for the one thing that he could do. The secret of the wisdom and skill he so desired.

The years passed and still he traveled on——along the roads and trails and half-forgotten paths——across plains and deserts and forests whose tangled growth held terrors that were sometimes real and sometimes even worse——over hills and cruel high mountain passes and down again perhaps along some unnamed sea——until at last, alone and old and tired, he reached the ramparts of the great capital city.

"I will never find wisdom," he sighed. "I'm a failure at everything."

At the edge of the market square Alberic set his bundle down and searched longingly as all the students, artisans and craftsmen went unconcernedly about their business. He wiped the dust from his eyes and sat for a moment, thinking of his future and his past. What a strange sight he was! His beard was now quite long and gray and the cloak and hat and shoes bore evidence of some repair from every place he'd been. His great bundle bulged with the debris of a lifetime's memories and disappointments and his face was a sad scramble of much the same. As he rummaged through his thoughts, a group of children, struck by his uncommon look, stopped and gathered close around him.

"Where have you come from?"

"What do you do?"

"Tell us what you've seen," they eagerly asked, and poised to listen or flee as his response required.

Alberic was puzzled. What could he tell them? No one had ever sought his conversation before, or asked his opinion on any question. He scratched his head and rubbed his knees, then slowly and hesitantly began to speak, and suddenly the sum of all those experiences, which lay packed up in his mind as in some disordered cupboard, came back to him. He told them of a place or two he'd been and of some lands they'd never known existed and creatures that all their wildest fancies could not invent, and then a story, a legend and three dark mysterious tales remembered from a thousand years before. As he spoke, the words began to come more easily and the pleasure of them eased away his weariness. Everything he'd ever seen or heard or touched or tried was suddenly fresh and clear in his memory, and when the children finally left for home, their faces glowing with excitement, it was to spread the news of the wonderful old man who knew so much.

Since he had no place else to go, Alberic returned to the square each day, and each day the crowds grew larger and larger around him. At first it was only the children, but soon everyone, regardless of age or size, crowded close to listen— and patiently he tried to tell them all they wished to hear. For many of their questions his own experience provided the answers, and for those he could not directly answer he always had a tale or story whose point or artifice led them to answers of their own. More and more he began to enjoy the days and soon he learned to embellish his tales with skillful detail, to pause at just the right time, to raise his voice to a roar or lower it to a whisper as the telling demanded. And the crowds grew even larger.

Workmen came to listen and stayed to learn the secret ways and methods of their own crafts. Artisans consulted him on questions of taste or skill and when they left they always knew more than when they came. Alberic told them everything he had learned or seen through all his failures and his wanderings, and before very long he became known throughout the realm as Alberic the Wise.

His fame spread so far that one day the King himself and several of his ministers came to the square to see for themselves. Cleverly disguised so as not to alert the old man to his purpose, the King posed several questions concerning matters of state and situations in far-off corners of the kingdom. Everything he asked, Alberic answered in great detail, enlarging each reply with accounts of the lore and customs of each region, condition of the crops and royal castles, local problems and controversies, reports on the annual rainfall and the latest depredations by various discontented barons. And for added measure, two songs and a short play (in which he acted all the parts) which he had learned before being dismissed from a traveling theater company.

"You are the wisest man in my kingdom," the astonished King proclaimed, throwing off his disguise, "and you shall have a palace of your own with servants and riches as befits a man of your accomplishments."

Alberic moved into the new palace at once and was more than content with his new life. He enjoyed the wealth and possessions he had never known before, slept on feather

beds, ate nothing but the most succulent and delicate foods and endlessly put on and took off the many cloaks, robes and caps the King had graciously provided. His beard was trimmed and curled and he spent his time strolling about the gardens and marble halls posing with proper dignity before each mirror and repeating to himself in various tones and accents, "Alberic the Wise, ALBERIC THE WISE, A-L-B-E-R-I-C T-H-E W-I-S-E!" in order to become accustomed to his new title.

After several weeks, however, the novelty began to wear thin, for a sable cloak is just a sable cloak and a *poulet poêla a l'estragon* is really just another roast chicken. Soon doubts began to crowd out pleasures and by degrees he grew first serious, then sober, then somber and then once again thoroughly discouraged.

"How is it possible to be a failure at everything one day and a wise man the next?" he inquired. "Am I not the same person?"

For weeks this question continued to trouble him deeply, and since he could not find a satisfactory answer he returned to the square with his doubts.

"Simply calling someone wise does not make him wise!" he announced to the eager crowd. "So you see, I am not wise." Then, feeling much better, he returned to the palace and began to make ready to leave.

"How modest," the crowd murmured. "The sign of a truly great man." And a delegation of prominent citizens was sent to prevail on him to stay.

Even after listening to their arguments Alberic continued to be troubled and the very next day he returned to the square again.

"Miscellaneous collections of fact and information are not wisdom," he declared fervently. "Therefore I am not wise!" And he returned and ordered workmen to begin boarding up the palace.

"Only the wisest of men would understand this," the people all agreed and petitions were circulated to prevent his leaving.

For several more days he paced the palace corridors unhappily and then returned for a third time.

"A wise man's words are rarely questioned," he counseled gently. "Therefore you must be very careful whom you call wise."

The crowd was so grateful for his timely warning that they cheered for fully fifteen minutes after he had returned to the palace.

Finally, in desperation, he reappeared that very afternoon and stated simply, "For all the years of my life I have sought wisdom and to this day I still do not know even the meaning of the word, or where to find it," and thinking that would convince them he ordered a carriage for six o'clock that afternoon.

The crowd gasped. "No one but a man of the most profound wisdom would ever dare to admit such a thing," they all agreed, and an epic poem was commissioned in his honor.

Once again Alberic returned to the palace. The carriage was canceled, the rooms were opened and aired. There was nothing he could say or do to convince them that he wasn't what they all thought him to be. Soon he refused to answer any more questions or, in fact, to speak at all and everyone agreed that because of the troubled times this was certainly the wisest thing to do. Each day he grew more morose and miserable, and though his fame continued to grow and spread he found no more satisfaction in his success than he had in all his failures. He slept little and ate less and his magnificent robes began to hang like shrouds. The bright optimism that had shone in his eyes through all his travels and hardships began to fade and as the months passed he took to spending all his time at the top of the great north tower, staring without any interest at nothing in particular.

"I am no wiser now than I was before," he said one afternoon, thinking back across the years. "For I still don't know what I am or what I'm looking for." But as he sat there remembering and regretting, he sensed in the air the barest suggestion of some subtle yet familiar scent that drifted in on the freshening breeze. What it was he didn't know——perhaps the pungent tangled aroma of some far eastern bazaar or the sharp and honest smell of a once-known workshop, or it might have been simply the sweet clean air of an upland field the memory of which had long been lost in detail yet retained in some more durable way; but whatever it was it grew stronger and stronger stirring something deep within him and taking hold of all his thoughts and feelings. His spirit suddenly quickened in response and each breath now came faster than the one before. And then for just a moment he sat quite still——and then at last he knew.

"I am not a glassmaker nor a stone cutter, nor a goldsmith, potter, weaver, tinker, scribe or chef," he shouted happily and he leaped up and bounded down the steep stone stairs. "Nor a vintner, carpenter, physician, armorer, astronomer, baker or boatman." Down and around he ran as fast as he could go, along the palace corridors until he reached the room in which all his old things had been stored. "Nor a blacksmith, merchant, musician or cabinetmaker," he continued as he put on the ragged cloak and shoes and hat. "Nor a wise man or a fool, success or failure, for no one but myself can tell me what I am or what I'm not." And when he'd finished he looked into the mirror and smiled and wondered why it had taken him so long to discover such a simple thing.

So Alberic picked up his bundle, took one last look through the palace and went down to the square for the last time.

"I have at last discovered one thing," he stated simply. "It is much better to look for what I may never find than to find what I do not really want." And with that he said goodbye and left the city as quietly as he'd come.

The crowd gasped and shook their heads in disbelief.

"He has given up his palace!"

"And his wealth and servants!"

"And the King's favor!"

"And he does not even know where he is going," they buzzed and mumbled. "How foolish, how very foolish! How could we ever have thought him wise?" And they all went home.

But Alberic didn't care at all, for now his thoughts were full of all the things he had yet to see and do and all the times he would stop to tell his stories and then move on again. Soon the walls were far behind and only his footsteps and the night were there to keep him company. Once again he felt the freedom and the joy of not knowing where each new step would take him, and as he walked along his stride was longer and stronger than was right somehow for a man his age.

Alberic the Wise

Meet the Author

Norton Juster, like his father before him, became an architect. However, he also had a love of telling stories that led him to become an author of children's books. One of his favorite things to write about is *"the awakening of the lazy mind."* His stories are often about people who have become bored by their lives because they are ignorant of all the possibilities that surround them. These characters often do not know how to relieve their boredom until they stumble across someone or something that teaches them how to learn. Once they begin to learn, they find that their lives will never be dull unless they stop pursuing knowledge.

Meet the Illustrator

Leonard Baskin first knew he wanted to be an artist when he was fourteen years old. He decided this after watching an artist, at Macy's department store, sculpt a human head out of clay. He bought five pounds of clay that day.

Baskin practiced sculpting and carving on his own for about a year. He wanted so much to learn more about it, that he "forced" himself on a well-known sculptor and asked for lessons. The sculptor decided to take him under his wing. Baskin studied with this sculptor for three years, and began to receive critical acclaim for his work. He continued his studies in art school and through research. He went on to become a successful painter, draftsman, and printmaker, as well as a sculptor.

Theme Connections

Within the Selection

Record your answers to the questions below in the Response Journal section of your Writer's Notebook. In small groups, report the ideas you wrote. Discuss your ideas with the rest of your group. Then choose a person to report your group's answers to the class.

- Why did Alberic leave his home and everything he knew to venture out into the unknown?
- Why did Alberic leave the wealth of the palace and the admiration of the people to travel from place to place?
- In what way are the old man from the beginning of the story and Alberic at the end of the story similar?

Across Selections

- Compare Alberic with Shlemiel in "When Shlemiel Went to Warsaw." What were the two men searching for and what did each one find?
- Select a character from another story in this unit or elsewhere in this book. Compare how that character changed to the way that Alberic changed. Which character changed the most? Whose changes will have the most long-lasting impact?

Beyond the Selection

- Think about how "Alberic the Wise" adds to what you know about journeys and quests.
- Add items to the Concept/Question Board about journeys and quests.

Wander-Thirst

Gerald Gould
illustrated by Jane Kendall

Beyond the East the sunrise, beyond the West the sea,
And East and West the wander-thirst that will not let me be;
It works in me like madness, dear, to bid me say good-by!
For the seas call and the stars call, and oh, the call of the sky!

I know not where the white road runs, nor what the blue hills are,
But man can have the sun for friend, and for his guide a star;
And there's no end to voyaging when once the voice is heard,
For the river calls and the road calls, and oh, the call of a bird!

Yonder the long horizon lies, and there by night and day
The old ships draw to home again, the young ships sail away;
And come I may, but go I must, and if men ask you why,
You may put the blame on the stars and the sun and the white
  road and the sky!

Roads Go Ever Ever On

J. R. R. Tolkien
illustrated by Jane Kendall

Roads go ever ever on,
Over rock and under tree,
By caves where never sun has shone,
By streams that never find the sea;
Over snow by winter sown,
And through the merry flowers of June,
Over grass and over stone,
And under mountains in the moon.

627

Pronunciation Key

a as in **a**t

ā as in l**a**te

â as in c**a**re

ä as in f**a**ther

e as in s**e**t

ē as in m**e**

i as in **i**t

ī as in k**i**te

o as in **o**x

ō as in r**o**se

ô as in b**ou**ght and r**aw**

oi as in c**oi**n

o͞o as in b**oo**k

o͞o as in t**oo**

or as in f**or**m

ou as in **ou**t

u as in **u**p

ū as in **u**se

ûr as in t**ur**n, g**er**m, l**ear**n, f**ir**m, w**or**k

ə as in **a**bout, chick**e**n, penc**i**l, cann**o**n, circ**u**s

ch as in **ch**air

hw as in w**hi**ch

ng as in ri**ng**

sh as in **sh**op

th as in **th**in

t͟h as in **th**ere

zh as in trea**s**ure

The mark (´) is placed after a syllable with a heavy accent, as in **chicken** (chik´ ən).

The mark (´) after a syllable shows a lighter accent, as in **disappear** (dis´ ə pēr´).

Glossary

A

abacus (aʹ bə kəs) *n.* A tool used to figure math problems by sliding counters.

abandon (ə banʹ dən) *v.* Leave something behind forever.

accomplish (ə komʹ plish) *v.* Do something successfully.

accuracy (aʹ kyə rə sē) *n.* Freedom from errors or mistakes; correctness.

ace (ās) *v.* To easily get all or most answers correct.

acquit (ə kwitʹ) *v.* Conduct oneself well, even in a stressful situation.

adjacent (ə jāʹ sənt) *adj.* Next to; touching.

adjourn (ə jûrnʹ) *v.* Bring to a temporary end; end for the present.

admission (əd mishʹ ən) *n.* The price paid to attend an event.

adobe (ə dōʹ bē) *n.* Sun-dried brick.

adventure (əd venʹ chər) *n.* A fun or exciting experience.

agate (aʹ gət) *n.* A striped marble.

aimlessly (āmʹ ləs lē) *adv.* Without purpose or direction.

alder (ôlʹ dər) *n.* A tree in the birch family.

align (ə līnʹ) *v.* To place in a straight line.

alignment (ə līnʹ mənt) *n.* The arrangement of things in a straight line.

altitude (alʹ tə to͞od) *n.* How high something is above Earth.

amiss (ə misʹ) *adv.* Wrong; not as expected.

ample (amʹ pəl) *adj.* More than enough.

ancestor (anʹ ses tər) *n.* A person from whom one is descended.

anticipation (an tisʹ ə pāʹ shən) *n.* A feeling of looking forward to something.

apparatus (aʹ pə raʹ təs) *n.* A piece of equipment that has a particular use.

appetite (apʹ ə tīt) *n.* Desire for food.

apprehension (apʹ ri henʹ shən) *n.* Fear.

apprentice (ə prenʹ tis) *v.* To bind oneself to a craft worker in order to learn a trade.—*n.* A person learning a trade or an art.

apt (aptʹ) *adj.* Inclined; likely.

arc (ärk) *v.* To move in a curved line. —*n.* A curve.

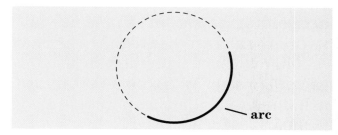

Word Derivations

Below are some words related to *arc*.

arcade	arcading	arcing
arcaded	arced	arcs

archaeoastronomy (ärʹ kē ō ə stronʹ ə mē) *n.* The study of ancient astronomical observatories.

archaeology or **archeology**
(är′ kē ol′ ə jē) *n.* The scientific study of people of the past by digging up things they left behind.

Word History

Archaeology, or archeology, came into English in the year 1837. It is from the Latin word *archaeologia,* meaning "knowledge gained through the study of ancient objects." This Latin word's origins are with the Greek words *archē,* meaning "beginning," and *logos,* meaning "word."

arm (ärm) *v.* Prepare for war; make weapons ready for use.

aroma (ə rō′ mə) *n.* A smell or odor, usually pleasant.

artifice (är′ tə fis) *n.* A clever trick in the way a story's plot is constructed.

artisan (är′ tə zən) *n.* A person who works at a craft that requires artistic skill or working with the hands.

ascend (ə send′) *v.* To climb up; to rise.

ashamed (ə shāmd′) *adj.* Embarrassed; not proud.

astronomical (as′ trə nom′ i kəl) *adj.* Having to do with the study of the stars and planets.

astronomy (ə stron′ ə mē) *n.* The scientific study of stars and planets.

athletic (ath le′ tik) *adj.* Having skill and strength in sports and other physical activities.

atmosphere (at′ mə sfir′) *n.* The gases that surround a planet or moon.

attendant (ə ten′ dənt) *n.* A person who waits on someone.

attitude (a′ tə tood′) *n.* A way of thinking, acting, or behaving.

avert (ə vûrt′) *v.* To avoid.

B

bamboo (bam′ boo′) *n.* A tropical, grass plant with long, stiff, hollow stems.

bandana (ban dan′ ə) *n.* A large, colorful handkerchief.

barrack (bar′ ək) *n.* A building where soldiers live.

bastion (bas′ chən) *n.* A part of a fortified structure that juts out so that defenders can fire at attackers from several angles.

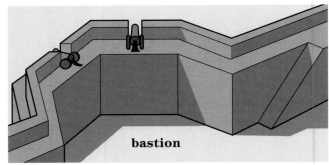

bastion

beanie (bē′ nē) *n.* A small bill-less cap worn on the crown of the head.

bedclothes (bed′ klōz) *n.* Items used to cover a bed, such as sheets, blankets, and quilts.

bedrock (bed′ rok) *n.* Solid rock.

benevolent (bə nev′ ə lənt) *adj.* Kind; generous.

berate (bi rāt′) *v.* To scold harshly.

bice (bīs) *adj.* Blue or blue-green.

biologist (bī o′ lə jəst) *n.* A person who studies plant and animal life specific to certain environments.

blemish (blem′ ish) *n.* A stain; a defect.

blintze (blints) *n.* Cheese or fruit wrapped in a thin pancake.

bloody (blu′ dē) *adj.* A word used to indicate an extremely negative feeling.

body (bo′ dē) *n.* An object such as a star or asteroid.

bombard (bom′ bärd) *n.* A leather jug or bottle.

booklet (bŏŏk′ lət) *n.* A small book, usually with a paper cover.

bore (bor) *v.* To drill into; to pierce.

bow (bou) *n.* The front part of a ship.

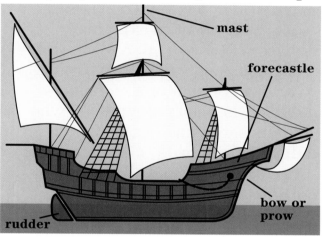

mast

forecastle

bow or prow

rudder

Word History

Bow came into English about 500 years ago. It probably came from the Dutch word *boech*, meaning "bow" or "shoulder." It is also related to *bōg*, a word meaning "bough" (a large tree branch) that dates back more than 800 years.

boycott (boi′ kot′) *v.* Join with others in refusing to buy from or deal with a person, nation, or business.

brazen (brā′ zən) *adj.* Bold; cocky.

breach (brēch) *n.* A violation of a law or agreement.

break (brāk) *v.* To tame a horse.

breakwater (brāk′ wô′ tər) *n.* Any structure that protects a harbor or beach from damage by waves.

brocade (brō kād′) *n.* Woven cloth that has a raised pattern.

bronc (bronk) *n.* A wild or poorly broken horse.

brushpopper (brush′ po pər) *n.* A person who works in an area covered with low-growing bushes and weeds.

bulldog (bŏŏl′ dôg′) *v.* To wrestle a steer, usually by grabbing its horns and twisting its neck.

buttress (bu′ tris) *n.* A structure built outside a wall to give the wall support.

C

cairn (kârn) *n.* A pile of stones left as a landmark or a monument.

cairn

calculation (kal′ kyə lā′ shən) *n.*
1. Counting, computing, or figuring.
2. The result of counting, computing, or figuring.

campaign (kam pān′) *n.* A series of actions planned and carried out to bring about a particular result; an organized effort to accomplish a purpose.

> **Pronunciation Key: a**t; l**ā**te; c**â**re; f**ä**ther; s**e**t; m**ē**; **i**t; k**ī**te; **o**x; r**ō**se; **ô** in b**ou**ght; c**oi**n; b**oo**k; t**oo**; f**or**m; **ou**t; **u**p; **ū**se; t**û**rn; **ə** sound in **a**bout, chick**e**n, penc**i**l, cann**o**n, circ**u**s; **ch**air; **hw** in **wh**ich; ri**ng**; **sh**op; **th**in; **th**ere; **zh** in trea**s**ure.

candidate (kan′ də dāt′) *n.* A person who is seeking an office, job, or position.

canyon (kan′ yən) *n.* A deep, narrow valley with high, steep sides.

capable (kā′ pə bəl) *adj.* Skilled or able to do something well.

capsule (kap′ səl) *n.* The top part of a rocket that is self-contained and holds astronauts and equipment.

capsize (kap′ sīz) *v.* To turn upside down.

captivity (kap ti′ və tē) *n.* Being held as prisoner.

carbon dating (kär′ bən dā′ ting) *v.* Using carbon 14 to find out the age of old material.

carcass (kär′ kəs) *n.* The body of a dead animal.

caribou (kar′ ə boo′) *n.* A reindeer.

cease (sēs) *v.* Bring an activity or action to an end.

celandine (sel′ ən dīn′) *n.* A plant in the buttercup family with single yellow flowers.

celestial (sə les′ chəl) *adj.* Relating to the sky.

ceremonial (ser′ ə mō′ nē əl) *adj.* Having to do with a formal celebration.

chance (chans) *v.* To take a risk and try something difficult.

challenge (chal′ ənj) *n.* Something that may be difficult to do.

chaparral (shap′ ə ral′) *n.* An area thick with shrubs and small trees.

cheder (kā′ dər) *n.* Religious school for teaching Judaism.

chives (chīvz) *n.* A food seasoning made from the leaves of a plant related to the onion.

cinder (sin′ dər) *n.* Ash or a piece of partially burnt coal or wood.

circumference (sər kum′ fər əns) *n.* The line that defines a circle.

claim (klām) *n.* A section of land declared as belonging to one person or group of people.

clamber (klam′ bər) *v.* To climb with difficulty.

clarify (klâr′ ə fī′) *v.* To make something clear; to explain.

cloister (kloi′ stər) *n.* A place where religious people live away from the world; a convent or a monastery.

cobbler (kob′ lər) *n.* A person who repairs shoes and boots.

collards (käl′ ərds) *n.* A green, leafy vegetable.

collide (kə līd′) *v.* Crash.

colonel (kûr′ nəl) *n.* A military officer; ranking between lieutenant and general.

commence (kə mens′) *v.* To begin.

Word History

Commence came into English about 600 years ago. It came from the French word *comencer*, and its assumed origin is the Latin word *cominitiare*. This Latin word is a derivative of *initiare*, meaning "to initiate." (Also note that the word *commence* contains the *-ence* suffix, which in this word means "the action of " or "the process of.")

commission (kə mi′ shən) *n.* An important task or assignment.

commotion (kə mō′ shən) *n.* Noise; excitement; disturbance.

communal (kə mū′ nəl) *adj.* Public; shared by all.

compassion (kəm pash′ ən) *n.* Sympathy; pity.

composition (kom′ pə zish′ ən) *n.* What something is made of.

comrade (kom′ rad′) *n.* Friend; companion.

concave (kon kāv′) *adj.* Curved inward; hollow; like the inner curve of a contact lens.

conceive (kən sēv′) *v.* 1. To start something with a certain point of view. 2. To understand.

conciliatory (kən sil′ ē ə tor′ ē) *adj.* Causing peace to be made.

condense (kən dens′) *v.* Change the physical state of something from a gas to a liquid or solid.

confederation (kən fe′ də rā′ shən) *n.* The act of joining states together for a common purpose.

confetti (kən fet′ ē) *n.* Tiny pieces of colored paper that are thrown during celebrations.

confidence (kon′ fə dəns) *n.* A belief in one's ability to do something.

confine (kən fīn′) *v.* 1. To limit. 2. To keep in a place.

confounded (kon foun′ did) *adj.* Darned.

confront (kən frunt′) *v.* To face.

congress (kong′ gris) *n.* An assembly of people who make laws.

constellation (kon′ stə lā′ shən) *n.* A group of stars that form shapes in the sky.

constituent (kən stich′ wənt) *n.* A voter in a particular area.

constitution (kon′ sti tōō′ shən) *n.* The basic principles used to govern a state, country, or organization.

content (kən tent′) *adj.* Happy or satisfied.

contest (kon′ test) *n.* A competition.

convention (kən ven′ shən) *n.* A formal meeting for some special purpose.

convex (kon veks′) *adj.* Curved outward; like the outer curve of a contact lens.

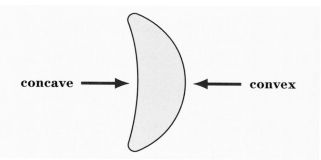

concave   →   ←   convex

conveyor belt (kən vā′ ər belt′) *n.* A device with a large looping belt used to move objects.

cordially (kor′ jə lē) *adj.* Sincerely; pleasantly.

corn pone (korn′ pōn′) *n.* Baked or fried corn bread.

cotangent (kō tan′ jənt) *n.* A term used in trigonometry.

course (kors) *v.* To flow.

cradleboard (krād′ l bord′) *n.* A wooden frame that Native American women wore on their backs to carry their babies.

cringe (krinj) *v.* To back away from something unpleasant; to physically shrink because of fear or excessive humility.

croaker-sack (krō′ kər sak) *n.* A sack usually made of burlap.

cultivate (kul′ tə vāt′) *v.* To till the ground; to grow crops.

curvilinear (kur′ və li′ nē ər) *adj.* Having rounded or curving lines.

D

decipher (dē sī′ fər) *v.* To read or translate something written in code; decode.

deduction (di duk′ shən) *n.* A fact or conclusion figured out by reasoning.

defeatist (di fē′ təst) *adj.* Expecting and accepting that one will lose or be defeated.

defect (di fekt′) *v.* To leave one's home country for another.

defiance (di fī′ əns) *n.* Bold refusal to obey or respect authority.

dehydration (dē′ hī drā′ shən) *n.* Loss of water in the body.

delegation (del′ i gā′ shēn) *n.* A group of people chosen to act for others; representatives.

deliberately (di li′ bə rət lē) *adv.* On purpose; meaning to.

Word History

Deliberately came into English about 500 years ago. It is the adverb form of the word *deliberate*, which came from the Latin word *deliberare*, meaning "to consider carefully." It is assumed that the Latin word *libra*, meaning "pound" or "scale," is also in its word history. This brings to mind the modern figure of speech "to weigh one's options." (Also note that *deliberately* contains the *-ly* suffix, which in this word means "in the manner of being.")

---

delta (del′ tə) *n.* Land formed at the mouth of a river by sediment carried in the water.

demolish (di mol′ ish) *v.* To do away with.

denounce (di nouns′) *v.* Openly condemn; declare disapproval.

deposits (di poz′ its) *n.* Valuables put away for safekeeping, as in a bank.

depredation (dep′ ri dā′ shən) *n.* The act of attacking and robbing.

descent (di sent′) *n.* A coming from a higher place to a lower one.

desert (dez′ ərt) *n.* A place where little or no rain falls.

deserted (də zər′ təd) *adj.* Not lived in; abandoned.

desist (di sist′) *v.* To stop.

desolation (des′ ə lā′ shən) *n.* Deserted condition.

desperation (des′ pə rā′ shən) *n.* A hopeless feeling, when you are ready to try anything to help the situation.

despotism (des′ pə ti′ zəm) *n.* A government run by a tyrannical ruler.

dialect (dī′ ə lekt′) *n.* A form of language that is spoken in a particular area or by a particular group of people.

diligence (dil´ i jens) *n.* Steady effort put forth to accomplish a task.

Word History

Diligence came into English about 600 years ago. It is a derivative of the word *diligent*, which has origins in the French word *diligere*, meaning "to love" or "to esteem." *Diligere* can also be divided into the word parts *di-*, meaning "apart," and *legere*, meaning "to select." (Also note that *diligence* contains the *-ence* suffix, which in this word means "the quality of" or "the state of.")

---

diminish (di min´ ish) *v.* To decrease; to lessen; to get smaller.

din (din) *n.* Clamor; uproar; racket.

diplomacy (di plō´ mə sē) *n.* The handling of relations between nations.

discernible (di sûrn´ ə bəl) *adj.* Easy to recognize as different.

disconsolately (dis kon´ sə lit lē) *adv.* In a very unhappy way; hopelessly.

disembodied (dis´ em bod´ ēd) *adj.* Without a body.

dismay (dis mā´) *n.* A sudden feeling of disappointment.

disown (di sōn´) *v.* To deny a connection to; to refuse to admit a relationship to.

distinct (di stingkt´) *adj.* 1. Clear; plain. 2. Separate.

district (dis´ trikt) *n.* A region that is part of some larger entity such as a city or county.

document (dok´ yə mənt) *n.* A written or printed statement that gives official proof and information about something.

dogie (dō´ gē) *n.* A calf with no mother.

domesticated (də mes´ ti kāt´ əd) *adj.* Able to exist closely with humans.

downpour (doun´ por´) *n.* A heavy rain.

dramatization (dram´ ə tə zā´ shən) *n.* An acting out of a story.

draught (draft) *n. chiefly British.* A liquid that is drunk; a dose.

dribble (dri´ bəl) *v.* In soccer, to move a ball down the field with a series of short, controlled kicks.

drill (dril) *n.* An exercise to increase mental or physical skills.

drought (drout) *n.* Dry weather that lasts a very long time.

dubiously (doo´ bē əs lē) *adv.* In a doubtful way.

dumpling (dum´ pling) *n.* A small pocket of dough filled with a meat or vegetable mixture and cooked by steaming or boiling it.

dwindle (dwin´ dl) *v.* To get smaller gradually.

E

---

eclipse (i klips´) *v.* To become more important than; to cover over.

ecstatically (ek stat´ ik lē) *adv.* With great joy.

eddy (ed´ ē) *n.* A small, circling current of water.

edible (ed´ ə bəl) *adj.* Eatable.

election (i lek´ shən) *n.* The act of choosing, by voting, someone to serve in an office, or whether to accept an idea.

elector (i lek´ tər) *n.* A qualified voter.

embarrassed (im bar´ əsd) *adj.* Feeling bad or silly about something one has done.

embellish (em bel´ ish) *v.* To make something better or more beautiful by adding to it.

emphatically (em fat´ ik lē) *adv.* With spoken firmness or force.

employee (em ploi´ ē´) *n.* One who works for pay.

encampment (en kamp´ mənt) *n.* A camp; a temporary stopping place.

encompass (en kum´ pəs) *v.* To include.

encounter (en koun´ tər) *v.* To meet by chance.

endurance (en dûr´ əns) *n.* The power to put up with hardships or difficulties.

energy (e´ nər jē) *n.* The strength or eagerness to work or do things.

enthusiastic (in thōō´ zē as´ tik) *adj.* Filled with excitement.

Equator (i kwā´ tər) *n.* The imaginary line that circles Earth's center; it is perpendicular to Earth's axis and equally distant from Earth's North and South Poles.

equinox (ē´ kwə noks´) *n.* The two times of the year when day and night are equal in length.

era (er´ ə) *n.* A period of time or of history, often beginning or ending with an historical event.

ermine (ûr´ min) *n.* A valuable white fur; the winter white fur coat of some weasels.

escort (e skort´) *v.* To go with and help or protect.

establish (i stab´ lish) *v.* To settle in a place.

Word Derivations

Below are some words related to *establish*.
establishable   establisher   establishment
established   establishes

estate (i stāt´) *n.* A large piece of land owned by one individual or family.

eternal (i tûr´ nl) *adj.* Everlasting; always; endless.

ewe (ū) *n.* A female sheep.

excursion (ik skûr´ zhən) *n.* A pleasure trip; an outing.

exhausted (ig zô´ stəd) *adj.* Very tired.

explorer (ik splor´ ər) *n.* A person who goes to a place one knows nothing about.

extraordinary (ik stror´ dən âr´ ē) *adj.* Unusual or amazing.

F

facility (fə sil´ ə tē) *n.* A place, such as a building, that serves a certain purpose.

Fahrenheit (fâr´ ən hīt) *adj.* Relating to a system for measuring temperature where water freezes at 32 degrees and water boils at 212 degrees.

fare (fâr) *n.* The cost to ride a bus, taxi, or other means of transportation.

feat (fēt) *n.* An act or deed that shows great courage, strength, or skill.

federal (fed´ ər əl) *adj.* Formed by an agreement of states or provinces to join together as one nation.

feisty (fī´ stē) *adj.* Having a lively and aggressive personality.

fervently (fûr´ vənt lē) *adv.* With great feeling; with emotion.

fidelity (fi del´ i tē) *n.* Faithfulness to duties or promises.

fife (fīf) *n.* A musical instrument like a flute that makes a high, clear sound and is often used with drums in a marching band.

floe (flō) *n.* A large sheet of floating ice.

flounder (floun´ dər) *v.* To struggle. —*n.* A type of flatfish that is good to eat.

forlornly (for lorn´ lē) *adv.* Sadly; hopelessly.

Word History

Forlornly is the adverb form of the word *forlorn*, which came into English more than 800 years ago. It is a derivative of the word *forlēosan*, which means "to lose." (Also note that *forlornly* contains the *-ly* suffix, which in this word means "in the manner of being.")

formation (for mā´ shən) *n.* A particular arrangement.

foundry (foun´ drē) *n.* A place where metal is melted and formed.

frantic (fran´ tik) *adj.* Very worried and afraid.

frantically (fran´ ti klē) *adv.* Quickly in a worried way.

frequency (frē´ kwən sē) *n.* The number of times something happens within a set period of time.

frigate (frig´ it) *n.* A type of tropical seabird with a hooked beak, webbed feet, and long wings and tail feathers.

fume (fūm) *v.* To mumble something in an angry or irritated way.

furrow (fûr´ ō) *n.* A trench cut by a plow.

fuse (fūz) *v.* To join together by melting.

gable (gā´ bəl) *n.* A part of a wall that is enclosed by sloping sides of a roof, making a triangle-shaped section on a building.

galaxy (gal´ ək sē) *n.* A large group of stars, dust, and gas.

gallinipper (gal´ ə nip´ ər) *n. informal.* Any of several insects that sting or bite.

garrison (gâr´ i sən) *n.* A military post or station.

genuine (jen´ yə wən) *adj.* Real.

geologist (jē o´ lə jist) *n.* A person who studies the solid matter on a moon or planet.

ginger (jin´ jər) *n.* A strong tasting spice made from ground ginger root.

gizzard (gi´ zərd) *n.* Intestine.

globular (glob´ yə lər) *adj.* Having the shape of a globe.

gore (gor) *v.* To pierce with an animal's horn or tusk.

gourd (gord) *n.* A melon-shaped fruit that can be dried and used as a bowl.

grenadier (gren´ ə dēr´) *n.* A soldier on foot; an infantry soldier.

groschen (grō´ shən) *n.* A form of money worth $\frac{1}{100}$ of a schilling. (A schilling is worth about $7\frac{1}{2}$ cents.)

grozing iron (grō´ zing ī´ ərn) *n.* A steel tool for cutting glass.

grueling (grōō´ ə ling) *adj.* Very difficult or exhausting.

guide (gīd) *v.* Lead someone along a path or to show the way.

H

haberdasher (ha′ bər da′ shər) *n. chiefly British.* One who sells men's clothing.

haint (hānt) *n.* A ghost.

hamlet (ham′ lit) *n.* A small village.

haughtily (hô′ təl ē) *adv.* In an overly proud way.

headquarters (hed′ kwor′ tərz) *n.* A center of operations where leaders work and give orders; a main office.

healer (hē′ lər) *n.* A doctor.

heavens (he′ vəns) *n.* The sky as viewed from earth.

hemisphere (hem′ ə sfir) *n.* Half of a sphere that results from cutting it through the center with a horizontal plane.

hesitate (hez′ ə tāt) *v.* Pause.

high-falutin' (hī′ fə loo′ tn) *adj.* Appealing to a higher class of people; fancy; showy.

hogan (hō′ gôn) *n.* A Navaho dwelling.

homespun (hōm′ spən) *adj.* Made at home.

hone (hōn) *v.* To sharpen.

honor (ä′ nər) *v.* Show respect.

horizon (hə rī′ zən) *n.* A line formed in the distance by an apparent meeting of Earth and sky.

horizontal (hor′ ə zon′ tl) *adj.* Along a line parallel to the horizon.

hospitable (hos pi′ tə bəl) *adj.* Kind and generous to guests.

hover (huv′ ər) *v.* To hang in the air.

Word History

Hover came from an older English word, *hoven*, which may have come into use as many as 800 years ago. Since the earliest records of this word, it has always had the same meaning.

humanity (hū man′ ə tē) *n.* People; all human beings.

hypotenuse (hī po′ tə noos′) *n.* In a right triangle, the side opposite the right angle.

I

ice floes (īs′ flōz′) *n.* Large sheets of floating ice.

immigrant (i′ mi grənt) *n.* A person who comes to live in a country in which he or she was not born.

impeach (im pēch′) *v.* Accuse of misconduct.

imperial (im pir′ ē əl) *adj.* Part of, or belonging to, a king's empire.

impetuous (im pech′ wəs) *adj.* Acting or done too quickly, without planning or thought.

impoverished (im pov′ risht) *adj.* Living in poverty.

impressed (im prest′) *adj.* Made to form a high opinion of someone or something.

inexorable (in ek′ sər ə bəl) *adj.* Absolute; unyielding.

infallibility (in fal′ ə bil′ ə tē) *n.* Assuredness or certainty of success.

inferno (in fûr´ nō) *n.* A place of extreme, almost unbearable, heat.

infirm (in fûrm´) *adj.* Weak; feeble; insecure.

ingenious (in jēn´ yəs) *adj.* Clever; skillful.

Word History

Ingenious came into English about 500 years ago. It comes from the Latin word *ingenium,* which means "natural capacity." Some meanings of the word *capacity* are "the amount that can be held in a space" and "ability or power." (Also note that *ingenious* contains the *in-* prefix, which in this word means "within," and the *-ous* suffix, which in this word means "having" or "possessing.")

ingot (ing´ gət) *n.* A piece of metal in the shape of a bar or a block.

ingratiate (in grā´ shē āt´) *v.* To put oneself in the good graces of others.

innovation (in´ ə vā´ shən) *n.* The act of creating something new or original.

insignificant (in´ sig ni´ fə kənt) *adj.* Not important.

intelligence (in tel´ ə jəns) *n.* 1. A network of people and resources working to gather secret information about an enemy. 2. The secret information about an enemy gathered by a spy.

intensity (in ten´ si tē) *n.* Great strength.

internal (in tûr´ nəl) *adj.* On the inside.

interplanetary (in´ tər pla´ nə târ´ ē) *adj.* Shared between the planets.

interrogation (in ter´ ə gā´ shən) *n.* Questioning.

interview (in´ tər vū´) *v.* Ask questions to find out about a person or what a person thinks.

intimacy (in´ tə mə sē) *n.* A closeness.

intricate (in´ tri kit) *adj.* Tangled; complicated.

investment (in vest´ mənt) *adj.* Using money to make a profit.

irrepressible (ir´ i pres´ ə bəl) *adj.* Unwilling to be controlled.

J

jabber (ja´ bər) *v.* Talk a lot and very fast.

journeyman (jûr´ nē mən) *n.* A person who has completed an apprenticeship and can now work in a trade under another person.

juggle (ju´ gəl) *v.* Handle more than one object or activity at one time; perform a clever trick.

juniper (jōō´ nə pər) *n.* An evergreen shrub with purple berries.

K

karate (kə rä´ tē) *n.* An Asian art of self-defense.

kasha (kä´ shə) *n.* A soft food made from a grain, usually buckwheat.

kayak (kī´ ak) *n.* A light Eskimo canoe having a wooden or bone framework and covered with skins.

kayak

keelboat (kēl′ bōt) *n.* A shallow boat built with a keel, or long beam, on the bottom.

kiln (kiln) *n.* An oven for firing glass, or heating it at very high temperatures, in order to make the color permanent.

kosher (kō′ shər) *adj.* Proper or acceptable according to Jewish law.

L

lambent (lam′ bənt) *adj.* Glowing softly.

lance (lans) *n.* A long-shafted spear.

lariat (lâr′ ē ət) *n.* A rope tied with a movable loop at one end, used to catch cows and horses; a lasso.

learned (lûrnd) *v.* Past tense of **learn:** To gain new knowledge or skill. —*adj.* (lûr′ nid) Educated.

legendary (lej′ ən der′ ē) *adj.* From a story that has been passed down from a people's earlier times.

legislature (lej′ i slā′ chər) *n.* A group of people who make or pass laws.

levee (le′ vē) *n.* An embankment built along a river to keep the river from overflowing.

levity (le′ və tē) *n.* A lighthearted attitude.

lieutenant (loo ten′ ənt) *n.* An officer in the armed forces.

lull (lul) *n.* A period of reduced noise or violence.

lumber (lum′ bər) *n.* Wood that has been cut into boards of various sizes for building.

lunar (loo′ nər) *adj.* Relating to the moon.

luxurious (lug zhoor′ ē əs) *adj.* Grand; rich; elegant.

lynx (lingks) *n.* A wildcat; a bobcat.

M

macaw (mə kô′) *n.* A large parrot that has bright colors and a long tail.

magnification (mag′ nə fi kā′ shən) *n.* The amount of enlargement possible; the amount something is enlarged.

magnificent (mag ni′ fə sənt) *adj.* Outstanding or inspiring.

mallet (ma′ lət) *n.* A type of hammer with a head made of wood or other soft material.

manager (ma′ ni gər) *n.* A person who takes care of or organizes something, like an office or a sports team.

maneuvering (mə noo′ vər ing) *n.* Planning and then acting according to plans.

manic (man′ ik) *adj.* Overly excited.

mantel (man′ təl) *n.* A shelf over a fireplace.

marrow (mar′ ō) *n.* 1. The soft substance in the hollow parts of bones. 2. The center; the core.

mast (mast) *n.* A pole that supports the sails of a ship or boat. See illustration of **bow.**

match (mach´) *n.* A contest, competition, or race.

Maya or **Mayan** (mä´ yə) or (mä´ yən) *n.* A member of a people who built an ancient civilization in Mexico and Central America. **Mayan** *adj.* Having to do with the civilization of the Mayas.

medley (med´ lē) *n.* A mixture; a jumble.

melodrama (mel´ ə drä´ mə) *n.* A play that exaggerates emotions and encourages the audience to be sympathetic.

menial (mē´ nē əl) *adj.* Humble; lowly; boring; tedious.

merciful (mûr´ si fəl) *adj.* Forgiving.

mesa (mā´ sə) *n.* A small, high plateau that stands alone, like a mountain with a flat top.

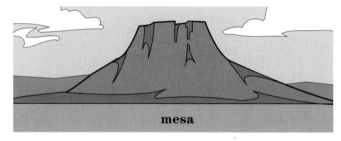

mesa

mesquite (me skēt´) *n.* A spiny shrub or tree in the legume, or pea and bean, family.

meteorite (mē´ tē ə rīt´) *n.* A piece of matter from the solar system that hits a planet or moon's surface.

microbes (mī´ krōbz) *n.* Living things that can only be seen with a microscope.

militia (mə lish´ ə) *n.* A group of citizens trained to fight and help in emergencies.

mill (mil) *n.* A factory.

mischievous (mis´ chə vəs) *adj.* Causing trouble in a playful way.

mission (mish´ ən) *n.* A special job or task.

module (mä´ jəl) *n.* A separate part of a rocket that is self-contained and serves a specific purpose.

monarch (mon´ ərk) *n.* A ruler; a king or a queen.

morale (mə ral´) *n.* The level of one's confidence.

morose (mə rōs´) *adj.* Sullen; gloomy.

mossback (môs´ bak) *n.* A wild bull or cow.

move (mo͞ov) *v.* To make a motion or a suggestion to act on something in a meeting.

muck (muk) *v.* To clean out.

muff (muf) *v.* To do an action poorly; to miss; to mess up.

musket (mus´ kət) *n.* A weapon, used in early American battles, which was aimed and fired from the shoulder. It fired a small, lead ball.

muster (mus´ tər) *v.* To work up; to gather a group in preparation for battle.

myriad (mir´ ē əd) *n.* An immense number; many.

mystified (mis´ tə fīd´) *adj.* Bewildered; baffled; puzzled.

mythology (mi thol´ ə jē) *n.* A collection of legends or fables.

N

nation (nā´ shən) *n.* A group of people living in a particular area under one government.

nebula (ne´ byə lə) *n.* Glowing clouds of gas and dust amidst the stars.

> **Pronunciation Key: a**t; lāte; câre; fäther; set; mē; it; kīte; ox; rōse; ô in bought; coin; boŏk; toō; form; out; up; ūse; tûrn; ə sound in about, chicken, pencil, cannon, circus; chair; hw in which; ring; shop; thin; thére; zh in treasure.

netherworld (neth´ ər wûrld´) *n.* The region below the ground; hell.

nomination (no´ mə nā´ shən) *n.* A proposal that someone could hold a government position or office.

Word History

Nomination is a derivative of the word *nominate*, which came into English about 500 years ago. It came from a derivation of the Latin word *nomen*, which means "name." (Also note that the word *nomination* contains the *-ation* suffix, which means "connected to the process of.")

novelty (no´ vəl tē) *n.* Something new or different.

nuclear reaction (noō´ klē ər rē ak´ shən) *n.* A process in which the centers or cores of atoms are changed.

nugget (nug´ ət) *n.* A solid lump of gold.

nylon (nī´ lon´) *adj.* A synthetic fiber that is strong and durable.

O

---

obliterate (ə blit´ ə rāt´) *v.* To destroy completely; to rub out; to erase.

Word Derivations

Below are some words related to *obliterate*.

obliterated	obliterating	obliterative
obliterates	obliteration	obliterator

oblong (ob´ lông) *adj.* Being longer than it is wide.

obscure (əb skyoōr´) *adj.* Not well known. —*v.* To hide; to cover up.

observatory (əb zûr´ və tor´ē) *n.* A place that is designed for astronomers to study the stars.

observatory

ocelot (o´ sə lot´) *n.* A small wildcat with black spots and a yellow coat.

optical (op´ ti kəl) *adj.* Having to do with sight.

optimism (op´ tə miz´ əm) *n.* The belief that everything will happen for the best.

optimistic (op´ tə mis´ tik) *adj.* Having a positive outlook.

organic (or gan´ ik) *adj.* Produced by living things; was once alive.

organism (or´ gə niz´ əm) *n.* Any living thing.

ornery (or´ nə rē) *adj.* Mean; grouchy; irritable.

oxlip (oks´ lip) *n.* A flowering herb with pale-colored flowers.

P

---

pantomime (pan´ tə mīm´) *v.* Use bodily movements or facial expressions, instead of speech, to tell a story.

parched (pärcht) *adj.* Very hot and dry.

parliamentary procedure
(pär´ lə men´ trē prə sē´ jər) *n.* A formal way to hold or conduct a meeting, following certain rules.

particle (pär´ ti kəl) *n.* A very small piece or portion of something.

partisan (pär´ tə zən) *n.* A committed supporter of a party, cause, person, or idea.

passion (pash´ ən) *n.* A strong liking or enthusiasm for something.

patchwork quilt (pach´ wûrk´ kwilt´) *n.* A blanket made from scraps of material sewn together.

peevishly (pē´ vish lē) *adv.* With irritation or lack of patience.

perimeter (pə rim´ i tər) *n.* The distance around the boundary of something.

persecute (pûr´ si kūt´) *v.* To torment; to oppress; to treat badly.

perspective (pər spek´ tiv) *n.* A way of looking at things in relation to each other.

Word History

Perspective came into English about 600 years ago. It came from the Latin word *perspectivus*, meaning "of sight" or "optical." This Latin word came from a derivation of *perspicere*, which can be broken into the word parts *per-*, meaning "through," and *specere*, meaning "to look." (Also note that the word *perspective* contains the *-ive* suffix, which means "performs the action of.")

persuade (pər swād´) *v.* To get others to think as you do about a subject or topic.

Word Derivations

Below are some words related to *persuade*.

persuaded	persuading	persuasively
persuader	persuasion	persuasiveness
persuades	persuasive	

pester (pes´ tər) *v.* To bother; to annoy.

petition (pə ti´ shən) *v.* Submit a formal request to someone in authority.

petroglyph (pe´ trə glif´) *n.* A drawing or word carved into a rock.

peyote (pā ō´ tē) *n.* A cactus plant.

piñon (pin´ yən) *n.* A kind of pine tree with edible seeds.

pity (pi´ tē) *v.* Feel sorry for.

plateau (pla tō´) *n.* A tract of high, flat land; a tableland.

player (plā´ ər) *n.* A person who takes part in, and plays against another person in, a match.

plummet (plum´ it) *v.* Fall suddenly.

pogrom (pō´ grəm) *n.* An organized attack on Jews in Russia in the late 1800s. Pogroms were encouraged by the Russian government at that time.

ponder (pon´ dər) *v.* To think about.

portage (pôr täzh´) *n.* The act of carrying boats and supplies from one waterway to another.

portage

portal (por′ təl) *n.* An entryway.

posterity (po ster′ ə tē) *n.* Future generations.

poultice (pōl′ tis) *n.* A wad of something soft and moist that is placed over a wound to heal it.

prairie (prâr′ ē) *n.* A large area of level or rolling land with grass and few or no trees.

prankster (prangk′ stər) *n.* A person who plays tricks on people for fun.

preamble (prē′ am′ bəl) *n.* The section of text at the beginning of a law document that states why the document was written.

precarious (pri kâr′ ē əs) *adj.* Lacking security or stability.

precaution (pri kô′ shən) *n.* Care taken beforehand.

prediction (pri dik′ shən) *n.* A statement about what someone thinks will happen in the future.

preserve (pri zərv′) *v.* 1. Protect and maintain. 2. Prepare food so that it can be eaten in the future.

pressure (pre′ shər) *v.* To force.

prevail (pri vāl′) *v.* To persuade.

primary (prī′ mâr ē) *adj.* Main.

prime (prīm) *n.* The most successful or important period of time.

primitive (prim′ ə tiv) *adj.* 1. Living in the ways of long ago. 2. In the earliest stages of development.

procedure (prə sē′ jər) *n.* The steps to follow in carrying out a routine or method.

proclaim (prō klām′) *v.* To announce publicly.

procure (prə kyûr′) *v.* Obtain by making a special effort.

profound (prə found′) *adj.* Deep.

prominence (prom′ ə nəns) *n.* Fame; importance.

prominent (prom′ ə nənt) *adj.* Famous; well-known.

proportions (prə por′ shənz) *n.* Amounts.

prospect (pros′ pekt′) *v.* Look for gold.

provisions (prə vizh′ ənz) *n.* Supplies, especially food or tools.

ptarmigan (tär′ mi gən) *n.* A bird also known as a grouse.

pun (pun) *n.* A joke made by using words that sound almost the same but have different meanings.

pungent (pun′ jənt) *adj.* Sharp or strong smelling or tasting.

Q

quarantine (kwor′ ən tēn′) *adj.* Involving the isolation of people from others to prevent the spreading of disease.

quiver (kwi′ vər) *v.* To shake slightly.

R

racquetball (ra′ kət bôl′) *n.* A sport played with a racket and small rubber ball in an enclosed room.

radiation (rā´ dē ā´ shən) *n.* Emitted energy that can be harmful.

radical (ra´ di kəl) *n.* A person who favors extreme changes or reforms.

rampart (ram´ pärt) *n.* A wall used as a defense for a city.

rancid (ran´ sid) *adj.* Stale; unpleasant.

rapscallion (rap skal´ yən) *n.* A rascal; a scamp.

ratification (rat´ ə fi kā´ shən) *n.* The formal approval of a law or laws.

ration (rash´ ən) *n.* A limited share of food.

ravage (ra´ vij) *v.* To damage heavily.

ravine (rə vēn´) *n.* A narrow, steep-sided valley worn into the earth by running water.

rebellion (ri bel´ yən) *n.* An uprising against a ruling authority; an act of defiance.

recede (ri sēd´) *v.* To go backward; to back away.

Word Derivations

Below are some words related to *recede*.

receded	recession	recessionary
receding	recessional	recessive
recess		

recognize (re´ kig nīz´) *v.* Know that you have seen someone or something before.

recoil (ri koil´) *v.* To spring back from.

reconciliation (rek´ ən sil´ ē ā´ shən) *n.* A restoration of agreement between two or more parties.

record (re´ kərd) *n.* A written account of the number of games a team won or lost during its season.

refracting (ri frak´ ting) *adj.* Passing through an object and changing direction, as a light ray passing into a lens at one angle and coming out at a different angle.

regard (re gärd´) *n.* Thought or care.

regiment (rej´ ə mənt) *n.* A large body of soldiers.

register (re´ jə stər) *v.* Officially record in order to protect.

rehearse (ri hûrs´) *v.* Practice.

remedy (rem´ ə dē) *n.* A cure; something that will make a sickness better.

remote (ri mōt´) *adj.* Far away and separate from others.

renounce (ri nouns´) *v.* To give up; to reject.

represent (re´ pri zent´) *v.* Speak or act for someone else.

resonance (rez´ ə nəns) *n.* Richness of sound; echoing.

resource (rē´ sors) *n.* Something that can be used.

reunion (rē ūn´ yən) *n.* A coming or bringing together of family, friends, or other groups of people.

reverie (rev´ ə rē) *n.* A daydream.

revolution (rev´ ə lōō´ shən) *n.* The overthrow of a system of government and the setting up of a new system of government.

revolutionize (re´ və lōō´ shə nīz´) *v.* Cause dramatic change.

rice paper (rīs´ pā´ pər) *n.* A thin paper produced from the stems of rice plants.

riddle (rid´ əl) *n.* A puzzle that appears as a statement or question.

ritual (rich´ ōō əl) *n.* A ceremony of worship; an act always performed on certain occasions.

roam (rōm) *v.* Wander.

rocker (ro´ kər) *n.* A device used to separate gold from sand and dirt.

rotate (rō´ tāt) *v.* To revolve; to turn around; to spin.

rowdy (rou´ dē) *adj.* Rough; disorderly.

rudder (rud´ ər) *n.* A broad, flat blade at the rear of a ship used to steer. See illustration of **bow.**

rutting (rut´ ing) *n.* Mating.

S

saber (sā´ bər) *n.* A heavy sword with a curved blade.

sabotage (sab´ ə täzh´) *v.* To damage purposely.

salutary (sal´ yə ter´ ē) *adj.* Favorable; positive.

salutation (sal´ yə tā´ shən) *n.* Greeting.

samovar (sam´ ə vär´) *n.* A decorative metal container with a spigot, or faucet, often used in Russia to heat water for tea.

Word History

Samovar came into English in the year 1830. It is a Russian word formed by joining the word parts *samo-*, meaning "self," and *varit'*, which means "to boil."

scallion (skal´ yən) *n.* A type of onion.

scout (skout) *v.* Go ahead of the group, while on a journey, to look for information.

scowl (skoul) *v.* Frown.

scythe (sīth) *n.* A tool with a long, curved blade for cutting grass or grain by hand.

scythe

sear (sēr) *v.* To roast; to burn.

seclude (si klōōd´) *v.* To keep away from others.

second (se´ kənd) *v.* To verbally agree with a motion or suggestion to do something in a meeting.

sect (sekt) *n.* A group of people bound together by common beliefs or ideals.

secure (sə kyōōr´) *adj.* Safe from harm or danger.

sentinel (sent´ nəl) *n.* A person who stands watch; a guard.

serve (sûrv) *n.* In volleyball and tennis, a way of putting the ball into play by sending it over the net.

shamefaced (shām´ fāst) *adj.* Embarrassed.

sharecropper (shâr´ krop´ ər) *n.* A farmer who gives part of his or her crop as rent to the owner of the land.

shlemiel (shlə mēl´) *n. slang.* A fool who is both awkward and unlucky.

shmendrick (shmen´ drik) *n. slang.* A nincompoop; a nobody.

short circuit (short´ sûr´ kət) *n.* A condition in which the path of an electrical current is obstructed.

shrill (shril) *adj.* High-pitched; piercing.

shroud (shroud) *n.* A covering for a dead body.

shy (shī´) *adj.* 1. Lacking; falling short. 2. Secretive; protective.

simultaneously (sī´ məl tā´ nē əs lē) *adv.* At exactly the same time.

singsong (sing´ sông´) *adj.* Having a repetitive musical sound.

skeeter (skē´ tər) *n. informal.* A mosquito.

slaughter (slô´ tər) *n.* The killing of a large number of animals.

slew (slo͞o) *n.* Many.

slump (slump) *v.* To sit with drooping shoulders.

Word History

Slump came into English in the year 1887. Its origins are probably in the Scandinavian languages. It is related to the Norwegian word *slumpa*, which means "to fall."

---

smithy (smith´ ē) *n.* A blacksmith's shop; a place where horseshoes are made.

solar system (sō´ lər sis´ təm) *n.* The sun and all the planets and other bodies that revolve around it.

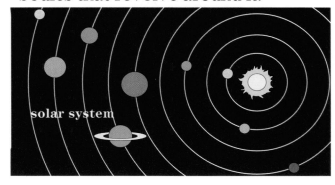

solar system

solder (sod´ ər) *v.* To join metal pieces together by using a highly heated liquid metal at a joint without heating the pieces themselves.

solitary (sol´ i ter´ ē) *adj.* Alone; single.

solstice (sol´ stis) *n.* The day of the year when the sun appears the farthest north and the day when it appears the farthest south in the sky.

sombre (som´ bər) *adj.* Dark or gloomy.

sovereign (so´ vrən) *adj.* Independent; self-governed.

span (span) *v.* To stretch across.

spar (spär) *n.* A pole or beam which supports the rigging on a ship; a mast.

spare (spâr) *adj.* Left over; remaining; extra.

spasm (spaz´ əm) *n.* A seizure; a fit.

spawn (spôn) *v.* To lay eggs and deposit them in water.

spectral (spek´ trəl) *adj.* Ghostly, eerie.

speculation (spek´ yə lā´ shən) *n.* Thinking about a subject; pondering.

spew (spū) *v.* To pour out; to squirt out.

spike (spīk) *v.* To forcefully hit a volleyball down the other side of the net.

spirit (spir´ ət) *n.* Enthusiasm; loyalty.

spirits (spir´ its) *n.* A liquid containing alcohol.

spooked (spo͞okt) *adj.* Scared.

stance (stans) *n.* A person's mental position on a subject.

Pronunciation Key: at; lāte; cåre; fäther; set; mē; it; kīte; ox; rōse; ô in bought; coin; book; too; form; out; up; ūse; tûrn; ə sound in about, chicken, pencil, cannon, circus; chair; hw in which; ring; shop; thin; there; zh in treasure.

staple (stā´ pəl) *n.* A basic, or necessary, food.

stockyard (stok´ yärd´) *n.* A place where livestock such as cattle, sheep, horses, and pigs that are to be bought or sold, slaughtered, or shipped are held.

Stonehenge (stōn´ henj) *n.* A group of large stones in England placed in circular formations around 3,500 years ago, possibly as an astronomical calendar.

Stonehenge

straddle (stra´ dəl) *v.* To sit with one's legs on each side of an object.

stroke (strōk) *n.* A sudden attack of illness caused by a blocked or broken blood vessel in or leading to the brain.

succession (sək sesh´ ən) *n.* One thing happening right after another.

substitute (sub´ stə toot) *n.* Anything that could take the place of something else.

succulent (suk´ yə lənt) *adj.* Juicy; tasty.

sufficient (sə fish´ ənt) *adj.* Enough.

suffocate (suf´ ə kāt´) *v.* To smother; to choke.

sull (sul) *v.* To balk; to stop suddenly and refuse to move.

summon (sum´ ən) *v.* Ask to come.

supple (sup´ əl) *adj.* Easily bent; not stiff.

sway (swā) *v.* To influence.

T

tan (tan) *v.* To turn animal hides into leather.

Word History

Tan came into English about 600 years ago, from the French word *tanner*, a derivation of the Latin word *tanum* or *tannum*. The Latin word means "tanbark," a type of bark that contains an astringent, or drying, substance used in the making of leather.

tangled-up (tang´ gəld up´) *adj.* Mixed-up and stuck together.

tantrum (tan´ trəm) *n.* A screaming, crying fit of childish anger.

tapir (tā´ pər) *n.* An animal similar to a pig, but with a long, flexible nose.

tariff (târ´ əf) *n.* A fee charged by a government on imports and exports.

teeming (tē´ ming) *adj.* Overflowing; swarming.

terminal (tûr´ mə nəl) *adj.* Eventually ending in death.

terrace (târ´ əs) *n.* A raised area with a series of level steps or surfaces cut into the side.

terrain (tə rān´) *n.* An area of land that is thought of in terms of its physical features.

tethered (teth´ ərd) *adj.* Tied by rope to a fixed object.

thresh (thresh) *v.* To separate grain from the stalk by beating it.

tidal flat (tī′ dəl flat) *n.* A flat area of land that is sometimes covered by tidal waters.

timpani (tim′ pə nē) *n.* A type of drum.

tipi (tē′ pē) *n.* A tent of the Native Americans of the Plains; a tepee.

Word History

Tipi, or **tepee,** came into English in the year 1743. It is a Native American word, meaning "to dwell," that originated with the Dakota tribe.

toboggan (tə bog′ ən) *n.* A long, narrow sled.

tome (tōm) *n.* One volume of a set of books.

tract (trakt) *n.* A large area of land.

traditional (trə di′ shən əl) *adj.* Passed from one generation to another.

traitor (trā′ tər) *n.* A person who betrays his or her country.

tranquility (tran kwil′ ə tē) *n.* Calmness.

transcribe (tran skrīb′) *v.* To change from one recorded form to another; to translate.

treason (trē′ zən) *n.* The act of betraying someone's trust.

treaty (trē′ tē) *n.* A formal agreement between two countries.

trek (trek) *n.* A long, slow journey.

trench (trench) *n.* A ditch; a long, narrow channel cut in the earth.

tributary (trib′ yə ter′ ē) *n.* A stream or river that flows into a larger one.

tribute (trib′ ūt) *n.* Praise, honor, or gifts given to show respect or to show thanks.

trifling (trī′ fling) *adj.* Small and unimportant.

trinket (tring′ kit) *n.* A small or cheap piece of jewelry.

tripod (trī′ pod) *n.* A three-legged table or stand.

tripod

troop (tro͞op) *n.* Soldiers.

tsar (zär) *n.* An emperor of Russia before 1918.

tsarina (zä rē′ nə) *n.* An empress of Russia before 1918.

tumult (to͞o′ mult) *n.* A great disorder; an uproar.

tundra (tun′ drə) *n.* A large, treeless plain in the arctic regions.

tunic (to͞o′ nik) *n.* A short coat.

tyranny (tir′ ə nē) *n.* The unjust use of power; harsh or cruel government.

U

unaccountably (un′ ə koun′ tə blē) *adv.* In a way that cannot be explained.

unalienable (un′ āl′ yə nə bəl) *adj.* Not capable of being given or taken away.

unanimity (ū′ nə ni′ mə tē) *n.* A condition of complete agreement.

unison (ū′ nə sən) *n.* Behaving the same way at the same time. **in unison** *idiom.* Two or more people saying or doing the same thing at the same time.

universe (ū′ nə vers′) *n.* Everything that exists, including the earth, the planets, the stars, and all of space.

unquenchably (un kwench′ ə blē) *adv.* Endlessly; in a persistent way.

V

vain (vān) *adj.* Conceited.

vagabond (va′ gə bond′) *n.* One who wanders from place to place.

valiant (val′ yənt) *adj.* Brave; fearless.

variable (vâr′ ē′ ə bəl) *adj.* Likely to change.

velocity (və los′ i tē) *n.* Speed.

vindicate (vin′ di kāt′) *v.* To prove innocent.

vintage (vin′ tij) *n.* The grapes or wine produced in a vineyard in one year.

vintner (vint′ nər) *n.* A person who makes wine for a living.

visible (vi′ zə bəl) *adj.* Able to be seen or noticed.

vocation (vō kā′ shən) *n.* An occupation; a profession.

voyage (voi′ ij) *n.* A journey by water.

W

water buffalo (wô′ tər buf′ ə lō′) *n.* A kind of oxen with large curved horns and a bluish-black hide. Water buffaloes are trained to work in rice fields in Asia.

whim (hwim) *n.* An impulsive thought, idea, or desire.

whopper (hwop′ ər) *n. informal.* A big lie.

wince (wins) *v.* To flinch; to start back from.

windlass (wind′ ləs) *n.* A roller turned with a handle used for lifting heavy weights.

windlass

winnow (win′ ō) *v.* To remove the chaff, or husks, from grain.

wrath (rath) *n.* Anger; rage.

Y

yarn (yärn) *n.* A made-up story.

yield (yēld) *v.* To give in; to stop arguing.

Z

Zulu (zoo′ loo) *n.* A person from KwaZulu Natal in South Africa.

From the book THE MIDNIGHT RIDE OF PAUL REVERE by Henry Wadsworth Longfellow, illustrated by Jeffrey Thompson. Illustrations copyright © 1999 National Geographic Society. Reprinted by permission.

THE DECLARATION OF INDEPENDENCE by R. Conrad Stein. Text copyright © 1995 by R. Conrad Stein. Reprinted by permission of Children's Press, a division of Grolier Publishing.

"The Master Spy of Yorktown" from BLACK HEROES OF THE AMERICAN REVOLUTION, copyright © 1976 BY Burke Davis, reproduced by permission of Harcourt, Inc.

From SHH! WE'RE WRITING THE CONSTITUTION by Jean Fritz, copyright © 1987 by Jean Fritz, text. Used by permission of G.P. Putnam's Sons, A division of Penguin Young Readers Group, A member of Penguin Group (USA) Inc., 345 Hudson St., New York, NY 10014. All rights reserved.

From SHH! WE'RE WRITING THE CONSTITUTION by Jean Fritz, illustrated by Tomie dePaola, copyright © 1987 by Whitebird, Inc. illustrations. Used by permission of G.P. Putnam's Sons, A division of Penguin Young Readers Group, A member of Penguin Group (USA) Inc., 345 Hudson St., New York, NY 10014. All rights reserved.

WE THE PEOPLE OF THE UNITED STATES COPYRIGHT © 1987 BY MILTON MELTZER. Used by permission of HarperCollins Publishers.

From SACAGAWEA by Betty Westrom Skold. Copyright © 1977 by Dillon Press. Reprinted with permission of the author.

Copyright © 1988 by Russell Freedman. All rights reserved. Reprinted from BUFFALO HUNT by permission of Holiday House, Inc.

SONGS OF THE DREAM PEOPLE: Chants and Images from the Indians and Eskimos of North America. Edited and illustrated by James Houston. Atheneum, New York, copyright © 1972 by James Houston.

"The Flower-Fed Buffaloes", from GOING TO THE STARS by Vachel Lindsay, copyright 1926 by D. Appleton & Co., renewed 1954 by Elizabeth C. Lindsay. A Hawthorn Book. Used by permission of Dutton Children's Books, an imprint of Penguin Putnam Books for Young Readers, a division of Penguin Putnam Inc.

From THE JOURNAL OF WONG MING-CHUNG by Laurence Yep. Copyright © 2000 by Laurence Yep. Reprinted by permission of Scholastic Inc.

Excerpt from SING DOWN THE MOON. Copyright © 1970 by Scott O'Dell. Reprinted by permission of Houghton Mifflin Co. All rights reserved.

"OLD YELLER AND THE BEAR", pages 32-39 from OLD YELLER by FRED GIPSON. COPYRIGHT © 1956 BY FRED GIPSON. Reprinted by permission of HarperCollins Publishers, Inc.

BILL PICKETT: RODEO RIDIN' COWBOY, text copyright © 1996 by Andrea Davis Pinkney, Illustrations copyright © 1996 by Brian Pinkney, reprinted by permission of Harcourt, Inc.

MCBROOM THE RAINMAKER TEXT COPYRIGHT © 1973 BY SID FLEISCHMAN. Used by permission HarperCollins Publishers.

THE STORY OF JUMPING MOUSE, A STORY FROM SEVEN ARROWS copyright © 1972 by Hymeyohsts Storm. Retold and illustrated for children copyright © 1984 by John Steptoe. USE LICENSED BY THE JOHN STEPTOE LITERARY TRUST AND HARPERCOLLINS PUBLISHERS.

TRAPPED BY ICE! Copyright © 1997 by Michael McCurdy. Printed by arrangement with Walker & Co.

"Maps" by Dorothy Brown Thompson reprinted by permission of University of Missouri-Kansas City, University Libraries.

"Travel" by Edna St. Vincent Millay. From COLLECTED POEMS, HarperCollins. Copyright 1921, 1948 by Edna St. Vincent Millay. All rights reserved. Reprinted by permission of Elizabeth Barnett, literary executor.

From APOLLO 11: FIRST MOON LANDING, copyright © 1995 by Michael D. Cole. Reprinted with permission of Enslow Publishers, Inc. All rights reserved.

"When Shlemiel Went to Warsaw" from WHEN SHLEMIEL WENT TO WARSAW AND OTHER STORIES by Isaac Bashevis Singer. Copyright © 1968 by Isaac Bashevis Singer. Reprinted by permission of Farrar, Straus & Giroux, LLC.

THE SEARCH COPYRIGHT © 1953 BY JOSEPH KRUMGOLD. Used by permission of HarperCollins Publishers.

From ALBERIC THE WISE reprinted with permission of Norton Juster, text copyright 1965 by Norton Juster. Illustrations from ALBERIC THE WISE AND OTHER JOURNEYS by Norton Juster, illustrated by Leonard Baskin © The Estate of Leonard Baskin.

"Wander-Thirst" reprinted by permission of Laurence S. Untermeyer. Copyright © 1941 by Harcourt, Brace and Company, Inc.

"Roads Go Ever On", from THE HOBBIT. Copyright © 1966 by J.R.R. Tolkien. Reprinted by permission of Houghton Mifflin Co. All rights reserved.

Photo Credits

Unit Opener Acknowledgements